# A ROAD,
# A CEMETERY,
# A PEOPLE

## Hayse Boyd, M.D.

*A Road, A Cemetery, A People*

Copyright © 2024
Hayse Boyd

All rights reserved. No part of this publication may be reproduced, stored in a retrieval system, or transmitted in any form or by any means, electronic, mechanical, photocopy, recording, or otherwise, without the prior written permission of the publisher.

# About the Author

Hayse Boyd was born in Tuscaloosa County on October 24, 1939. In 1940 his parents bought a farm near North River on the Crabbe Road ten miles north of Tuscaloosa. He was reared in a large beautiful home on the farm that had been built in 1896 by Eugene B. Tierce.

In 1962, he married the love of his life, Peggy Rushing, a neighbor who lived on the Crabbe Road three miles south of the Boyd farm. They are the parents of three children: Tara Boyd Thornhill; Cinda Boyd Perry; and Denson Hayse Boyd. They have five grandchildren and two great grandchildren.

Dr. Boyd earned a Doctor of Medicine degree from the Medical College of Alabama in Birmingham in 1965. He enjoyed a long and fruitful career as a doctor of internal medicine in Northport.

Ill health resulted in his retirement from medical practice in 1995. Life in retirement allowed him to devote more time to ministry to his Lord and Savior Jesus Christ through involvement in the First Baptist Church of Tuscaloosa where he has served in leadership roles. He authors a weekly Bible lesson that is distributed not only to members of his Sunday School class but is shared on-line to all who wish to receive it.

From childhood, history had been a favorite subject, but the desire to become an author had never entered his mind until 2000. That year ushered in a writing career that has resulted in the publication of 8 books that include an autobiography, biographies of two Northport men (Sonny Booth and Jack Dyer), the history of the hospital in Northport, books that tell many humorous experiences incurred in his medical practice, two carefully researched histories of Tuscaloosa County, and the story of a daughter's near-death experience from bacterial endocarditis.

At age 85 and with the completion of *A Road, A Cemetery, A People,* he is undecided as to what will be his next writing project.

# Acknowledgements

I am deeply indebted to Dr. David Sloan, a retired University of Alabama Professor of Journalism. This dear friend took my manuscript with its innumerable errors and formatted it into a book that is well-organized and will hold the attention of the reader as one reads about the history of the North River area traversed by the Crabbe Road in Tuscaloosa County during the period 1839-1960. His patience in working with me is sincerely appreciated.

Sonya Booth Davis, a Northport native and retired English teacher from Samford University, provided expertise in editing Chapter 22 "Marjorie Shipp" and Chapter 23 "Dr. Joseph Calvin Shipp." Sonya, along with her deceased parents Betty and Sonny Booth were dear friends to Dr. and Mrs. Shipp. Sonya holds a special place of love in my heart.

**Resource material**
Much of *A Road, A Cemetery, A people* is memoir. My family and I have been residents of the Crabbe Road since 1940 when I was six months old. I witnessed firsthand many of the stories that I tell.

A am indebted to my neighbors and friends including members of the LaFoy, Hamner, Shirley, Tierce, Hagler, Adams, Rushing and Chism families who shared their memories and photos from family albums. In particular I thank Brenda LaFoy and her mother Jeanie Rushing LaFoy Lancaster for sharing their extensive genealogy research.

William Taylor Hamner, Sr. was one of the first men to arrive in the North River area on the Crabbe Road. He fathered sixteen children by three wives; a fourth wife produced no children. The story of the William Taylor Hamner, Sr. family is recorded in *Hamner Heritage-Beginning Without End* written by two of Hamner's descendants Geneal Hamner Black and Mary Clark Ryan. The book was published in 1979 and was an invaluable resource.

I quote extensively from local newspapers that date to 1911—*The Northport Gazette, the Tuscaloosa Breeze, The Tuscaloosa News*.

Valeria Brown is church secretary and record custodian for Macedonia Church and Cemetery. She allowed me unlimited access to old church records dating to 1886.

To my wife, Peggy Rushing Boyd, the love of my life who stood beside and encouraged me during the past five years as I spent countless hours at the word processor. She was solace in lifting my spirits during periods of frustration. I cherish the sixty-two plus years God has granted to us in marriage.

Most importantly, I thank God for giving me life to complete this project. Without Jesus Christ as the Lord of my life, this work would never have come to fruition.

# Table of Contents

| | | |
|---|---|---|
| 1 | Introduction | 1 |
| 2 | The Crabbe Road and the Boyd Family | 5 |
| 3 | Macedonia Cemetery | 23 |
| 4 | Churches | 85 |
| 5 | Crabbe Road, First Settlers | 95 |
| 6 | The Lafoy School | 109 |
| 7 | Growing up on a Cotton Farm | 127 |
| 8 | Dock "Doc" Bigham (1869-1918) | 137 |
| 9 | Moonshining on the Crabbe Road | 143 |
| 10 | The Murder of Pricey Shirley White | 149 |
| 11 | Politics along the Crabbe Road | 153 |
| 12 | Recreation on the Crabbe Road | 169 |
| 13 | The Curb Market | 189 |
| 14 | The History of the Crabbe Road | 201 |
| 15 | The LaFoy Family | 211 |
| 16 | Cost of Living | 215 |
| 17 | Windham Springs | 231 |
| 18 | The Joseph Enoch Rushing Family | 233 |
| 19 | The Mitt Lary Family | 247 |
| 20 | The Joel T. Shirley Family | 251 |
| 21 | The Byrd Franklin Shirley, Sr., Family | 267 |
| 22 | Marjorie Shipp | 291 |
| 23 | Dr. Joseph Calvin Shipp | 295 |

# A ROAD,
# A CEMETERY,
# A PEOPLE

## Hayse Boyd, M.D.

CHAPTER 1

# Introduction

A *Road* (the Crabbe Road) *A Cemetery* (Macedonia Cemetery) *A People* (the residents of the Lafoy Community) is a memoir of my life on the Crabbe Road known today as Alabama Highway 69 North. I have devoted five years to the writing of this book. It is a joy to share intriguing stories of the area and its people to all who read this book.

In 1940, when I was six months old, my parents purchased a one-hundred twenty-acre farm on the Crabbe Road ten miles north of Tuscaloosa from Mrs. Lela Tierce, the widow of Mr. Eugene B. Tierce, Sr. The Tierce home on the property was built in 1897, and it was in that house that I spent the first eighteen years of my life. In 1958, I entered the University of Alabama, and upon graduation in 1961, I enrolled in the Medical College of Alabama in Birmingham. Following several years of medical training in Birmingham, my family and I moved back to the farm on the Crabbe Road, and I entered the private practice of internal medicine in Northport. It is my hope to spend the remainder of my days enjoying life on the Boyd far.

**Lafoy families**
It is impossible to include all the Crabbe Road family stories about my neighbors, friends, and relatives who influenced my life during childhood. Among others, I tell the story of the W. A. Boyd family (my grandfather), the Byrd Franklin Shirley family, the Joel Tom Shirley family, the Thomas D. LaFoy family, the William T. Hamner, Sr. family, the Benjamin Tucker Tierce family, the James Martin Hagler family, the Joseph Enoch Rushing family, the Ezra Jonah Shipp family, along with others. The story of several of these families occupy an entire chapter in *A Road, A Cemetery, A People*.

**Churches**
Carrolls Creek Baptist Church was founded in 1842. The Presbytery was composed of John H. Hamner and Samuel W. Hassell. No one knows how often the church met or whether there was a regular pastor. The church was not actually constituted until 1877. It was accepted into the Tuscaloosa County Baptist Association in 1878. The church's history is rich.

Macedonia Church was established in the late 1880s, and its history, too, is rich. Macedonia Cemetery was a burial ground prior to the establishment of Macedonia Church. The first documented burial in Macedonia Cemetery occurred April 27, 1862. The names of all interred there, along with a brief bio of many, is given.

**Lafoy School**
Lafoy School was located on the Crabbe Road eight miles north of Northport across the high-

way from the current site of Carrolls Creek Baptist Church. The school opened circa 1910. The earliest information I have found about the school is in the February 11, 1911 *Northport Gazette*. Many news articles from the 1910s through the 1940s about the school give priceless information about it.

The school closed in 1941. In 1942, the property was bought by Carrolls Creek Baptist Church to be used as a temporary home while a new church was built directly across Highway 69. Later, the old building was used as a community center.

**Recreation**
Life was lived to the fullest on the Crabbe Road during the first half of the 20th century. Most of the citizens were honest, hardworking, religious people who lived on small farms, held public jobs, and were people whom I loved and admired. Despite having little spare time, they found recreation through such activities as cow-pasture softball games on Sunday afternoons, community picnics, hunting and fishing, and just visiting each other.

The most famous sports family on the Crabbe Road was the Mitt Lary family. The story began with Mitt, the daddy. In 1916, he was promised a tryout for both the New York Yankees and the Boston Red Sox. However, when the United States declared war on Germany on April 7, 1917, Mitt enlisted in the US Army.

After the war, Mitt met the love of his life, Margaret Rancher, in New York. They married and rather than pursuing professional baseball, Mitt returned to his roots in Tuscaloosa County and to life on the farm growing peaches and other crops including cotton and corn.

Seven sons were born to Mitt and Margaret—Joe, Jr., Frank, Al, Gene, Ed, Raymond, and James. The first son, Joseph Milton Lary, Jr. was born in 1922, and six of Mitts's seven boys followed in their father's footsteps and perfected their craft as baseball pitchers. James was the designated catcher in the bunch. James, the second son born in 1923, was also a musician and an all-state tuba player while a student at Tuscaloosa County High School.

Patriotism ran strong in the blood of the Lary family. Like their father, the Lary brothers served their country in its armed forces. James served in the US Army in Italy. Joe Jr., Raymond, and Ed served in the US Navy. Frank was a member of the Alabama National Guard and Al served in the Korean War. The boys joked that Al was the luckiest as he was assigned the duty of being Marilyn Monroe's personal escort during her trips to Korea.

Each of the Lary boys attended the University of Alabama all earing prestigious sports awards. Joe Jr. was the first Lary to enter the University of Alabama after World War II ended. He earned two letters in baseball and was a part of the 1947 Alabama SEC championship team. Joe Jr., Al, Ed, Frank, and Gene earned athletic scholarships to the University of Alabama. Frank and Al were part of the 1950 SEC championship team and secured a spot in the university's first college world series. Ed and Al were the only two brothers who also played football at Alabama. Al became a first-team All-SEC and All-American selection in 1950 and held almost every receiving record at Alabama during his time on campus. He was named the top all-around athlete at Alabama in 1950. Gene was the last Lary to attend the University of Alabama. He earned four letters in baseball and helped lead Alabama to the 1955 SEC championship.

**Politics**
Politics played an important role in the lives of the people of the Lafoy Community. On election years, political rallies at the Lafoy Community Center attracted large crowds. Several residents were elected to public office and the stories of their journey to political success is intriguing. Three of the most notable were my father, Herman C. Boyd who served on the Tuscaloosa

# INTRODUCTION

County Board of Revenue, Nathan Chism who was sheriff of Tuscaloosa County, and Magaria Bobo who currently serves as Circuit Clerk Tuscaloosa County.

**A small dirt road**
The Crabbe Road was a narrow dirt road hardly wide enough to accommodate two-way traffic during my early childhood. In 1947, the road was paved from Two-mile Creek in Northport to North River. One of the happiest events of my childhood was watching the road in front of our house being blacktopped. In the early 1950s, the remainder of the Crabbe Road from North River to Jasper was paved.

**Shootings and killings**
As with any community, everything that occurred on the Crabbe Road and in the Lafoy Community was not good. Murders were committed including the shooting death of Tuscaloosa County Sheriff P. M. Watts by Doc Bigham as the sheriff raided Bigham's whiskey still in Piney Woods in 1918. Pricey Shirley Gibson White was shot dead by her husband at the front door of Woolworth Store in downtown Tuscaloosa. Lillie Boyd Gast was shot dead by her husband Wheeler Gast in front of two of their children. The details of these murders are included within these pages.

**Moonshining**
Moonshining flourished on the Crabbe Road between 1920-1950. Many stories are included. The following article appeared in the "Tuscaloosa News" July 25, 1929.

"County officers last night seized near Windham Springs on the Crabbe Road one of the most complete and best equipped liquor plants in the history of this county. Two trucks were required to haul in the contents comprising one hundred twenty-five 5-gallon cans, 500 one-gallon containers, two 1,500-gallon stills, two 2,000-gallon stills, one ton of sugar and 1,000 pounds of meal and shorts.

More than 250 gallons of liquor and 4,000 gallons of beer were poured out on the hillside in the raid.

Officers found five men at work at the stills, but they made good their escape after officers had surrounded the plant and fired sixteen shots to frighten them.

The four stills were less than "ten" feet apart and a 150-foot hose line had been laid to a creek to furnish water. A pump to provide an adequate flow of water to the still was taken in by the officers.

Officers of the raiding party included Deputies John Payne, C. L. Lawrence, Sr., Louis King, W. I. Huff, Will Kuykendall, and Will Wilcutt.

All the liquor found was stored in new tin cans and officers pointed out the danger of allowing it to remain in tin containers for any length of time. It is believed that it was being manufactured for sale in other counties. All the containers were packed ready for shipment.

The road to the still made a secret entrance through the garage of a man's house. The rear wall of the garage was converted into a door, and a road led from there through a cotton field to the stills. A car was usually left parked in the garage while the still was in operation to conceal the entrance to the road, said officers."

**Life on a cotton farm**
I grew up on a cotton farm. My father was not a farmer; he was an automobile salesman at Tucker Motor Company, the Tuscaloosa Ford dealership. The farm work was done by tenant farmers. Within this chapter, I present a summary of the role cotton farming played in the economic history of Alabama during the first half of the twentieth century.

**Tuscaloosa County Curb Market**
Many people in the Lafoy Community were members of the Tuscaloosa County Curb Market. I have many wonderful memories of the market and of those who were venders there. Our next-

door neighbors John and Octavia Tierce Hagler were venders. Their story is told in another chapter.

The first record of a curb market in Tuscaloosa dates to 1924. Its location is said to have been on Broad Street (identified as University Boulevard today) at its intersection with 21st Avenue. By 1929, the facility had been moved to 7th Street on the north lawn of the Tuscaloosa County courthouse.

Between its opening in 1924 and its closure in the early 2000s, the curb market has occupied six locations. The curb market remained beside the courthouse until the early 1950s when it was moved to 4th Street between Greensboro Avenue and 23rd Avenue near Tanner Brothers Produce Company behind the First National Bank Building.

The next move of the curb market came in 1982. The Tuscaloosa Truck Growers Association, the parent organization of the curb market, moved the facility to the intersection of Jack Warner Parkway and Greensboro Avenue a few yards from the banks of the Warrior River. The site was almost under the northbound lane of the Hugh Thomas Bridge. Locals refer to the area as at the bottom of "River Hill."

**Dr. Joseph Shipp**

An entire chapter in *A Road, A Cemetery, A People* is devoted to Dr. Joseph Shipp. He was born February 10, 1927 in a house that sat across the Crabbe Road from Macedonia Methodist Church. The reader will be inspired as he reads the story of this great physician who was recognized internationally for his pioneer work in juvenile diabetes.

CHAPTER 2

# The Crabbe Road and the Boyd Family

Topics discussed in this chapter: W.A. Boyd and family move to Lafoy Community circa 1910
Two-mile Creek lumber mill circa 1920
Purchase house 515 18th Street late 1930s
Birth of Herman Boyd, Jr. and death of his mother 1934
Herman Boyd, Sr. marries Lucille Farquhar 1935
Introduction to Tierce family and house 1940
Death of John Howard Boyd 1942; Dr. Ruby Tyler
Old wall-mounted crank telephone dating prior to 1918
Birth Peggy Rushing 1940
Death of my mother 1958
Death of my father 1964
My father's remarriage and divorce, Ruth Warren 1963
Boyds on the Crabbe Road in the future
W. A. Boyd's benevolence 1932
W. A. Boyd's death 1944
The death of Aney Beck Boyd 1947
The murder of Lillie Boyd Gast 1935
The execution of Wheeler Gast 1937

**THE EARLY YEARS OF THE 1900S**

**The W. A. Boyd, Jr. family, my grandparents**
I do not know when the W. A. Boyd, Jr. family moved into the Lafoy Community. Macedonia Methodist Church records reveal that he and his wife Aney Lou Virgie Beck Boyd, along with three of their six children were members of Macedonia Church in 1916. Their children listed on the church roll included: Lee Boyd (December 10, 1897-February 28, 1944); Earl Boyd (January 2, 1900-March 29, 1976); and Lillie Boyd (April 2, 1905-April 1, 1935). No mention is made of the three younger children: Eldon Boyd (June 25, 1902-January 30, 1964); Herman Boyd (March 20, 1908-January 11, 1964); and Woodrow Boyd (July 3, 1912-August 19, 1982).

The house the Boyd family lived in was a well-constructed house with big rooms on what in 2024 is Four Winds Road. It is less than a quarter mile north of Macedonia Church.

The old house was torn down in the late 1900s, but in 1955, Ollie and Emma Hamner lived there. Ollie and Emma lost a young child, Richard Bruce Hamner, to pneumonia on January 12, 1955. When my parents went to the house to offer condolences, I was with them. As we were leaving, Daddy said, "Hayse, our family lived in this house when I was a child. I attended Turner School on the Crabbe Road that sat on a bluff near the bridge over North River. The small school was a mile north of this house. Octavia Tierce Hagler was my teacher. During the winter months when the temperature was cold, I nearly froze to death as we walked to school."

In the early decades of his life, Granddaddy

5

# A ROAD, A CEMETERY, A PEOPLE

The W. A. Boyd saw mill and home on Crabbe Road at Two Mile Creek, circa 1920.

was in the lumber and real estate business. Circa 1920, he owned and operated a large and very profitable sawmill at Two Mile Creek on the Crabbe Road, the site that in 2024 is home to the Presbyterian Apartments at 3845 Highway 69 North. This photograph of the house and sawmill shows my grandmother standing on the front porch.

**No Boyds on the Crabbe Road 1920s-1940**
Granddaddy's business interests in farming, lumber, real estate, and in insurance endeavors resulted in his being a man on the move. To my knowledge, he never lived on the Crabbe Road after he sold the lumber mill and house at Twomile Creek in the early 1920s. His next move was to a large farm six miles south of Tuscaloosa on the Eutaw Road near the Warrior River. The river bottom land was fertile and excellent for farming and growing cattle. When I was a child, he took me to the farm and showed me the house the family lived in during the early and mid-1920s.

The date is not known, but in the late 1920s or early 1930s, my grandparents purchased a lovely two-story house at the intersection of 18th Street and Hackberry Lane in the Forest Lake area of Tuscaloosa. They lived there until Granddaddy died on September 13, 1944.

During the "roaring twenties," Granddaddy's business endeavors were very successful. His office was on the fourth floor of the Alston Building at the intersection of Greensboro Avenue and 6th Street in downtown Tuscaloosa. During the Great Depression of the 1930s, there is a wonderful story of how he shared his wealth with others were had fallen on very hard times. That story is told later in this chapter.

**My father's life during the years he did not live on the Crabbe Road, 1920-1940**
Daddy was born on March 20, 1908 during the years the Boyd family lived on the Crabbe Road near Macedonia Church. For reasons that are not clear to me, Daddy did not attend a local high school but my grandparents enrolled him in Tupelo Mississippi Institute (TMI) from which he graduated in 1926.

In the early 1930s, he was employed as a salesman by Tucker Motor Company, the Tuscaloosa Ford dealership. He enjoyed a very successful career there and eventually was promoted to the position of general sales manager in charge of all sales. He remained in that position until his death on January 11, 1964.

**Daddy's 1st marriage and the death of his wife**
In the early 1930s, Daddy married a young lady from Fayette, Elsie Dyer. They became the proud parents of a baby boy, Herman C. Boyd, Jr., who was born on May 31, 1934. Sadly, Elsie died

# THE CRABBE ROAD AND THE BOYD FAMILY

three weeks later on June 24, 1934 the result of post-delivery complications.

Daddy was devastated. A widower with a three-week-old baby to care far, he turned to his dear friends W. C. Warren and his wife Anabel. The Warrens took the baby in as one of their own and assumed the role of "grandparents." They lovingly cared for Herman Jr. until Daddy remarried in 1935. Mrs. Warren had become so attached to the baby that she cried when the ten-month-old baby went to live with his parents. During the years of my childhood, Mrs. Warren visited our home frequently. I recall her telling wonderful stories about caring for a motherless young child.

On March 2, 1935, the young widower with a little baby to care for married Grace Lucille Farquhar. To that marriage, I was born on October 24, 1939.

During the years 1935-1940, Daddy and my mother-to-be lived in several locations in and near Tuscaloosa. When I was born, he and Mother lived in Alberta City. When I was six months old, Mother and Daddy bought a 120-acre farm from the Tierce family on the Crabbe Road ten miles north of downtown Tuscaloosa.

**The Tierce family**
Benjamin Tucker Tierce (1785-February 18, 1869) and Susannah Clardy Tierce (June 13, 1787-April 27, 1862) arrived in the North River area on the Crabbe Road circa 1830. They acquired a lot of land. Benjamin Tucker and Susannah had only one child, Elliott Catlett Tierce (December 17, 1827-March 21, 1906). Elliott Catlett Tierce had two sons, Elliott Lee Tierce (March 18, 1863-October 17, 1938) and Eugene Benjamin Tierce, Sr. (May 15, 1865-August 30, 1918).

The Tierce-Boyd house built 1896 is shown in 2024.

In 1896, Eugene Benjamin Tierce, Sr. built a beautiful eight-room, four-porch house with a large center hallway that originally was a dogtrot. The house faced due east and sat about twenty yards from the Crabbe Road. Unfortunately, Mr. Tierce met an accidental death in 1918 when he was chopping firewood and the axe blade slipped and severed blood vessels in his neck. He quickly bled to death in the yard of his home. His widow, Mrs. Lela Hyche Tierce, continued to live in the house with the younger two children (Eugene B. Tierce, Jr. (October 30, 1908-December 31, 1970), and Louise Tierce (March 31, 1910-Febraury 11, 1983).

**My life in the Tierce-Boyd house**
The story of my life in the Tierce-Boyd house from age six-months until I entered college in 1958 is told in chapters "Cotton farming on the Crabbe Road" and "Politics on the Crabbe Road.". After Daddy's death in 1964, ownership of the house left the Boyd family. New owners have done a wonderful job of restoration and maintaining the house.

**Death and grief come to the Boyd family on the Crabbe Road in 1942.**
In February 1942, Mother gave birth to John

My parents, Herman and Lucille Farquhar Boyd

Howard Boyd. The little baby died two weeks later of whooping cough.

The following article appeared on page 2 of the March 11, 1942 issue of *The Tuscaloosa News*.

"John Howard Boyd, two-week-old son of Mr. and Mrs. Herman Boyd of this city died early today at his home after a sudden illness. The infant is survived by his parents and two brothers, Herman Boyd, Jr., and David Hayse Boyd. His father is associated with Tucker Motor Company.

Funeral services will be held Thursday, March 12 at Macedonia Methodist Church on the Crabbe Road."

**The effect of my brother's death on me**
I was told in childhood that John Howard appeared normal at birth. However, within a few days he developed a severe case of whooping cough. Mother used the old crank telephone in our hallway to call Dr. Ruby Tyler, Tuscaloosa's only pediatrician at the time.

Dr. Tyler immediately left her office for started for our house that lay ten miles away on a winding, narrow, dirt road that was almost impassable when muddy during the winter months of February and March. Upon arrival, Dr. Tyler quickly wrapped the baby in a thick blanket, placed him on the front seat of her car bedside her and drove as fast as was safe to Druid City Hospital. John Howard died enroute.

Dr. Tyler served as my pediatrician in childhood. I was sickly as a child and had pneumonia five times before I entered first grade. Being a patient in her office frequently and observing her practice medicine helped mold my desire to become a physician. She was a great mentor. When she retired from private practice many years later, she joined the medical staff at Partlow Hospital.

All members of the medical staff at DCH Hospital and the medical staff at Partlow Hospital were required to attend a joint meeting each month at DCH to discuss relevant current medical issues. She and I often sat at the same table and reminisced those long-ago years when I was a patient in her pediatric practice. She was a great doctor and a lovely lady.

Second:

By the time I was eight years old, I had the freedom to wander over our entire farm alone. That included walking up to Macedonia Cemetery and looking at the tombstones scattered over the area. When I would come to John Howard's grave, I would stop and just ponder many things. What would my life have been like if he had lived and I had had a little brother with whom I could have shared the experiences of life?

**The old crank wall-mounted telephone**
The old crank wall-mounted telephone that Mother used to call Dr. Tyler has its own story.

Commercial telephone service on the Crabbe Road did not arrive until the early 1950s. However, the Tierce-Boyd house had telephone service that dated to prior to the 1918 death of Eugene B. Tierce, Sr.

Mr. Tierce paid to have a private telephone line run from the telephone switchboard in Northport to his house. Three or four other families in the community paid to tap into Mr.

# THE CRABBE ROAD AND THE BOYD FAMILY

Tierce's telephone line thus creating a party line.

The telephone in our house was the last phone on the line, the one farthest from town and the first phone available to people who lived beyond us when emergencies arose. On several occasions I remember strangers appearing at our front door asking for permission to call the sheriff if a shooting was taking place or to call the undertaker to come and pick up a corpse. People appeared at all hours of the day or night. At times it frightened me to have strangers in the house especially if Daddy was not at home.

This old crank phone was installed in the Eugene B. Tierce, Sr., house prior to his death in 1918. Today it is mounted on the wall beside my computer.

### The arrival of Peggy Ann Rushing on the Crabbe Road 1940
Two momentous occasions occurred in 1940 on the Crabbe Road that shaped my life forever—our family moved to the Tierce-Boyd home and Peggy Ann Rushing, the wonderful person who would become my wife on June 2, 1962, was born. While researching on-line *Tuscaloosa News* articles for material to use in this memoir, I came across the following article announcing her birth.

### January 16, 1940: Peggy Ann Rushing arrives at the hospital
Mr. and Mrs. Roy Rushing, nee Faith Ramsey, announce the birth of a 7 ¾ pound baby girl at the Druid City Hospital on Saturday January 13. The baby has been named Peggy Ann. Both mother and daughter have been removed to their home in Lafoy where they are receiving congratulations.

The story of Peggy's life and our marriage is woven throughout *A Road, A Cemetery, A People*.

### The death of my mother, 1958
I share the story of my parents' involvement in church, civic, cultural, and political spheres in other chapters and is not repeated here except to note events relating to their deaths.

God blessed me with two wonderful parents. From the time of my earliest memory, they set me upon a path that led to a fulfilled life for which I am deeply grateful.

In 1953, the year I was in the seventh grade at Tuscaloosa County High School, Mother was diagnosed with breast cancer. Her battle with illness included multiple surgeries, chemo therapy, irradiation therapy, and entailed tremendous pain. She died on October 6, 1958. At the time of her death, I was in my second week as a freshman at the University of Alabama. The story of my life between 1958 and 1961 is shared in the chapter, "Crabbe Road and the W. C. Warren family."

### Obit for Mrs. Lucille Boyd
Mrs. Lucille Boyd, wife of Herman Clory Boyd, Sr., died last night at Druid City Hospital after a long illness. Before her marriage, she was Grace Lucille Farquhar, a former teacher in the Fayette City School System.

She was an active member of the Macedonia Methodist Church where she taught an adult Bible class.

Funeral services will be held at 3:00 p.m. Tuesday at the Macedonia Church with the Reverend Wayne Graham and the Reverend Billy Prickett officiating. Burial will be in the church cemetery by Jones-Seigner.

Survivors include her husband, Herman Boyd, Sr., a former member of the Tuscaloosa

County Board of Revenue and now sales manager of Tucker Motor Company; two sons, Herman Boyd, Jr., and David Hayse Boyd of Northport; three sisters, Mrs. G. E. "Lula" Roberts of Mobile, Mrs. J. R. "Carrie" Kemp of Fayette, and Mrs. Virgie Dyer of Fayette, and one grandson, David Herman Boyd of Northport.

Active pallbearers for the funeral will be John Shirley, Roy Rushing, Tucker Mathis, Leslie Gaddy, Devon Black, and Thomas Lake.

Honorary pallbearers are Pruitt Hamner, Clifton Turner, Polk Rushing, Robert Rushing, B. F. Shirley, Howard Hagler, Eugene Tierce, J. D. Hamner, Wilton Gay, Clyde Utley, Judge W. C. Warren, Grover Pearson, Gay Dorroh, Nathan Chism, Dawson Chism, Hershel Shirley, Dr. J. H. Thomas, Frank Harrell, Hayse Tucker, James Rushing, Ellis Franklin, Dee Hamner, Neil Snow, Bruce Hamner, John Hagler, Lonnie Shirley, Grady Shirley, and employees of Ticker Motor Company.

**Tribute to Mother by the Women's Society of Christian Service of Macedonia Methodist Church.**
We, the members of the W.S.C.S. of the Macedonia Methodist Church do hereby wish to pay tribute to the memory of our beloved Christian friend and co-worker.

Active in all phases of the W.S.C.S., she was Spiritual Life Chairman at the time of her death. A devout Christian who daily lived her religion and who constantly worked for the church and community, she was an adult Sunday school teacher until ill health forced her retirement. For the last three years, she had been in constant pain but cheerfully served the Lord every day and looked forward to being once again in God's house, the placed she loved so well.

Not only has our W.S.C.S suffered a great loss, but also has our church and community. In sickness or sorrow, she was always on hand to bring comfort, kindness, and assistance as only she could. Regardless of the needs, great or small, she was always there.

Her life greatly enriched the lives of others with her Christian guidance, leadership, cheerfulness, and kindness. Though her active life has ended, her works continue through the love and inspiration she gave to us all.

Therefore, may a copy of this tribute be posted in the minutes of the W.S.C.S. and a copy sent to the *Christian Advocate*, the news magazine serving Methodists in the State of Alabama, and a copy to members of her family. Signed by Mrs. B. F. Shirley, Macedonia W.S.C.S secretary.

**The death of my father, January 11, 1964**
Daddy died of a sudden heart attack while riding in a car on University Boulevard in downtown Tuscaloosa on a cold winter Saturday afternoon in January 1964. Smut Smitherman, a fellow salesman at Tucker Motor Company was driving. Daddy suddenly slumped over in his seat and immediately became unresponsive. Smut sped to Druid City Hospital, but Daddy was pronounced dead on arrival.

Dad had many risk factors for coronary artery disease—a long history of smoking cigarettes, hypertension, a stressful lifestyle, and was slightly overweight. At 6 feet, he weighed 220 pounds. His first heart attack occurred in September 1963. In those days, the only treatment for a heart attack was limited to sedation, putting the patient to bed, placing him in an oxygen tent, administering digitalis to regulate heart rhythm, and prescribing a diuretic to relieve the body of excess fluid. At the time, the five-year mortality rate for heart attacks in a person his age was 98 percent.

***Tuscaloosa News*, January 11, 1964, front page:**
**Herman C. Boyd, Sr. dies, Former County Official**
Herman C. Boyd, Sr., 55, of Northport Route 2 (Crabbe Road), a former member of the Tuscaloosa County Board of Revenue, died Saturday

# THE CRABBE ROAD AND THE BOYD FAMILY

afternoon of a heart attack suffered while riding in a car in downtown Tuscaloosa.

Mr. Boyd, who served on the County Board of Revenue 1944-1952, had been an employee of Tucker Motor company for more than 30 years. He was general sales manager at the time of his death.

He was a member of Macedonia Methodist Church where he was a former member of the Official Board and a Sunday School teacher.

Funeral services will be held Monday afternoon at 2:00 p.m. at Macedonia Church with Dr. J. H. Chitwood, pastor of Tuscaloosa First Methodist Church, and the Reverends Bob Maxwell and Wayne Graham, former pastors of Macedonia Methodist Church officiating. Burial will follow in the church cemetery with Spigener Browne-Service in charge of arrangements.

Survivors include his wife, Ruth Warren Boyd; two sons, Herman Boyd, Jr. of Northport, and David Hayse Boyd of Birmingham; three step-sons, Tommy Burch of Northport, James Burch of Lawton, Oklahoma, and John Burch of Peru, Indiana; three brothers, Eldon Boyd of Tuscaloosa, Woodrow Boyd of Northport, and Early Boyd of Pensacola, Florida; and a grandson, David Herman Boyd of Northport.

Active pallbearers will be: Jody Allen, John Shirley, Roy Rushing, Grady Shirley, Ralph Dorroh, Clyde Utley, Nathan Chism and Devaughn Black.

Honorary pallbearers will be: Dr. Eric Rodgers, Hayse Tucker, Robert Williamson, Johnny Tinklepaugh, Neal Snow, Judge W. C. Warren, Tuck Mathis, Dr. Maxwell Moody, Jr., Dr. K. H. Patrick, Dr. James Thomas, John Hagler, B. F. Shirley, Lonnie Shirley, J. D. Hamner, Dee Hamner, Eugene Tierce, Bruce Hamner, Ellis Franklin, James Rushing, Howard Hagler, Howard Rushing, Dr. A. K. Patton, Robert Rushing, Dr. Howard Holley, Ollie Hamner, Neal Palmer, Dwight Tanner, John Walker, Truman Gray, Charlie Gross, Hal McCall, Chester Walker, Cliff Lindsey, Marshall Walker, Raymond Guy, Albert Hagler, Dawson Chism, Hershel Shirley, Cecil Gray, Barnard Rushing, James "Kid" Hamner and employees of Tucker Motor Company.

**Daddy's 1963 marriage and divorce**

Daddy's obit states that he was survived by a wife, Ruth, and stepsons Tommy Burch, James Burch, and John Burch, along with sons Herman Boyd Jr. and me. Because *A Road, A Cemetery, A People* serves as a documentary of Boyd family history and is written primarily for the benefit of my children and grandchildren, I include the story of Daddy's marriage to Ruth even though it is painful.

After Mother's death in 1958, Daddy, a handsome fifty-year-old man with a great personality and who was making a comfortable living in the automobile business would naturally capture the attention of widows or divorcees who might be interested in dating him.

Daddy occasionally went out with several very nice ladies all of whom I met and respected. In August 1963, five years after Mother's death, he married Ruth Warren Burch, a beautiful, smart, and loving widow. Ruth was the daughter of Judge and Mrs. W. C. Warren, a couple that is introduced earlier.

Ruth was one of four daughters born to Circuit Judge and Mrs. W. C. Warren. In the 1920s and 1930s, Warren had served in the Alabama Senate 1926-1934. In 1940, he was elected Circuit Judge of Tuscaloosa County a position he held for almost three decades. The intellectual atmosphere of the Warren home shaped Ruth's life in many positive ways. She was a very creative person busily involved in local civic and religious affairs. Soon after Ruth finished college, she married _____ Burch. They moved to Cleveland, Tennessee. The marriage produced three sons. Ruth's husband died circa 1956 at which time her two older sons, John and Jim, were married and were pursuing life careers in the US AirForce. Having only ten-year-old Tommy at home and being 300 miles from her aging parents, Ruth and Tommy moved back to Tuscaloosa circa 1960. She parked a nice house trailer in the side yard of her parents' home at 515 on 18th Street. However, she and Tommy lived for the most part in her parents' house next door, a lovely two-story five bedroom house the Warrens purchased from the W. A. Boyd estate following Granddaddy's death in 1944.

After Ruth moved back to Tuscaloosa circa 1960, she and Daddy renewed a friendship they had shared during earlier years when they were much younger. They fell in love. However, there was a problem.

Daddy was already dating another person, Nell McDuff, a divorced lady, who, like Ruth, was a fine person. Daddy was faced with a choice—continue to see Nell and put an end to the developing relationship with Ruth or drop his relationship with Nell and marry Ruth. In July 1963, Daddy married Ruth.

For a honeymoon, the newly-weds began a tour of the west by automobile. While they were gone, I, an upcoming junior medical student in Birmingham, underwent surgery at UAB for g-i bleeding. Several feet of small intestine were removed. When Daddy and Ruth learned of my hospitalization, they cut short their vacation and returned home. I was delighted to see them.

A few weeks later in September 1963, Daddy had a major heart attack. He never recovered to the point that he could return to work. He was mentally and emotionally devastated. Even so, Ruth and Daddy found happiness in their short-lived marriage of five months.

Lingering consequences of having a third party involved, Nell McDuff, created problems. When Peggy and I came home for Christmas in 1963, Daddy and Ruth told us they had decided to go separate ways and were to get a divorce. We were heartbroken, but there was an even darker cloud hovering over Daddy. He was dying of cardiac disease. He knew it and it was obvious to others.

Like most medical students, I looked upon my father's physical condition through the eyes of an "up-and-coming doctor." I noted Daddy's skin had the ashen appearance of a man with a low blood oxygen level. His voice was weak. He could barely walk across the room. I called his cardiologist, Dr. Max Moody, and told him I had checked Daddy's blood pressure and it was very high. I also had auscultated his heart and the rhythm was very irregular due to frequent premature ventricular contractions, a very ominous sign. Dr. Moody was courteous but he made it clear that all available treatment had been given and there was nothing more to do. Fourteen days later, Herman called me and said Daddy was dead. I was sad, but not shocked.

Daddy's death created potential significant legal hurdles. Having been married to Ruth for just a few months, he had not gotten around to drawing up a new *Last Will and Testament*. The old will he had made after Mother died in 1958 was no longer valid since he had remarried. Ruth and Daddy had discussed a divorce settlement in general terms but had given little attention to details.

As widow of the deceased, Ruth, by law, was entitled to a large part of Daddy's estate. However, her request was for a small monetary settlement in cash and a few acres of land on the Boyd farm on which she planned to move the house trailer from her daddy's yard and make it her home.

My brother, Herman Jr., the older son, served as administrator in settling Daddy's estate. I was a struggling junior medical student and still suffering with chronic g-i bleeding. I had little time to meet with Herman to discuss the division of Boyd property. Herman made those decisions, decisions that I later learned were opposite to Daddy's wishes as expressed in his will of 1958. I never saw the 1958 will until 2023. When I read of Daddy's instructions that Herman ignored, I was disappointed.

Lest the reader misunderstands my love for Herman, the two of us shared a deep love as

# THE CRABBE ROAD AND THE BOYD FAMILY

The Hayse and Peggy Boyd home on Lake Tuscaloosa was built in 1977.

The home of our daughter Cinda and her husband Allan

brothers, but our interests and goals in life were quite different. I hold no ill will toward him. In *Physician or Parson? One Moan's Search for the Answer* a memoir I wrote in 2000, I lovingly devote and an entire chapter to my brother.

**Boyds on the Crabbe Road in the Future**
It has been one of God's greatest gifts of my life to have spent my entire life on the Crabbe Road except for the years 1961-1977 during which I lived in Birmingham. I love the Boyd farm and am happy that our three children have been given parcels of the farm with the hopes that one day they may live on this sacred land.

In 1997, our middle child, Cinda Boyd Perry and her husband Allan built a lovely home next door to us. Allan did most of the construction on the house. It was a great joy having their children, Brooke and Brett, grow up so close to us. In 2024, Brett is building a home on a lot on Rushing family land three miles from our house that we bought from Peggy's parents many years ago. Brooke and her husband Kyle Sanford live about eight miles from our home on US Highway 43 North. Maybe one day they will choose to build on Boyd property.

Denson, our youngest child, lives in Atlanta. He has been given a beautiful lot next to Cinda's lot. He hopes one day to retire and spend his last years on Boyd property.

Tara, our oldest, also has a beautiful lot next to Cinda's. She and her husband make her home in McCalla, Alabama. Possibly one day she may desire to relocate to the farm on which she grew up. Tara's children, Savannah, is married and lives in Paris, France. Marshall is to be married in March, 2024. He lives in Dallas, Texas. Tara's children's career goals will probably prevent them from ever living on the Boyd farm.

**Burial sites on the Crabbe Road**
Burial plots for Peggy, me, Tara and her husband, Cinda and her husband, and Denson have been purchased in Macedonia Methodist Church Cemetery, a place that is only a quarter mile from the Boyd farm. I take comfort in knowing my final resting place will be on the Crabbe Road and adjacent to the church that I attended in childhood and the place where I confessed Jesus

# A ROAD, A CEMETERY, A PEOPLE

The six-story Alston Building

Christ as Lord and Savior.

**William Aaron Boyd, Jr.: A benevolent man**
Granddaddy's success as a business man in timber, real estate, and insurance during the 1920s-1940s is noted earlier in this chapter. His office was on the fourth floor in the six-story Auston building in downtown Tuscaloosa, a building completed in 1909 and is considered Tuscaloosa's first skyscraper.

During the years prior to the American Great Depression of the 1930s, friends periodically borrowed money in times of need from Granddaddy. He was honest, generous, and lent money at standard interest rates or at no interest at all. Following the stock market crash in October 1929, many banks locked their doors in bankruptcy. Bank customers lost their cash reserves held in banks. Included in that number were people indebted to Granddaddy. With their money in the bank unavailable to them, they had no way to repay their loans to Grandaddy. He could have done what banks and many private lenders did, foreclose on the loans and take possession of people's homes and properties. If he had done that, he would have greatly increased his own wealth. He did not take advantage of those unfortunate friends. He refused to foreclose on loans and leave debtors without homes and deprived of the bare necessities of life. His action speaks volumes about his compassion toward his fellow man. The story of his benevolence captured national attention.

Our family keepsakes contain a transcript of an interview in which a news reporter questioned Granddaddy about debt and its dangers. W. A. Boyd, Jr. believed that debt was one of the greatest robbers of human happiness. He rendered sound advice on this subject, counsel that is greatly needed in the 21st century. Many marriages have been ruined due to the inability of the partners to control spending. The same applies to nations. It is sad that many in today's world no longer save money for "rainy days." Those days surely come to each of us.

In 1932, Granddaddy went to the public steps of the Tuscaloosa County Courthouse and set fire to I.O.U. notes in the amount of $50,000 that was owed him by borrowers. According to current economic calculations, $50,000 in 1932 would have a purchasing power of $1,115,660 in 2024.

The following photo was made of W. A. Boyd and broadcaster Philip Lord at the national headquarters of NBC radio in New York City in 1932.

**Granddaddy's Death**

**Tuscaloosa News September 13, 1944 page 1**
**W. A. Boyd, 68**
**Succumbs here**
**Funeral services are to be held Thursday**
William A. Boyd, Jr. 68, resident of 515 18th Street in this city, died early this morning at his home after an illness lasting several weeks.

Mr. Boyd was stricken with a heart attack in late July and had been seriously ill since. He was widely known throughout Tuscaloosa County. During most of his life, he operated a farm, but in recent years, he was prominent in real estate transactions and the lumber business. He was a member of the First Methodist Church of Tusca-

14

# THE CRABBE ROAD AND THE BOYD FAMILY

In case you heard the "We, the People" broadcast over NBC Sunday, you heard William A. Boyd, of Tuscaloosa, Ala., tell how back in 1932 he tore up $50,000 worth of I. O. U. notes, bounding checks and difficult debts, inserting an ad in the Tuscaloosa paper asking all his debtors to come by and renew their friendship and business with him. Boyd recommended this as a swell Christmas or New Year's gift ... if you can afford it. Here's a cut of Boyd, with Phillips Lord leaning over his shoulder as he told the nation-wide network of his Good Samaritan deed.

The caption below this photograph reads, "In case you heard the 'We, the People' broadcast over NBC on Sunday, you heard William A. Boyd of Tuscaloosa, Alabama, tell how back in 1932, he tore up $50,000 worth of I. O. U. notes, binding the checks and difficult debts, inserting an ad in the Tuscaloosa paper asking all his debtors to come by and renew their friendship and business with him. Boyd recommended this as a swell Christmas or New Year's gift ... if you can afford it. Boyd is shown with Phillip Lord leaning over his shoulder as he told the nation-wide network of his Good Samaritan Gift."

loosa.

Survivors include: his widow, Mrs. Aney Beck Boyd; four sons, Herman Boyd, Sr. who was re-elected as a member of the Tuscaloosa County Board of Revenue last May; Eldon Boyd, also of Tuscaloosa; Early Boyd of Mobile; Woodrow Boyd of Mobile; two sisters, Mrs. John Snow of Brookwood and Mrs. Johnnie Guin of Johns, Alabama.

Funeral services will be held at 3:00 p.m. from First Methodist Church with Dr. C. C. Daniel officiating assisted by the Rev. Marvin Park. Burial will be in the Tuscaloosa Memorial Park by Mathis-Jones.

Active pallbearers for the rites will be: Sgt. J.B. Gregory, A. Parker Mize, Henry Taylor, C. B. Hinton, E. L. Dodson, and M.C. Fitts.

Honorary pallbearers will be: Dr. John Shamblin, Dr. S.T. Hardin, Dr. R.M. Wallace, W.W. Deal, Bruce Shelton, James McCollum, Judge W. C. Warren, Cliff Lindsey, Frank Rice, Judge Chester Walker, L. C. Smitherman, Charlie Wright, Herman Noland, J. B. Clements, John Hagler, Thurman James, Lonnie Shirley, Howard Hagler, C. D. Newman, Julius H. Allen, C. W. Gross, Victor Holman, John E. Walker, and Pat Lancaster.

Honorary pallbearers are requested to be at the church by 2:40 p.m. Thursday.

Note: Parker Mize was grandaddy's partner in a local insurance agency.

I was four years and ten months old when Grandaddy died. I have vague memory of being in his home only once or twice. The two-story house had a wide front porch extending across the entire front of the house. I remember him sitting at his rolltop desk near the stairwell in the entrance hall.

I do have vivid recall of walking up the front steps of First Methodist Church at the time of the funeral service. Mother was holding one hand and my first cousin, Jenelle Thomas, daughter of Daddy's deceased sister, Lille Boyd Gast was holding my other hand.

After he died, his big desk came to our house and my grandmother moved in with us until her death from leukemia in 1947. I often just sat and looked at that old desk and pondered the hundreds of papers that he had written, read, and signed while sitting at the desk.

15

# A ROAD, A CEMETERY, A PEOPLE

**The death of Anie Beck Boyd**

It is interesting that Grandmother Boyd spent the final years of her life following Granddaddy's death in 1944 on the Crabbe Road, a stone's throw from the house where she and her family lived in the early 1900s.

Following Grandaddy's death, she broke up housekeeping in the big house on 18th St. and made her home with us until her death in 1947. As a result, much of the time, I had two grandmothers living with us. Grandmother Farquhar had broken up housekeeping in 1936 following the death of Granddaddy Farquhar. She lived until 1957 and lived with us several months out of the year spending the other months living with my Aunt Lula Roberts in Mobile and Aunt Carrie Kemp in Fayette. Our house was large enough that we had plenty of room for these two dear loved ones.

Grandmother Boyd developed leukemia in 1947. There was little treatment available at the time. She received treatment at University Hospital in Birmingham. I remember riding in the car when Daddy took her to see the doctor there. In those days, US Highway 11 followed the route that today is Alabama Highway 215, a very crooked and narrow road. She died August 12, 1947.

**August 13, 1947** *The Tuscaloosa News* **Front page**
**Mrs. W. A. Boyd, succumbs at 66**
**Rites on Thursday**
**Lifelong resident of Tuscaloosa County**

Mrs. W. A. Boyd, Jr. died Tuesday afternoon at Druid City Hospital after an extended illness. She had been undergoing treatment for leukemia for several months, relatives said.

The deceased was the widow of W. A. Boyd, Jr. and the mother of Hermas Boyd, a member of the Tuscaloosa County Board of Revenue. She was 66 years old.

Since the death of her husband three years ago, Mrs. Boyd had made her home with Herman Boyd and his family on the Crabbe Road. She was a lifelong resident of Tuscaloosa County and leaves a host of friends who will mourn her passing. Mrs. Boyd was a member of the First Methodist Church of Tuscaloosa.

Funeral services will be held at 4:00 p.m. Thursday at Macedonia Methodist Church with the Rev. E. S. Jackson officiating. Interment will be in Tuscaloosa Memorial Park by Memory Chapel.

The body will lie in state in the Herman Boyd residence until time of the funeral.

Mrs. Boyd leaves four sons, Herman, Eldon, and Woodrow of Tuscaloosa County and Early Boyd who is in the US Army. She also leaves three sisters, Mrs. Dosie Oswalt of Northport, Mrs. Maude Watkins of Samantha, and Mrs. Charles King of Louisville, Kentucky, and two brothers Will Beck of Louisville, Kentucky, and E. A. Beck of Ralph.

Active pallbearers for the funeral will be Judge W. C. Warren, John Hagler, John and Lonnie Shirley, Eugene Tierce, and Roy Rushing.

Honorary pallbearers will include Henry Taylor, Abe Williams, Houston Wood, Dr. R. M. Wallace, Pat Lancaster, Judge Chester Walker, John E. Walker, Cliff Lindsey, Frank Rice, Spurgeon Black, Hugh Spencer, Grady Shirley, Charlie Newman, Bailey Thompson, Nathan Chism, T. L. James, and Matt T. Maxwell.

**The practice of lying in state in the home of the deceased**

Grandmother's obituary notes that her body would lie in state in our home until the time of the funeral. It was a common practice in the Lafoy Community and widespread throughout the South that after the body of the deceased was embalmed at the funeral home, it was brought back to the family residence where it would lie in state with the casket open until the day of the funeral which was usually the next day.

While lying in state, friends and family members would call expressing condolences. Foods of

# THE CRABBE ROAD AND THE BOYD FAMILY

all descriptions were brought in for the grieving family. In some ways, it was a social event as many in attendance rarely saw each other in the work-a-day world.

Around bedtime as people began to leave the home, two or three visitors would volunteer to stay the night beside the casket while family members tried to get some sleep. I have clear memories of Grandmother's open casket positioned in the wide hallway of our house that extended from the front door to a small back porch next to the dining room. I, too, in my teenage years later volunteered to stay the night at our next-door neighbor's house when Mrs. Lela Hyche Tierce Clements lay in state on August 23, 1958.

People did not regard this as a burden. Rather, it was a time during the quietness of the night for those keeping watch to reminisce and talk and ponder the meaning of life. I treasure such memories.

**The murder of Lillie Vera Boyd Gast**
The following event did not occur on the Crabbe Road, but it is an important part of my Boyd family history.

It is noted at the beginning of this chapter, that Lillie Boyd, born April 2, 1905, was the daughter of W. A. and Anie Beck Boyd. She was a member of Macedonia Methodist Church in 1915 when the family lived just off the Crabbe Road near the church.

Lillie married Joseph Wheeler Gast, born March 13, 1898, and together they had six children, the first being Evelyn Jenelle, born January 16, 1921. Other children included: Colleen Boyd, born October 18, 1923; William Aaron Boyd, born April 23, 1926; Jacqueline Boyd, born August 15, 1928; Jimmy Lee Boyd, born July 5, 1930; Glenaves Ann Boyd, born October 4, 1932.

On April 1, 1935, Wheeler Gast shot and killed Lillie in their home in front of the two youngest children. The other children were just a short distance away at school. The following *Tuscaloosa News* article tells the sad story.

***The Tuscaloosa News*, April 2, 1935, page 1**
**Services held for slain wife, Lillie Boyd Gast**
**Neighbors relate she told of Gast's threats on her life**
A story of almost incessant domestic discord, spun with threads of threats of death, was unwound Tuesday as officers continued to build up a case of what they believe will be premediated murder against Joe Wheeler Gast who struck his wife over the head with a blunt instrument and then fired a pistol bullet into her body with fatal results Monday afternoon in their home in Ralph.

Meanwhile six minor children, two of them too young to realize the import of the tragedy that struck with lightening swiftness in the little house blurred by a smoking pistol, remain to mourn the loss of their mother.

Their father, stoic and tight lipped in his cell at the county jail, admitted that "I killed her" but would add no word that would enlighten officers in the overt act that drove him to his berserk sway on Monday.

Services for the slain young matron were to be held at 4 o'clock this afternoon from the home of her brother, Earl Boyd, at 1915 Broad Street. Officiating will be Rev. Charles R. Oakley and Rev. J. T. Beale. Interment will be in Tuscaloosa Memorial Park, Foster's Funeral Home in charge.

Pall bearers will be A. P. Mize, Sgt. J. B. Gregory, H. C. Bell, W. Charles Warren, E. L. Dodson, and L. E. McGraw. (A. P. Mize was W. A. Boyd's partner in a local insurance agency).

The slaying victim was the daughter of Mr. and Mrs. W. A. Boyd and was born and reared in Tuscaloosa as a member of a well-known family. For the past two years, the couple and their six children had made their home in Ralph. The children are: Jenelle, 14; Colleen, 12; Aaron, 9; Jacklyn, 7; Jimmy Lee, 5; Ann, 3.

Surviving are five brothers: Lee, Earl, Eldon,

# A ROAD, A CEMETERY, A PEOPLE

Herman, and Woodrow Boyd.

A neighbor of the Gasts reported to the authorities the harassed woman had come to his house on Sunday to tell him and his family of several threats of death that had been made to her and to relate alleged abuses.

After killing his wife on Monday, Gast fled from a deputy sheriff and caught a ride to town to surrender to Sheriff Festus Shamblin.

**Boyd family account of the murder**
Boyd family tradition holds that the murder occurred during the hours that the older children were in school a short distance away. As the ruckus broke out, little Jimmy Lee and Ann were hiding under the bed but were in the room during the crime.

For a period of about six weeks, all six children were taken to the home of their uncle, Cornelius Addalee "Lee" Boyd and his wife Una. Afterwards, Janelle lived with another aunt and uncle, Eldon and Annie Mae Boyd until she married James Thomas on January 16, 1937. It is not clear where Colleen lived after her stay with Lee and Una. She married Jimmy Rouse in 1942. William Aaron lived with another aunt and uncle, Early and Ethel Boyd until 1942 when at the age of 15 he joined the US Navy. His grandfather, W. A. Boyd, signed the papers falsifying his age in order to join the Navy. Family rumor is that he and his Aunt Ethel did not get along and that led to his desire to leave Tuscaloosa. Lee Boyd died February 28, 1944.

After the six-week period, Jacqueline lived with her Boyd grandparents until 1946 when she married Walter Dodson Rankin. Jimmy Lee, after the six-week stay with Lee Boyd, lived in our home. It was not a happy situation. The mental trauma of his past affected him greatly. He ran away from our house as a teenager and joined the Navy. He never married and was killed in a motorcycle accident in Oregon in 1969. His body was returned to Tuscaloosa where he is buried in Tuscaloosa Memorial Park next to his mother and his Boyd grandparents. As with all her siblings, Ann was taken to the home of Lee and Una Boyd and was legally adopted by them. Lee died February 28, 1944.

In 2024, the great-grandson of Lillie Boyd Gast, Stanley Michal Adams, lives on the Crabbe Road beside Carrolls Creek Baptist Church.

The *Tuscaloosa Magazine*, based in Northport was a publication that featured stories of local and Alabama history in the late 20th century. An article on the trial of Joseph Wheeler Gast ail was published in the magazine entitled "Man of Sorrows." It was written by Clint Cargile. Much of the information was the result of research done by Stan Adams, grandson of Jenelle Gast Thomas. For many years, Stan has made his home on the Crabbe Road directly across the road from the site of Lafoy School and only a mile from the site where Lillie Boyd lived in 1915 when her name appeared on the church roll of Macedonia Methodist Church, along with W. A. Boyd and Aney Beck Boyd.

**Man of Constant Sorrows**
In the summer of 1936 amongst a three-month drought across most of Alabama, Joseph wheeler Gast took the long walk into Kilby Prison's death cell to meet Alabama newest form of execution, the electric chair, "Big Yellow." He had no hope for clemency as a yard of appeals and two claims of insanity proved fruitless. Govern Bibb Graves had already stated he would not intervene and the fateful time was set for just after midnight on Friday, June 4. But Joe Wheeler Gast appeared calm as the warden entered his cell, displaying no outward show of emotion of excitement. He closed his Bible, the source of much comfort over the past year, rose quietly off the bed, and followed the officer out of his cell.

As he was led to the chair, Joe glanced at Homer McGraw, a Tuscaloosa funeral director and a person known by Gast and simply said, "Goodbye." He also bid goodbye to the warden and several others present. He sat still as the

# THE CRABBE ROAD AND THE BOYD FAMILY

straps were fastened around his arms and legs. Just before the mask was placed over his eyes, Gast gave his final words, "I'm sorry for what I've done, but I know in my heart God has forgiven me." At 12:15 a.m. the switch was thrown and again at 12:17 at which time Gast was proceeded dead, earning himself the dubious honor the first person from Tuscaloosa County to die in Big Yellow.

The story of Joseph Wheeler Gast first made headlines on April 1st 1935, just days after his return from the Civilian Conservative Corps at Chatom, Alabama where he had been working for several months. Many friends of the Ralph farmer and his wife, Mrs. Lillie Vera Boyd Gast, hoped that the evening headline was some sort of April Fools' Day prank. Unfortunately, it was anything but. The headline read, "Ralph Farmer Murders Wife."

Joe Gast came to Alabama by way of his father, Edward H. Gast, Jr., a gunsmith and blacksmith. Edward Sr. was a prominent citizen of Gainesville, Florida, who disapproved of Edward Jr.'s marriage to Ella Grower, an Indian and housekeep for the Gast family. Ed and Ella raised eight boys who gained a reputation as a rowdy bunch. The Gast brothers were a group of "good ol' boys" who liked to drink and fight. They found work as skilled laborers, doing odd jobs in carpentry and roofing. Joseph served in the military during the First World art, but was stationed in Florida and never went overseas. He and his brothers were also talented musicians, once traveling to Meridian, Mississippi to play with the legendary Jimmie Rodgers. They also called many local square dances.

It was at one of these dances that Joe Gast met his future wife, Lille Vera Boyd, the only daughter of William Aaron Boyd, Jr. a prominent businessman in the Tuscaloosa area. After the First World War, Mr. Boyd made a fortune buying and clearing property around Tuscaloosa and selling it to farmers. By the 1930s, he had gained a considerable amount of political pull in the area. He even received a writeup in the *Wall Street Journal*. Soon after, he was invited to New York to ring the opening bell at the New York Stock Exchange. It's easy to see why a man of his wealth and statue didn't want his only daughter hanging around at country square dances and spending her time with a known troublemaker such as Joe Gast.

Joe and Lillie tried to elope several times, but her father always sent her five brothers to track them down and bring her back. Eventually, they managed a successful elopement and lived several years in Mississippi and Tuscaloosa before relocating with their six children to a little farm in Ralph twenty miles south of Tuscaloosa in 1933.

Trouble began soon afterward when, in November 1933, Joe took a job with a CCC camp at Fort Barrancas, Florida, later transferring to the Chatom camp in North Alabama. During her husband's absence, Lille Gast began attending square dances and returning to the free-spirited life she had enjoyed before meeting Gast. There were also rumors of an affair with a prominent Tuscaloosa businessman. While Gast was still away at the CCC camp, he received an anonymous letter telling him "Come home if you think anything of your family." The letter, later revealed to have been written by his oldest daughter Evenly Janelle Gast, was intended to save the family, but it turned out to be its undoing.

Gast returned home on the last weekend of March 1935 to confront his wife. He stopped at a friend's house on the way, borrowing a German Ruger pistol. No one is quite sure of the events that took place upon his return, but a neighbor reported that Lillie came to his house on Sunday, March 31, to tell him and his family about several threats of death. She also related to him several alleged abuses since Gast's return. Lillie Gast had already been in contact with a lawyer and many believe that it was on that Sunday that Lillie told Gast of her plans to divorce him. Due to the prominence of her family and Gast's frequent absence, she would most likely gain custody of her children as well.

This was all too much for Joe Gast, and on Monday, April 1, 1935, one day before his wife's 30th birthday, he struck her on the head with the German pistol, then shot her in the chest, killing her instantly. He left her lying on her side across their bed, blood streaming from both the gunshot wound and the gash across her head. Their two youngest children, Jimmy Lee, 4, and Glenaves Ann, 2, were still at home at the time and hid under a bed. The other four chidden were in the school building just across the street. They undoubtedly heard the fatal shot, as did several neighbors who reported seeing Gast flee from the house moments later.

Gast called on prominent Ralph citizen, Matt Taylor, and reported what he had done. Then he fled into the nearby swamp, pursued by Deputy Sheriff Murray Pate and two of Lillie's brothers. While in the swamp, Gast disposed of the pistol and made his way to the home of his friend Shepshed Park. Park convinced him to turn himself in and offered to give him a ride to Tuscaloosa. Gast, realizing the gravity of the situation he had put himself in accepted Park's offer. They rode into town where he surrendered to Sheriff Festus Shamblin and was locked in the jail.

He agreed to an interview with *The Tuscaloosa News* and readily admitted the crime. "I killed her," he said through a small window in the jail. Asked how he did it, he merely replied, "I shot her and hit her over the head." Remaining stoical and tightlipped, he gave no further details, asking only, "How are my children?"

Gast's children were sent to live with their grandparents William Aaron and Aney Boyd. The very next day rather than celebrating their mother's birthday, they attend her memorial service at their uncle Early Boyd's home at 1915 Broad Street in downtown Tuscaloosa. Later she was interred in Tuscaloosa Memorial Park Cemetery.

Joe Wheeler Gast was indicted on charges of first-degree murder. The trial began on April 25, 1935, with Judge Henry B. Foster presiding. The newspapers had already reported Gast's intention to plead not guilty by reason of insanity. His attorneys, Fred Nichol, Liston Bell, and John Leland had spent the last three weeks gathering evidence to prove Gast's alleged insanity. The only evidence the defense could offer was a stint Gast served in a Florida insane asylum almost 20 years before after his discharge from the military.

On the day of the trial, the defendant, a study in somber and gray, sat with wrinkled and downcast brow in the midst of his defense council, occasionally tapping nervously on the table and whispering to his attorneys behind his palm. He was attired in a gray denim work shirt, open at the throat, and rough, gray trousers, the same ensemble he had worn since entering the county jail. He fingered an unlighted cigarette, casting longing glances toward a place to smoke it.

His eyes seemed to avoid the occasional gaze of the father of the slain woman, who sat with the prosecutor, not six feet away. The fact that he was allowed to sit at the prosecution table was a testament to his prominence and influence in Tuscaloosa. William A. Boyd had already made it known he intended to push prosecution to the limit and seek the death penalty. The elder Boyd was with the state's imposing solicitor Gordan Davis and Robert A. Wright, John Bealle, and Charles Warren. Two seats to the left of Gast sat his mother, Mrs. Ella Gast, wearing a dark frock, white straw hat and white shoes, her eyes dim behind gold-trimmed spectacles.

The courtroom overflowed as more than 400 people filled the seats and overflowed into the aisles. As the jury was selected and seated, Gast was examined by three court appointed physicians. They made a preliminary probe to determine his mental condition at the time of, and prior to, the murder.

Before 2 o'clock, Gast's insanity defense was already thrown out. The doctors had examined the defendant and concluded, "He was sane at the time of the commission of the crime and is

# THE CRABBE ROAD AND THE BOYD FAMILY

sane at this time." His alleged insanity was also overshadowed by numerous stories of almost incessant domestic discord, spun with threads of threat and death. The largest hurdle to Gast's insanity plea was the murder weapon. It was impossible to prove him mentally incompetent when he had stopped at a friend's house to borrow the gun two days before the murder. This not only threw out the insanity defense, it also gave persecutors ample evidence of premediated murder.

Ninety witnesses were summoned to the trial, 57 of them for the defense. The prosecutor's battle plan presented Gast as being "just as mean as he can be." Wright described him as "having hell in his heart." He sketched Gast's 15-year marriage to Lilli Vera as one of constant abuses and terror for the poor woman and her children. "Who knows how many times the hand of that man has been at her throat? He made her leave her children and drove her out! He robbed those children of the best friend they've got!" Wright thundered at the jury and packed courtroom.

A neighbor of Gast's testified the defendant had told him of his plans to kill his wife. When the man remonstrated with him over this possible fate on the children, he claimed Gast told him, "William A. Boyd will take care of them."

The defense presented a picture to the jury aimed at strengthening the insanity pleas by enlarging upon the unnaturalness and heinousness of the killing. They pictured Mrs. Gast as a model wife and devoted to her home and family. The only item varying from this defense was their asking a witness, "Did Gast tell you that his wife ought to stay at home with the children and quit running around to dances?" The question brought quick objecting from the state.

On the second day of the trial, Friday, June 26, Gast took the stand and astounded the overflowing courtroom as he testified, "I refuse to drag my wife's name into this because I loved her too much and she is not here to strike back." He gave no further details. When asked of his alleged insanity at the time of the murder, Gast replied, momentarily breaking into a frenzy, "Insanity? Of course, I was insane when I killed her and broke all those hearts. I was madly insane. If I hadn't been, I would never have done it. I loved my wife insanely, and if I could dig the eath from over her with these fingers and have her again, I would gladly do it."

The jury received the case at 6:40 Friday night and retired at 10:45 to sleep on it. The next morning, they had a verdict. As the jury filed into the courtroom, Wheeler Gast at last raised his head from his arms. His mother who had suffered through the whole ordeal downcast as the state had pleaded for the death penalty for her son was not there to learn her son's fate. She was home ill. The jury foreman, James R. Maxwell, rose to his feet and announced the verdict, "Guilty of murder, as charged."

There were no softening words of mercy. Gast sobbed softly, but otherwise showed little emotion. There was no outburst from the rest of the court. "Have you anything to say before sentence is pronounced upon you?" asked Judge Foster? Gast hesitated for just second, flinched slightly and shook his head in negation with a few mumbled words that were not audible at the bench. Judge Foster passed down a death in the electric chair sentence on Joseph Wheeler Gast, the first such sentence given to any man from Tuscaloosa County. It was also the first death sentence given in Tuscaloosa County in 15 years since outlaw Dock Bigham was hanged outside the county jail for the murder of Sheriff P. M. Watts in 1920. Gast took a few nervous paces, nodded his head slightly as if receiving the confirmation of his worse fears, and was lead, manacled, from the courtroom with head high. Friends of graying Boyd immediately forged to him behind the railings, clasping his hand and offered words of congratulations.

Later that day, Gast met with reporters at his jail cell prior to his transfer to Alabama's death row at Kilby Prison. "I forgive everybody who may have done me injustice, and I am asking them to likewise forgive me," he said, clutching the bars of his cell and lighting cigarettes in chain fashion. "I have no ill will toward anybody and I pray to God I will be forgiven." When asked why he refused to "drag my good wife's name into this," Gast simply replied, "Rather than tell what I know, I changed my defense." But he hoped his fate would be a warning to others. "I hope that my death will heal some of the heartaches that I have caused, and discourage anybody who would do wrong," he said.

Harrowing too was the thought of his six children. "I want you to tell the public not to point the finger of scorn at these children," he choked. "After all, they are not responsible for anything we have done. I want people to help them and encourage them to grow up and be ladies and gentlemen and to be respected by people worth knowing."

Profuse was Gast in his appeal to Mr. and Mrs. Boyd. "I broke the heart of one of the best women who ever lived with all respect to my splendid mother." He said of Mrs. Boyd, "If she forgives me, I can go to my death with a better soul. I hold no ill will toward anybody, and I hope they will come to hold none against me."

The following Monday, Gast, who was sentenced to die on June 28, was transferred out of Tuscaloosa to Kilby Prison. The four deputies responsible for his transfer said Gas appeared hopeful throughout the long auto trip, chain smoking the entire way despite his handcuffs.

Gast would find himself back in Tuscaloosa over a month later only to hear Judge Foster throw out any chance of a retrial. He was in good spirits, chatting with his mother and two devoted sisters, but after Judge Foster's ruling, he was quickly taken back to his death cell at Kilby. On June 25, three days before his scheduled execution, Gast was granted a reprieve by the Alabama Supreme Court until they could review is case sometime in early 1936.

Execution of Wheeler Gast was delayed a year by the process of law. The circuit jury verdict was confirmed by the Supreme Court twice, and two sanity hearings were held to test the claim of the defense that Gast was insane at the time the crime was committee. Several expert witnesses held him sane, and the governor made it clear that he would not interne in the execution. "I will go to the electric chair like a man. It won't hurt me," Gast declared. Regarding his refusal to give a motive behind his crime, Gast stuck by his decision, "I'm glad from the very bottom of my heart that I did not drag her name into this, and disgrace her family and our children," he said with rising fervor. "What I know will go with me!" He impaled one reporter with eyes that gleamed with something akin to fanatic zeal and excitement, "I hope anybody that utters a harmful word against her other than to her and my family—I hope God will strike such a person dead."

On the early June Sunday following Joseph Wheeler Gast's meeting with Big Yellow Mama, the 37-year-old war veteran was buried at Tuscaloosa Memorial Park in an area reserved for Veterans. Members of the Frank W. Moody Post No. 32 American Legion served as pallbearers, and the color guard accorded military honors to the deceased was used. According to a family story, which has not been confirmed, William Aaron Boyd, on his deathbed, called Ella Gast and confessed to having paid five thousand dollars to someone to ensure Gast received the death sentence.

CHAPTER 3

# Macedonia Cemetery

~~~

Macedonia Methodist Church Cemetery located on the Crabbe Road nine miles north of Northport is the burial site of approximately 500 individuals most of whom lived within ten miles of the cemetery. My childhood home was a quarter mile north of the cemetery. I passed by it every time I went to town or to school. In addition, as a child sitting in the sanctuary of Macedonia Church each Sunday, I gazed out the clear-glass church windows and pondered the lives of the people buried there. By the age of nine or ten, I often rode my bike to the cemetery and walked through the burial ground and read inscriptions on the tomb stones. I asked my parents many questions about the history of those buried there. When visiting the cemetery, I lingered longer at the grave of John Howard Boyd, my baby brother who died of whooping cough at age three weeks in 1942. The cemetery became even more special in 1958 when my mother died and was buried next to John Howard. Then in 1964, my father was buried beside Mother and John Howard. The area is indeed sacred ground. I write this history to give identity and honor to those whose earthly remains rest there until the second coming of the Lord at which time they will arise to meet Jesus in clouds of glory.

Macedonia Methodist Church was established in 1902, but burials in the cemetery occurred many years before the church was organized. The grave with the oldest grave marker giving the name and date of the person interred is that of Susannah Tierce who was buried on April 27, 1862. In addition to Susannah Tierce, there are 18 other graves with tombstones giving the names of the interred persons and the dates of burial that occurred prior to 1902 and the organization of the church.

There are 128 graves in the cemetery marked only by a small rock that has no name or date on them. It is possible some of these burials occurred prior to 1902.

**The William Taylor Hamner, Sr. legacy**
One of the early families to settle near North River on the Crabbe Road was William Taylor Hamner, Sr. who along with his first wife settled here circa 1830. An entire chapter in *A Road, A Cemetery, A People* is devoted to the Hamner family.

In the 1970s, two of William T. Hamner, Sr.'s descendants, Geneal Hamner Black and Mary Clark Ryan, wrote a well-researched book, *Hamner Heritage—Beginning Without End,* about the Hamner family. According to Hamner family belief, William Taylor Hamner, Sr.'s first wife died circa 1840 and was buried in what would later be known as Macedonia Cemetery. Her name remains a mystery.

Following the death of his first wife, William Taylor Hamner, Sr. married Permelia Chism. Per-

# Macedonia Methodist Church Cemetery

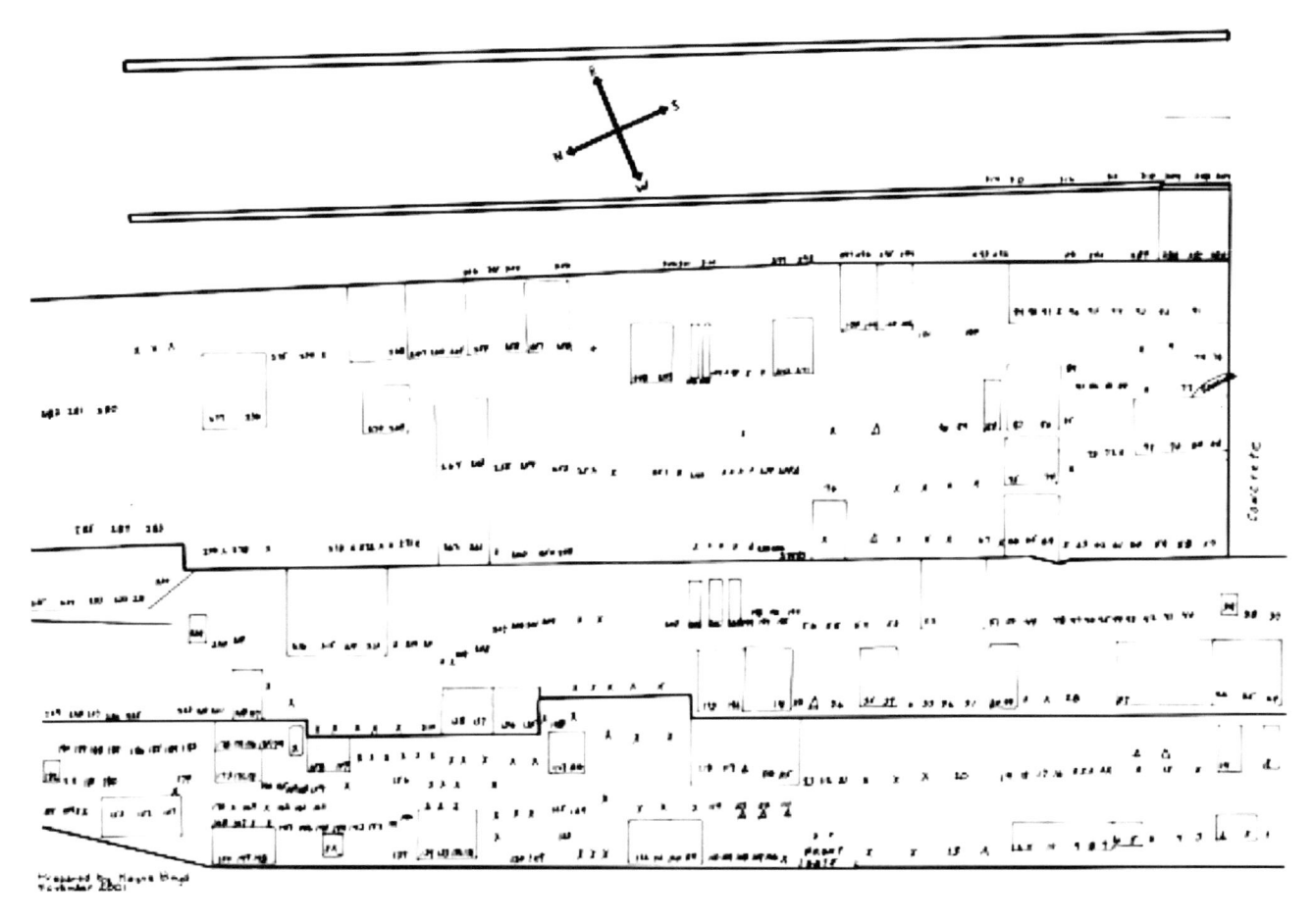

melia Chism Hamner died on August 10, 1874. She was buried in Macedonia Cemetery. William Taylor Hamner, Sr. died on July 10, 1889 and was buried in Macedonia Cemetery. His grave has a tombstone, grave # 2 on the map of the cemetery, giving his name and dates of birth and death. On either side of his grave, there are graves marked only by a slab of rock. Hamner tradition holds that these are the graves of his first two wives. He eventually married four times and fathered sixteen children by three of the four wives.

In 2001, 31 grave markers carried the name "Hamner." Others have been added since then.

**The legacy of the Benjamin Tucker Tierce family**

Benjamin Tucker Tierce (1785-1869) and his wife Susannah Clardy Tierce (June 13, 1787- April 27, 1862) were the patriarchal Tierce family in the Lafoy Community. It is thought they arrived here in the early 1830s. Public records show that on March 27, 1833, Mr. Tierce bought land from Jacob Clements on the Crabbe Road near North River. Tierce lands eventually included a thousand or so acres of land. The Tierce property included the site that later became Macedonia Church and Macedonia Cemetery.

Susannah Clary Tierce died on April 27, 1862 and was buried in what would be later known as Macedonia Cemetery. As noted, her grave marker carries the oldest date in the cemetery. Benjamin Tucker Tierce died on February 18, 1869 and was buried beside Susannah. Many other Tierce family members are buried in the cemetery. In 2001, there were 28 grave markers that carried the name "Tierce." Others have been

# MACEDONIA CEMETERY

added since then.

**Legacy of other families**
In addition to the Hamner and Tierce families, many other Lafoy Community families have multiple family members buried in Macedonia Cemetery. In 2001, twenty members of the Rushing family, fifteen members of the Clements family, twelve members of the Gay family, twelve members of the Shirley family, and eleven members of the LaFoy family are buried in there. Many additional members of these families have been buried there since 2001. Individual chapters in *A Road, A Cemetery, A People* are devoted to the Hamner, LaFoy, Rushing, Shirley, and Tierce families.

**Veterans of the Civil War**
Three tomb markers identify the interred as a veteran of the Civil War. They are: grave 2, William T. Hamner, Sr. (1814-1889); grave 238, John P. Hamner (October 4, 1845-December 18, 1905); grave 15, Nicholas House (1847-1917).

**Caretakers of the cemetery**
**John Hagler and his wife Octavia Tierce Hagler**
John Hagler and his wife Octavia Tierce Hagler had a deep and abiding love for the sacred spot that held the earthly remains of their loved ones and friends. Octavia's father, Eugene Benjamin Tierce, Sr., donated the land for Macedonia Church and Cemetery. Octavia was the great granddaughter of Benjamin Tucker Tierce and Susannah Clardy Tierce. Her Tierce linage is as follows.

Benjamin Tucker Tierce (1785-1869) and his wife Susannah Clardy Tierce (June 13, 1787-April 27, 1862) were parents to Elliott Catlett Tierce (December 17, 1827-March 21, 1906) His tombstone reads "E. C."

Elliott Catlett Tierce married Frances Caroline Doss (December 3, 1831-March 13, 1900). They were the parents of f Eugene Benjamin Tierce, Sr. (May 15, 1865-Augsut 30, 1918.) Eugene Benjamin Tierce, Sr. married Veturia Scales (November 22, 1869—June 21, 1907). They were Octavia Tierce Hagler's parents.

John and Octavia's house was across the Crabbe Road from the cemetery. It fell John's lot to oversee the digging of graves when the need occurred. Neighbors would join in and soon the task was done. No charge for grave digging was made to the deceased's family.

The original cemetery nearest the Crabbe Road has never been sodded. When I was growing up, dense woods enclosed the cemetery's north and east boundaries. Two big oak trees stood in the church parking lot at the cemetery's south end. Three or four ancient cedar trees were scattered throughout the cemetery. Cedar trees were often found in Christian graveyards, their year-round greenery symbolic of everlasting life in Christ.

The maintenance of the cemetery prior to the 1960s was performed by families of those whose loved ones were buried there. A big cleanup was done just prior to Homecoming, or Decoration Day, the first Sunday in May each year.

The spring cleaning of the entire cemetery included raking dead leaves, scraping the ground clear of weeds, putting dirt in sunken graves, and removing debris and clutter. This was done by volunteers. The cleanup was no small task; it required a community effort. Families would clean their family plots of graves and then they would clean other graves that needed attention. The process was repeated until the entire cemetery was clean. Unfortunately, in the months following the First Sunday in May celebration, weeds and grass grew back and cemetery maintenance was lax except for those family spots that continued to be well-kept by individual families. It was my responsibility and joy every few weeks to clean the Boyd plot where my little brother John Howard was buried.

### B. F. Shirley

One of the earliest families to settle in Lafoy Community was the Byrd Franklin Shirley family. An entire chapter in *A Road, A Cemetery, A People* is devoted to the Shirley family. B. F. Shirley, Jr. was born July 4, 1921, the ninth of twelve children born to Byrd Shirley and his wife Matilda Smith Shirley. When B. F. retired from his job at Gulf States Paper Corporation circa 1970s, he became custodian of the cemetery and lovingly cared for it until poor health prevented him from working. B. F. knew the background and family connections of most of the people interred there. He had assisted in digging the graves of many. I, too, know the background of many of those who are buried there and attended the funeral of many. Working together, he and I spent many hours walking over the burial sites while the two of us shared information that is included in this chapter. B. F. died February 17, 2003.

### Gary Rice

Gary Rice became cemetery custodian following B. F. and held the job for several years until he moved to another city. By marriage, Gary had family connections to the cemetery. His wife, Sharon Kay Guy Rice, was the daughter of Elsie Tierce who was the daughter of Collier Tierce who was the son of Eugene Benjamin Tierce, Sr. who was the son of E. C. Tierce who was the son of the Tierce patriarch Benjamin Tucker Tierce.

### Billy Brown

Billy Brown followed Gary Rice as custodian. He, too, is a descendant of another family of long-standing presence in Lafoy. He is the son of Nina Sue Hagler Brown who is the daughter of Albert Hagler. Albert Hagler was a brother to John Hagler, the original cemetery caretaker. In 2023, Billy is doing an excellent job of caring for the cemetery.

### Mapping the old cemetery

Graves in the original part of Macedonia Cemetery, the section that is not covered with sod and is nearest the highway, are not laid out in neat rows. This makes mapping very difficult. The first map was composed by B. F. Shirley, the then-cemetery caretaker, and me in 2001. It is shown at the beginning of this chapter.

Grave #1 is located at the southwest corner of the cemetery adjacent to the church parking lot and Highway 69. Graves 1-105 are located within the section of the old cemetery that is to the south of the front gate of the cemetery. Graves 106-285 (including 186A and 243A) are found within the section of the old cemetery that is to the north of the front gate.

There are 128 graves in the old cemetery that are identified only by a rock marker; the identity of the interred one is unknown. On the accompanying map, these graves are marked with an "x."

There are 8 graves in the old cemetery that are covered with two slabs of hewn rock resulting in a tent formation over the grave. On the accompanying map, these graves are identified with a D. Certain graves or groups of graves (family plots) are bordered by a curb of concrete or a row of blocks. On the map, all such curbs of concrete or block are shown as dark solid lines forming rectangles or squares.

### Mapping the new section of the cemetery

In 1959, available grave space in the old cemetery became scarce and a new section was opened on the east side of the cemetery, the area farthest from the highway. The first person buried in the new section was Larkin Hamner who was buried on April 19, 1955. His grave was assigned the number 286 on the cemetery map. Subsequent grave sites in the new sodded cemetery assumed numbers 287-323.

# MACEDONIA CEMETERY

**An alphabetical listing of those interred in the cemetery**

Using the grave numbers shown on the map of the cemetery at the beginning of this chapter and the information engraved on the tombstones, the following alphabetical list gives the names, along with birth and death dates as seen on the tombstones.

Because *A Road, A Cemetery, A People* is written as a history of the Crabbe Road and Lafoy Community, additional information about some individuals is given, if known. I wish I had been able to give such information for all, but my limited knowledge and lack of available research material prevents that.

The information comes from my personal experience and two books: *Hamner Heritage—Beginning Without End; 1816, a Tierce Comes to Tuscaloosa.* I also interviewed members of the Gay, Hamner, LaFoy, Rushing and Shirley families. Old *Tuscaloosa News* clippings were very helpful.

Note: If a footnote is given, it refers to the page in the book *Hamner Heritage—Beginning Without End.*

**Disclaimer**

No work such as this can be produced without typographical mistakes and errors of fact. I apologize and ask the reader's forgiveness.

**Aaron, Jessie W.**: May 28, 1912-December 27, 1912 Grave # 147

**Adams, James Monroe:** October 24, 1896-June 10, 1955 Grave # 237. He was the husband of Valda Lee House.

**Adams, Valda Lee House**: May 1, 1896-January 7, 1929 Grave # 236.

Valda is the daughter of Dovie Ann Hamner and Nicholas House.[1] Dovy Ann was the 8th child of William T. Hamner, Sr. and his second wife Permelia Chism.

**Adcox, Martha Jane Gay**: July 26, 1886-May 6, 1959.

Grave # 210.

Martha was the wife of John Adcox and the daughter of Lewellen Sydney Gay and Julie E. Gay. Martha Jane was a granddaughter of Callow "Cap" Gay and Jane Palmer Gay. She was a sister to Fanny Lee Gay Rushing, J. R. "Dick" Gay, Sam H. Gay, Robert B. Gay, Annie Pearl Gay, and Josephine Gay. All are buried in Macedonia except for John Adcox.

**Anders, E. Jr.**: March 26, 1807-August 19, 1881. Grave 140.

**Ballenger, William H.**: April 17, 1871-August 10, 1933. Grave # 180.

**Barger, Dorothy M.**: September 30, 1929-October 16, 1973. Grave # 308.

**Barger, Marvin T.**: June 10, 1947-May 23, 1965.

Grave # 307.

**Barger, Samuel**: March 17, 1919-May 6, 1981.

Grave # 309.

**Barringer, infant**: No date given.

Grave # 312B.

She is the infant daughter of Meredith Booth Barringer and Danny Barringer. Meredith is the daughter of Carol Shirley Booth and Randy Booth. Carol is the daughter of Margaret and Grady Shirly who are buried next to the infant.

**Bigham, Dock "Doc"**: 1869-1919

Grave # 250.

Dock was hanged on June 19, 1919 for the August 15, 1918 killing of Tuscaloosa County Sheriff P. M. Watts during a raid on Bigham's moonshine still in Pinney Woods. He was the last man to be publicly hanged in Tuscaloosa County. He was the father of Dugs Bigham who was killed at age seventeen in a shootout with law enforcement officers.

The story of "Doc Bigham is told in the chapter, "Crabbe Road, Doc Bigham."

**Bigham, Dugs**: May 15, 1897-November 10, 1914. Grave # 260.

He was the son of Doc Bigham and was killed

---
[1] Page 304-309

in a shootout with law enforcement officers who were searching for his father on charges of escaping from the state penitentiary where Doc was serving time for burning a tenant house belonging to Eugene B. Tierce, Sr. Three years later, Doc would kill Sheriff Watts.

**Bigham, Joe**: 1873-1917
Grave # 249.
He was a brother to Doc Bigham.

**Bigham, Johnny Ray**: August 12, 1958-June 16, 2017. Grave # 306 A.

Johnny was married to Tracey Brown, the widow of Brett Brown. Brett was the son of Naomia Shirley Brown and Jack Brown and the grandson of Lonnie and Estelle Wedgeworth Shirley. Lonnie was the son of Byrd and Matilda Shirley.

**Black, Constance Pamala Stamps**: February 13, 1955-December 28, 2022.
Grave # 310C.
Connie was the wife of Don Micheal Black who was the son of Mary Ann Geneal Hamner Black and Marion DeVaughn Black.

**Black, Mary Ann Geneal Hamner**: November 22, 1930-April 29, 2007. Grave # 310A.

Geneal was the wife of Marion DeVaughn Black and daughter of Edward Bruce Hamner and Fannie Lou Shirley Hamner. Entire chapters in *A Road, A Cemetery, A People* are devoted to the genealogy of the Hamner and Shirley families many of whom are buried in Macedonia Cemetery.

**Black, Johnnye**: August 28, 1920-December 20, 1987. Grave # 297.
She was the wife of William B. Black.

**Black, Marion DeVaughn**: November 29, 1923-July 17, 1990. Grave # 310.
He was the husband of Many Ann Geneal Hamner and the father-in-law of Constance Stamps Black. He was the son of Lena Bell Newman and Spurgeon Black.

**Black, William B.**: December 17, 1917-April 2, 1987. Grave # 296.
He was the husband of Johnnye Black.

**Blake, Albert Lee:** October 5, 1894-February 15, 1958. Grave # 221.

**Blake, David Oneal**: November 22, 1938-September 23, 1941. Grave # 223.

**Blake, Infant Mary Elois**: March 22, 1933 Grave # 222

**Boyd, Herman C. Sr.:** March 20, 1908-January 11, 1964. Grave # 23.
He was the husband of Lucille Farquhar Boyd and was my father.

**Obit for Herman Boyd, Sr.**

Herman C. Boyd, Sr., 55, of Crabbe Road and a former member of the Tuscaloosa County Board of Revenue, died Saturday afternoon of a heart attack suffered while riding in a car in downtown Tuscaloosa.

Mr. Boyd served on the Board of Revenue 1944-1952 and has been an employee of Tucker Motor Company for more than 30 years. He was general sales manager at the time of his death.

He was a member of the Macedonia Methodist Church where he was formerly a member of the official board and an adult Sunday School teacher.

He was a native of Tuscaloosa County.

Funeral services will be held Monday afternoon at 2:00 o'clock at Macedonia Methodist Church with Dr. J. H. Chitwood, the Reverend Bob Maxwell, and the Reverend Wayne Graham officiating. Burial will be in the church cemetery with Speigner-Brown Service in charge of arrangements.

Survivors include his second wife, Ruth Warren Burch Boyd; two sons, Herman Boyd, Jr. of Northport, and Hayse Boyd of Birmingham; a grandson, David Heath Boyd of Northport; three stepsons, Thomas Burch of Northport, James Burch of Lawton, Oklahoma, John Burch of Peru, Indiana; three brothers, Woodrow Boyd of Echola, Eldon Boyd of Tuscaloosa and Early Boyd of Pensacola, Florida.

Active pallbearers will be Jody Allen, John Shirley, Roy Rushing, Grady Shirley, Ralph Dorroh, Clyde Utley, Nathan Chism and DeVaughn

# MACEDONIA CEMETERY

Black.

Honorary pallbearers will be Dr. Eric Rodgers, Mr. Hayse Tucker, Robert Williamson, Johnny Tinklepaugh, Neil Snow, Judge W. C. Warren, Tuck Mathis, Dr. Maxwell Moody, Jr., Dr. Killough Patrick, Dr. Jim Thomas, John Hagler, B. F. Shirley, Lonnie Shirley, J. D. Hamner, Dee Hamner, Eugene Tierce, Bruce Hamner, Ellis Franklin, James Rushing, Howard Hagler, Howard Rushing, Dr. A. K. Patton, Sr., Robert Rushing, Dr. Howard Holley, Ollie Tanner, Neal Palmer, Dwight Tanner, John Walker, Truman Gray, Charlie Gross, Hal McCall, Chester Walker, Cliff Lindsey, Marshall Walker, Raymond Guy, Albert Hagler, Dawson Chism, Hershel Shirley, Cecil Gray, Bernard Rushing, James Hamner, and the employees of Tucker Motor Company.

**Boyd, John Howard:** 1942-1942
Grave # 21.

**Obit for John Howard Boyd**

John Howard Boyd, 2-week-old son of Mr. and Mrs. Herman Boyd, Sr. of the Crabbe Road died early today at his home after a sudden illness. The infant is survived by two brothers, Herman Boyd, Jr. and David Hayse Boyd and his parents. His father is employed by Tucker Motor Company.

Funeral services will be held at 11:00 a.m. Thursday at Macedonia Methodist Church with internment in Macedonia Cemetery.

**Boyd, Lucille Farquhar**: August 23, 1907-October 6, 1958. Grave # 22.

**Obit for Mrs. Lucille Boyd.**

Mrs. Lucille Boyd, wife of Herman Clory Boyd, Sr., died last night at Druid City Hospital after a long illness. Before her marriage, she was Grace Lucille Farquhar, a former teacher in the Fayette City School System.

She was an active member of the Macedonia Methodist Church where she taught an adult Bible class.

Funeral services will be held at 3:00 p.m. Tuesday at the Macedonia Church with the Reverend Wayne Graham and the Reverend Billy Prickett officiating. Burial will be in the church cemetery by Jones-Seigner.

Survivors include her husband, Herman Boyd, Sr., a former member of the Tuscaloosa County Board of Revenue and now sales manager of Tucker Motor Company; two sons, Herman Boyd, Jr. and David Hayse Boyd of Northport; three sisters, Mrs. G. E. "Lula" Roberts of Mobile, Mrs. J. R. "Carrie" Kemp of Fayette and Mrs. Virgie Dyer of Fayette; and one grandson, David Herman Boyd of Northport.

Active pallbearers for the funeral will be John Shirley, Roy Rushing, Tucker Mathis, Leslie Gaddy, DeVaughn Black, and Thomas Lake.

Honorary pallbearers are Pruitt Hamner, Clifton Turner, Polk Rushing, Robert Rushing, B. F. Shirley, Howard Hagler, Eugene Tierce, J. D. Hamner, Wilton Gay, Clyde Utley, Judge W. C. Warren, Grover Pearson, Gay Dorroh, Nathan Chism, Dawson Chism, Hershel Shirley, Dr. J. H. Thomas, Frank Harrell, Hayse Tucker, James Rushing, Ellis Franklin, Dee Hamner, Neil Snow, Bruce Hamner, John Hagler, Lonnie Shirley, Grady Shirley, and employees of Ticker Motor Company.

**Brooks, Dovie**: 1875-1915
Grave # 176.

**Brown, Brett:** December 2, 1964-March 6, 2010. Grave # 139A.

Brett was the son of Naomia Shirley Brown and Jack Brown and the grandson of Lonnie and Estelle Wedgeworth Shirley. Lonnie was the son of Byrd and Matilda Shirley.

**The Joe Ed Brown family burials**

Joe Ed Brown and Nina Sue Hagler Brown were the parents of four sons: Tommy; Billy; Mickey; and Scottie. Each member of the family will be cremated and their ashes interred in and near grave # 328. As of 2024, the following family members are deceased.

**Brown, Joe Ed** (November 3, 1934-August 8, 2022)
Grave # 328 C.

Joe Ed was the husband of Nina Sue Hagler Brown and the father of Tommy, Billy, Mickey, and Scottie Brown.

**Brown, Nina Sue Hagler**: 10, 1936-January 13, 2021.

Grave # 328.

Nina Sue was the daughter of Henry Albert Hagler and Kelen Elizabeth "Patty" Parizek. Henry Albert Hagler was the son of James Martin Hagler and Permelia Elizabeth Hamner.[2]

Permelia was the daughter of Louis Alfred Hamner and Penina Wilson Clements.

Louis Alfred Hamner was the son of William Taylor Hamner, Sr. and his second wife Permelia Chism.

Penina Clements was the daughter of Thomas Clements and Elizabeth Simpson.

All the above are buried in Macedonia Cemetery except for Henry Albert Hagler and Kelen Elizabeth "Patty" Parizek who are buried in Memory Hills Gardens.:

**Brown, Mickey**: (February 9, 1957-October 11, 2022).

Grave 328 A.

Mickey was the son of Joe Ed and Nina Sue Hagler Brown.

**Brown, Scottie** April 8, 1964-Augsut 13, 2018.

Grave 328 B.

Scottie was the son of Joe Ed and Nina Sue Hagler Brown.

**Cannon, Chestley Guy:** November 12, 1931-November 21, 1954. Grave # 146.

**Cannon, Guy:** May 21, 1901-January 30, 1948.

Grave # 145.

**Cannon, Jackie**: 1909-1958

Grave # 144

**Chism, Archie G.**: 1878-1949

Grave # 16

Archie G. was the son of George Washington Chism and Dovy Ann Hamner and the husband of Buna Vista Hamner who was his first cousin.[3]

Buna Vista Hamner was the daughter of John Pruitt Hamner and Annie Margaret Hall and the granddaughter of William Taylor Hamner, Sr. and his second wife Permelia Chism.

Dovy Ann Hamner was the daughter of William Taylor Hamner, Sr. and his second wife Permelia Chisms. She was born in October 1856 and died sometime between 1901-1903 and is buried in Macedonia Cemetery in a grave with no identifying headstone.[4]

George Washington Chism is buried in Macedonia Cemetery in a grave with no identifying headstone.

Archie George Chism was a brother to Bascom Virgil Chism and Harvey Morgan Chism.

All the above are buried in Macedonia Cemetery except for Bascom Chism.

**Obit for Archie George Chism**

Archie George Chism, 76, of Northport Route 1 died Sunday morning at Druid City Hospital.

He is survived by: his widow; one son, L. A. Chism, Northport; four daughters, Mrs. R. E. Nash, Atlanta; Mrs. W. C. Taylor, Rogers, Arkansas; Mrs. S. V. Sanders, Sentinel, Oklahoma; and Mrs. A. E. Newman, Gadsden; a stepson, James Monroe House; a brother, Marvin Chism.

Funeral services will be held at Macedonia Methodist Church at 11:00 a.m. Tuesday with burial in the church cemetery by Jones and Spigener.

Active pallbearers will be Bradford and Howard Hamner, Woodrow and Roy Rushing, Preston House, and Nathan Chism.

Honoree pallbearers will be L. W. White, Dr. G. W. Hall, Joe Wilson, Sellie Long, Joe Rice, James Anders, H. O. Junkin, W. J. Squires, L. H. Sellers, and W. I. Brandon.

**Chism, Archie Lewis:** October 2, 1913-March 16, 1960. Grave #19. (In *Hamner Her-*

---

[2] Page 255

[3] Page 212
[4] Pages 304-309

# MACEDONIA CEMETERY

*itage-Beginning Without End,* his name is listed as Lewis Archie) He was the son of Archie George Chism and Buena Vista Hamner Chism; the husband of Minnie Waldrop who was the daughter of Walch Waldrop and Luella Williamson. Minnie Waldrop Chism is buried in Nazareth Primitive Baptist Cemetery off Highway 43.[5]

Buena Vista Hamner Chism was the daughter of John Pruitt Hamner and Annie Margret Hall and the granddaughter of William Taylor Hamner, Sr. and Permelia Chism all of whom are buried in Macedonia Cemetery.

**Chism, Bascom Virgil**: 1882-1945
Grave # 62.

He was the husband of Mittie Etta Rigsby and the son of George Washington Chism and Dovy Ann Hamner. Bascom was a brother to Archie George Chism and Harvey Morgan Chism.

Mittie Etta Rigsby (September 21, 1886-1970) was the daughter of Jessie Tyson Rigsby and Nancy Elizabeth White and a sister to James Tyson Rigsby. James Tyson is buried in Macedonia Cemetery

Dovy Ann Hamner was the daughter of William Taylor Hamner, Sr. and his second wife Permelia Chisms. She was born in October 1856 and died sometime between 1901-1903 and is buried in Macedonia Cemetery in a grave with no identifying headstone.

George Washington Chism is buried in Macedonia Cemetery in a grave with no identifying headstone.

**Obit for B. V. Chism**

B. V. Chism, 63, prominent farmer of Northport Star Route died Thursday morning after having been ill for several months. Although Mr. Chism had been afflicted with heart trouble for some time, his sudden death came as a surprise to family and friends.

Mr. Chism for several years had engaged in in the lumber business of Tuscaloosa County being in partnership with Largus Barnes.

The deceased leaves his widow, Mrs. Mittie Rigsby Chism; one daughter, Mrs. Clyde Deal of Fayette; three sones, Eddie Chism who is with the armed forces in New Zealand; Glen Chism of Atlanta; John Chism of Northport Star Route; two brothers, Arch Chism of Northport Route 1, and Marvin Chism of Coker; one grandson.

Funeral services will be held from Macedonia Methodist Church on the Crabbe Road Saturday afternoon at 2:00 p.m.

Active pallbearers will be Nathan Chism, Dawson Chism, Howard Rigsby, Lester Appling, and Fletcher Barnes.

Honorary pallbearers will be Largus F. Barnes, J. S. Morris, Glenn Rice, Frank Rice, Dr. G. W. Hall, James Anders, Jim McCullen, C. S. Hinton, M. O. Clements, Jim Clements, and Festus Deal. Jones and Spigener will be in charge of burial.

**Chism, Buna Vista**: January 27, 1877-Februay 11, 1965). Grave # 17.

Buna Vista was the 6th child of John Pruitt Hamner and Annie Margaret Hall and the granddaughter of William Taylor Hamner, Sr. and his second wife Permelia Chism.[6]

Buena Vista Hamner married first to John Monroe House on September 9, 1894. Buna Vista and John Monroe House had one child, John Monroe House, Jr. who was born July 9, 1895. The date of death of John Monroe House, Sr. is not given nor is there a mention of a divorce from Buena Vista. But, Buena Vista Hamner House married a second time on June 14, 1900 to Archie George Chism who was her first cousin. All the above are buried in Macedonia Cemetery.

Archie George Chism and Buena Vista House Hamner had five children: (1) Maggie Lee Chism; (2) Ursula Judson Chism; (3) Ida Bell Chism; (4) Margaret Elizabeth Chism; (5) Lewis Arch Chism. Only Lewis Arch Chism is buried in Macedonia Cemetery.

**Obit for Mrs. Archie (Beuna Vista) Chism**

Mrs. Archie Chism, 88, died Thursday at

[5] Page 304

[6] Page 212

Oak Hill Nursing Home after a lengthy illness. She was a native of Tuscaloosa County and a member of Carrolls Creek Baptist Church.

Survivors include four daughters; Mrs. Margaret Walton of Atlanta; Mrs. Maggie Sanders of Sentinel, Oklahoma; Mrs. Bill Taylor of Roger, Arkansas; Mrs. Ed Newman of Orlando Florida; two sisters, Mrs. Alma Rushing of Northport, and Mrs. Ozella Rushing of Tuscaloosa. A brother J. C. Hamner and 9 grandchildren and 14 great grandchildren.

Services will be at Spigener Brown Service Chapel with burial in Macedonia Methodist Cemetery.

**Chism, Harvey M.:** December 26, 1885-July 31, 1924.

Grave # 65.

Harvey Morgan was the son of George Washington Chism and Dovy Hamner and the grandson of William Taylor Hamner, Sr. and his second wife Permelia Chism.[7]

Harvey Morgan Chism married his first cousin Ullie Mae Hamner who was the daughter of John Pruitt Hamner and Annie Margaret Hall and the granddaughter of William Taylor Hamner, Sr. and his second wife Permelia Chism.[8]

Harvey was a brother to Archie George Chism and Bascom Virgil Chism.

Harvey was the father of Virda Mae Chism.

All the above are buried in Macedonia Cemetery.

**Chism, Mittie Etta:** September 21, 1886-1970. Grave # 63.

Mittie was the wife of Bascom Virgil Chism and the daughter of Jessie Tyson Rigsby and Nancy Elizabeth White. Mittie was a sister to James Tyson Rigsby. James Tyson Rigsby is buried in Macedonia Cemetery.

**Chism, Robert Lee:** June 12, 1914-November 19, 1915. Grave # 67.

**Chism, Ullie Mae**: May 25, 1889-July 5, 1936.

Grave # 64.

Her grave marker in the in cemetery reads, "Ullie M. Hamner Chism Junkin."

Ullie Mae was the 13th child of John Pruitt Hamner and Annie Margaret Hall and the granddaughter of William Taylor Hamner, Sr. and his second wife Permelia Chism.[9]

Ullie Mae first married her first cousin Harvey Morgan Chism, son of George Washington Chism and Dovy Ann Hamner. Ullie Mae and Harvey Morgan had six children: (1) Clarence Hagler Chism who died at age one year and is buried in Macedonia Cemetery in a grave with no identification; (2) George Nathan Chism; (3) Virda Mae Chism, a child buried in Macedonia Cemetery; (4) Harvey Dawson Chism; (5) Annie Ruth Chism; (6) John Autry Chism killed in action in Germany during World War II.

Harvey Morgan Chism died July 31, 1924. After his death, Ullie Mae married a second time to Oscar Junkin. Therefore, her tombstone in Macedonia Cemetery reads Ullie M. Hamner Chism Junkin.

Dovy Ann Hamner was the daughter of William Taylor Hamner, Sr. and Permelia Chism. She married George Washington Chism who was the son of Lewis David Chism and Marilla Freeman. Dovy Ann and George Washington Chism had four children: (1) Archie George Chism; (2) Bascom Virgil Chism; (3) Harvey Morgan Chism; (4) Marvin Chism. All are buried in Macedonia Cemetery except for Marvin Chism who is buried in Arbor Springs Baptist Church Cemetery on Highway 43 North.[10]

**Chism, Virda:** July 7, 1912-June 12, 1921.

Grave # 66.

She was the daughter of Harvey Morgan Chism and Ullie Mae Hamner and is buried by her parents.

Ullie Mae Hamner was the daughter of John Pruitt Hamner and Annie Margaret Hall and the granddaughter of William T. Hamner, Sr. and his

---

[7] Page 235
[8] Page 306
[9] Page 306
[10] Page 304-309

# MACEDONIA CEMETERY

second wife Permelia Chism.

**Christian, Addie L.:** April 5, 1896-October 9, 1977. Grave # 234

**Christian, J. Riley**: August 10, 1887-January 18, 1974. Grave # 235

**Clements, Benjamin Jackson "Jack"**: March 1, 1889-June 12, 1944. Grave # 102.

Jack married Brazzie Mae Hall. Jack was the 5th child of Thomas Clements and Frances Ann Hamner and was a brother to James "Jim" S. Clements.[11]

Frances Ann Hamner was the daughter of John A. Hamner and Mary Amanda Rose.

John A. Hamner lived in Windham Springs and was the son of Turner Hamner, Jr. and Martha "Betsy Cooper.[12] He was a brother to William Taylor Hamner, Sr.[13]

**Obit for B. J. Clements**

B. J. Clements, 55, widely known resident of the Samantha Community, died unexpectedly of a heart attack yesterday at his home.

Mr. Clements was a native of this county and served for several years as a representative from Beat 7 on the County Democratic Executive Committee. He was a successful farmer and operated a school bus for the county.

Mr. Clements was also widely known as a song writer and harmony student.

He leaves his widow, Mrs. Brazzie Clements; four daughters, Mrs. Marjorie Fortenberry; Mrs. Frances Appling; and Misses Pauline and Emogene Clements; one son, Cecil Clements of the US Navy; two brothers, Tom Clements of Tuscaloosa, and Jim Clements of the Crabbe Road; a half-brother John Clements and one sister.

Funeral arraignments will be held at Macedonia Methodist Church on the Crabbe Road. Time of the rites will be announced by Jones and Spigener, depending arrival of relatives.

**Clements, Brazzie M.:** May 1, 1903-1996. Grave # 103.

She was the wife of Benjamin Jackson "Jack" Clements and the daughter of Charlie Avery Hall and Rebecca Smalley.

**Clements, David A.:** June 19, 1950-September 20, 1950. Grave # 124.

**Clements, David Sampson**: October 8, 1883-September 16, 1946. Grave # 126

**Clements, Francis:** 1846-1927 Grave # 89.

Francis was the daughter of John A. Hamner and Mary Amanda Rose and the granddaughter of Turner Hamner, Jr. and Martha "Betsy" Cooper who are buried on Hamner property in Windham Springs.

Frances was the second wife of Thomas Clements. His first wife was Elizabeth Simpson who died in 1870 and is buried in Macedonia in a grave next to Thomas Clements with only a rock as a headstone.[14]

Warren Calvin Clements, son of Frances Hamner and Jack Clements, is buried in Macedonia Cemetery.

**Clements, Georgia E. Crump:** June 23, 1889-April 24, 1971. Grave # 127.

**Clements, Ida Mae:** December 17, 1902-May 1, 1975. Grave # 108.

She was the daughter of James S. "Jim" Clements and Mary Etta Hamner.[15]

Ida was crippled in an accident when she was young that resulted in a life spent in a wheelchair. She was known for her "La Foy News" articles about social activities in the Lafoy Community. The column was printed regularly in *The Tuscaloosa News*. She never married.

Ida Mae lived with her parents until their deaths. Her mother died in 1940 and her father died in 1945. After James "Jim," Clements died, Ida's sister Vera Virginia Clements LeSueur and her husband Bernard LeSueur moved into the Clements house and Ida lived there until the house burned in the late 1960s. She was rescued from the burning house by a passing neighbor,

---

[11] Page 350
[12] Page 350
[13] Page 125

[14] Pages 342-343
[15] Page 345

Grady Shirley.

Mary Etta Hamner was the daughter of George Harrison Hamner who was born in the Lafoy Community in 1837. George Harrison Hamner was the first son William Taylor Hamner, Sr. and his first wife whose name is unknown.[16]

**Clements, James S.**: July 31, 1877-1945. Grave # 109.

James was the son of Thomas Clements and Frances Ann Hamner Clements and the grandson of John A. Hamner and Martha "Betsy" Cooper. His home was a few yards south of Lafoy School. He operated a small rural grocery store across the Crabbe Road from his home.

James Clements was a brother to Jack Clements.

James married Mary Etta Hamner the daughter of George Harrison Hamner and Sarah "Sally" McGee. James was the father of Ida Mae Clements and Vera Virginia Clements LeSueur.

Mary Etta Hamner Clements died March 3, 1940. After Mary Etta's death, James S. Clements married Lela Hyche Tierce the widow of Eugene Benjamin Tierce, Sr.

**Obit for James S. Clements**

James B. Clements, 67, well-known farmer of the Crabbe Road died last night at Saint Vincent's Hospital in Birmingham where he had been confined since last Thursday. Mr. Clements failed to rally following a major operation. He was the son of Tom and Frances Hamner Clements and a lifeline resident of the Lafoy Community.

Surviving is his widow, Mrs. Lela Hyche Tierce Clements; two daughters, Miss Ida Clements, and Mrs. Bernard LeSueur; one brother, Tom Clements of Alberta City; and a sister Mrs. Mary Strasburg of Ohio.

Funeral services will be held Wednesday afternoon at 3:00 o'clock at Macedonia Methodist Church on the Crabbe Road with internment in Macedonia Cemetery by Jones and Spigener. Rev. J. C. Maske and Rev. G. B. Davidson will officiate.

Active pallbearers will be nephews of the deceased, Woodrow, T. M. Eddie, James T. and Houston Clements and Earnest Compton.

Honorary pallbearers will be: Roy Faucett; Dr. S. T. Hardin; Charles Newman; T. D. Lafoy; Frank Fitts; T. W. Christian; Herman Boyd; E. J. Shipp; John Shirley; B. A. Renfro; Tom Morrison; Joe Christian; Frank Rice; Judge Chester Walker.

**Clements, Manen**:: January 17, 1833-May 8, 1907. Grave # 101.

**Clements, Mary Etta:** 1881-March 3, 1940. Grave # 110.

Mary Etta Hamner was the daughter of George Harrison Hamner and Sarah "Sally" McGee. She was the wife of James "Jim" S. Clements and the mother of Ida Clements and Vera Virginia Clements LeSueur. All except Vera LeSueur are buried in Macedonia Cemetery.

George Harrison Hamner was the son of William Taylor Hamner, Sr. and his first wife, whose name is not known. Hamner family tradition holds that she died circa 1840 and is buried in a grave with no inscribed identification beside her husband in Macedonia Cemetery. If that is true, her grave is the oldest in the cemetery.

**Obit for Mary Etta Clements:**

Mrs. J. S. Clements, a resident of the Crabbe Road near Northport, died Sunday night at Druid City Hospital after a short illness. Mrs. Clements was fifty-five years old and had resided in Tuscaloosa County all her life. Before her marriage, she was Miss Mary Etta Hamner, daughter of the late Mr. and Mrs. George Hamner.

She was a member of the Macedonia Methodist Church. A private funeral will be held at the graveside at Macedonia Cemetery this afternoon at 3:00 o'clock with the Rev. T. L. Selman and the Rev. C. L. Hollis officiating. A private funeral was necessary because Mrs. Clements died of spinal meningitis.

---

[16] Page 155

# MACEDONIA CEMETERY

Survivors include her husband, J. S. Clements, prominent groceryman; two daughters, Miss Ida Mae Clements and Miss Vera Virginia Clements; one brother, N.J. Hamner of the Crabbe Road; three sisters, Mrs. Nina Cooper of Birmingham, Mrs. E. L. Turner of Northport Route 1 and Mrs. Harvey Stine of Echola.

Pallbearers for the funeral are nephews of the deceased, Dewey Smith, Eddie Clements, Ike Cain, Clinton Strickland, Otis Turner and Venois Turner.

Honorary pallbearers are Judge Chester Walker, J. A. Savage, B. A. Renfro, M. Tierce, T. W. Christian, Roy Faucett, Frank Fitts, Reuben Wright, Charles Newman, Thomas D. LaFoy, Jack Rushing and Josh Rushing.

**Clements, Myrtie Loice**: October 6, 1907-May 12, 1909. Grave # 100.

**Clements, Roma:** April 19, 1921 Grave # 125.

**Clements, Thomas**: 1829-1900 Grave # 90.

His first wife was Elizabeth Simpson who died in 1870 and is buried in Macedonia in a grave next to Thomas Clements with only a rock as a headstone.

After the death of Elizabeth Simpson Clements, Thomas Clements married Frances Ann Hamner the daughter of John A. Hamner and Mary Amanda Rose.

All the above are buried in Macedonia Cemetery.

John A. Turner was the son of Turner Hamner, Jr. and Martha "Betsy" Cooper.[17] He and Martha "Betsy" Cooper are buried on Hamner property in Windham Springs.

**Clements, Thomas Robert:** October 23, 1946-September 8, 2004. Grave # 128A.:

**Clements, Warren Calvin**: November 16, 1920-May 20, 1930. Grave # 88.

He was the son of Benjamin Jackson "Jack" Clements and Brazzie Mae Hall and the grandson of Thomas Clements and Frances Ann Hamner and is buried beside his grandparents.

**Clements, Winfield Frank:** December 23, 1928-September 29, 1995. Grave # 130.

**Cooper, Dorothy B.:** August 24, 1926-January 31, 1935. Grave # 224.

### Obit for Dorothy B. Cooper (February 2, 1935 *Tuscaloosa News*):

Eight-year-old daughter of Mr. and Mrs. Wilson Cooper died Thursday at the home of her parents in Anniston. The little girl who formerly made her home in Northport with her parents will be brought back here for funeral services. The body will arrive this afternoon and will be carried to the home of her great grandmother, Mrs. Chris Thomas in Northport. Burial will take place at Macedonia Church at 11 o'clock Saturday morning.

**Cooper, Thelma Rushing:** September 29, 1906-December 8, 1932. Grave # 84.

She was the wife of William Morgan Cooper who is buried in Piney Woods Baptist Church Cemetery. She was the daughter of Marvin Goldman Rushing and Ozella Judson "Juddie" Hamner and the granddaughter of Joseph Enoch Rushing and Samantha Lenora Deason.

Ozella Judson "Juddie" Hamner Rushing was the daughter of John Pruitt Hamner and Annie Margaret Hall and the granddaughter of William T. Hamner, Sr. and his second wife Permelia Chism all of whom are buried in Macedonia Cemetery.

### Obit for Mrs. Thelma Rushing Cooper

Funeral services for Mrs. Thelma Rushing Cooper, 26-year-old resident of the Crabbe Road were held this morning at 11:00 o'clock at Macedonia Methodist Church with the Reverends C. L. and Marvin Manderson officiating and Foster's Funeral Home directing internment in the church cemetery.

Mrs. Cooper died at the home of her parents Mr. and Mrs. Goldman Rushing on the Crabbe at 9:00 a.m. on Thursday morning after a four-month illness. She was vising her parents when

---
[17] Page 342

death overtook her. She was well-known in the community and an active member of Macedonia Church and her death is mourned by many friends and relatives.

Surviving are her husband William Morgan Cooper and two children, James, age 5 and Lamar age 6 months; her parents; three sisters, Alda, Lenora, and Etteline and two brothers Preston, and Billy, all of the Crabbe Road.

Active pallbearers for the rites are Nathan Chism, Dee Hamner, Curtis Hamner, Melvin Hamner, Howard Rushing, Woodrow Rushing, Wayland Hyche, and Cullen Hamner.

Honorary pallbearers are Tom Morrison, S. S. McGee, Charles Newman, D. J. Bolton, Hiram Darden, Frank Rice, Largus Barnes, H. G. Shepherd, Jim Driver.

**Crawford, Lucille Wilson Hagler:** May 20, 1914-May 29, 1994. Grave # 41.

She was the wife of Sterling Pleasant Crawford and was the ninth of ten children born to Permelia Elizabeth Hamner and James Martin Hagler. Lucille has four siblings buried in Macedonia Cemetery. They are: John Martin Hagler; Minnie Lula Hagler Taylor; Gladys Hagler Struck; Wiley Pruitt Hagler.

Permelia Elizabeth Hamner Hagler was the daughter of Louis Alfred Hamner and Penina Wilson Clements

Louis Alfred Hamner was the fourth child of William Taylor Hamner, Sr. and his second wife Permelia Chism.

Penina Wilson Clements was the daughter of Thomas Clements and Elizabeth Simpson.[18]

All the above are buried in Macedonia Cemetery.[19]

James Martin Hagler was the son of John Pruitt Hagler and Sallie Ann Martin. They are not buried in Macedonia Cemetery.

**Crawford, R. E.:** December 31, 1848-April 11, 1902. Grave # 42.

**Crawford, Sarah Elizabeth.** December 29, 1937.

Grave # 43.

She was infant daughter of Sterling and Lucille Hagler Crawford who was born and died on December 29, 1937.

**Crawford, Sterling Pleasan**t: October 18, 1898-February 4, 1965. Grave # 40.

He was the husband of Lucille Wilson Hagler and the father of Sarah Elizabeth Craw.

**Criss, Charlotte Deann**: June 4, 1940-December 12, 1941. Grave # 230.

**Criss, Holdridge C. Jr.**: June 12, 1940-December 26, 1963. Grave # 231.

**Criss, Holdridge C. Sr.**: May 25, 1916-August 9, 1968. Grave # 232.

**Criss, Wilma Naugher**: March 17, 1923-June 5, 2004. Grave # 233A.

**Criswell, Ellen King**: 1890-1928 Grave # 166.

She was the wife of Will Criswell. Ellen was the daughter of Andy J. King and Hester J. Hathcock King both of whom are buried in Macedonia Cemetery.

**Criswell, an infant daughter** of Tom and Fannie King who died in 1920. Grave # 170.

**Criswell, Will**: 1889-April 5, 1956.

Grave # 170. He was the husband of Ellen King.

**Dawson, Maude:** 1889-1893 Grave # 46

**Dawson, Maybelle**: May 9, 1893-January 12, 1960. Grave # 47.

**Dawson, Riley**: 1891-1893 Grave # 45

**Dawson, Sara**: 1823-1896 Grave # 44.

**Dawson, Stella:** 1887-1891 Grave # 48

**Earnest, Edward Earl:** August 13, 1943-January 5, 2005. Grave # 59A.

He was the son of Lenora Bell Hyche and Ed Wilson Earnest.

Lenora Bell Hyche was the daughter of Lenora Belle "Lou" Rushing and Early Monroe

---
[18] Page 247
[19] Page 255

# MACEDONIA CEMETERY

Hyche and the granddaughter of Joseph Enoch Rushing and Samantha Lenora Deason.

All the above except Ed Wilson Earnest are buried in Macedonia Cemetery.

**Edmonds, Annie Barbara:** December 24, 1888-July 17, 1974. Grave # 190.

**Edmonds, Annie S.:** January 7, 1905-July 4, 1982. Grave # 220.

**Edmonds, Frank C.:** December 2, 1917-December 28, 1981. Grave # 218.

**Edmonds, Hester Jane**: April 19, 1920-April 2, 1975. Grave # 217.

**Edmonds, "Jim" Ola, Jr.:** May 15, 1925-June 2, 1973. Grave # 181.

**Edmonds, Joseph E.:** February 24, 1886-December 5, 1976. Grave # 219.

**Edmonds, Ola R.:** October 13, 1890-November 11, 1952. Grave # 189.

**Edmonds, Patton M.:** February 14, 1929-September 6, 1947. Grave # 154.

**Gay, Annie Pearl**: May 15, 1894-December 19, 1969. Grave # 205. She was the daughter of Lewellen Sydney Gay and Julie Elizabeth Shirley Gay.

Annie Pearl Gay was a sister to Fanny Lee Gay Rushing, J. R. "Dick" Gay, Sam H. Gay, Robert B. Gay, and Josephine Gay.

Anne Pearl Gay and J. R. "Dick" Gay never married.

All the above are buried in Macedonia Cemetery.

**Gay, Callaway H.**: 1824-1894
Grave # 137.

Calloway H. Gay was the patriarch of the Gay family in the Lafoy Community. He married Jane Palmer and was the father of Lewellen Sydney Gay.

Lewellen Sydney Gay married Julie Elizabeth Shirley. He was the father of Fanny Lee Gay Rushing, J. R. "Dick" Gay, Sam H. Gay, Robert B. Gay, Annie Pearl Gay, Martha Jane Gay Adcock, and Josephine Gay.

All the above are buried in Macedonia Cemetery.

**Gay, an infant boy.:** May 3, 1922.
Grave # 208.

He was the infant son of Robert and Janie Vista Scott.

**Gay, John Richard "Dick":** April 20, 1885-January 17, 1953. Grave # 204.

He was the son of Lewellen Sydney Gay and Julie Elizabeth Shirley, the brother of Fanny Lee Gay Rushing, Sam H. Gay, Robert B. Gay, Annie Pearl Gay, Martha Jane Gay Adcock, and Josephine Gay all of whom are buried in Macedonia Cemetery.

John Richard "Dick" Gay never married.

**Gay, Jane Palmer**: 1830-1894
Grave # 138.

She was the wife of Callaway "Capp" Gay and the mother of Lewellen Sydney Gay.

Jane Palmer Gay was the grandmother of Fanny Lee Gay Rushing, J. R. "Dick" Gay, Sam H. Gay, Robert B. Gay, Annie Pearl Gay, Martha Jane Gay Adcock, and Josephine Gay.

All the above are buried in Macedonia Cemetery.

**Gay, Janie Vista Scott:** December 22, 1894-December 30, 1958. Grave # 212.

She was the wife of Robert Gay and the mother of an infant son who died in 1922 and is buried in Macedonia Cemetery.

**Gay, Josephine:** January 6, 1897-August 10, 1935.
Grave # 136.

She was the daughter of Lewellen Sydney Gay and Julie Elizabeth Shirley, the sister of Fanny Lee Gay Rushing, Sam H. Gay, Robert B. Gay, Annie Pearl Gay, and Martha Jane Gay Adcock. Josephine never married. All the above are buried in Macedonia Cemetery.

**Gay, Julie Elizabeth Shirley:** September 6, 1861-October 19, 1937. Grave # 135.

She was the wife of Lewellen Sydney Gay and the mother of Fanny Lee Gay Rushing, J.R. "Dick" Gay, Sam H. Gay, Robert B. Gay, Annie Pearl Gay, Martha Jane Gay Adcock, and Josephine Gay.

All the above are buried in Macedonia Cemetery.

**Obit for Mrs. Julie Elizabeth Shirley Gay,** *Tuscaloosa News,* **page 3, October 29, 1937.**

Mrs. Julie Elizabeth Gay, 76, died at her home in Northport Tuesday morning following a lengthy illness. She was widely known and loved throughout the Northport section and had been a member of the Methodist Church for 67 years.

Funeral services will be at 11:00 o'clock Thursday morning from Macedonia Methodist Church with the Rev. I. T. Carlton and Rev. B. F. Atkins officiating. Jones and Spigener will be in charge of internment in the church cemetery.

Surviving are five daughters, Mrs. Will Rushing, of Northport, Mrs. J. Adcox of Gordo, Mrs. Linnie Laycock of Northport, Mrs. Thad Wallace of Birmingham, and Miss Pearl Gay of Northport; three sons, Bob Gay of Northport, Sam Gay of Romulus, Dick Gay of Northport; one brother, J. T. Shirley of Northport; 16 grandchildren and 1 great grandchild.

Pallbearers will be Luther Davis, George Johnson, Gary McGee, Clyde Daniel, Alf Powell, and W. W. Deal.

Honorary pallbearers will be A. Laycock, R. L. Shamblin, Q. S. Hinton, Lewis Angers, Clint Deason, and H. G. Shepherd.

**Gay, Lewellen Sydney:** January 5, 1851-August 12, 1914. Grave # 209.

Lewellen married Julie Elizabeth Shirley. He was the father of Fanny Lee Gay Rushing, J.R. "Dick" Gay, Sam H. Gay, Robert B. Gay, Annie Pearl Gay, Martha Jane Gay Adcock, and Josephine Gay all of whom are buried in Macedonia Cemetery.

**Obit for Lewellen Sydney Gay:**

On last Wednesday, August 12, 1914, Mr. Sydney L. Gay passed away at his home in Northport after an illness of about 15 months.

He was born in this county January 5, 1850, and if he had lived until next January, he would have been 64 years of age. In 1880 he was married to Miss Julia Shirley who survived him until his death.

Mr. Gay lived for years about 6 miles up on the Crabbe Road near Carrolls Creek, but a few months ago he moved with his family to town. (His home on the Crabbe Road is the current site of Publix Grocery store at the intersection of the Crabbe Road and Mitt Lary Road.) Few men were more devoted to their family than he, and he spent most of his time at home.

**Gay, Ora:** November 12, 1902-March 26, 1991.

Grave # 207.

She was the wife of Sam H. Gay.

**Gay, Robert B.:** March 10, 1892-November 8, 1957. Grave # 211.

Robert was married to Janie Vista Scott Gay. He was the son of Lewellen Sydney Gay and Julie Elizabeth Shirley and a brother to Fanny Lee Gay Rushing, J. R. "Dick" Gay, Sam H. Gay, Annie Pearl Gay, Martha Jane Gay Adcock, and Josephine Gay all of whom are buried in Macedonia Cemetery.

**Gay, Sam H.:** November 23, 1889-October 10, 1976. Grave # 206.

Sam was married to Ora Gay. He was the son of Lewellen Sydney Gay and Julie Elizabeth Shirley and a brother to Fanny Lee Gay Rushing, J.R. "Dick" Gay, Robert B. Gay, Annie Pearl Gay, Martha Jane Gay Adcock, and Josephine Gay all of whom are buried in Macedonia Cemetery.

**Gibson (Pricey Shirley Gibson White)**

Grave # 179. Note: please see comments for Estelle Shirley Robertson under grave #172. Estelle Shirley and Pricey are one and the same person. Pricey Shirley was the daughter of Joel Tom and Ida Shirley. She first married W. Brady Robertson by whom she had a son, W. Brady Robertson, Jr. They divorced and she married Joe Dawson White. Joe Dawson White shot and killed Pricey in Woolworth Store on Broad Street in downtown Tuscaloosa. An entire chapter in a *Road, A Cemetery, A People* is devoted to Pricey's murder.

# MACEDONIA CEMETERY

**Grammer, Alice G.:** 1923-1980. Grave # 107

**Grammer, Henry:** September 14, 1877-March 13, 1902. Grave # 1. The grave is covered by a tent made of rock slabs.

**Grammer, Jack:** April 10, 1911-April 26, 1977.
Grave # 279.

**Grammer, Louise:** 1928-1941
Grave # 106.

**Grammer, Martha Ann:** February 17, 1905
Grave # 278.

**Guy, Raymond:** March 13, 1928-November 26, 1994. Grave # 191.

Raymond was the husband of Elsie Tierce and the father of Kay Guy Rice both of whom are buried in Macedonia Cemetery.

Elsie Tierce Guy was the wife of Raymond Guy and the mother of Kay Guy Rice and the daughter of Benjamin Collier Tierce and Nellie F. Tierce.

Benjamin Collier Tierce was the son of Eugene Benjamin Tierce, Sr. and Veturia Scales Tierce.

Eugene Benjamin Tierce, Sr. was the son of Elliot Catlett Tierce and Frances Caroline Doss Tierce.

Elliott Catlett Tierce was the son of Benjamin Tucker Tierce and Susannah Clardy Tierce.

All the above are buried in Macedonia Cemetery.

**Hagler, Howard Houston:** 1936-1953.
Grave # 27.

Houston was killed in a motorcycle accident in Northport. He was the son of Howard Theron Hagler and Marvel Josephine Randolph.

Howard Theron Hagler was the son of James Martin Hagler and Permelia Elizabeth Hamner.[20]

Permelia Elizabeth Hamner was the daughter of Louis Alfred Hamner and Penina Wilson Clements.

Louis Alfred Hamner was the son of William Taylor Hamner, Sr. and his second wife Permelia Chism.[21]

All the above except Howard Theron Hagler and Marvel Hagler are buried in Macedonia Cemetery.

**Obit for Howard Houston Hagler**

Sixteen-year-old Howard Houston Hagler, student at Tuscaloosa County High School, was killed instantly early last night in a motorcycle accident which occurred on Main Avenue and Park Street in Northport. A companion of the motorcycle, Sammy Harper, 17, suffered a fractured toe and arm but did not require hospitalization

County Deputy Sheriff W. F. Wright's investigation showed the motorcycle driver swerved the vehicle to avoid a collision with an automobile that was driving onto Main Avenue from Park Street and crashed into a utility pole. The driver of the car was listed as Eddy Dunn. Wright said the motorcycle was driven by young Hagler. The Hagler youth lived on the Crabbe Road four miles from Northport. Coroner R. N. Wallace said the youth's neck was broken, and he suffered a concussion.

Funeral services will be held from Macedonia Methodist Church on Thursday at 4:00 p.m. with the Rev. Wayne Graham officiating. Burial will be in the church cemetery with Jones and Spigener in charge.

Young Hagler was a member of the Methodist Church, a member and past president to the 4-H Club at Tuscaloosa County High School and in the junior class at the school.

Survivors include: his parents; a brother, James Martin Hagler; his grandmothers Mrs. James Martin Hagler, and Mrs. T. A. Randolph and a great grandmother, Mrs. Belle Randolph.

**Hagler, James A. "Duffy":** died June 20, 2017 at age 84 . Grave # 320B.

Duffy was the husband of Sara Jo Bean and the son of James Lewis "Dick" Hagler and Maria Theresa Innes Hagler who are buried in Memory Hills Gardens.

---

[20] Page 255

[21] Page 130

James Lewis Hagler was the son of James Martin Hagler and Permelia Elizabeth Hamner Hagler.[22]

Permelia Elizabeth Hamner was the daughter of Louis Alfred Hamner and Penina Wilson Clements.

Louis Alfred Hamner was the son of William T. Hamner, Sr. and his second wife Permelia Chism.

Penina Wilson Clements was the daughter of Thomas Clements and Elizabeth Simpson.

All the above except for James Lewis and Maria Hagler are buried in Macedonia Cemetery.

**Hagler, James Martin:** April 10, 1871-July 31, 1935. Grave # 34.

He was married to Permelia Elizabeth Hamner. Of their ten children, five are buried in Macedonia Cemetery: John Martin Hagler; Minnie Lula Hagler Taylor; Gladys Hagler Stuck; Lucille Hagler Crawford; Wiley Pruitt Hagler. In addition, a granddaughter Nina Sue Hagler Brown and great grandsons Scottie Brown and Mickey Brown are buried in Macedonia Cemetery.[23]

Permelia Elizabeth Hamner was the daughter of Louis Alfred Hamner and Penina Wilson Clements.

Louis Alfred Hamner was the son of William T. Hamner, Sr. and his second wife Permelia Chism. All the above are buried in Macedonia Cemetery.

Penina Wilson Clements was the daughter of Thomas Clements and Elizabeth Simpson.

Children of Permelia Elizabeth Hamner and James Martin Hagler not buried in Macedonia Cemetery include: Henry Albert Hagler; James Lewis "Dick" Hagler; Frank Verner Hagler; Howard Theron Hagler; Lizzie Mae Hagler.[24]

**Obit for James Martin Hagler**

James Martin Hagler, prominent Tuscaloosa County planter and a lifelong resident of Northport, died late yesterday afternoon at a Birmingham hospital after brief illness. He was widely known throughout this section and is survived by his widow, 10 children, a number of grandchildren, five brothers and two sisters.

Funeral services will be held at 11:00 a.m. Friday at Macedonia Methodist Church on the Crabbe Road officiated by Rev. Trimm Powell.

Pallbearers will be Largus F. Barnes, Joe Rice, R. L. Shamblin, John M. Burchfield, Sr., Monroe Ward, and George J. Johnston.

Honorary pallbearers will be Frank Rice, Fleetwood Rice, Howard Maxwell, James Maxwell, Mems Tierce, Reuben Wright, Joe A. Searcy and George Daniel.

Surviving Mr. Hagler are his widow, formerly Miss Permelia Hamner of Northport; six sons, John M. Hagler, Willey P. Hagler, and James "Dick" L. Hamner all of the Crabbe Road, Frank B. Hagler of the US Navy stationed in California, and Howard Hagler of Coker; four daughters, Mrs. J. Albert Taylor of the Crabbe Road, Mrs. E. M. Denny of Elliott, Ohio, and Miss Lucille Hagler and Mrs. Aubrey Clements both of Northport Route 1.

**Hagler, John M.:** September 25, 1898-July 5, 1980. Grave # 32.

As noted near the beginning of this chapter, John was the caretaker of Macedonia Cemetery during the first decades of the 20th century. His home was across the Crabbe Road from the cemetery.

John was married to Octavia Tierce Hagler and was the second of ten children born to Permelia Elizabeth Hamner and James Martin Hagler. Five of the ten children are buried in Macedonia Cemetery: John Martin Hagler; Lucille Hagler Crawford; Gladys Hagler Struck; Wiley Pruitt Hagler; Minnie Lou Hagler Taylor.[25]

Permelia Elizabeth Hamner was the daughter of Louis Alfred Hamner and Penina Wilson Clements.

Louis Alfred Hamner was the son of William

---

[22] Page 255
[23] Page 255
[24] Page 255
[25] Page 255

# MACEDONIA CEMETERY

T. Hamner, Sr. and his second wife Permelia Chism. All the above are buried in Macedonia Cemetery.

Penina Wilson Clements was the daughter of Thomas Clements and Elizabeth Simpson.[26]

All the above are buried in Macedonia Cemetery except for Louis Alfred Hamner and Penina Wilson Clements. They are buried in the old Alberta Methodist Church Cemetery.[27]

James Martin Hagler was the son of John Pruitt Hagler and Sallie Ann Martin. They are not buried in Macedonia Cemetery.

**Hagler, Octavia Tierce:** October 26, 1894-April 6, 1983. Grave # 33.

Octavia was the wife of John Martin Hagler. She was the daughter of Eugene Benjamin Tierce, Sr. and Veturia Scales Tierce.

Eugene Benjamin Tierce, Sr. was the son of Elliott Catlett Tierce and Frances Caroline Doss.

Elliott Catlett Tierce was the son of Benjamin Tucker Tierce and Susannah Clardy Tierce.

Octavia Tierce Hagler was a sister to Victor Tierce, Festus Tierce, Memnon Tierce, Sr. Collier Tierce, and Hester _____. She was a half-sister to Louise Tierce Mathis and Eugene Benjamin Tierce, Jr.

All but Memnon and Hester are buried in Macedonia Cemetery.

**Hagler, Pamelia Elizabeth:** August 7, 1877-November 16, 1959. Grave # 35.

Pamelia was married to James Martin Hagler and was the daughter of Louis Alfred Hamner and Penina Wilson Clements.

Penina Wilson Clements was the daughter of Thomas Clements and Elizabeth Simpson.[28]

Louise Alfred Hamner was the son of William T. Hamner, Sr. and Permelia Chism.

Of Permelia Elizabeth Hamner Hagler's ten children, five are buried in Macedonia: John Martin Hagler; Gladys Hagler Struck; Minnie Lula Hagler Taylor; Lucille Hagler Crawford; Wiley Pruitt Hamner. In addition, a granddaughter, Nina Sue Hagler Brown, daughter of Henry Albert Hagler and Helen Elizabeth "Patty" Parizek, and two great grandsons, Scottie Brown and Mickey Brown, sons of Nina Sue Hagler Brown, are buried in Macedonia Cemetery.

Henry Albert and Helen Elizabeth Hagler are buried in Memory Hills Gardens.

**Obit for Mrs. Pamela Elizabeth Hamner Hagler**

Mrs. Pamela Elizabeth Hagler, 82, of Northport Route Two died at her home Monday about 4 p.m. She was a lifelong resident of the community.

Funeral services are to be held Wednesday at 2:00 p.m. at Macedonia Methodist Church with the Rev. T. H. Wilson and the Rev. L. B. Stewart in charge.

Surviving are six sons, John, Wiley, Albert, and J. L. Hagler all of Northport, Howard of Tuscaloosa, and Frank of Pensacola; four daughters, Mrs. Albert Taylor, Mrs. Sterling Crawford, and Mrs. A. B. Clements all of Northport and Mrs. E. M. Denny of Palatka, Florida; 33 grandchildren and 42 great grandchildren.

Pallbearers will be Robert Hagler, Gorman Hagler, Alvin Hagler, Roy Whatley, Woodrow Hagler, and Tommy Hagler.

Honorary pallbearers will be Bryce Broughton, John Rushing, Belvie Broughton, Houston Thomas, James R. Maxwell, Dr. Joe Shamblin, Nathan Chism, Grady Shirley, Albert Billings, Festus Tierce, and stewards of Union Chapel Church.

**Hagler, Sara Jo**: March 22, 1932-January 18, 2010. Grave # 320.

She was the wife of James A. "Duffy" Hagler.

**Hagler, Theo Mae Rushing:** October 4, 1907-May 22, 1995. Grave # 132.

She was the wife of Wiley Pruitt Hagler and the daughter of Joseph David "Gin" Rushing and Permelia Alma Hamner.

Joseph David "Gin" Rushing was the son of Joseph Enoch Rushing and Samantha Lenora

---

[26] Page 247
[27] Page 247
[28] Page 247

# A ROAD, A CEMETERY, A PEOPLE

Deason.

Permelia Alma Hamner was the daughter of John Pruitt Hamner and Annie Margaret Hall.

John Pruitt Hamner was the son of William Taylor Hamner, Sr. and his second wife Permelia Chism.

Theo Mae Rushing Hagler was a sister to Etta Alma Rushing Thomas and Ozella Judson "Juddie" Hamner Rushing.

All the above are buried in Macedonia Cemetery.

**Hagler, Wiley P.:** August 25, 1904-July 7, 1976. Grave # 131.

He was the husband of Theo Mae Rushing and the son of James Martin Hagler and Permelia Elizabeth Hamner.

Of the ten children born to Permelia Elizabeth Hamner and James Martin Hagler, five are buried in Macedonia Cemetery. In addition to Wiley Pruitt, they are: John Martin Hagler; Lucille Hagler Crawford; Gladys Hagler Struck; Minnie Lou Hagler Taylor.[29]

Permelia Elizabeth Hamner was the daughter of Louis Alfred Hamner and Penina Wilson Clements.

Louis Alfred Hamner was the son of William T. Hamner, Sr. and his second wife Permelia Chism.

Penina Wilson Clements was the daughter of Thomas Clements and Elizabeth Simpson.[30]

All the above are buried in Macedonia Cemetery except for Louis Alfred Hamner and Penina Wilson Clements. They are buried in the old Albert Methodist Church Cemetery.[31]

James Martin Hagler was the son of John Pruitt Hagler and Sallie Ann Martin. They are not buried in Macedonia Cemetery.

**Hamner, Annie M.:** January 10, 1846-January 3, 1931.

Grave # 239.

**Hamner, Annie Mable:** April 7, 1907-May 18, 1988. Grave # 288.

Mable was the daughter of Larkin "Lark" Rogers Hamner and Bertice Josephine "Joe" Smith.[32]

Lark was the son of John Pruitt Hamner and Annie Margaret Hall.

John Pruitt Hamner was the son of William T. Hamner, Sr. and his second wife Permelia Chism.

All the above are buried in Macedonia Cemetery.

Annie Mable never married.

**Hamner, Annie Margaret Hall:** January 10, 1846-January 3, 1931. Grave # 239.

Annie Margaret Hall was the wife of John Pruitt Hamner and the mother of thirteen of his children.

Eleven of the thirteen children are buried in Macedonia Cemetery: (1) an infant daughter who died in 1867; (2) Mary Ulalah Virginia Hamner, a child; (3) Ollie Jackson "Ollie" Hamner (married to Louise Rigsby); (4) John Early Hamner (married to Rose Annie Viella "Ella" Rigsby); (5) Buena Vista Hamner Chism (married first to John Monroe House and married second to Archie George Chism); (6) Larkin "Lark" Rogers (married to Beatrice Josephine Smith); (7) Annie Brazile Hamner Rushing (married to Thomas Hillman "Jack" Rushing); (8) Ozella Judson Hamner Rushing (married to Marvin Goldman Rushing); (9) Permelia Alma Hamner married to Joseph David "Gin" Rushing; (10) Ullie Mae Hamner Chism (married to her first cousin Harvey Morgan Chism); (11) Edward "Dock" Hamner (married to Fannie Mae Duncan who is not buried in Macedonia Cemetery).

The two children of Annie Margaret Hall and John Pruitt Hamner not buried in Macedonia Cemetery are: (1) Gillie Pruitt Hamner (married to Hassie Lou Lewis) who are buried in Tuscaloosa Memorial Park (2) Jacob Cullen Hamner (married to Jessie Florence Lewis) who are buried in Tuscaloosa Memorial Park.

---

[29] Page 255
[30] Page 247
[31] Page 247

[32] Page 214

Annie Margaret Hall lived to within one month of her 85th birthday. At her death, ten of her thirteen children were still living.[33]

Nothing is known of Annie Margaret Hall's parents.

**Hamner, Bertice Josephine "Jo":** December 23, 1884- January 18, 1976. Grave # 287.

Josephine was the wife of Larkin "Lark" Rogers Hamner. She was the daughter of Daniel R. Smith and Emma Frances Smith.

Larkin "Lark" Rogers Hamner was the seventh child of John Pruitt Hamner and Anne Margaret Hall.

John Pruitt Hamner was the son of William T. Hamner, Sr. and his second wife Permelia Chism.

Beatrice "Joe" Hamner was the mother of Annie Mable Hamner.

All the above are buried in Macedonia Cemetery.

Beatrice was also the mother of William Trimm Hamner, John Curtis Hamner and James Lando "Kid" Hamner who are buried in Carrolls Creek Baptist Church Cemetery.

**Hamner, Edward Bruce:** August 25, 1901- February 12, 1986. Grave # 304.

Bruce married Fannie Lou Shirley the daughter of Byrdie "Byrd" Shirley and Matilda Ann Smith.[34]

Members of Edward Bruce Hamner's family who are buried in Macedonia Cemetery include: a daughter, Geneal Hamner Black; a son, Ollie Bruce "Doc" Hamner; a grandson John Howard Hewitt.

Edward Bruce Hamner was the son of Oliver "Ollie" Jackson Hamner and Mary Louise Rigsby.

Oliver "Ollie" Jackson Hamner was the son of John Pruitt Hamner and Annie Margaret Hall.

John Pruitt Hamner was the son of William T. Hamner, Sr. and his second wife Permelia Chism.

Edward Bruce Hamner was a brother to Lou Bell Hamner Rushing, Vera Mae Hamner, Ollie Lee Hamner (a child) and Oll Dee Hamner.

All the above are buried in Macedonia Cemetery.

Edward Bruce Hamner was also a brother to Jessie Pruitt Hamner, James Webster "Jay" Hamner, and Hollis Harwood "Woody" Hamner who are buried in Carrolls Creek Baptist Church Cemetery.

Edward Bruce was also a brother to John O'Neal Hamner who is buried in Sunset Cemetery.

**Hamner, Edward Powell "Dock":** April 18, 1875-December 30, 1936. Grave # 253.

He was the son of John Pruitt Hamner and Annie Margaret Hall.

John Pruitt Hamner was the son of William Taylor Hamner, Sr. and his second wife Permelia Chism.

"Dock" married Fannie Maybell Duncan. Early in their marriage, they moved to Texas, but when "Dock" died, his body was brought back to Macedonia Cemetery for burial. Later when his wife died, she was buried in Oklahoma.

All the above except for Fannie Maybell are buried in Macedonia Cemetery.[35]

**Obit for Edward Powell "Dock" Hamner**

Funeral services for Edward Powell "Dock" Hamner who was murdered in Plainview, Texas last Wednesday will be held this morning at 10:00 o'clock at Macedonia Methodist Church with the Rev. C. L. Manderson officiating. The body arrived here Saturday but relatives in Northport have not been notified regarding the particulars of the tragedy. He was 62 years old.

Survivors of Mr. Hamner of Plainview, Texas include: his wife, Mrs. Finnie Duncan Hamner; three daughters, Misses Ester, Martha Lee, and Viola all of whom reside in Texas or Oklahoma; three sisters Mrs. Joseph David "Gib" Rushing, Mrs. Goldman Rushing, Mrs. A. G. Chism; five brothers, O. J., J.E., L. R., J. C. and G. C., all

---

[33] Page 183
[34] Page 194
[35] Page 211

residents of Northport.

**A subsequent article reads:**

Circumstances surrounding the recent murder of Edward Power "Dock" Hamner in a filling station near Plainview, Texas was received here today with receipt of a Plainview newspaper by Northport relatives of Mr. Hamner.

The paper states that he apparently was robbed and killed early in the morning of December 30.

Hamner was found dead in his filling station three miles east of Plainview. His head was crushed as though struck with a heavy blunt weapon.

**Hamner, Ella**: 1880-1940
Grave # 256

**Hamner, Emma Louise Estes:** October 20, 1930-December 31, 1998. Grave # 266.

Emma was the wife of Ollie Bruce "Doc" Hamner and the mother of Richard Bruce Hamner.

Ollie Bruce "Doc" Hamner was the son of Edward Bruce Hamner and Fannie Lou Shirley Hamner.

Edward Bruce Hamner was the son of Oliver "Ollie" Jackson Hamner and Mary Louise Rigsby and the grandson of John Pruitt Hamner and Annie Margaret Hall and the great grandson of William T. Hamner, Sr. and his second wife Permelia Chism.

Fannie Lou Shirley Hamner was the daughter of Byrdie "Byrd" Franklin Shirley and Matilda Smith Shirley.

All the above are buried in Macedonia Cemetery.

**Hamner, Fannie Lou Shirley**: April 30, 1908-August 17, 1988. Grave # 305.

Fannie Lou was the wife of Edward Bruce Hamner. Members of her family buried in Macedonia Cemetery include her son Ollie Bruce "Doc" Hamner, her daughter Mary Ann Geneal Hamner Black, and her grandson John Howard Hewitt who was the son of Glenda Sheryl Hamner Hewett.

Fannie Lou Shirley Hamner was the daughter of Byrdie "Byrd" Franklin Shirley and Matilda Ann Smith. She was a sister to John Ester Shirley, Lonnie Lee Shirley, B. F. Shirley, Grady Edward Shirley, Bobby Renzo "Buddy" Shirley, Ruby Shirley Mills, Martha Shirley Turner, and Frances Shirley Hamner.

All the above are buried in Macedonia Cemetery.

Fannie Lou was also a sister to Sue Lake and Joan Davis who are not buried in Macedonia Cemetery.

Edward Bruce Hamner was the son of Oliver "Ollie" Jackson Hamner and Mary Louise Rigsby.

Oliver "Ollie" Jackson Hamner was the son of John Pruitt Hamner and Annie Margaret Hall.

John Pruitt Hamner was the son of William Taylor Hamner, Sr. and his second wife Permelia Chism.

Edward Bruce was a brother to Lou Bell Hamner Rushing, Vera Mae Hamner and Oll Dee Hamner all of whom are buried in Macedonia Cemetery.[36]

Edward Bruce Hamner was a brother to Jessie Pruitt Hamner, James Webster "Jay" Hamner and Hollis Harwood "Woody" Hamner. They are buried in Carrolls Creek Baptist Church Cemetery.

Edward Bruce was a brother to John O'Neal Hamner who is buried in Sunset Cemetery.

**Hamner, Frances Shirley**: June 9, 1913-March 10, 2008. Grave # 311A.

She was the wife of Oll Dee Hamner and the daughter of Byrdie "Byrd" Franklin Shirley and Matilda Ann Smith.

Frances Shirley Hamner was a sister to John Ester Shirley, Lonnie Lee Shirley, B. F. Shirley, Grady Edward Shirley, Bobby Renzo "Buddy" Shirley, Martha Shirley Turner, Ruby Shirley Mills, and Fanny Lou Shirley Hamner all of whom are buried in Macedonia Cemetery. She was also a sister to Sue Lake and Joan Davis who

---
[36] Page 194

are not buried in Macedonia Cemetery.

Oll Dee Hamner was the son of Oliver "Ollie" Jackson Hamner and Mary Louise Rigsby.

Oliver "Ollie" Jackson Hamner was the son of John Pruitt Hamner and Permelia Chism.

John Pruitt Hamner was the son of William Taylor Hamner, Sr. and his second wife Permelia Chism.

All the above are buried in Macedonia Cemetery.[37]

**Hamner, George Harrison:** March 12, 1837-Febraury 13, 1909

Grave # 74.

He was the son of William Taylor Hamner, Sr. by his first wife whose name is not known.[38]

George Harrison Hamner married Sarah "Sally" McGee who was the daughter of Joseph and Mary McGee. Joseph and Mary are buried in Bethel Presbyterian Church Cemetery.

George Harrison Hamner was the father of Frances Ann Hamner who married James S. Clements all of whom are buried in Macedonia Cemetery.

Hamner family tradition holds that George Harrison Hamner's mother is buried in a grave marked only by a stone with no name inscribed on it in Macedonia Cemetery beside William Taylor Hamner, Sr.'s grave. If this is true, her grave is likely the oldest in the cemetery.

**Hamner, Hettie:** August 16, 1906-September 8, 1989. Grave # 261.

**Hamner, Infant daughter** of William C.: no date

Grave # 264.

**Hamner, Infant son** of William C.: no date
Grave # 264.

**Hamner, John Earley:** September 21, 1873-November 7, 1952. Grave # 257.

He was the husband of Rose Anie Viella "Ella" Rigsby and the son of John Pruitt Hamner and Annie Margaret Hall.

John Pruitt Hamner was the son of William T. Taylor, Sr. and his second wife Permelia Chism.[39]

John Early Hamner's siblings buried in Macedonia Cemetery include: an infant sister born and died June 8, 1876; Mary Ulalah Virginia Hamner, a child; Edward Powell "Dock" Hamner; Buena Vista Hamner Chism; Larkin "Lark" Rogers Hamner; Annie Brazeal Hamner Rushing; Ozella Judson Hamner Rushing; Permelia Alma Hamner Rushing and Ullie Mae Hamner Chism.

**Hamner, John Pruitt:** October 4, 1845-December 18, 1905. Grave # 238.

He was the husband of Anne Margaret Hall and the son of William Taylor Hamner, Sr. and his second wife Permelia Chism.[40]

Eleven of their thirteen children are buried in Macedonia Cemetery: (1) an infant daughter in 1867; (2) Mary Ulalah Virginia Hamner, a child; (3) Ollie Jackson "Ollie" (married to Louise Rigsby); (4) John Early Hamner (married to Rose Annie Viella "Ella" Rigsby); (5) Buena Vista Hamner Chism (married first to John Monroe House and married second to Archie George Chism); (6) Larkin "Lark" Rogers (married to Beatrice Josephine Smith); (7) Annie Brazile Hamner Rushing (married to Thomas Hillman Rushing); (8) Ozella Judson Hamner Rushing (married to Marvin Goldman Rushing); (9) Permelia Alma Hamner married to Joseph David "Gin" Rushing; (10) Ullie Mae Hamner Chism (married to her first cousin Harvey Morgan Chism); (11) Edward "Dock" Hamner (married to Fannie Mae Duncan who is not buried in Macedonia Cemetery).

The two children of Annie Margaret Hall and John Pruitt Hamner not buried in Macedonia Cemetery are: (1) Gillie Pruitt Hamner (married to Hassie Lou Lewis) who are buried in Tuscaloosa Memorial Park (2) Jacob Cullen Hamner (married to Jessie Florence Lewis) who are buried

---

[37] Page 197
[38] Page 155
[39] Page 199
[40] Page 184

in Tuscaloosa Memorial Park.

John Pruitt Hamner served in the Confederate Army.

**Hamner, Larkin Rogers:** February 2, 1879-April 19, 1955. Grave # 286.

He was the seventh child of John Pruitt Hamner and Annie Margaret Hall.[41]

Lark Hamner married Beatrice Josephine "Jo" Smith and was the father of Annie Mable Hamner, William Trimm Hamner, John Curtis Hamner and James Lando "Kid" Hamner.

Lark Hamner was a brother to: Mary Ulalah Virginia Hamner, a child who died in childhood; Ollie Jackson "Ollie" Hamner (married to Louise Rigsby); John Earl Hamner (married to Rose Anne Viella Rigsby); Buena Vista Hamner Chism (she married first to John Monroe House and married second to her first cousin Archie George Chism); Annie Brazeal Hamner Rushing (married to Thomas Hillman "Jack" Rushing); Ozella Judson Hamner (married to Marvin Goldman Rushing); Permelia Alma Hamner (married to Joseph David "Gin" Rushing; Ullie Mae Hamner Chism (married to her first cousin Harvey Morgan Chism).

All the above except William Trimm Hamner, John Curtis Hamner and James Lando "Kid" Hamner are buried in Macedonia Cemetery.

**Hamner, Lewis Daniel**: December 10, 1920-May 13, 1924. Grave # 240.

**Hamner, Lillian Kirk:** February 19, 1919-December 21, 1925. Grave # 268

**Hamner, Louvenia Jene Logan**: December 14, 1891-October 19, 1979. Grave # 87.

Jene was the wife of Newton Jessie Hamner and the daughter of William H. Logan and Nancy Rebecca Watts Logan.[42]

Louvenia Jene Logan was the mother of Mary Eunice Hamner who died in childhood.

Newton Jessie Hamner was the son of George Harrison Hamner and Sarah "Sallie" McGee.

George Harrison Hamner was the son of William Taylor Hamner, Sr. by his first wife whose name is not known.[43]

All the above are buried in Macedonia Cemetery.

**Hammer, Lular:** August 14, 1876-December 14, 1879. Grave # 76. She was the daughter of Louis Alfred Hamner and Penina Wilson Clements.

Penina Wilson Clements was the daughter of Thomas Clements and Elizabeth Simpson.

Louis Alfred Hamner was the fourth son of William Taylor Hamner, Sr. and his second wife Permelia Chism.

All the above are buried in Macedonia Cemetery except for Louis Alfred Hamner and Penina Wilson Clements who are buried in the old Alberta City Methodist Cemetery.[44]

**Hamner, Mary Eunice:** August 16, 1920-December 13, 1929. Grave # 85.

She was the daughter of Newton Jessie Hamner and Louvenia Jene Logan.

Newton Jessie Hamner was the son of George Harrison Hamner and Sarah "Sally" McGee and the grandson of William Taylor Hamner, Sr. and his first wife whose name is not known.

Louvenia Jene Logan was the daughter of William H. Logan and Nancy Rebecca Watts Logan.

All the above are buried in Macedonia Cemetery.

**Hamner, Mary Louise Rigsby:** February 7, 1875-March 30, 1954. Grave # 255.

She was the wife of Oliver Jackson "Ollie" Hamner.[45]

Mary Louise Rigsby was the daughter Jesse Tyson Rigsby and Nancy Elizabeth White. Jesse Tyson Rigsby is buried in Macedonia Cemetery.

Mary Louise Rigsby was the mother of Jessie Pruitt Hamner, James Webster "Jay" Hamner, Loubelle Hamner Rushing, Edward Bruce Hamner, Vera Mae Hamner, Ollie Lee Hamner, Oll

---

[41] Page 214
[42] Page 214
[43] Page 155
[44] Page 247
[45] Page 186

# MACEDONIA CEMETERY

Dee Hamner, Hollis Harwood "Woody" Hamner; John O'Neal Hamner.

Oliver Jackson "Ollie" Hamner, Mary Louise Rigsby Hamner's husband, was the son of John Pruitt Hamner and Annie Margaret Hall and the grandson of William T. Hamner, Sr. and his second wife Permelia Chism.

Oliver Jackson "Ollie" Hamner was a brother to John Early Hamner (married to Rose Anne Viella Rigsby), Edward Powell "Dock" Hamner (married to Fannie Maybelle Duncan), Buena Vista Hamner Chism (married first to John Monroe House and married second to her first cousin Archie George Chism), Larkin Rogers "Lark" Hamner (married to Beatrice Josephine "Joe" Smith), Annie Brazeal Hamner Rushing (married to Thomas Hillman Rushing), Ozella Judson Hamner Rushing (married to Marvin Goldman Rushing), Permelia Alma Hamner (married to Joseph David "Gin" Rushing and Ullie Mae Hamner Chism (married to her first cousin Harvey Morgan Chism).

All the above are buried in Macedonia Cemetery except for Jessie Pruitt Hamner, James Webster "Jay" Hamner and Hollis Harwood "Woody" Hamner who are buried in Carrolls Creek Baptist Church Cemetery. John O'Neal Hamner is buried in Sunset Cemetery.

**Obit for Mary Louise Rigsby Hamner:**

Mrs. Mary Rigsby Hamner, 79, of the Crabbe Road died last night at Druid City Hospital. Funeral services will be held at 3:00 p.m. today from Macedonia Methodist Church with the Rev. J. E. Horton officiating. Burial will be in the church cemetery by Jones and Spigener.

Surviving is one daughter, Mrs. Robert "Lou Bell" Rushing of Northport; five sons, Pruett, J. W., Bruce, John O., and Dee, all of Northport; a brother Lattie L. Rigsby of Northport; three sisters, Mrs. Minnie Chism, Fayette, Mrs. Alda Wyjack, Iowa City, and Mrs. Susie Skelton; thirteen grandchildren and thirteen great grandchildren.

Pallbearers will be Roy Rushing, Dawson Chism, James Rushing, Bradford Hamner, Vester Rigsby, and Cullen Hamner.

Honorary pallbearers will be Herman Boyd, John and Grady Shirley, T. S. Black, Ed Earnest, A. E. Yow, B. A. Renfro, Hugh Spencer, Fletcher Barens, John Hagler, Joe Jobson, and Dr. John Shamblin.

**Hamner, Newt Jesse:** January 16, 1889-July 23, 1969. Grave # 86.

Newt was married to Louvenia Jene Logan the daughter of William H. Logan and Nancy Rebecca Watts who are buried in Macedonia Cemetery.[46]

Newton Jessie Hamner was the son of George Harrison Hamner and Sarah "Sally" McGee.

George Harrison Hamner was the son of William Taylor Hamner, Sr. and his first wife whose name is not known. Hamner family tradition holds that George Harrison Hamner's mother is buried in a grave marked by a stone with no name engraved next to William Taylor Hamner, Sr.'s grave in Macedonia Cemetery. If this is true, her grave is likely the oldest in the cemetery.

Mary Eunice Hamner, a daughter of Newton Jessie Hamner and Louvenia Jene Logan who died in childhood, is buried in Macedonia Cemetery.

**Obit for Newton J. Hamner**

Newton J. Hamner, 80, of the Crabbe Road died last night at a local nursing home.

Funeral services will be held Friday at 10:00 a.m. at the Macedonia Methodist Church with the Rev. Bob Maxwell and Rev. Lynwood Sudduth officiating. Burial will be in the church cemetery by Memory Chapel Funeral Home.

Surviving is his wife, three daughters, Mrs. Clara Sudduth, Mrs. Nora Watson, and Mrs. Myrtle Kincaid of Tuscaloosa; a sister, Mrs. Nina Cooper of Birmingham and three grandchildren.

Active pallbearers will be Oniest Boyd, Troy Criss, Otis Turner, Gene Turner, Hilary Shirley, and Mark Shirley.

Honorary pallbearers will be Tom Clements,

---

[46] Page 170

Jim Smith, John Chism, Reuben Hamner, Bill and Lewis Faucett, Paul Putman, Grady, John, Lonnie, and B. F. Shirley, Albert and John Hagler, Elbert Ransey, John Christian, Spurgeon Black, B. R. Holston, Jack Cook, Jay, Bruce, and Dee Hamner, Robert Rushing, Frank Lafoy, and Dr. Sam Davis.

**Hamner, Ollie Bruce "Doc"**: February 24, 1927-July 5, 1980. Grave # 265.

Ollie was the husband of Emma Louise Estes and the son of Edward Bruce Hamner and Fannie Lou Shirley Hamner. He was killed in a tractor accident.[47]

Edward Bruce Hamner was the son of Oliver Jackson "Ollie" Hamner and Mary Louise Rigsby.

Oliver Jackson "Ollie" Hamner was the son of John Pruitt Hamner and Annie Margaret Hall.

John Pruitt Hamner was the son of William Taylor Hamner, Sr. and his second wife Permelia Chism.

Fannie Lou Shirley Hamner was the daughter of Byrdie "Byrd" Franklin Shirley and Matilda Ann Smith.

All the above are buried in Macedonia Cemetery.

**Hamner, Oll Dee**: November 6, 1907-September 8, 1993. Grave # 311.

He was the husband of Frances Shirley and the son of Oliver "Ollie" Jackson Hamner and Mary Louise Rigsby.

Oliver "Ollie" Jackson Hamner was the son of John Pruitt Hamner and Annie Margaret Hall.[48]

John Pruitt Hamner was the son of William Taylor Hamner, Sr. and his second wife Permelia Chism.

Mary Louise Rigsby was the daughter of Jesse Tyson Rigsby and Nancy Elizabeth White.[49]

Oll Dee was a brother to Edward Bruce Hamner (married to Fannie Lou Shirley), Lou Bell Hamner Rushing (married to Robert E. Lee Rushing) and Vera Mae Hamner (a child) all of whom are buried in Macedonia Cemetery. He was also a brother to Jessie Pruitt Hamner (married to Ruby Pearson); James Webster "Jay" Hamner (married to Essie Queen Lafoy); Hollis Harwood Hamner (married to Elsie Yow) all of whom are buried in Carrolls Creek Baptist Church Cemetery.

Oll Dee Hamner was also a brother to John O'Neal Hamner who is buried in Sunset Cemetery.

**Hamner, Oliver Jackson "Ollie"**: September 1, 1871-October 11, 1938. Grave # 254.

He was the husband of Mary Louise Rigsby and the son of John Pruitt Hamner and Annie Margaret Hall.

John Pruitt Hamner was the son of William T. Hamner, Sr. and his second wife Permelia Chism.[50]

Oliver Jackson "Ollie" Jackson was the father of Jessie Pruitt Hamner (married to Ruby Pearson), James Webster "Jay" Hamner (married to Essie Queen LaFoy), Loubelle Hamner Rushing (married to Robert E. Lee Rushing), Edward Bruce Hamner (married to Fannie Lou Shirley), Hollis Harwood Hamner (married to Elsie Yow), Vera Mae Hamner who died in childhood, Ollie Lee Hamner who died in childhood and Oll Dee Hamner (married to Frances Shirley Hamner) and John O'Neal Hamner.

Oliver Jackson "Ollie" Hamner was a brother to John Early Hamner, Edward Powell "Dock" Hamner, Buena Vista Hamner Chism, Larkin Rogers Hamner, Annie Brazeal Hamner Rushing, Ozella Judson Hamner Rushing, Permelia Alma Hamner Rushing, and Ullie Mae Hamner Chism.

John O'Neal Hamner is buried in Sunset Cemetery.

Jessie Pruitt Hamner, James Webster and Hollis Harwood are buried in Carrolls Creek Baptist Church Cemetery. The others listed above

---

[47] Page 194
[48] Page 197
[49] Page 186

[50] Page 186

# MACEDONIA CEMETERY

are buried in Macedonia Cemetery.

Mary Louise Rigsby was the daughter of Jesse Tyson Rigsby and Nancy Elizabeth White who are not buried in Macedonia Cemetery.[51]

**Hamner, Ollie Lee:** April 25, 1906-January 4, 1907. Grave # 251. No date is given on the tombstone but *Hamner Heritage—Beginning Without End* gives the dates of April 25, 1906-January 4, 1907.[52]

**Hamner, Richard Bruce:** December 31, 1953-January 12, 1955. Grave # 267.

He was the son of Ollie Bruce Hamner and Emma Louise Estes and died of pneumonia.

Ollie Bruce Hamner was the son of Edward Bruce Hamner and Fannie Lou Shirley.

Edward Bruce Hamner was the son of Oliver Jackson "Ollie" Hamner and Mary Louise Rigsby.

Oliver Jackson "Ollie" Hamner was the son of John Pruitt Hamner and Annie Margaret Hall.

John Pruitt Hamner was the son of William Taylor Hamner, Sr. and his second wife Permelia Chism.

**Hamner, Rose Anie Viella "Ella" Rigsby:** March 26, 1880-June 7, 1940. Grave # 256.

She was the wife of John Early Hamner and the daughter of Jesse Tyson Rigsby and Nancy Elizabeth White. She was a sister to Mary Louise Rigsby Hamner the wife of Oliver Jackson "Ollie" Hamner.[53]

John Early Hamner was the son of John Pruitt Hamner and Annie Margaret Hall.

John Pruitt Hamner was the son of William Taylor Hamner, Sr. and his second wife Permelia Chism.

John Early Hamner's siblings buried in Macedonia Cemetery include: an infant sister who was born and died June 8, 1876; Mary Ulalah Virginia Hamner, a child; Edward Powell "Dock" Hamner; Buena Vista Hamner Chism; Larkin "Lark" Rogers Hamner; Annie Brazeal Hamner Rushing; Ozella Judson Hamner Rushing; Permelia Alma Hamner Rushing; Ullie Mae Hamner Chism.

**Hamner, Sallie:** October 11, 1848-July 28, 1931. Grave # 75.

She was the wife of George Harrison Hamner and the mother of Newton Jessie Hamner.

George Harrison Taylor was the son of William Taylor Hamner, Sr. and his first wife whose name is not known.

**Hamner, Vera Mae:** December 29, 1905-January 27, 1911.

Grave # 252

She was the fifth child of Ollie Jackson Hamner and Mary Louise Rigsby. She had an abscessed tooth pulled and died of a following infection.[54]

**Hamner, William Claude:** March 29, 1900-February 15, 1978. Grave # 262.

He was the son of John Early Hamner and Rose Anie Viella Rigsby. He married Hettie Mable Cook.[55]

**Hamner, William Taylor Sr.:** 1814-July 10, 1889.

Grave # 2.

He is the patriarch of all the Hamner's buried in Macedonia. He was married four times and fathered sixteen children by three wives.

William Taylor Hamner, Sr.'s first wife's name is unknown.

His second wife was Permelia Chism. Permelia Chism was born in 1825 in South Carolina and was the daughter of Middleton Chism and Lucrecia "Creazy" _____ Chism. It is thought that the Chism family first arrived in Northport in the late 1820s.[56]

According to Hamner family tradition, William T. Hamner, Sr.'s first two wives are buried on either side of his grave. The graves are marked only by rocks with no names. The first wife died circa 1840. If Hamner tradition is true, her grave

---

[51] Page 186
[52] Page 197
[53] Page 199
[54] Page 197
[55] Page 206
[56] Page 126

49

might be the oldest in the cemetery. The oldest tombstone giving identity of the person interred and the date of death is that of Susannah Tierce, April 27, 1862,

William Taylor Hamner, Sr.'s third wife by whom he had no children was Ella Hester Johns Stanley. They divorced. She is buried in Texas.

William Taylor Hamner's fourth wife was Eglantine Ellen "Tiny" Brittain. This marriage produced one child Mary Ann Matilda Hamner. Eglantine Ellen "Tiny" Brittain is buried in Mount Olive Baptist Church Cemetery.

The following children of William Taylor Hamner, Sr. are buried in Macedonia Cemetery: George Harrison Hamner by first wife.

By his second wife Permelia Chism, the following children are buried in Macedonia Cemetery: Mary Ulalah Virginia Hamner; Oliver "Ollie" Jackson Hamner; John Early Hamner; Edward Powell "Dock" Hamner; Buena Vista Hamner Chism; Larkin "Lark" Rogers Hamner; Annie Brazeal Hamner Rushing; Permelia Alma Hamner Chism; Ozella Judson Hamner Rushing; Ulla Mae Hamner Chism.

The only children of William T. Hamner, Sr. and Permelia Chism not buried in Macedonia Cemetery are Gillie Pruitt Hamner and his wife Hassie Lou Lewis who are buried in Tuscaloosa Memorial Park and Jacob Cullen Hamner and his wife Jessie Florence Lewis who are also buried in Tuscaloosa Memorial Park.

**Hannah, Jessie Mae Rigsby:** June 9, 1908-April 3, 1994. Grave # 276

**Hathcock, Granny:** 1835-1915

Grave # 169. She was the mother of Hester J. Hathcock King and the grandmother of Ella King Criswell.

**Hewitt, John Howard Jr.:** April 25, 1961-___, 1983.

Grave # 306.

He was the son of Glenda Sheryl Hamner Hewett who is still living in 2024.

Glenda Sheryl Hamner is the daughter of Edward Bruce Hamner and Fannie Lou Shirley Hamner.

Fannie Lou Shirley Hamner was the daughter of Byrdie "Byrd" Franklin Shirley and Matilda Smith Shirley.

Edward Bruce Hamner was the son of Oliver Jackson " Ollie" Hamner and Mary Louise Rigsby. Oliver Jackson "Ollie" Hamner was the son of John Pruitt Hamner and Annie Margaret Hall and the son of William T. Hamner and Permelia Chism.

All the above are buried in Macedonia Cemetery.

**House, Allie Lee Hamner:** September 16, 1889-April 5, 1958. Grave # 25.

She was the daughter of William Taylor Hamner, Jr. and Emma Alabama Shirley.

Allie Lee Hamner married Simon Henry House and was the mother of Samuel Tillman House both of whom are buried in Macedonia Cemetery.

William Taylor Hamner, Jr. was the third child of William Taylor Hamner, Sr. and his second wife Permelia Chism. William Taylor Hamner, Jr. (April 2, 1847-December 28, 1928) married Emma Alabama Shirley the daughter of John Lewis Shirley on March 3, 1890. They had nine children. William Taylor Hamner, Jr. taught school at Lafoy School.

William Taylor Hamner, Jr. and Emma Alabama Shirley Hamner are buried in Bethel Cemetery.[57]

**House, Ben F.:** December 8, 1877-January 23, 1953. Grave # 5.

He was the son of Nicholas L. "Nick" House (1847-1917). Ben was married to Donnie Cooper (1880-1946).[58]

The death date of Nicholas House's first wife is not clear. After her death, Nicholas House married Dovy Hamner (1856-1909) the eighth child of William T. Hamner, Sr. and his second wife Permelia Chism.

Dovy Ann Hamner first married George

---

[57] Page 237
[58] Page 309

# MACEDONIA CEMETERY

Washington Chism on November 9, 1876. They had four children: Archie George Chism (1878); Marvin A. Chism (1880); Bascom Chism (1882); Henry Morgan Chism (1885). Dovy Ann married second to Nicholas L. "Nick" House on December 9, 1888. Dovy Ann and Nicholas had two children: Simon Henry House (b. July 8, 1889) and Valda Lee House (b. May 1, 1896). Valda Lee married James Monroe Adams.[59]

**House, Donie Cooper:** She died 1900-1903. Grave # 6.

She was the wife of Ben House. She died 1900-1903. She was a sister to Willie Bea Cooper who was married to Marvin Chism.[60]

**House, John Monroe**, Jr.: July 9, 1895-December 1, 1959. Grave # 18. He is the son of John Monroe House, Sr., and Buna Vista Hamner.[61]

John Monroe House was blinded early in life when he walked into a fire (per B. F. Shirley).

Buena Vista Hamner was the daughter of John Pruitt Hamner and Annie Margaret Hall.

John Pruitt Hamner was the son of William T. Hamner, Sr. and his second wife Permelia Chisms.

Buena Vista married first to John Monroe House on September 9, 1894. Buna Vista and John Monroe House had one child, John Monroe House, Jr. who was born July 9, 1895. The date of death of John Monroe House, Sr. is not given nor is there a mention of a divorce from Buena Vista. However, Buena Vista Hamner House married a second time on June 14, 1900 to Archie George Chism, her first cousin. All the above are buried in Macedonia Cemetery.

Archie George Chism and Buena Vista House Hamner had five children: (1) Maggie Lee Chism; (2) Ursula Judson Chism; (3) Ida Bell Chism; (4) Margaret Elizabeth Chism; (5) Lewis Arch Chism. Only Lewis Arch Chism is buried in Macedonia Cemetery.[62]

**Obit for John Monroe House, Sr.**

John M. House, 64, of Northport died at a local hospital Tuesday afternoon.

Funeral services will be held Thursday at 11:00 a.m. at Macedonia Methodist Church with the Rev. W. K. E. James officiating. Burial will follow in the church cemetery with Speigner-Brown-Service in charge.

Survivors include his mother, Mrs. Buna Vista Chism of Northport; four sisters, Volon Sanders of Sentinel, Ohio, Mrs. Bill Taylor of Roger, Arkansas, Mrs. A. E. Newman of Orlando, Florida, and Mrs. J.C. Walton of Atlanta; one brother, L. A. Chism of Tacoma, Washington.

Active pallbearers will be Houston Hamner, C. Hamner, Preston Rushing, Dee Hamner, Roy Rushing, Dawson Chism and James Rushing.

Honorary pallbearers will be Willis Skelton, John Chism. R. D. Hamner, Louis Sanders, Claude Hamner, Pruitt Hamner, Wash Petty, Roy Hutchins, James Anders, Eldon Boyd, Wylie Hagler, Woodrow Rushing, and Trimm Hamner.

**House, Maggie**: 1908-1913
Grave # 14.

**House, Nicholas**: 1847-1917
Grave # 14
1847-1917.

The name of Nicholas' first wife is unclear. Nicholas and his first wife had one child, Ben House. After the death of his first wife, Nicholas House married Dovy Hamner on December 9, 1876. Dovy was the eighth child of William Taylor Hamner, Sr. and his second wife Permelia Chism.[63]

Dovy and Nicholas House had two children: (1) Simon Henry House who married Allie Lee Hamner daughter of William Taylor Hamner, Jr. and granddaughter of William T. Taylor, Sr. and Permelia Chism; (2) Valda Lee House who married James Monroe Adams, all of whom are

---

[59] Page 311
[60] Page 309
[61] Page 212

[62] Page 212
[63] Page 309

buried in Macedonia Cemetery.

In 2001, B.F. Shirley, the then-current cemetery caretaker, told Hayse Boyd at the time of the original mapping of the cemetery, that Nicholas House was killed by Eugene Benjamin Tierce, Sr.

Nicholas House's grave marker shows that he served in Co. G 3 Ala Reg Confederate Army.

**House, Samuel Tillman:** 1916-1937

Grave # 24.

He was the son of Simon Tillman House and grandson of William Taylor Hamner, Jr. and Emma Alabama Shirley and great grandson of William T. Hamner, Sr. and Permelia Chism. He never married. It is

said that he died following surgery for a ruptured appendix.

William Taylor Hamner, Jr. (April 2, 1847- December 28, 1928) on March 3, 1890 married Emma Alabama Shirley the daughter of John Lewis Shirley. They had nine children. William Taylor Hamner, Jr. taught school at Lafoy School. William Taylor Hamner, Jr. and Emma Alabama Shirley Hamner are buried in Bethel Cemetery.[64]

**Obit for Samuel Tillman House**

Samuel Tillman House, 21-year-old Northport Route 1, died Monday night at Druid City Hospital after a one-week illness. Funeral services will be held this afternoon at 4:30 at Macedonia Methodist Church with Elder George B. Davison officiating. Interment will be in the church cemetery by Mathis-Jones.

Mr. House is survived by his parents, Mr. and Mrs. Simeon House, and three brothers, Emil House, Preston House and Adrian House.

**House, Simon Henry:** July 8, 1889-July 4, 1973. Grave # 26.

He was the son of Nicholas House and Dovy Hamner Chism. Dovy was the daughter of William T. Hamner, Sr. and his second wife Permelia Chism. Simon Henry House married Allie Lee Hamner the daughter of William T. Hamner, Jr. and Emma Alabama Shirley.

William T. Hamner, Jr, was the son of William T. Hamner, Sr. and his second wife Permelia Chism.

Simon Henry was the father of Samuel Tillman House.

**Hyche, Early Monroe:** January 11, 1878- March 9, 1923. Grave # 57

He was the husband of Lenora Belle "Lou" Rushing and the father of Lenora Belle "Lou" Rushing and Waylon Hyche.

Lenora Belle "Lou" Rushing was the daughter of Joseph Enoch Rushing and Samantha Lenora Deason both of whom are buried in Macedonia Cemetery.

Siblings of Lenora Belle "Lou" Rushing Hyche buried in Macedonia Cemetery include Joseph David "Gin" Rushing and his wife Permelia Alma Hamner, Thomas Hillman "Jack" Rushing and his wife Annie Brazile Hamner Rushing, James Willie Snow Rushing and his wife Fannie Lee Gay, Marvin Goldman Rushing and his wife Ozella Judson "Juddie" Hamner, Sylvester Hayes Rushing (he never married), James Knox Polk Rushing and his wife Annie Elizabeth Turner and Robert E. Lee Rushing and his wife Loubelle Hamner Rushing. Siblings not buried in Macedonia Cemetery include John Gilbert "Gib" Rushing and his wife Minnie Williamson Snyder, Joshua Mills "Josh" Rushing and his wife Clara Barton Shirley and Hewitt Ashley Rushing and his wife Nora V. Turner.

**Hyche, Lenora Belle "Lou" Rushing:** February 14, 1882-March 19, 1954. Grave # 58.

She was the wife of Early Monroe Hyche. She was the daughter of Joseph Enoch Rushing and Samantha Lenora Deason both of whom are buried in Macedonia Cemetery.

Siblings of Lenora Belle "Lou" Rushing Hyche buried in Macedonia Cemetery include Joseph David "Gin" Rushing and his wife Permelia Alma Hamner, Thomas Hillman "Jack" Rushing and his wife Annie Brazile Hamner, James Willie Snow Rushing and his wife Fannie Lee Gay, Marvin Goldman Rushing and his wife Ozella Judson "Juddie" Hamner, Sylvester Hayes

[64] Page 237

# MACEDONIA CEMETERY

Rushing (Hayes never married), James Knox Polk Rushing and his wife Annie Elizabeth Turner and Robert E. Lee Rushing and his wife Loubelle Hamner.

Siblings not buried in Macedonia Cemetery include John Gilbert "Gib" Rushing and his wife Minnie Williamson Snyder (buried in Williamson Cemetery), Joshua Mills "Josh" Rushing and his wife Clara Barton Shirley (buried in Memory Hills Gardens) and Hewitt Ashley Rushing and his wife Nora V. Turner (buried in Bethel Cemetery).

**Obit for Mrs. Lou Rushing Hyche**

Mrs. Lou Bell Rushing Hyche, 72, of the Crabbe Road died Thursday afternoon at Druid City Hospital. A funeral service will be held March 20 at Macedonia Methodist Church with the Rev. J. E. Horton and Rev. Tim Powell officiating with burial in the church cemetery with Jones and Spigener in charge.

Surviving is one son, Wayland Hyche; a daughter, Mrs. Ed Earnest; three brothers, Polk, Josh, and Robert Rushing; seven grandchildren.

Active pallbearers will be nephews, Roy Rushing, John Rushing, Preston Rushing, Minor Medders and David Rushing.

Honorary pallbearers will be Dr. Luther Davis, Spurgeon Black, Gil Hamner, Anthony Renfro, Ed Turner, Nathan Chism, Sam Palmer, Carl Adams, Belton and Elmer Earnest and Curtis Hamner.

**Jones, Annie Bigham:** 1868-1939 Grave # 272.

**Jones, Foster:** August 28, 1890-September 20, 1967.
Grave # 273

**Jones, Hunter:** 1892-1917
Grave # 271.

**Junkin, Ullie Mae Hamner Chism:** May 25, 1889-July 5, 1936. Grave # 64.

She was the 13th child of John Pruitt Hamner and Annie Margaret Hall. Ullie Mae married her first cousin Harvey Morgan Chism a son of George Washington Chism and Dovy Ann Hamner. After Harvey Morgan Chism died, she married Oscar Junkin. [65]

John Pruitt Hamner was the son of William T. Hamner, Sr. and his second wife Permelia Chism.

Dovy Ann was the daughter of William Taylor Hamner, Sr. and Permelia Chism. She first married George Washington Chism who was the son of Lewis David Chism and Marilla Freeman. Dovy Ann and George Washington Chism had four children: (1) Arch George Chism; (2) Bascom Virgil Chism; (3) Harvey Morgan Chism; (4) Marvin Chism. All are buried in Macedonia Cemetery.

Dovy married second to Nicholas House. See *House* for additional information.

**Keene, Alda Mae. Clements**: May 28, 1935-August 29, 1993. Grave 129.

**Keeth, Carl Jr.**: February 27, 1931-December 30, 1952. Grave # 277.

**King Andy J.**: August 11, 1850-November 4, 1934. Grave # 165.

He was the husband of Hester J. Hathcock and the father of Ellen King Criswell both of whom are buried in Macedonia Cemetery.

**Obit for Andrew King:**

Services for Andrew King, 73, who died yesterday afternoon on the Crabbe Road will be held at 2:30 p.m. this afternoon at Macedonia Methodist Church with the Rev. Mr. Marvin Manderson officiating. Burial will follow in the church cemetery by Jones and Spigener.

Mr. King is survived on his widow; one son, Oliver King of Tuscaloosa; two daughters, Mrs. Frances Criswell of Northport, and Mrs. Cora Cannon of Tuscaloosa; four brothers: Jim; Dock; Rufus; and John King all of Oneonta, Alabama.

**King, Hester J. Hathcock**: March 12, 1871-June 2, 1936. Grave # 164.

She was the wife of Andy J. King and the mother of Ellen King Criswell.

**King, James Oliver**: September 20, 1923-September 20, 1923. Grave # 168.

---
[65] Page 236

He was the grandson of Andrew and Hester King who are buried in Macedonia and the son of Oliver King who is not buried in Macedonia Cemetery.

**LaFoy, Addie:** December 29, 1867-February 17, 1924.

Grave # 114

**LaFoy, Frances Albert**: October 26, 1824-December 1, 1887. Grave # 113.

Frances Albert LaFoy was the son of William H. LaFoy and Sarah Cottrell.

Frances Albert LaFoy was born in South Carolina. He married Elizabeth Caroline Cottrell who was born in Georgia prior to February 10, 1851, the exact date not known. In 1860, they lived in Fort Motley, Greenville, South Carolina where he worked as a blacksmith and farmer. The 1880 Federal Census showed they lived in Tuscaloosa County near Northport. Frances Albert LaFoy married Elizabeth Caroline Cottrell prior to February 1851. Elizabeth Caroline Cottrell was born June 30, 1830 in Georgia. She died on December 29, 1906, and is buried in grave # 112 in Macedonia Cemetery.

Frances Albert LaFoy and Elizabeth Caroline Cottrell were the parents of thirteen children: (1) Mary F. Taylor LaFoy; (2) Henry Clay LaFoy; (3) Thomas Daniel LaFoy; (4) Sarah Elizabeth LaFoy; (5) Martha C. LaFoy; (6) Nancy A. LaFoy; (7) William LaFoy; (8) Susan C. LaFoy; (9) John Albert LaFoy; (10) William R. LaFoy; (11) John M. LaFoy; (12) John Henry LaFoy; (13) William H. LaFoy

**LaFoy, Elizabeth Carolyn Cottrell:** June 30, 1830-December 29, 1906. Grave # 112.

She was the wife of Frances Albert LaFoy and the mother of thirteen children: (1) Mary F. Taylor LaFoy; (2) Henry Clay LaFoy; (3) Thomas Daniel LaFoy; (4) Sarah Elizabeth LaFoy; (5) Martha C. LaFoy; (6) Nancy A. LaFoy; (7) William LaFoy; (8) Susan C. LaFoy; (9) John Albert LaFoy; (10) William R. LaFoy; (11) John M. LaFoy; (12) John Henry LaFoy; (13) William H. LaFoy

**LaFoy, Addie Elizabeth Brown:** July 24, 1879-April 2, 1961. Grave # 122.

**LaFoy, Emil Frances:** December 2, 1910-May 24, 1983. Grave # 284.

Emil Frances LaFoy was the son of Thomas Daniel LaFoy and Addie Elizabeth "Lizzie" Brown LaFoy. Emil Frances "Frank" married Frances America Broughton who was born in the Cowden Community near Samantha on May 1, 1914. Frances America died June 2, 2005, and is buried in grave # 284 in Macedonia Cemetery.

**LaFoy, Frances America Broughton:** May 1, 1914-June 2, 2005. Grave # 285.

Frances America Broughton was born in the Cowden Community near Samantha. She married Emil Francs "Frank" L LaFoy.

Frances America and Frank were the parents of three sons: Tony LaFoy (November 18, 1936-February 4, 2021.) He is buried in Sunset Cemetery; Charles Ray LaFoy (July 5, 1938-March 16, 1992). He is buried in Salem Cemetery in New Lexington; William Thomas LaFoy. He died at the age of one month on January 27, 1941, and is buried in Macedonia Cemetery in grave # 283 beside his parents.

**LaFoy, Maggie:** February 20, 1902-June 9, 1903. Grave # 120. An infant girl.

**LaFoy, Thomas:** May 1905-August 1906 Grave # 119. An infant male.

**LaFoy, Thomas Daniel:** July 3, 1871-November 11, 1946. Grave # 121.

Thomas Daniel LaFoy was the third child of Frances Albert LaFoy and his wife Elizabeth Caroline Cottrell LaFoy.

He married Addie Elizabeth "Lizzie" Brown on August 24, 1896. Thomas Daniel died on November 11, 1946, and is buried in grave # 121 in Macedonia Cemetery. Addie Elizabeth "Lizzie Brown LaFoy died on April 2, 1961 and is buried in grave # 122 in Macedonia Cemetery. Their daughter Essie Queen LaFoy married James Webster "Jay" Hamner the son of Oliver Jackson "Ollie" Hamner and Mary Louise Rigsby. Jay and Queen are buried in Carrolls Creek Baptist

# MACEDONIA CEMETERY

Church Cemetery.

**Obit for Thomas Daniel LaFoy**

Funeral services for Thomas D. LaFoy who died Monday at his home on Northport Route 2 will be held at 2:00 p. m. Wednesday at Macedonia Methodist Church with burial in the church cemetery, Jones and Spigener in charge.

Mr. LaFoy was 76 years old and a lifelong resident of this county.

He leaves: his widow; three daughters, Mrs. Tom Morrison, Mrs. J. W. Hamner, and Mrs. Nannie Walters all of Northport Route 2; four sons, Verner, of Tuscaloosa, Thurman, Frank, and John of Northport Route 2; 17 grandchildren, and one great grandchild; a niece Mrs. Queen Walton of Mississippi; a nephew, Lasco Watkins of Birmingham.

Active pallbearers for the funeral will be Herman Boyd, Pruett Hamner, Lonnie Shirley, James Hamner, Roy Rushing, and Devaughn Black.

Honorary pallbearers will be B. A. Renfro, Larkin R. Hamner, Hugh Spencer, Dr. S. T. Hardin, Newton J. Hamner, Roy Faucett, Charlie Newman, J. D. Homan, and Hayes Rushing.

**LaFoy, Will**: date unknown
Grave 111. He was accidentally killed in a shotgun accident while hunting according to B.F. Shirley.

**LaFoy, William T.**: December 21, 1940-January 27, 1941. Grave # 283.

He was the infant son of Emil Frances LaFoy and Frances America Broughton LaFoy.

**Langley, Susie**: May 1841-April 1913 Grave # 97.

**Lewis, Malinda Mustin**: October 10, 1855-February 28, 1928. Grave # 275.

**Lewis, Oliver Bennet**: died May 19, 1923 Grave # 274.

**Logan, Daniel**: March 9, 1894-July 1, 1940. Grave # 187.

**Logan, Herman B.**: April 4, 1899-July 5, 1924. Grave # 160.

**Logan, Jewell F.**: July 28, 1914-March 16, 1991. Grave # 183.

**Logan, Nancy A.**: November 15, 1898-January 11, 1975. Grave # 188.

**Logan, Nancy Rebecca Watts**: February 8, 1860-July 13, 1935. Grave # 161.

She was the wife of William H. Logan and the mother of Louvenia Jene Logan Hamner.

Louvenia Jene Logan was the wife of Newton Jesse Hamner.

Newton Jessie Hamner was the son of George Harrison Hamner and Sarah "Sally" McGee.

George Harrison Hamner was the son of William Taylor Hamner, Sr. and his first wife whose name is not known. Hamner family tradition holds that George Harrison Hamner's mother is buried in a grave marked only by a stone with no name on it in Macedonia Cemetery beside the grave of William Taylor Hamner, Sr. If this is true, her grave is likely the oldest in the cemetery.

All the above are buried in Macedonia Cemetery.

**Logan, Rosa Franklin**: September 6, 1890-July 28, 1931. Grave # 185.

**Logan, Samuel G.**: October 21, 1920-January 26, 1951. Grave # 184.

**Logan, William H.**: May 9, 1860-March 18, 1943. Grave # 162.

He was the husband of Nancy Rebecca Watts.

**Mathis, Louise Tierce**: March 31, 1910-Febraury 11, 1983.

Grave # 203.

Louise was the wife of Tucker Mathis who is buried in Sunset Memorial Park in Northport. Tuck and Louise had no children.

Louise was the daughter of Eugene Benjamin Tierce, Sr. and Lela Hyche Tierce.

Eugene Benjamin Tierce, Sr. was the son of Elliott Catlett Tierce and Frances Caroline Doss.

Elliott Catlett Tierce was the son of Benjamin Tucker Tierce and Susannah Clardy Tierce.

Louise was a sister to Eugene Benjamin Tierce, Jr. and a half-sister to Octavia Tierce Hagler, Victor Tierce, Festus Tierce, Memnon Tierce, Sr., Collier Tierce, Hester _____.

All the above except for Memnon and Hester are buried in Macedonia Cemetery.

**McAllister, Lenora Hyche Earnest**: July 14, 1917-July 20, 1990. Grave # 59.

She was the daughter of Lenora Belle "Lou" Rushing Hyche and Early Monroe Hyche. She was the mother of Edward Earl Earnest, all of whom are buried in Macedonia Cemetery. In addition, part of the ashes of her daughter Mona Lisa Valles were scattered over Lenora's grave.

Lenora was first married to Ed Earnest. After they divorced, she married Roy McAllister.

Lenora Belle "Lou" Hyche was the daughter of Joseph Enoch Rushing and Samantha Lenora Deason both of which are buried in Macedonia Cemetery.

Siblings of Lenora Belle "Lou" Rushing Hyche buried in Macedonia Cemetery include Joseph David "Gin" Rushing and his wife Permelia Alma Hamner, Thomas Hillman "Jack" Rushing and his wife Annie Brazile Hamner, James Willie Snow Rushing and his wife Fannie Lee Gay, Marvin Goldman Rushing and his wife Ozella Judson "Juddie" Hamner, Sylvester Hayes Rushing (Hayes never married), Permelia Alma Hamner Rushing and her husband Joseph David "Gin" Rushing, James Knox Polk Rushing and his wife Annie Elizabeth Turner, Robert E. Lee Rushing and his wife Loubelle Hamner and two infants Edward Nathan Rushing and Anthony Leon Rushing.

All the above are buried in Macedonia Cemetery.

**McDaniel, Bobby Tierce**: February 27, 1949-October 31, 2011. Grave # 27A.

**McDaniel, Curtis**: August 31, 1933-January 17, 2008.

Grave # 27B.

**Medders, Mary E. (Cricket) Rushing**: February 2, 1929-April 12, 2012. Grave # 322.

She married Minor Seay Medders on January 21, 1950 in Columbus, Mississippi. They had one child, Debra Kay "Debbie" Medders.

Crickett was the daughter of Robert E. Lee Rushing and Loubelle Hamner Rushing.

Robert E. Lee Rushing was the son of Joseph Enoch Rushing and Samantha Lenora Deason.

Loubelle Hamner Rushing was the daughter of Oliver "Ollie" Jackson Hamner and Mary Louise Rigsby.

Oliver "Ollie" Jackson Hamner was the son of John Pruitt Hamner and Annie Margaret Hall.

John Pruitt Hamner was the son of William T. Hamner and his second wife Permelia Chism.

All the above are buried in Macedonia Cemetery.

**Medders, Minor Seay:** February 2, 1929-April 12, 2012. Grave # 323.

He married Mary E. (Cricket) Rushing. They had one child, Debra Kay "Debbie" Medders.

**Mills, Erma Shirley**: March 26, 1950-February 11, 1970. Grave # 303.

She was the daughter of Erman and Ruby Shirley Mills.

Ruby Shirley Mills was the daughter of Byrdie "Byrd" Franklin Shirley and Matilda Ann Smith.

All the above are buried in Macedonia Cemetery.

**Mills, Erman Wesley**: June 19, 1918-May 13, 2002. Grave # 303A

He was the husband of Ruby Shirley Mills and the father of Erma Mills both of whom are buried in Macedonia Cemetery.

**Mills, Ruby Shirley**: June 8, 1918-January 3, 2006. Grave # 303 B.

Ruby Shirley was the daughter of Byrdie "Byrd" Franklin Shirley and Matilda Ann Smith Shirley.

Ruby was a sister to John Ester Shirley (married to Annie Snow Rushing); Lonnie Lee Shirley (married to Estelle Wedgeworth); B. F. Shirley (married to Mary Alice Turner); Grady Edward Shirley (married to Margaret Watkins); Bobby Renzo "Buddy" Shirley; Fannie Lou Shirley Hamner (married to Edward Bruce Hamner); Martha Shirley Turner (married to Clifton Turner); Frances Shirley Hamner (married to Oll Dee Hamner).

# MACEDONIA CEMETERY

All the above are buried in Macedonia Cemetery.

Ruby was also a sister to Sue Lake and Joan Davis who are not buried in Macedonia Cemetery.

**Morrow, James Hershel**: November 6, 1928-October 3, 2012. Grave # 247A. He was the husband of Bobbie Morrow.

**Morrow, Bobbie:** birth date _____ - February 9, 2017. Grave # 247.

She was the wife of James Hershel Morrow.

**Naramore, Ella E.:** January 22, 1888-October 27, 1972. Grave # 247.

**Naramore, Reuben:** December 23, 1870-October 19, 1958. Grave # 269.

**Newman, Brenda Joyce**: 1940-1942

Grave # 31.

She was the daughter Ida Bell Chism and Edward "Ed" Newman.

Ida Bell Chism was the daughter of Buna Vista Hamner and Archie George Chism.

Buna Vista Hamner was the daughter of John Pruitt Hamner and Annie Margaret Hall.

John Pruitt Hamner was the son of William Taylor Hamner, Sr. and his second wife Permelia Chism.

**Obit for Brenda Joyce Newman:**

Little Brenda Joyce Newman, 21-month-old daughter of Mr. and Mrs. Ed Newman of 512 26th Avenue died Saturday at a hospital in Birmingham as a result of having swallowed a bobby pin. Two operations were performed.

Surviving besides the parents are the grandparents, Mr. and Mrs. Archie Chism of Northport and C. J. Newman of Fayette and other relatives. She was the niece of Mrs. Margaret Chism of this city.

Funeral services will be held at 4:00 o'clock this afternoon from the Northport Methodist Church with Rev. J. S. Sturdivant officiating assisted by the Rev. B. F. Atkins. Burial will be in the Macedonia Methodist Cemetery by Mathis-Jones.

**Ormond, M. T.:** 1909-1911.

Grave # 171.

**Owens, Adera Dee**: March 11, 1990-March 21, 1990. Grave # 182.

**Patterson, Martha Jane**: 1867-1961.

Grave # 3.

She was the wife of William Patterson.

**Patterson, Sim:** 1882-June 10, 1957.

Grave # 20. He was a brother to William Patterson.

**Patterson, William:** 1880-1927

Grave # 20. He was the husband of Martha Jane

**Pearce. John A.**: January 24, 1942-April 25, 1981. Grave # 298.

He was married to Judy Arnell Crawford. Judy was to be buried in the grave next to her husband, but when she died, she was cremated and as of 2024 her ashes have not been buried anywhere.

Judy was the daughter of Lucille Wilson Hagler and Sterling Pleasant Crawford.

Lucille Wilson Hagler Crawford was the daughter of Permelia Elizabeth Hamner and James Martin Hagler.

Permelia was the daughter of Louis Alfred Hamner and Penina Wilson Clements.

Louis Alfred Hamner was the son of William T. Hamner, Sr. and his second wife Permelia Chism.

**Renfro, Benjamin Anthony:** 1872-1957

Grave # 226.

**Renfro, Susan Margaret Tierce:** January 2, 1851-December 31, 1936. Grave # 225.

**#225 Renfro, Susan Margaret Tierce:** January 2, 1851-December 31, 1936.

**Her obituary reads,** "Mrs. Susie Renfro, 86-yesr-old-resident of Northport died early today at the home of Mrs. Lester Taylor in Northport. She had been ill for only a short time. Surviving her is one son, B. A. Renfro of Northport. Funeral services were to be held from Macedonia Church with the Reverend Mr. Selman officiating. Burial in the church cemetery is to be directed by Jones and Spigener."

In the Mem Tierce book *1816 A Tierce Comes to Tuscaloosa* on page 39 the statement is given "Mother Renfro (Susan Martha Tierce placed flowers on the graves with no flowers on Decoration Day."

**Rice, Sharon Kay Guy:** March 4, 1953-July 19, 2009. Grave # 51A

She was the wife of Gary Rice one of the cemetery caretakers noted near the beginning of this chapter. In 2023, Gary is still living.

Sharon was the daughter of Raymond Guy and Elsie Tierce Guy.

Elsie Tierce Guy was the daughter of Benjamin Collier Tierce and Nellie F. Tierce.

Benjamin Collier Tierce was the son of Eugene B. Tierce, Sr. and Veturia Scales Tierce.

Eugene B. Tierce, Sr. was the son of Elliott Catlett Tierce and Frances Caroline Doss.

Elliott Catlett Tierce was the son of Benjamin Tucker Tierce and Susannah Clardy Tierce.

All the above are buried in Macedonia Cemetery.

**Rigsby, Amon L.:** February 9, 1910-June 29, 1970. Grave # 245.

**Rigsby, Charlie Patton:** November 9, 1914-April 4, 1989. Grave # 242.

He was a brother to Mary Rigsby Hamner, wife of Ollie Jay Hamner who is buried in Macedonia Cemetery.

**Rigsby, Clarence Woodrow:** March 13, 1913-December 15, 1992. Grave # 241.

**Rigsby, James Tyson:** October 5, 1877-June 4, 1949. Grave #248.

James married Jenter Mae Hall who was born on July 31, 1884 and died on October 5, 1946.

**Rigsby, Jenter Mae Hall:** July 31, 1884-October 5 1946. Grave # 247.

Jenter was the wife of James Tyson Rigsby.

**Robertson, Andre Brian:** December 8, 1962-August 21, 2013. Grave # 323B

Andre was the son of Joe and Sirley Robertson.

Andre taught Computer Science at Holt High School, but his first love was farming, especially growing tomatoes and other vegetables.

Andre served in leadership roles as president of the Tuscaloosa County Farmers Curb Market Association.

**Robertson, Pricey Gibson Estelle Shirley White:** May 9, 1905-July 25, 1929. Grave # 172.

Pricey was the daughter of Joel T. Shirley and Sarah Curry Shirley and a sister to Clara Barton Shirley Rushing, Emile Mae Shirley Snow, Maude Shirley Bobo, and Mary Irene Shirley Pierre.

She was the mother of a baby who died in infancy and is buried in Macedonia Cemetery.

Pricey Gibson Shirley first married W. Brady Robertson. They had a son W. Brady Robertson, Jr. who died in infancy and is buried in Macedonia Cemetery. Pricey and Brady divorced and afterward left for parts unknown.

Pricey then married Joe Dawson White, a professional boxer. Dawson shot and killed Pricey in front of Woolworth Department Store in downtown Tuscaloosa on a Saturday morning. Pricey's grave stone intentionally omits the name "White."

**Robertson, Joseph A.:** February 25, 1934-August 13, 2013. Grave # 323.

He was the father of Andre Brian Robertson who is buried in Macedonia Cemetery.

**Robertson, Thomas P.:** February 19, 1824-August 6, 1908. Grave # 13

**Robertson, W. Brady, Jr.:** 1929-1929 Grave # 173.

He was the infant son of Pricey Gibson Estelle Shirley and W. Brady Robertson, Sr. See comments under Robertson, Pricey Gibson Estelle Shirley White.

**Rosman, Mary S.:** February 22, 1822-July 22, 1881. Grave # 36.

**Rushing, Annie Brazile "Brizzie" Peggy Hamner:** April 10, 1882-May 21, 1927. Grave # 72.

She was the wife of Thomas Hillman "Jack" Rushing (October 15, 1876-November 19, 1942) and the daughter of John Pruitt Hamner and Annie Margaret Hall.

John Pruitt Hamner was the son of William T. Hamner, Sr. and his second wife Permelia Chism.

Annie Brazile and Thomas Hillman Rushing had ten children of whom three are buried in Macedonia Cemetery. They include: Roy Marshall Rushing (September 11, 1912-May 1, 2001) who was married to Faith Vivian Ramsey); Edward Nathan Rushing (July 2, 1908-July 4, 1908) and Anthony Leon Rushing (March 9, 1921-January 12, 1922). The graves of Edward Nathan and Anthony Leon are marked by rock stones with no names or dates.

Children of Annie Brazile and Thomas Hillman Rushing not buried in Macedonia Cemetery include: Ozella Bertice "Bert" Rushing (married to Herman Payne Thomas); Clara Bell "Jim" Utley (married to Clyde Buel Utley); Joseph Howard "Runt" Rushing (unmarried); Temperance Hagler "Temp" Rushing (married to Floyd Alton Maughn); Nell Irene Rushing (married to Edwin George Owens); Truman Hillman "Buck" Rushing (married to Corendene Edwina Tierce); Annie Gladys Rushing (married to Robert James Romaine).

**Rushing, Annie Turner**: October 13, 1898-October 8, 1990. Grave # 38.

She was the wife of James Knox Polk Rushing and the mother of Eddie Ormand Rushing both of whom are buried in Macedonia Cemetery.

Annie Elizabeth Turner Rushing was the daughter of James Valentino Turner and Matilda Ann Cooper.

James Knox Polk Rushing was a brother to Joseph David "Gin" Rushing (married to Permelia Alma Hamner), Thomas Hillman "Jack" Rushing (married to Annie Brazile Hamner), James Willie "Will" Snow Rushing (married to Fannie Gay), Lenora Bell "Lou" Rushing Hyche (married to Early M. Hyche), Marvin Goldman Rushing (married to Ozella Judson "Juddie" Hamner) and Robert Edward Lee Rushing (married to Loubelle Hamner).

All the above are buried in Macedonia Cemetery.

**Rushing, Eddie Ormond**: April 3, 1927-April 17, 1927. Grave # 39.

He was the infant son of James Knox Polk Rushing and Annie Elizabeth Turner Rushing.

**Rushing, Vivian Faith Ramsey**: December 21, 1918-May 20, 2007. Grave # 314A.

She was the daughter of James Early Ramsey and Susan Roberta Baggett.

She was the wife of Roy Marshall Rushing (September 11, 1912-May 1, 2001) and the grandmother of William Aaron Strickland both of whom are buried in Macedonia Cemetery.

Roy Marshall Rushing was the son of Annie Brazile Annie Brazile "Brizzie" or "Peggy" Hamner, the daughter of John Pruitt Hammer and Annie Margaret Hall, and Thomas Hillman Rushing.

Thomas Hillman Rushing was the son of Joseph Enoch Rushing and Samantha Lenora Deason.

William Aaron Strickland was the son of Tara Boyd Strickland, daughter of Peggy Rushing Boyd and Hayse Boyd.

**Obit for Faith Ramsey**

Faith Ramsey Rushing, age 88, long time resident of Northport died Sunday, May 20, 2007 at Forest Manor Nursing Home. The funeral service will be at Macedonia Methodist Church at 3:30 p.m. Thursday, May 24, 2007 with the Rev. Paul Peoples, the Rev. Rock Stone, and son-in-law Dr. Hayse Boyd officiating. Magnolia North Funeral Home will direct services. The body will lie in state one hour prior to the service. Visitation will be from 6:00 p.m. to 8:00 p.m. Wednesday at the funeral home.

She was preceded in death by her husband of sixty-two years, Roy Marshall Rushing, her parents James Early Ramsey and Susan Roberta Baggett and two brothers, Murrell, and Jack Ramsey.

She is survived by four children: Peggy Boyd (Hayse); Larry Rushing (Pat); Linda Harding

(Linda); Randy Rushing (Sherry) and ten grandchildren and eleven great grandchildren and one sister Doris May and one brother Dr. Charles Ramsey.

Faith loved her family, her church, and the Home Demonstration Club. She was a faithful servant to her Christ, the best cook in the world and a beloved mother and granny.

In 1994, she suffered a stroke that resulted in thirteen years of invalidism.

Pallbearers will be four grandsons: Denson Hayse Boyd, Shane Rushing, Lance Rushing, and Jason Rushing; four grandsons-in-law: Bill Strickland, Paul Smith, Patrick Howell, and Allan Perry.

Honorary pallbearers will be: Members of Macedonia United Methodist Church; friends and neighbors of Lafoy Community; employees of Rushing Concrete; Dorothy Binns; Dr.
John Summerford.

The family expresses appreciation to caregivers Eloise Taylor and others.

**Rushing, Fannie Gay**: December 30, 1881-January 1, 1967. Grave # 214.

She was the wife of James Willie "Will" Snow Rushing and the mother of Annie Snow Rushing Shirley.

Fannie Gay Rushing was the daughter of Lewellen Sydney Gay and Julie Elizabeth Shirley Gay and the granddaughter of Callaway "Capp" H. Gay and Jane Palmer and a sister to J. R. "Dick" Gay, Sam H. Gay, Robert B. Gay, Annie Pearl Gay, and Josephine Gay.

James Willie "Will" Rushing was the son of Joseph Enoch Rushing and Samantha Lenora Deason. He was a brother to Lenora Belle "Lou" Rushing Hyche (married to Early M. Hyche), Joseph David "Gin" Rushing (married to Permelia Alma Hamner), Thomas Hillman "Jack" Rushing (married to Annie Brazile Hamner), Marvin Goldman Rushing (married to Ozella Judson "Juddie" Hamner), Sylvester Hayes Rushing (he never married), James Knox Polk Rushing (married to Annie Elizabeth Turner) and Robert E. Lee Rushing (married to Loubelle Hamner).

All the above are buried in Macedonia Cemetery.

**Obit for Mrs. Fannie Gay Rushing**

Funeral services for Mrs. Fannie Gay Rushing, 88, a lifelong resident of the Crabbe Road who died last night at Druid City Hospital will be held Tuesday at 2:00 p.m. at Macedonia Methodist Church with the Rev. Robert H. Maxwell officiating. Burial will be in the church cemetery with Memory Chapel Funeral Home in charge.

She was the oldest living member of Macedonia Methodist Church.

She is survived by two daughters, Mrs. Glyndon Newman of Birmingham, and Mrs. John Shirley of the Crabbe Road; three sisters, Miss Pearl Gay and Mrs. Beuna Laycock of Northport and Mrs. T. F. Wallace of Birmingham; a brother, Sam H. Gay of Berry and five grandchildren and two great grandchildren and several nieces and nephews.

Active pallbearers are Roy Rushing, Hayse Boyd, James Rushing, Bernard Rushing, and Lonnie Shirley, and Joe Robertson.

Honorary pallbearers are Jody W. Allen, Jay Hamner, Prewitt Hamner, John Hagler, Spurgeon Black, members of the official board of Macedonia Church and friends.

The body will remain at the funeral home until 1:00 p.m. Thursday.

**Rushing James Knox Polk**: September 9, 1892-August 18, 1967. Grave # 37

Polk was the son of Joseph Enoch Rushing (January 14, 1850-November 28, 1936) and Samantha Lenora Deason (May 16, 1852-August 5, 1911) the Rushing patriarchal couple in the Lafoy Community.

Polk was married to Annie Elizabeth Turner the daughter of James Valentino Turner and Matilda Ann Cooper. He was the father of Eddie Ormand Rushing.

James Knox Polk Rushing was a brother to Joseph David "Gin" Rushing (married to Permelia Alma Hamner), Thomas Hillman "Jack" Rushing (married to Annie Brazile Hamner), James Willie "Will" Snow Rushing (married to Fannie Gay), Lenora Bell "Lou" Rushing Hyche (married to Early M. Hyche), Marvin Goldman Rushing (married to Ozella Judson "Juddie" Hamner) and Robert Edward Lee Rushing (married to Loubelle Hamner).

All the above are buried in Macedonia Cemetery.

**Rushing, James Willie "Will" Snow:** August 20, 1879-January 1, 1934. Grave # 213.

Will was the son of Joseph Enoch Rushing (January 14, 1850-November 28, 1936) and Samantha Lenora Deason (May 16, 1852,-August 5, 1911) the Rushing patriarchal couple in the Lafoy Community.

He was the husband of Fannie Gay and the father of Annie Snow Rushing Shirley and Azilee Shirley Newman.

James Willie Snow Rushing was a brother to Joseph David "Gin" Rushing (married to Permelia Alma Hamner), Thomas Hillman "Jack" Rushing (married to Annie Brazile Hamner), Lenora Bell "Lou" Rushing Hyche (married to Early M. Hyche), Marvin Goldman Rushing (married to Ozella Judson "Juddie" Hamner), Robert Edward Lee Rushing (married to Loubelle Hamner), Sylvester Hayes Rushing (he never married), James Knox Polk Rushing (married to Annie Elizabeth Turner).

Fannie Gay Rushing was the daughter of Lewellen Sydney Gay and Julie Elizabeth Shirley.

Annie Snow Rushing was the wife of John Ester Shirley.

All the above are buried in Macedonia Cemetery.

**Obit for Will Rushing:**

An extended illness resulted in the death this morning at 3:00 o'clock for Will Rushing, widely known Tuscaloosa County resident at his home on the Crabbe Road. His passing is mourned by a large number of friends and family.

He is survived by his widow, Mrs. Fannie Gay Rushing; two daughters, Azilee and Annie Snow Rushing; nine brothers, Gilbert, Jack, Gin, Goldman, Polk, Hewitt, Josh, Hayes and Robert; one sister, Mrs. "Lou" Early Hyche and several nieces and nephews.

Funeral services will be held Tuesday at 11:00 o'clock in Macedonia Methodist Church of which he was a member. The Rev. Trimm Powell, the Rev. M. R. Smith and the Rev. C. L. Manderson will officiate with Jones and Spigener in charge.

Pallbearers will be B. A. Renfro, Roy Faucett, Lev Anders, Jimmy Maxwell, Charlie Shirley, and B. V. Chism.

**Rushing, Joseph Enoch:** January 14, 1850-November 28, 1936. Grave # 70

He was married to Samantha Lenora Deason (May 16, 1852-August 5, 1911.) They had thirteen children of whom ten are buried in Macedonia Cemetery. They are: (1) Joseph David "Gin" Rushing (married to Permelia Alma Hamner); (2) James Willie "Will" Rushing (married to Fannie Gay); (3) Thomas Hillman "Jack" Rushing (married to Annie Brazile Hamner); (4) Lenora Bell "Lou" Rushing Hyche (married to Early M. Hyche); (5) Marvin Goldman Rushing (married to Ozella Judson "Juddie" Hamner); (6) Robert Edward Lee Rushing (married to Loubelle Hamner); (7) Sylvester Hayes Rushing (never married); (8) James Knox Polk Rushing (married to Annie Elizabeth Turner); (9) Eddie Ormand Rushing, an infant; (10) Lottie Snow Rushing, a child that died a one-year-old.

Eddie Ormand Rushing and Lottie Snow Rushing's graves are marked only by stones with no name inscribed.

The three children of Joseph Enoch Rushing and Samantha Lenora Deason not buried in Macedonia Cemetery are: (1) John Gilbert Rushing and his wife Mittie Williamson Snyder. They are buried in Williamson Cemetery in Northport. (2) Joshua Mills "Josh" Rushing and his wife Clara Barton Shirley. They are buried in Memory Hills Gardens in Tuscaloosa; (3) Hewitt

Ashley Rushing and his wife Nora V. Turner. They are buried in Bethel Cemetery.

**Obit for Joseph Enoch "Joe" Rushing**

Joseph Enoch Rushing, prominent Tuscaloosa County farmer and known by many as "Uncle Joe," was buried Saturday afternoon in Macedonia Cemetery following services in the church there. He died at his home on the Crabbe Road on Friday after a prolonged illness.

Mr. Rushing, who was 85 years old, was a lifelong resident of this county and prominent in all community activities at Macedonia. He was a trustee of the church for many years and active in church life. He was also a trustee of Lafoy School for many years and active in school affairs. Friends from all parts of the county gathered for the last rites.

Surviving Mr. Rushing are 10 children and 41 grandchildren and 11 great grandchildren. The children include one daughter, Mrs. Lou Rushing Hyche and nine sons: Gilbert "Gib," Joseph David "Gin," Thomas Hillman "Jack," Goldman, Josh, Hayes, Polk, Hewitt, and Robert.

Pallbearers for the funeral were grandsons Howard, John, Roy, James and Joe Rushing and Wayland Hyche.

Honorary pallbearers were Joe Rice, R. L. Shamblin, Frank Rice, L. C. Curry, Hull Cummins, O. J. Hamner, B. A. Renfro, C. S. "Boss" Hinton, Bill Koster, J. I. McGee, H. G. Shepherd, and Gary MaGee. Foster's Funeral Home was in charge.

**Rushing, Joseph David** "Gin": October 15, 1876-April 22, 1943. Grave # 152.

He was the son of Joseph Enoch Rushing (January 14, 1850-November 28, 1936) and Samantha Lenora Deason (May 16, 1852-Aug. 5, 1911) the Rushing patriarchal couple in the Lafoy Community.

He married Permelia Alma Hamner and was the father of Margaret Lucille Rushing Speed.

Joseph David was a brother to James Willie "Will" Rushing (married to Fannie Gay), Thomas Hillman "Jack" Rushing (married to Annie Brazile Hamner), Lenora Bell "Lou" Rushing Hyche (married to Early M. Hyche), Marvin Goldman Rushing (married to Ozella Judson "Juddie" Hamner), Robert Edward Lee Rushing (married to Loubelle Hamner), Sylvester Hayes Rushing (he never married), James Knox Polk Rushing (married to Annie Elizabeth Turner), and James Willie Snow married to Fanny Gay.

Permelia Alma Hamner Rushing was the daughter of John Pruitt Hamner and Annie Margaret Hall.

John Pruitt Hamner was the son of William T. Hamner, Sr. and his second wife Permelia Chism.

All the above are buried in Macedonia Cemetery.

**Rushing, Samantha Lenora Deason**: May 16, 1852-August 5, 1911. Grave # 71.

She was the wife of Joseph Enoch Rushing (January 14, 1850-November 28, 1936). They had thirteen children of whom nine are buried in Macedonia Cemetery: (1) Joseph David "Gin" Rushing (married to Permelia Alma Hamner); (2) James Willie "Will" Rushing (married to Fannie Gay); (3) Thomas Hillman "Jack" Rushing (married to Annie Brazile Hamner); (4) Lenora Bell "Lou" Rushing Hyche (married to Early M. Hyche); (5) Marvin Goldman Rushing (married to Ozella Judson "Juddie" Hamner); (6) Robert Edward Lee Rushing (married to Loubelle Hamner); (7) Sylvester Hayes Rushing (never married); (8) James Knox Polk Rushing (married to Anne Elizabeth Turner); (9) Edward Nathan Rushing, a child; (10) Anthony Leon Rushing, a child.

The three children not buried in Macedonia Cemetery are John Gilbert Rushing and his wife Mittie Williamson Snyder who are buried in Williamson Cemetery in Northport, Joshua Mills "Josh" Rushing and his wife Clara Barton Shirley who are buried in Memory Hills Gardens in Tuscaloosa and Hewitt Ashley Rushing and his wife Nora V. Turner who are buried in Bethel Cemetery

# MACEDONIA CEMETERY

**Rushing, Lottie Snow:** October 5, 1908-1909

Grave # 80.

She was the daughter of Marvin Goldman Rushing and Ozella Judson "Juddie" Hamner.

Marvin Goldman Rushing was the son of Joseph Enoch Rushing and Samantha Lenora Deason.

Ozella Judson "Juddie" Hamner Rushing was the daughter of John Pruitt Hamner and Anne Margaret Hall.

John Pruitt Hamner was the son of William T. Hamner, Sr. and his second wife Permelia Chism.

All the above are buried in Macedonia Cemetery.

**Rushing, Loubelle Hamner:** December 5, 1899-October 3, 1979. Grave # 258.

She was married to Robert E. Lee Rushing.

Loubelle Hamner Rushing was the daughter of Oliver "Ollie" Jackson Hamner and Mary Louise Rigsby. Mary Louise Rigsby was the daughter of Jesse Tyson Rigsby (September 29, 1852-April 4, 1884) and Nancy Elizabeth White (July 26, 1858-March 3, 1932).

Oliver "Ollie" Jackson Hamner was the son of John Pruitt Hamner and Annie Margaret Hall.

John Pruitt Hamner was the son of William T. Hamner, Sr. and his second wife Permelia Chism.

Loubelle was a sister to Edward Bruce Hamner (married to Fannie Lou Shirley), Vera Mae Hamner (a child), Ollie Lee Hamner (a child), and Oll Dee Hamner (married to Frances Shirley). All the above are buried in Macedonia Cemetery.

Loubelle Hamner Rushing also was a sister to Jessie Pruitt Hamner (married to Ruby Pearson, James Webster "Jay" Hamner (married to Queen Lafoy) and Hollis Harwood "Woody" Hamner (married to Elsie Yow). They are buried in Carrolls Creek Baptist Church Cemetery.

Loubelle Hamner was a sister to John O'Neal Hamner who is buried in Sunset Cemetery.

Loubelle Hamner Rushing was the mother of Mary Evelyn "Cricket" Rushing Medders who is buried in Macedonia Cemetery.

Robert E. Lee Rushing was the son of Joseph Enoch Rushing (January 14, 1850-November 28, 1936) and Samantha Lenora Deason (May 16, 1852-Aug. 5, 1911) the Rushing patriarchal couple in the Lafoy Community.

Robert E. Lee Rushing was a brother to Joseph David Rushing (married to Permelia Alma Hamner); James Willie "Will" Rushing (married to Fannie Gay), Thomas Hillman "Jack" Rushing (married to Annie Brazile Hamner), Lenora Bell "Lou" Rushing Hyche (married to Early M. Hyche), Marvin Goldman Rushing (married to Ozella Judson "Juddie" Hamner), Sylvester Hayes Rushing (he never married), James Knox Polk Rushing (married to Annie Elizabeth Turner), and James Willie Snow married to Fanny Gay.

All the above are buried in Macedonia Cemetery.

**Rushing, Marvin Bernard:** July 3. 1911-1915

Grave # 81.

He was the son of Marvin Goldman Rushing and Ozella Judson "Juddie" Hamner.

Marvin Goldman Rushing was the son of Joseph Enoch Rushing and Samantha Lenora Deason.

Ozella Judson "Juddie" Hamner Rushing was the daughter of John Pruitt Hamner and Annie Margaret Hall.

John Pruitt Hamner was the son of William T. Hamner, Sr. and his second wife Permelia Chism.

All the above are buried in Macedonia Cemetery.

**Rushing, Marvin Goldman:** October 8, 1884-February 17, 1947. Grav e # 83.

He was the husband of Ozella Judson "Juddie" Hamner and the son of Joseph Enoch Rushing and Samantha Lenora Deason.

Marvin Goldman was the son of Joseph Enoch Rushing, (January 14, 1850-November

28, 1936) and Samantha Lenora Deason (May 16, 1852-August 5, 1911), the Rushing patriarchal couple in the Lafoy Community.

Marvin Goldman Rushing was a brother to James Willie "Will" Rushing (married to Fannie Gay), Thomas Hillman "Jack" Rushing (married to Annie Brazile Hamner), Lenora Bell "Lou" Rushing Hyche (married to Early M. Hyche), Robert Edward Lee Rushing (married to Loubelle Hamner), Sylvester Hayes Rushing (never married), James Knox Polk Rushing (married to Annie Elizabeth Turner) and Joseph David "Gin" Rushing (married to Permelia Alma Hamner).

All the above are buried in Macedonia Cemetery.

Marvin Goldman Rushing was also a brother to John Gilbert Rushing and his wife Mittie Williamson Snyder who are buried in Williamson Cemetery in Northport and to Joshua Mills "Josh" Rushing and his wife Clara Barton Shirley who are buried in Memory Hills Gardens in Tuscaloosa and to Hewitt Ashley Rushing and his wife Nora V. Turner who are buried in Bethel Cemetery.

Goldman's wife Ozella Judson "Juddie" Hamner Rushing was the daughter of John Pruitt Hamner and Annie Margaret Hall.

John Pruitt Hamner was the son of William T. Hamner, Sr. and his second wife Permelia Chism. All the above are buried in Macedonia Cemetery.

Marvin Bernard and Lottie Snow Rushing are children of Ozella and Marvin Goldman. They, too, are buried in Macedonia Cemetery.

**Rushing, Melvina "Sook":** died October 1917

Grave # 69.

She was a sister to Joseph Enoch Rushing and never married. Family tradition holds that she was blind.

**Rushing, Ozella Judson "Juddie" Hamner:** October 4, 1887-July 2, 1973.

Grave # 82.

She was the wife of Marvin Goldman Rushing and the daughter of John Pruitt Hamner and Annie Margaret Hall. She was the mother of Marvin Bernard and Lottie Snow Rushing both of whom died young.

John Pruitt Hamner was the son of William T. Hamner, Sr. and his second wife Permelia Chism.

Marvin Goldman Rushing was the son of Joseph Enoch Rushing and Samantha Lenora Deason. He was a brother to James Willie "Will" Rushing (married to Fannie Gay), Thomas Hillman "Jack" Rushing (married to Annie Brazile Hamner), Lenora Bell "Lou" Rushing Hyche (married to Early M. Hyche), Robert Edward Lee Rushing (married to Loubelle Hamner), Sylvester Hayes Rushing (he never married), James Knox Polk Rushing (married to Anne Elizabeth Turner) and Joseph David "Gin" Rushing (married to Permelia Alma Hamner).

All of the above are buried in Macedonia Cemetery.

**Rushing, Pamelia Alma:** January 15, 1884-February 3, 1970. Grave # 153.

She was the wife of Joseph David "Gin" Rushing and the mother of Margaret Lucille Rushing Speed.

Permelia Alma was the daughter of John Pruitt Hamner and Annie Margaret Hall.

John Pruitt Hamner was the son of William T. Hamner, Sr. and Permelia Chism all of whom are buried in Macedonia Cemetery.

Siblings of Permelia Alma Hamner buried in Macedonia Cemetery include: (1) an infant sister, in 1867; (2) Mary Ulalah Virginia Hamner, a child; (3) Ollie Jackson "Ollie" (married to Louise Rigsby); (4) John Early Hamner (married to Rose Annie Viella "Ella" Rigsby); (5) Buena Vista Hamner Chism (married first to John Monroe House and married second to Archie George Chism); (6) Larkin "Lark" Rogers (married to Beatrice Josephine Smith); (7) Annie Brazile Hamner Rushing (married to Thomas Hillman Rushing); (8) Ozella Judson Hamner Rushing (married to Marvin Goldman Rushing);

(9) Ullie Mae Hamner Chism (married to her first cousin Harvey Morgan Chism); (10) Edward "Dock" Hamner (married to Fannie Mae Duncan. Fannie Mae is not buried in Macedonia Cemetery).

**Obit for Mrs. Permelia Alma Rushing:**

Funeral services for Mrs. Alma Rushing, 88, of Northport will be held at 11:00 a.m. Thursday at Macedonia Methodist Church with Rev. B. F. Atkins officiating.

Burial will be in the church cemetery with Strickland-Hayes Funeral Home in charge.

Mrs. Rushing died Thursday morning at the home of a son.

She is survived by two daughters, Mrs. Wiley Hagler, and Mrs. Houston Thomas, both of Northport; three sons, Woodrow C. Rushing, James C. Rushing, both of Northport and J. D. Rushing of Cullman; one sister, Mrs. Ozella Rushing; 14 grandchildren and 10 great grandchildren.

Pallbearers will be James V. Rushing, Nathan Chism, Preston Rushing, Dee Hamner, Roy Rushing, Melvin Hamner, Cullen Hamner and Curtis Hamner.

**Rushing, Robert E. Lee**: May 15, 1895-March 16, 1982. Grave # 259.

He was the son of Joseph Enoch Rushing and Samantha Lenora Deason.

Robert E. Lee Rushing was the husband of Loubelle Hamner and the father of Mary E. "Cricket" Rushing Medders. All are buried in Macedonia Cemetery.

Robert E. Lee Rushing was a brother to Marvin Goldman Rushing (married to Ozella Judson "Juddie" Hamner), James Willie "Will" Rushing (married to Fannie Gay), Thomas Hillman "Jack" Rushing (married to Annie Brazile Hamner), Lenora Bell "Lou" Rushing Hyche (married to Early M. Hyche), Sylvester Hayes Rushing (never married), James Knox Polk Rushing (married to Anne Elizabeth Turner), Joseph David "Gin" Rushing (married to Permelia Alma Hamner).

All the above are buried in Macedonia Cemetery.

Robert E. Lee Rushing is also a brother to John Gilbert Rushing and his wife Mittie Williamson Snyder who are buried in Williamson Cemetery in Northport and to Joshua Mills "Josh" Rushing and his wife Clara Barton Shirley who are buried in Memory Hills Gardens in Tuscaloosa and Hewitt Ashley Rushing and his wife Nora V. Turner who are buried in Bethel Cemetery.

**Rushing, Roy Marshall**: September 11, 1912-May 1, 2001. Grave # 314.

Roy was the husband of Faith Vivian Ramsay (December 21, 1918-May 20, 2007) and the son of Thomas Hillman "Jack" Rushing and Annie Brazile Hamner.

Thomas Hillman "Jack" Rushing was the son of Joseph Enoch Rushing and Samantha Lenora Deason.

Roy Marshall Rushing was the grandfather of William Aaron Strickland, the son of Tara Boyd Strickland, who is buried in Macedonia Cemetery.

Annie Brazeal Rushing was the daughter of John Pruitt Hamner and Annie Margaret Hall.

John Pruitt Hamner was the son of William T. Hamner, Sr. and his second wife Permelia Chism.

All the above are buried in Macedonia Cemetery.

**Rushing, Sylvesta Hayes**: November 11, 1889-May 25, 1953. Grave # 68.

Sylvester never married. He was the ninth child of Joseph Enoch Rushing and Samantha Lenora Deason.

Sylvester Hayes Rushing was the brother of Joseph David "Gin" Rushing (married to Permelia Alma Hamner), James Willie "Will" Rushing (married to Fannie Gay), Thomas Hillman "Jack" Rushing (married to Annie Brazile Hamner), Lenora Bell "Lou" Rushing Hyche (married to Early M. Hyche), Marvin Goldman Rushing (married to Ozella Judson "Juddie" Hamner), Robert Edward Lee Rushing (married to Loubelle

Hamner), James Knox Polk Rushing (married to Anne Elizabeth Turner) and Joseph David "Gin" Rushing (married to Permelia Alma Hamner).

All the above are buried in Macedonia Cemetery.

Sylvester Hayes Rushing was also a brother to John Gilbert Rushing and his wife Mittie Williamson Snyder who are buried in Williamson Cemetery in Northport and to Joshua Mills "Josh" Rushing and his wife Clara Barton Shirley who are buried in Memory Hills Gardens in Tuscaloosa and to Hewitt Ashley Rushing and his wife Nora V. Turner who are buried in Bethel Cemetery.

**Obit for Sylvester Hayes Rushing**

Sylvester Hayes Rushing, 63, of the Crabbe Road died last night at Druid City Hospital about 9:30 p.m. after suffering a heart attack at his home.

A lifelong resident of Tuscaloosa County, he was the son of the late Joseph Enoch Rushing and Samantha Lenora Deason. He never married.

Funeral services will be held tomorrow at 2:00 p. m. at Macedonia Methodist Church with the Rev. Trimm Powell and the Rev. Wayne Graham officiating. Burial will follow in the church cemetery.

Survivors include a sister, Mrs. Lou Bell Hyche and brothers Joshua Mills "Josh Rushing, Polk Rushing and Robert Rushing; and 38 nieces and nephews.

Active pallbearers will be Fletcher Barnes, Joe Jobson, Lester Taylor, Belton Earnest, B. R. Holston, and George W. Christian.

Honorary pallbearers will be Anthony Renfro, Ray Farebee, Charles Clark, Dr. Luther Davis, Moody Fields, Bill Squires, Tom Christian, Glen Rice, Hoyt Frazer, Bill Hitt, T. S. Black, Lonnie Shirley, Largus Barnes, George Watson, Herman Boyd, Vester Gray, Adam Lesly, Monroe Ward, Sam Gay, Leon Chism, Hugh Spencer, and Delma Earnest.

**Rushing, Thomas Hillman "Jack"**: October 15, 1876-November 19, 1942. Grave # 73

Thomas Hillman Rushing was the son of Joseph Enoch Rushing, January 14, 1850-November 28, 1936, and Samantha Lenora Deason b. May 16, 1852, d. Aug. 5, 1911, the Rushing patriarchal couple in the Lafoy Community.

Thomas Hillman Rushing married Annie Brazile Hamner who was the daughter of John Pruitt Hamner and Annie Margaret Hall.

John Pruitt Hamner was the son of William T. Hamner, Sr. and his second wife Permelia Chism.

Annie Brazile Hamner and Thomas Hillman Rushing had ten children of whom three are buried in Macedonia Cemetery. They are Roy Marshall Rushing (married to Faith Vivian Ramsey), Edward Nathan Rushing—July 2, 1908-July 4, 1908 and Anthony Leon Rushing—March 9, 1921-January 12, 1922. The graves of Edward Nathan and Anthony Leon are marked by rock stones with no names.

Children of Annie Brazile and Thomas Hillman Rushing not buried in Macedonia Cemetery include Ozella Bertice "Bert" Rushing (married to Herman Payne Thomas), Clara Bell "Jim" Utley (married to Clyde Buel Utley), Joseph Howard "Runt" Rushing (unmarried), Temperance Hagler "Temp" Rushing (married to Floyd Alton Maughn), Nell Irene Rushing (married to Edwin George Owens), Truman Hillman "Buck" Rushing (married to Corendene Edwina Tierce) and Annie Gladys Rushing (married to Robert James Romaine).

**Savage, Mary:** March 9, 1839-July 5, 1871. Grave 156.

**Sellers, Luther**: December 19, 1900-December 22, 1930. Grave # 128.

**Shaw Infant**: 1909

Grave # 77. Parents not known.

**Sherer, James Goodwin:** October 15, 1968-January 7, 1969. Grave # 289.

October 15, 1968-Januay 7, 1969.

He is the son of Shirley Turner Sherer and Joe Sherer. Shirley Turner was the daughter of Martha Shirley Turner and Clifton Turner. Mar-

# MACEDONIA CEMETERY

tha Shirley was the daughter of Byrd Franklin Shirley and Matilda Smith Shirley.

**Shirley, Annie Snow Rushing:** May 13, 1913-April 20, 1980. Grave # 215.

She was the wife of John Ester Shirley (January 17, 1907-June 5, 1996) and the daughter of James Willie "Will" Snow Rushing and Fannie Gay.

Fannie Gay was the daughter of Lewellen Sydney Gay and Julie Elizabeth Shirley.

Lewellen Sydney Gay was the daughter of Callaway "Capp" Gay and Jane Palmer.

James Willie "Will" Rushing was the son of Joseph Enoch Rushing and Samantha Lenora Deason.

John Ester Shirley was the son of Byrdie "Byrd" Franklin Shirley (March 17, 1880-November 17, 1932) and Matilda Ann Smith (September 9, 1886-January 6, 1957).

All the above are buried in Macedonia Cemetery.

**Shirley, Jean Rose:** December, 14, 1949-October 22, 2009. Grave # 319A.

She was the wife of Hilary Joe Shirley who in 2024 is still living.

Jean died of ovarian cancer and her twin sister Joan Rose Nicholson died of the same disease.

**Shirley, John Ester:** January 17, 1907-June 5, 1996. Grave # 216.

He was the husband of Anne Snow Rushing Shirley (May 13, 1913-April 20, 1980).

He was the son of Byrdie "Byrd" Franklin Shirley, Sr. (March 17, 1880-November 17, 1932) and Matilda Ann Smith Shirley (September 9, 1886-January 6, 1957).

John Ester Shirley was a brother to Lonnie Lee Shirley (married to Estelle Wedgeworth), Grady Edward Shirley (married to Margaret Watkins), Fannie Lou Shirley Hamner (married to Edward Bruce Hamner), Martha Nell Shirley Turner (married to Clifton Turner), Ruby Alene Shirley Mills (married to Erman Mills), B. F. Shirley (married to Mary Alice Turner) and Emma Frances Shirley Hamner (married to Oll Dee Hamner).

All the above are buried in Macedonia Cemetery.

He was also a brother to Sue Lake and Joan Davis who are not buried in Macedonia Cemetery.

**Shirley, B.F. Jr.:** July 4, 1921-February 17, 2003. Grave # 315.

He was the husband of Mary Alice Turner (June 10, 1925-August 8, 2009) and the son of Byrdie "Byrd" Franklin Shirley (March 17, 1880-November 17, 1932) and Matilda Ann Smith (September 9, 1886-January 6, 1957).

B. F. Shirley was a brother to John Ester Shirley (married to Annie Snow Rushing), Lonnie Lee Shirley (married to Estelle Wedgeworth), Grady Edward Shirley (married to Margaret Watkins), Fannie Lou Shirley Hamner (married to Edward Bruce Hamner), Martha Nell Shirley Turner (married to Clifton Turner), Ruby Alene Shirley Mills (married to Erman Mills), and Emma Frances Shirley Hamner (married to Oll Dee Hamner.

All the above are buried in Macedonia Cemetery.

He was also a brother to Sue Lake and Joan Davis who are not buried in Macedonia Cemetery.

**Obit for B. F. Shirley, Jr.**

B. F. Shirley, age 81, died February 17, 2003 at DCH Regional Medical Center. Graveside services will be held Thursday, February 20, 2003 at Macedonia Methodist Cemetery with Rev. Tim Bailey and Rev. Mike Skelton officiating. Visitation is tonight 6:00 p.m. to 8:00 p.m. at Magnolia Funeral Home North directing.

Survivors include his wife of 53 years, Mary Alice Turner Shirley, Northport; daughter Leigh Ann Rice of Northport; Robert (Sheri) Shirley, of Northport; sisters Frances Hamner, Ruby Mills, Martha Turner of Northport; Joan Davis Tuscaloosa; grandchildren Sara and Tyler Rice.

Mr. Shirley served in the Navy during World War II. He worked for Gulf States Paper Mill for

29 years. He was an active member of Macedonia Methodist Church where he served as custodian of the cemetery for many years. He enjoyed hunting, fishing and especially gardening. He loved his family and those in the community. He was a wonderful husband, father, and grandfather.

Pallbearers will be Robert Shirley, Joe Rice, James Shirley, Ronald Davis Johnny Shirley, Jerry Turner, Charles Mills, Alvin Hamner and Hilary Shirley.

**Shirley, Byrdie Franklin, Sr.:** March 17, 1880-November 17, 1932. Grave # 149.

Byrdie Franklin Shirley, Sr. was the son of John Lewis Shirley and Anna Key Chism Shirley. At the time of his birth, his parents lived in what in 2023 is part of the Northwood Lake subdivision in Northport near the Shirley Cemetery that is located on Union Chapel Road West.

Byrd married Matilda Ann Smith (September 9, 1886-January 6, 1957). The names of her parents are not known. The Smith family lived in the vicinity of Piney Woods/Windham Springs twenty miles north of Northport on the Crabbe Road. Byrd and Matilda were the parents of twelve children, eleven of whom lived to adulthood.

"Byrd" was killed as a pedestrian in downtown Northport by a drunk driver.

Byrdie Franklin Shirley, Sr. was the father of John Ester Shirley (married to Annie Snow Rushing), Lonnie Lee Shirley (married to Estelle Wedgeworth), Grady Edward Shirley (married to Margaret Watkins), Fannie Lou Shirley Hamner (married to Edward Bruce Hamner), Martha Nell Shirley Turner (married to Clifton Turner), Ruby Alene Shirley Mills (married to Erman Mills), B. F. Shirley (married to Mary Alice Turner), Emma Frances Shirley Hamner (married to Oll Dee Hamner) and to James W. Shirley who died at age three in 1914.

Byrd was the grandfather of Lonnie Lee Shirley, Jr. the son of Lonnie Lee Shirley and Estelle Wedgeworth Shirley. He was also the grandfather of James Gary Shirley, Edward Wendell Shirley, and George Mark Shirley, all sons of Grady Edward Shirley and Margaret Watkins Shirley. "Byrd" was the grandfather of Erma Shirley Mills the daughter of Erman Mills and Ruby Shirley Mills. "Byrd" was the grandfather of Ollie Bruce Hamner the son of Edward Bruce Hamner and Fannie Lou Shirley Hamner. "Byrd" was the great grandfather of Brett Jeffery Brown the grandson of Lonnie Lee Shirley and Estelle Wedgeworth Shirley. Byrd was the great grandfather of John Howard Hewett, Jr. the grandson of Edward Bruce Hamner and Fannie Lou Shirley Hamner.

All the above are buried in Macedonia Cemetery.

Byrd Shirley was the father of Sue Shirley Lake (married to Thomas Lake) who are buried in Memory Hills Gardens and Joan Shirley Davis (married to Howard Davis) who are buried in Tuscaloosa Memorial Park.

**Shirley, Bobby Renzo "Buddy":** February 4, 1933-March 15, 1999. Grave # 313.

He was the son of Byrdie "Byrd" Franklin Shirley (March 17, 1880-November 17, 1932) and Matilda Ann Smith (September 9, 1886-January 6, 1957).

"Buddy" was a brother to John Ester Shirley (married to Annie Snow Rushing, Lonnie Lee Shirley (married to Estelle Wedgeworth), Grady Edward Shirley (married to Margaret Watkins), Fannie Lou Shirley Hamner (married to Edward Bruce Hamner), Martha Nell Shirley Turner (married to Clifton Turner), Ruby Alene Shirley Mills (married to Erman Mills), Emma Frances Shirley Hamner (married to Oll Dee Hamner) and B.F. Shirley (married to Mary Alice Turner).

All the above are buried in Macedonia Cemetery.

He also was a brother to Sue Lake and Joan Davis who are not buried in Macedonia Cemetery.

**Shirley, Estelle Wedgeworth:** September 1, 1915-December 1, 2000. Grave # 141.

She was the wife of Lonnie Lee Shirley Sr.

# MACEDONIA CEMETERY

(December 9, 1909-June 10, 1975) and the mother of Lonnie Lee Shirley, Jr. (August 3, 1942-February 16, 1943) and the grandmother of Brett Jeffry Brown (December 2, 1964-March 6, 2010).

All the above are buried in Macedonia Cemetery.

Brett Jeffery Brown was the son of Naomia Shirley Brown (the daughter of Lonnie Lee Shirley and Estelle Wedgeworth Shirley) and Jack Brown. Jack Brown and Naomia Shirley Brown are buried in Memory Hills Gardens.

**Shirley, Grady Edward**: February 20, 1915-July 10, 1994. Grave # 312.

Grady was the husband of Margaret Watkins (August 27, 1918-August 10, 2003), the father of George Mark Shirley (November 22, 1950-December 19, 2020), James Gary Shirley (December 1, 1942-June 23, 2020), and Edward Wendall Shirley (September 4, 1939-July 23, 2019) all of whom are buried in Macedonia Cemetery.

Grady was the son of Byrdie "Byrd" Franklin Shirley (March 17, 1880-November 17, 1932) and Matilda Ann Smith (September 9, 1886-January 6, 1957).

Grady was a brother to John Ester Shirley (married to Annie Snow Rushing, Lonnie Lee Shirley (married to Estelle Wedgeworth), "Buddy" Shirley, Fannie Lou Shirley Hamner (married to Edward Bruce Hamner), Martha Nell Shirley Turner (married to Clifton Turner), Ruby Alene Shirley Mills (married to Erman Mills), Emma Frances Shirley Hamner (married to Oll Dee Hamner) and B.F. Shirley (married to Mary Alice Turner). .

All the above are buried in Macedonia Cemetery.

He was also a brother to Sue Lake and Joan Davis who are not buried in Macedonia Cemetery

**Shirley, Inf. of Virgil Festus and Nancy**: 1920

Grave # 167.

This baby was the product V. F. Shirley and Nancy Shirley. Virgil Festus "V.F." Shirley (December 12, 1882-November 19, 1959) was a brother to Byrdie "Byrd" Shirley. He married Nancy Hocutt (February 11, 1887-Augsut 18, 1965). They are buried in Sand Springs Cemetery.

**Shirley, James Wesley**: September 2, 1911-February 2, 1914. Grave # 150.

He was the son of Byrdie "Byrd" Franklin Shirley and Matilda Ann Smith and died at age 3 the result of pneumonia that followed a severe burn when his gown caught fire standing before an open fire in the yard of the Byrd Shirley house.

**Shirley, Jean Rose**: December 14, 1949-October 22, 2009. Grave # 319A

Jean was the wife of Joe Hiliary Shirley who in 2023 is still living. Hiliary is the son of Grady Shirley (February 20, 1915-July 10, 1994) and Margaret Watkins (August 27, 1918-August 10, 2003). Jean, along with her twin sister, Joan Rose Nicholson, died of ovarian cancer.

**Shirley, Lonnie Lee, Sr.**: December 9, 1909-June 10, 1975.Grave # 142.

Lonnie was the husband of Estelle Wedgeworth Shirley (September 1, 1915-December 1, 2000) and the father of Lonnie Lee Shirley, Jr. (August 3, 1942-February 16, 1943) and the grandfather of Brett Jeffry Brown (December 2, 1964-March 6, 2010). Brett was the son of Naomia Shirley Brown (daughter of Lonnie Lee Shirley, Sr. and Estelle Wedgeworth Shirley) and Jack Brown. They are buried in Memory Hills Gardens in Tuscaloosa.

Lonnie Lee Shirley, Sr, was the son of Byrdie "Byrd" Franklin Shirley (March 17, 1880-November 17, 1932) and Matilda Ann Smith (September 9, 1886-January 6, 1957)

Lonnie Lee Shirley, Sr. was a brother to John Ester Shirley (married to Annie Snow Rushing), Grady Edward Shirley (married to Margaret Watkins), Fannie Lou Shirley Hamner (married to Edward Bruce Hamner), Martha Nell Shirley Turner (married to Clifton Turner), Ruby Alene

Shirley Mills (married to Erman Mills), B. F. Shirley (married to Mary Alice Turner), Emma Frances Shirley Hamner (married to Oll Dee Hamner).

All the above are buried in Macedonia Cemetery.

He was also a brother to Sue Lake and Joan Davis who are not buried in Macedonia Cemetery.

**Shirley, Lonnie Lee Jr.**: August 3, 1942-February 16, 1943. Grave # 143.

He was the son of Lonnie Lee Shirley, Sr. (December 9, 1909-June 10, 1975) and Estelle Wedgeworth Shirley (September 1, 1915-December 1, 2000).

**Obit for Lonnie Lee Shirley, Jr.**

Services for Lonnie Lee Shirley age six and a half months will be held at 11:00 a. m. Wednesday from the Macedonia Methodist Church on the Crabbe Road with interment in the church cemetery by Jones and Spigener. The child died early today at his home.

Surviving are the parents, Mr. and Mrs. Lonnie Lee Shirley, Sr. a sister Naomia Shirley, and his grandmother Mrs. Matilda Shirley and his grandfather N. A. Wedgeworth.

**Shirley, Matilda Ann Smith:** September 9, 1886-January 6, 1957. Grave # 148.

Matilda was the wife of Byrdie "Byrd" Franklin Shirley (March 17, 1880-November 17, 1932) and the mother of their twelve children.

Matilda Ann Smith Shirley was the mother of John Ester Shirley (married to Annie Snow Rushing), Lonnie Lee Shirley (married to Estelle Wedgeworth), Grady Edward Shirley (married to Margaret Watkins), Fannie Lou Shirley Hamner (married to Edward Bruce Hamner), Martha Nell Shirley Turner (married to Clifton Turner), Ruby Alene Shirley Mills (married to Erman Mills), B. F. Shirley (married to Mary Alice Turner) and Emma Frances Shirley Hamner (married to Oll Dee Hamner).

Matilda Ann Smith Shirley was the grandmother of Lonnie Lee Shirley, Jr. the son of Lonnie Lee Shirley and Estelle Wedgeworth and to James Gary Shirley, Edward Wendell Shirley and George Mark Shirley, sons of Grady Edward Shirley and Margaret Watkins Shirley.

Matilda Ann Smith was also the grandmother of Erma Shirley Mills (daughter of Erman Mills and Ruby Shirley Mills) and to Ollie Bruce Hamner (son of Edward Bruce Hamner and Fannie Lou Shirley Hamner).

Matilda was the great grandmother of Brett Brown the grandson of Lonnie Lee Shirley, Sr. and Estelle Wedgeworth Shirley.

All the above are buried in Macedonia Cemetery

She was also the mother of Sue Lake and Joan Davis who are not buried in Macedonia Cemetery.

**Obit for Matilda Ann Smith Shirley**

Funeral services for Mrs. Matilda Ann Smith Shirley, 70, widow of Byrd Franklin Shirley, Sr. who died Sunday afternoon at her residence on Northport Route 2 were held today at 3:00 p.m. at Macedonia Methodist Church nine miles north of Tuscaloosa on the Crabbe Road with burial in the church cemetery by Jones and Spigener.

Active pallbearers were John Hagler, Herman Boyd, Pruitt Hamner, Frank Rutner, Polk Rushing, and Newt Hamner.

Honorary pallbearers were Lester Taylor, Lattie Rigsby, Memnon Tierce, Robert Rushing, Frank Clements, Albert Taylor, Spurgeon Black, M.L. Lake, Dr. Sam Davis, and Jay Henry.

Surviving are six daughters, Mrs. Bruce Hamner, Mrs. Dee Hamner, Mrs. Howard Davis, Mrs. Erman Mills and Mrs. Clifton Turner all of this area; five sons John Ester, Lonnie Lee, Grady Edward, B. F. and Bobby Renzo, all of this area; a sister Mrs. L. R. Hamner; eight brothers, John H. Smith of Fosters, T. W. Smith of Holt, John, Will and Ed Smith of Northport, Searcy Smith of Abernant, Frank and Fred Smith of Smith, Arkansas, 28 grandchildren and 4 great grandchildren.

# MACEDONIA CEMETERY

**Shirley, Margaret Watkins:** August 27, 1918-August 10, 2003. Grave # 312A.

Margaret was the wife of Grady Edward Shirley (February 20, 1915-July 10, 1994) and the mother of their five children.

Margaret was the mother of Edward Wendell Shirley (September 4, 1939-July 23, 2019), George Mark Shirley (November 22, 1950-December 19, 2020), and James Gary Shirley (December 1, 1942-June 23, 2020). She was the great grandmother of a stillborn infant daughter born to Meredith Booth Barringer and Danny Barringer. Meredith is the daughter of Carol Shirley Booth, Margaret's daughter. The great grandchild's grave is beside Margaret's.

All the above are buried in Macedonia Cemetery except Meredith and Danny Barringer who are living.

**Shirley, Mary Alice Turner:** June 10, 1925-August 8, 2009. Grave # 315A.

She was the wife of B. F. Shirley (July 4, 1921-February 17, 2003) and the daughter of Mr. and Mrs. Festus Turner and the mother of two children.

**Obit for Mary Alice Turner Shirley:**

Mary Alice Shirley, age 84, of Northport died August 8, 2009 at Forest Manor Nursing Home. Graveside services will be held Tuesday at 11:00 a.m. at Macedonia Methodist Church Cemetery with Rev. Rock Stone and Rev. Mike Skelton officiating with Magnolia Funeral Home North directing. Visitation will be 6:000-8:00 p.m. tonight the funeral home.

Her husband, B. F. Shirley and her parents Mr. and Mrs. Festus Turner preceded her in death.

Survivors include: her daughter Leigh Ann Shirley Rice; son, Robert F. (Cherie) Shirley; sisters Ida Grace Stuckey; grandchildren Sara Hughes and Tyler Rice; and great granddaughter Emma Kate Hughes.

Mrs. Shirley was a devoted wife, mother, and grandmother. She was a faithful member of Macedonia Methodist Church where she taught a Sunday School class for over 40 years.

Pallbearers will be Robert Shirley, Tyler Rice, Hilary Shirley, James Shirley, John David Hughes, Russell Wilcutt, Nick Strong and Dan Turner.

**Shirley, Pricie Gibson:** 1903-1933
Grave # 179.

Pricie was the daughter of Mr. and Mrs. Joel Tom Shirley and sister to Mrs. Irene Pierre, Mrs. Maude Saye, Mrs. Emil Snow, and Mrs. Josh Rushing.

Pricie was married to Joe Dawson White, widely recognized "White hope" for the world heavyweight boxing championship. He shot his estranged wife in the back as she walked into Woolworth Store on Broad Street on a Saturday morning. She died later that day. (An entire chapter is devoted to the Joel Tom Shirley family elsewhere in this memoir.)

**Skelton, Inf. daughter of Cecil and Etteline Rushing:** 1941
Grave # 79.

Buna Etteline "Dick" Rushing was the sixth child of Marvin Goldman Rushing (October 8, 1884-February 17, 1947) and Ozella Judson "Juddie" Hamner (October 4, 1887-July 2, 1973). She was married to Cecil Wayne Skelton. She was a sister to Thelma Ann Rushing who married William Morgan Cooper. Thelma Ann Cooper is buried in Macedonia Cemetery, but Morgan Cooper is buried in Piney Woods Baptist Church Cemetery.

Marvin Goldman Rushing was the son of Joseph Enoch Rushing and Samantha Lenora Deason. He was a brother to James Willie "Will" Rushing (married to Fannie Gay), Thomas Hillman "Jack" Rushing (married to Annie Brazile Hamner), Lenora Bell "Lou" Rushing Hyche (married to Early M. Hyche), Robert Edward Lee Rushing (married to Loubelle Hamner), Sylvester Hayes Rushing (never married), James Knox Polk Rushing (married to Anne Elizabeth Turner) and Joseph David "Gin" Rushing (married to Permelia Alma Hamner).

Ozella Judson "Juddie" Hamner Rushing was the daughter of John Pruitt Hamner and Annie Margaret Hall and the granddaughter of William T. Hamner, Sr. and his second wife Permelia Chism.

All the above are buried in Macedonia Cemetery.

**Skelton, Inf. son of Cecil and Etteline Rushing**: 1943

Grave # 78.

Buna Etteline "Dick" Rushing was the sixth child of Marvin Goldman Rushing (October 8, 1884-February 17, 1947) and Ozella Judson "Juddie" Hamner (October 4, 1887-July 2, 1973). She was married to Cecil Wayne Skelton. She was a sister to Thelma Ann Rushing who married William Morgan Cooper. Thelma Ann Cooper is buried in Macedonia Cemetery, but Morgan Cooper is buried in Piney Woods Baptist Church Cemetery.

Marvin Goldman Rushing was the son of Joseph Enoch Rushing and Samantha Lenora Deason. He was a brother to James Willie "Will" Rushing (married to Fannie Gay), Thomas Hillman "Jack" Rushing (married to Annie Brazile Hamner), Lenora Bell "Lou" Rushing Hyche (married to Early M. Hyche), Robert Edward Lee Rushing (married to Loubelle Hamner), Sylvester Hayes Rushing (never married), James Knox Polk Rushing (married to Anne Elizabeth Turner) and Joseph David "Gin" Rushing (married to Permelia Alma Hamner).

Ozella Judson "Juddie" Hamner Rushing was the daughter of John Pruitt Hamner and Annie Margaret Hall and the granddaughter of William T. Hamner, Sr. and his second wife Permelia Chism.

All the above are buried in Macedonia Cemetery.

**Smalley, Ida:** July 23, 1901-November 26, 1939. Grave # 155

**Smith, Charles Edward**: May 5, 1896-June 3, 1970. Grave # 99. He is a brother to Matilda Ann Smith Shirley, the wife of Byrd Shirley, Sr.

**Smith, Emma Frances:** September 12, 1868-November 19, 1919. Grave # 95.

She was the mother of Beatrice Josephine "Joe" Smith Hamner who was the wife of Larkin "Lark" Rogers Hamner.

Larkin "Lark" Rogers Hamner and Beatrice Josephine "Joe" Smith were the parents of Annie Mable Hamner, William Trimm Hamner, John Curtis Hamner and James Lando "Kid" Hamner.

All the above are buried in Macedonia Cemetery except for William Trimm Hamner, John Curtis Hamner and James Lando "Kid" Hamner. William Trimm and James Lando are buried in Carrolls Creek Baptist Church Cemetery.

Lark Hamner was the seventh child of John Pruitt Hamner and Annie Margaret Hall.

John Pruitt Hamner was the son of William Taylor Hamner, Sr. and his second wife Permelia Chism. Lark Hamner was a brother to Mary Ulalah Virginia Hamner, a child who died in childhood, Ollie Jackson "Ollie" Hamner (married to Louise Rigsby), John Earl Hamner (married to Rose Anne Viella Rigsby), Buena Vista Hamner Chism (she married first to John Monroe House and married second to her first cousin Archie George Chism), Annie Brazile Hamner Rushing (married to Thomas Hillman Rushing), Ozella Judson Hamner (married to Marvin Goldman Rushing, Ullie Mae Hamner Chism (married to her first cousin Harvey Morgan Chism) and Permelia Alma Hamner (married to Joseph David "Gin" Rushing.

All the above are buried in Macedonia Cemetery except as noted with Trimm Hamner, James Lando Hamner and John Curtis Hamner.

**Smith, Etta Mae:** May 5, 1911. Grave # 96.

**Smith, James Elmer:** February 1, 1931-January 9, 2006. Grave # 229A.

**Smith, Jessie Crimm:** February 18, 1900-March 6, 1927. Grave # 98.

He was a brother to Matilda Ann Smith Shirley the wife of Byrd Shirley, Sr.

**Smith, Leona Grammer:** August 7, 1907-September 12, 1981. Grave # 228.

# MACEDONIA CEMETERY

She was the wife of William S. "Will' Smith.

**Smith, Troy David:** May 30, 1927-July 3, 1945. Grave # 229.

**Smith, William S. "Will":** December 15, 1898-September 24, 1982. Grave # 227.

Will was married to Leona Grammer Smith. Will was a brother to Matilda Smith Shirley, wife of Byrd Shirley.

Will was the husband of Leona G. Smith.

**Smith, Daniel William R.:** March 8, 1857-March 7, 1935. Grave # 94.

He was the husband of Emma Frances Smith, and the father of father of Beatrice Josephine "Joe" Smith Hamner the wife of Larkin "Lark" Rogers Hamner and the grandfather of Annie Mable Hamner, William Trimm Hamner, John Curtis Hamner and James Lando "Kid" Hamner. All are buried in Macedonia Cemetery except for William Trimm Hamner and James Lando "Kid" Hamner who are buried in Carrolls Creek Baptist Church Cemetery. The burial site for John Curtis Hamner is missing. He is also the father of Matilda Ann Smith Shirley, wife of Byrd Shirley.

**Speed, Margaret Lucile:** 1910-1934 Grave #151.

Margaret was the daughter of Joseph David "Gin" Rushing

(October 15, 1876-April 22, 1943) and Permelia Alma Hamner (January 15, 1884-February 3, 1970).

Joseph David Rushing was the son of Joseph Enoch Rushing and Samantha Lenora Deason.

Permelia Alma Hamner was the daughter of John Pruitt Hamner and Annie Margaret Hall.

John Pruitt Hamner was the son of William T. Hamner, Sr. and his second wife Permelia Chism.

All the above are buried in Macedonia Cemetery.

Margaret married Walter Lee Speed who is not buried in Macedonia Cemetery.

**Obit for Margaret Lucille Speed**

Mrs. Margaret Lucille Rushing Speed, 24, daughter of Mr. and Mrs. Joseph David "Gib" Rushing, died Sunday morning at 11:30 o'clock in an Anniston hospital. The remains reached Tuscaloosa at 10.40 p.m. Sunday night and were taken to the home of her parents at Northport to await the funeral.

Mrs. Speed is survived by her husband, Walter Lee Speed of Anniston, three brothers, Woodrow, James and David Rushing and two sisters, Mrs. Theo Hagler, and Mrs. Houston Thomas, all of Northport. She had made her home in Anniston for the post three years.

Funeral services were to be held at Macedonia Methodist Church at 2:00 o'clock with the Rev. C. L. Manderson officiating with internment to take place in the church cemetery with Mathis-Jones Mortuary in charge.

Pallbearers were Melvin Hamner, John Rushing Nathan Chism, Harwood Hamner, Howard Rushing and Curtis Hamner.

**Stamps, Early Edward:** February 6, 1882-June 3, 1948. Grave # 281.

**Stamps, Jeryl O'Neal:** August 27, 1944-August 30, 1944. Grave #280.

**Stephens, Mary Etta Rigsby:** 1926-1955 Grave #246.

**Stine, Elizabeth Fendley:** August 16, 1864-February 9, 1926. Grave # 244.

She was the wife of John H. Stine and the mother of Harvey Franklin Stine who married Sarah Elizabeth Hamner the seventh child of George Harrison Hamner and Sarah "Sallie" McGee.

George Harrison Hamner was the son of William Taylor Hamner, Sr. by his first wife whose name is not known. Hamner family tradition holds that George Harrison Hamner's mother is buried in a grave in Macedonia Cemetery that is marked only by a stone with no name inscribed. It is located beside William Taylor Hamner, Sr.'s grave. If this is true, her grave is likely the oldest in the cemetery.[66]

All the above except Harvey Franklin Stine are buried in Macedonia Cemetery.

---

[66] Page 155

Sarah "Sallie" McGee was the daughter of Joseph and Mary McGee who are buried in Bethel Presbyterian Church Cemetery.

**Stine, John F.:** September 2, 1864-August 28, 1922. Grave # 243.

He was the husband of Elizabeth Fendley and the father of Harvey Franklin Stine who married Sarah Elizabeth Hamner the seventh child of George Harrison Hamner and Sarah "Sallie" McGee all of whom except Harvey Franklin Stine are buried in Macedonia Cemetery.

**Stine, Jester:** date not readable. Grave # 243A

**Strickland, William Aaron:** June 26, 1990-June 26, 1990. Grave #299.

He was the still-born son of Tara Boyd Strickland and Bill Strickland. He also is the grandson of Herman and Lucile Boyd and Faith and Roy Rushing.

**Strunk, Gladys Hagler:** July 19, 1902-September 16, 1991. Grave #53.

(Check this date on tombstone. In Hamner book on page 259 the date of birth is given as May 14, 1900.) Gladys Hagler was the daughter of Permelia Elizabeth Hamner and James Martin Hagler.

Permelia Elizabeth Hamner was the daughter of Louis Alfred Hamner and Penina Wilson Clements.

Louis Alfred Hamner was the son of William T. Hamner, Sr. and his second wife Permelia Chism.

Of the ten children born to Permelia Elizabeth Hamner and James Martin Hagler, five are buried in Macedonia Cemetery. They are: (1) John Martin Hagler (married to Octavia Tierce); (2) Lucille Hagler Crawford (married to Sterling Crawford); (3) Gladys Hagler Struck (divorced); (4) Wiley Pruitt Hagler (married to Theo Rushing); (5) Minnie Lou Hagler Taylor (married to James Albert Taylor).[67]

Penina Wilson Clements was the daughter of Thomas Clements and his first wife Elizabeth Simpson.[68]

All the above are buried in Macedonia Cemetery except for Louis Alfred Hamner and Penina Wilson Clements. They are buried in the old Albert Methodist Church Cemetery.[69]

James Martin Hagler was the son of John Pruitt Hagler and Sallie Ann Martin. They are not buried in Macedonia Cemetery.

**Sullivan, Elmer E.:** December 10, 1926-April 18, 2006. Grave # 317.

**Sutton, Burnice:** April 20, 1893
Grave # 104

**Sutton, Eula Lee:** August 23, 1893-January 7, 1962. Grave # 105.

**Taylor, Inez:** September 6, 1920- September 7, 1920. Grave # 8

She was the daughter of James Albert Taylor and Minnie Lula Hagler Taylor all of whom are buried in Macedonia Cemetery.

**Taylor, an Infant daughter:** July 23, 1933. Grave #7

**Taylor, James Albert:** May 16, 1894-March 21, 1973. Grave # 1

He was the husband of Minnie Lula Hagler Taylor and the father of Inez Taylor and Thelma Taylor.

Minnie Lula Hagler Taylor was the first child of Permelia Elizabeth Hamner and James Martin Hagler.

Permelia Elizabeth Hamner was the daughter of Louis Alfred Hamner and Penina Wilson Clements.

Louis Alfred Hamner was the son of William T. Hamner, Sr. and his second wife Permelia Chism.

Penina Wilson Clements was the daughter of Thomas Clements and Elizabeth Simpson.

Minnie Lula was a sister to John Martin Hagler (married to Octavia Tierce), Lucille Hagler Crawford (married to Sterling Crawford) and Gladys Hagler Struck and Wiley Pruitt Hagler (married to Theo Rushing).

---

[67] Page 255
[68] Page 247
[69] Page 247

# MACEDONIA CEMETERY

All the above are buried in Macedonia Cemetery.

James Martin Hagler was the son of John Pruitt Hagler and Sallie Ann Martin who are not buried in Macedonia Cemetery.

**Taylor, Mary Ellen Offel**: January 11, 1918-August 10, 1941. Grave # 10.

Mary Ellen was the wife of Arthur Virgil Taylor the son of James Albert and Minnie Lula Taylor. Mary Ellen was born January 11, 1918 in Ohio and died August 10, 1941. After Mary Ellen's death, Arthur Virgil Taylor married Gertrude Martin. He is not buried in Macedonia Cemetery.

**Obit for Mrs. R. V. Taylor**

Funeral services for Mrs. R. V. (Mary Ellen Offel) Taylor, 33, who died Tuesday at Marine Hospital in Staten Island, New York, will be held Thruway afternoon at 4:00 o'clock at Macedonia Methodist Church with internment in the church cemetery by Jones and Spigener.

Mrs. Taylor had been ill for about four weeks, the illness developing while visiting her husband who is connected with US Navy at Staten Island. She was a native of Ohio and is survived by a number of relatives there in addition to her husband who formerly resided in this county.

Active pallbearers will be John Hagler, Albert Hagler, Sterling Crawford, Wiley Hagler, and Howard Hagler.

Macedonia Church is 10 miles north of Tuscaloosa on the Crabbe Road. The body will arrive here on the train Thursday Morning at 10:00 a.m.

**Taylor, Minnie Lula Hagler**: November 1, 1896-November 8, 1971

Grave # 12

Minnie was the wife James Albert Taylor and the mother of Inez Taylor and Thelma Taylor.[70]

Minnie Lula Hagler Taylor was the first child of Permelia Elizabeth Hamner and James Martin Hagler.

Permelia Elizabeth Hamner was the daughter of Louis Alfred Hamner and Penina Wilson Clements.

Louis Alfred Hamner was the son of William T. Hamner, Sr. and his second wife Permelia Chism.

Penina Wilson Clements was the daughter of Thomas Clements and his first wife Elizabeth Simpson.

Minnie Lula Hagler Taylor was a sister to John Martin Hagler (married to Octavia Tierce), Lucille Hagler Crawford (married to Sterling Crawford), Gladys Hagler Struck (divorced), Wiley Pruitt Hagler (married to Theo Rushing) and Albert Hagler married to Helen Elizabeth "Patty" Parizek.

All the above are buried in Macedonia Cemetery except for Albert Hagler and Patty Parizek.

Minnie Lula was a granddaughter to John Pruitt Hagler and Sallie Ann Martin who are not buried in Macedonia Cemetery.

**Taylor, Thelma**: July 8, 1916-November 2, 1919

Grave # 9.

Thelma was the daughter James Albert and Minnie Lula Hagler Taylor.

**Thomas, Baxter Irwin**: October 1, 1871-July 27, 1908.

Grave # 60

Baxter was the husband of Myrtie Hyche Thomas. He was the father of Houston Lonzo Thomas who married Etta Alma Rushing who is buried in Macedonia Cemetery.

Etta Alma Rushing was the daughter of Joseph David "Gin" Rushing and Permelia Alma Hamner.

Joseph David "Gin" Rushing was the son of Joseph Enoch Rushing and Samantha Lenora Deason.

Permelia Alma Hamner was the daughter of John Pruitt Hamner and Annie Margaret Hall.

John Pruitt Hamner was the son of William T. Hamner, Sr. and his second wife Permelia Chism.

**Thomas, Etta Alma Rushing**: May 17,

---

[70] Page 255

1906-December 15, 1980

Grave # 133

Etta was the wife of Houston Lonzo Thomas.

Etta Alma Rushing was the daughter of Joseph David "Gin" Rushing and Permelia Alma Hamner.

Joseph David "Gin" Rushing was the son of Joseph Enoch Rushing and Samantha Lenora Deason.

Permelia Alma Hamner was the daughter of John Pruitt Hamner and Annie Margaret Hall.

John Pruitt Hamner was the son of William T. Hamner, Sr. and his second wife Permelia Chism.

All the above are buried in Macedonia Cemetery including the following siblings of Etta Alma Rushing Thomas: (1) Theo Rushing Hagler (married to Wiley Pruitt Hagler) (2) Goldman Rushing (married to Ozella Judson "Juddie" Hamner); (3) James Polk Rushing (married to Annie Turner); (4) Hayes Rushing (unmarried); (5) Robert E. Lee Rushing (married to Loubelle Hamner (6) Thomas Hillman "Jack" Rushing (married Mary Brazile Hamner); (7) Willie Snow "Will" Rushing (married to Fannie Gay).

**Thomas, Houston:** February 14, 1903-July 3, 1960.

Grave # 134.

Houston was the husband of Etta Alma Rushing and the son of Baxter Thomas and Myrtie Hyche all of whom are buried in Macedonia Cemetery.

**Thomas, J. R.:** June 22, 1922 D.O.B. I need the date of death Grave # 2 94

**Thomas, Maude E.:** October 28, 1920-January 16, 1979

Grave # 295

**Thomas, Myrtie Hyche:** August 27, 1870-May 6, 1926.

Grave # 61

Myrtie was the wife of Baxter Irwin Thomas and the mother of Houston Lonzo Thomas who married Etta Alma Rushing all of whom are buried in Macedonia Cemetery. Her obituary reads:

"Mrs. Myrtie Thomas, age fifty-five, died at her home five miles from Northport on the Byler Road at about 5:00 o'clock yesterday morning. Funeral services followed by internment took place this morning at 10 o'clock at the Macedonia Church. Mrs. Thomas left two sons, one daughter, three brothers and two sisters to mourn her loss."

**Ronie Thomas:** November 12, 1949-June 24, 2004

Grave # 316 in new part of cemetery. Check for dates.

**Tierce, Benjamin Collier:** June 6, 1890-August 15, 1946.

Grave # 192

Collier was the husband of Nellie F. Tierce and the son of Eugene Benjamin Tierce, Sr. (May 15, 1865-August 30, 1918) and his first wife Veturia Scales (November 22, 1869-June 21, 1907).

Eugene Benjamin Tierce, Sr. was the son of Elliott Catlett Tierce (tombstone reads "E.C. Tierce" December 17, 1827-March 21, 1906) and Frances Caroline Doss (December 3, 1831-March 13, 1900).

Elliott Catlett Tierce was the son of Benjamin Tucker Tierce (1785-February 18, 1869) and Susannah Clardy Tierce (June 13, 1787-April 27, 1862). Susannah's tomb stone is the oldest in the cemetery.

Benjamin Collier Tierce was the father of Elsie Tierce Guy, Evelyn Tierce and Katherine Tierce and the grandfather of Kay Guy Rice.

Benjamin Collier Tierce was a brother to Memnon Tierce, Sr., Victor Tierce, Festus Tierce, Octavia Tierce Hagler (married to John Martin Hagler), Hester _____. He was a half-brother to Louise Tierce Mathis and Eugene Benjamin Tierce, Jr. (married to Lillie Stine). All the above are buried in Macedonia Cemetery except for Memnon and Hester. Collier was also the father of Buster Tierce who is not buried in Macedonia Cemetery.

# MACEDONIA CEMETERY

**Obit for Collier Tierce**

Funeral services for Collier Tierce, 56, who was accidentally killed Wednesday morning while working at a sawmill on the Crabbe Road when he was drawn into the machine when a piece of his clothing became entangled will be held Saturday afternoon at 3:00 p.m. from Macedonia Methodist Church on the Crabbe Road with the Rev. Mr. Powell officiating assisted by the Rev. Mr. Jackson Jones and Spigener Funeral Home will direct internment in the church cemetery.

Surviving Mr. Tierce is his widow; six children, Collier "Buster" Jr., E. W., Elsie, Evelyn, Pauline, and Kathleen; a grandson, Daniel; three brothers, a half-brother, two sisters, and a half-sister and his stepmother, Mrs. Lela Tierce. (See above for their names.)

Active pallbearers for the rites will be Lattie Rigsby, Robert Rushing, Pruitt Hamner, Herman Boyd, Frank Turner, Albert Blake.

Honorary pallbearers will be Judge Reuben Wright, Bernard Collier, Dr. J. E. Shirley, Frank Rice, Largus Barnes, Judge Chester Walker, John E. Walker, Judge W. C. Warren, T. E. Christian, Sam Palmer, Monroe Ward, Tom B. Ward, Cliff Lindsay, James Anders, Nathan Chism, and Tunstall Searcy.

**Tierce, Benjamin Tucker:** 1785-February 18, 1869

Grave # 56.

Benjamin Tucker was the patriarch of the Tierce family in the Lafoy Community and is thought to have arrived here in the early 1830s. Public records show that on March 27, 1833, he bought land from Jacob Clements on the Crabbe Road near North River.

Benjamin Tucker Tierce was the husband of Susannah Clardy Tierce (June 13, 1787-April 27, 1862) and the father of Elliott Catlett Tierce whose tombstone reads "E.C." Tierce (December 17, 1827-March 21, 1906).

Susannah Clardy Tierce's grave marker reads "April 27, 1862." It is the oldest grave marker in the cemetery.

**Tierce, Daniel:** June 17, 1942-December 17, 2022

Need grave # in new section of cemetery

Daniel was the son of one of Collier Tierce's daughters.

**Tierce, Donald**: March 8, 1933-November 1, 2003

Grave # 300A

Donald was the son of Eugene Benjamin Tierce, Jr. (October 30, 1908-December 31, 1970) and Lillie Snow Chastine Tierce (July 30, 1908-January 19, 2000.)

Eugene Benjamin Tierce, Jr. was the son of Eugene Benjamin Tierce, Sr. (May 15, 1865-August 30, 1918) and his second wife Lela Hyche Tierce (August 6, 1885-August 23, 1958).

Eugene Benjamin Tierce, Sr. was the son of Elliott Catlett Tierce (tombstone reads "E.C. Tierce") and Frances Caroline Doss.

Elliott Catlett Tierce was the son of Benjamin Tucker Tierce and Susannah Clardy.

Donald was a brother to Rogene Tierce.

All the above are buried in Macedonia Cemetery.

**Tierce, Elliott Catlett "E. C.":** December 17, 1827-March 21, 1906.

Grave # 197

Elliott Catlett was the son of Benjamin Tucker Tierce (1785-February 18, 1869) and Susannah Clardy Tierce (June 13, 1787-April 27, 1862).

Elliott Catlett Tierce was the husband of Frances Caroline Doss Tierce (December 3, 1831-March 13, 1900). He was the father of Eugene Benjamin Tierce, Sr. (May 15, 1865-August 30, 1918) and Elliott Lee Tierce (March 18, 1863-October 17, 1938).

Elliott Lee Tierce was the father of Joe T. Tierce and George Culver Tierce.

All the above are buried in Macedonia Cemetery.

**Tierce, Elliott**: 1890-1974

Grave # 50

Elliott A. (tombstone reads "Elliott") was the

son of Elliott Catlett Tierce (tombstone reads "E.C. Tierce" December 17, 1827-March 21, 1906.) and Frances Caroline Doss (December 3, 1831-March 13, 1900).

Elliott Catlett Tierce was the son of Benjamin Tucker Tierce and Susannah Clardy Tierce.

Elliott A. Tierce married Molly Snyder (November 11, 1895-September 23, 1937.

All the above are buried in Macedonia Cemetery.

**Tierce, Elliott Lee**: March 18, 1863-October 17, 1938

Grave # 54

Elliott Lee was the son of Elliott Catlett Tierce (tombstone reads "E.C." December 17, 1827-March 21, 1906) and Frances Caroline Doss (December 3, 1831-March 13, 1900).

Elliott Lee Tierce married Julia Frances Watson (January 28, 1868-April 7, 1904).

Elliott Lee and Julia Frances had five sons (two of whom are Elliott A. Tierce and Joe Tierce) and three daughters (page 85 in *A Tierce Comes to Tuscaloosa*.) Julia Frances died April 7, 1904 and is buried in Macedonia Cemetery. Elliott Lee then married Mrs. Verona Bedford (see his obit in the October 18, 1938 *Tuscaloosa News*). *A Tierce Comes to Tuscaloosa* states that Verona had two sons and one daughter. Were they by a previous marriage or by her marriage to Elliott Lee? I find no record of Verona's death or place of burial. There is no tombstone in Macedonia with her name on it. The October 18, 1938 issue of *The Tuscaloosa News* obit states, "Elliott Lee Tierce is survived by six sons: E.A. Tierce, Joe Tierce, Robert Tierce, G. C. Tierce, all of Northport and Howard Tierce, of Louisiana and Verner Tierce of Tuscaloosa and four daughters: Mrs. W. A. Carr of Florida, Mrs. Walter Shamblin of Tuscaloosa and Mrs. Earnest Carr of North Carolina, and Miss Eunice Tierce of Tuscaloosa.

Elliott Lee Tierce was a brother to Eugene Benjamin Tierce, Sr.

Elliott Lee Tierce, along with Elliott Catlett Tierce (tombstone reads "E.C.") were two of the seven trustees of Macedonia Methodist Church when the Tierce family deeded part of the Tierce property on which to build Macedonia Church on June 12, 1902.

**Tierce, Eugene Benjamin Sr.:** May 15, 1865-August 30, 1918

Grave # 200.

Eugene Sr. was the son of Elliott Catlett Tierce (tombstone reads "E.C." Tierce December 17, 1827-March 21, 1906.) and Frances Caroline Doss (December 3, 1831-March 13, 1900).

Elliott Catlett Tierce was the son of Benjamin Tucker Tierce (1785-February 18, 1869) and Susannah Clardy Tierce (June 13, 1787-April 27, 1862).

Eugene Benjamin Tierce, Sr. was a brother to Elliott Tierce.

Eugene Benjamin Tierce, Sr. was married first to Veturia Scales and this marriage produced Victor Tierce, Festus Tierce, Collier Tierce (married to Nellie Tierce), Memnon Tierce, Sr, Octavia Tierce Hagler (married to John Martin Hagler) and Hester _____.

Eugene Benjamin Tierce, Sr. married a second time after the death of Susannah to Lela Hyche. This marriage produced Eugene Benjamin Tierce, Jr. (October 30, 1908-December 31, 1970) who married Lillie Stine Tierce and Louise Tierce Mathis (March 31, 1910-Febraury 11, 1983.) All the above except Memnon and Hester _____ are buried in Macedonia Cemetery

**Tierce, Eugene Benjamin, Jr.:** October 30, 1908-December 31, 1970.

Grave #301.

Eugene Jr. was the husband of Lillie Snow Chastine (July 30, 1908-January 19, 2000).

Eugene Benjamin Tierce, Jr. was the son of Eugene Benjamin Tierce, Sr. and his second wife Lela Hyche.

Eugene Benjamin Tierce, Sr. was the son of Elliott Catlett Tierce (tombstone reads "E.C." Tierce) and Frances Caroline Doss.

Elliott Catlett Tierce was the son of Benjamin

# MACEDONIA CEMETERY

Tucker Tierce and Susannah Clardy Tierce.

Eugene Benjamin Tierce, Jr. was a brother to Octavia Tierce Hagler (married to John Martin Hagler) and Louise Tierce Mathis.

Eugene Benjamin Tierce, Jr. was a half-brother to Victor Tierce, Festus Tierce, Collier Tierce (married to Nellie Tierce), Memnon Tierce, Sr.; and Hester_____.

Eugene Benjamin Tierce, Jr, was the father of Donald Tierce and Rogene Tierce. All the above are buried in Macedonia Cemetery except for Memnon and Hester.

Eugene was also the father of Corendene (June 19, 1928-September 23, 2015) Rushing, Cordelia Rushing (February 1, 1931-January 13, 2008) and Ophelia Harrison who is still living in 2023.

**Tierce, Eugene Benjamin "B.J.":** March 16, 1984-April 29, 1984. Grave # 300.

B. J. was the son of Benjamin Tierce.

Benjamin Tierce was the son of Eugene Benjamin Tierce, Jr. and Lillie Snow Tierce and the grandson of Eugene Benjamin Tierce, Sr. and Lela Hyche Tierce and the great grandson of Elliott Catlett Tierce and Frances Caroline Doss and the great, great grandson of Benjamin Tucker Tierce and Susannah Clary Tierce.

All the above except Benjamin who is 2023 is still living are buried in Macedonia Cemetery.

**Tierce, Evelyn:** April 24, 1916-August 23, 1972

Grave # 117

Evelyn was the daughter of Benjamin Collier Tierce (June 6, 1890-August 15, 1946) and Nellie F. Tierce (November 30, 1897-January 7, 1974).

Benjamin Collier Tierce was the son of Eugene Benjamin Tierce, Sr. and Veturia Scales Tierce.

Eugene Benjamin Tierce, Sr. was the son of Elliott Catlett Tierce (tombstone reads "E.C." Tierce) and Frances Caroline Doss.

Elliott Catlett Tierce was the son of Benjamin Tucker Tierce and Susannah Clardy

Evelyn Tierce was a sister to Katherine Tierce and Elsie Tierce Guy.

**Tierce, Festus:** June 25, 1901-February 3, 1988

Grave # 116

Festus was the son of Eugene Benjamin Tierce, Sr. and Veturia Scales Tierce.

Eugene Benjamin Tierce, Sr. was the son of Elliott Catlett Tierce (tombstone reads "E.C." Tierce) and Frances Caroline Doss.

Elliott Catlett Tierce was the son of Benjamin Tucker Tierce and Susannah Clardy.

Festus Tierce was a brother to Victor Tierce, Memnon Tierce, Sr. Collier Tierce (married to Nellie Tierce), Octavia Tierce Hagler (married to John Martin Hagler) and Hester _____.

Festus was a half-brother to Louise Tierce Mathis and Eugene Benjamin Tierce, Jr. (married to Lillie Snow Chastine).

All but Memnon and Hester are buried in Macedonia Cemetery.

**Tierce, Frances Caroline Doss:** December 3, 1831-March 13, 1900. Grave # 199.

Frances was the wife of Elliott Catlett Tierce (tombstone reads "E.C." Tierce December 17, 1827-March 21, 1906.) and the mother of Elliott Lee Tierce (March 18, 1863-October 17, 1938) and Eugene Benjamin Tierce, Sr. (May 15, 1865-August 30, 1918)

Elliott Catlett Tierce was the son of Benjamin Tucker Tierce (1785-February 18, 1869) and Susannah Clardy Tierce (June 13, 1787-April 27, 1862).

**Tierce, George Culver:** June 21, 1902-April 10,1951

Grave # 28.

George was the son of Elliott Lee Tierce (March 18, 1863-October 17, 1938) and Julia Francis Tierce (January 28, 1868-April 7, 1904) and a brother to Joe T. Tierce (January 14, 1896-May 16, 1965).

**Tierce, Infant daughter of Memnon Tierce (son of Eugene B. Tierce, Sr.) and Willie Koster Tierce.** The baby was born and died on October

14, 1921. Grave # 198

**Tierce, Infant son of Elliott A. and Molly Synder: July 28, 1924**

Grave # 196.

**Tierce, Joe T.:** January 14, 1896-May 16, 1965. Grave # 30

Joe was the husband of Lillie M. Tierce and a brother to George Culver Tierce and the son of Elliott Lee Tierce.

**Tierce, Julia Frances:** January 28, 1868-April 7, 1904

Grave # 55.

Julia was the first wife of Elliott Lee Tierce and the mother of Elliott Tierce and Joe T. Tierce. After her death, Elliott Lee married a second time to Verona Bedford.

**Tierce, Katherine:** January 19, 1925-June 21, 1971

Grave # 118.

Katherine was the daughter of Benjamin Collier Tierce and Nellie F. Tierce.

Benjamin Collier Tierce was the son of Eugene Benjamin Tierce, Sr. and his first wife Veturia Scales Tierce.

Eugene Benjamin Tierce, Sr. was the son of Elliott Catlett Tierce (tombstone reads "E.C." Tierce) and Frances Caroline Doss.

Elliott Catlett Tierce was the son of Benjamin Tucker Tierce and Susannah Clardy.

Katherine Tierce was a sister to Evelyn Tierce and Elsie Tierce Guy.

**Tierce, Lela A. Hyche:** August 6, 1885-August 23, 1958

Grave # 202

Lela Hyche was the second wife of Eugene Benjamin Tierce, Sr. (May 15, 1865-August 30, 1918). After Veturia Scales Tierce, the first wife of Eugene Benjamin Tierce, Sr. died in the 1907, he married Lela Hyche. That marriage produced Louise Tierce Mathis and Eugene Benjamin Tierce, Jr. (married to Lillie Snow Chastine).

Eugene Benjamin Tierce, Sr. died in 1918. After his death, Lela Hyche Tierce continued to live in the Tierce home on the Crabbe Road built in 1896 with her daughter Louise and son Eugene Benjamin Tierce, Jr. until they married. In 1940, Mrs. Tierce sold the house and most of the Tierce farm to my parents Herman C. Boyd, Sr. and Lucille Farquhar Boyd. I was six months old at the time. It was in this house that I spent my growing up years.

In 1940, Lela Hyche Tierce married James S. Clements after the death of his wife Mary Etta Hamner Clements. James and Lela lived in the James S. Clements house adjacent to the Lafoy School until James died in 1945. Lela Hyche then made her home with her daughter Louise Mathis until her death in 1958.

All the above are buried in Macedonia Cemetery.

**Tierce, Lillie M.:** May 13, 1898-May 10, 1971

Grave # 29.

Lillie M. Tierce was the wife of Joe T. Tierce who was the son of Elliott Lee Tierce.

Elliott Lee was the son of Elliott Catlett Tierce (tombstone reads "E.C." December 17, 1827-March 21, 1906) and Frances Caroline Doss (December 3, 1831-March 13, 1900).

Elliott Lee Tierce married Julia Frances Watson (January 28, 1868-April 7, 1904).

**Tierce, Lillie Snow Chastine**: July 30, 1908-January 19, 2000. Grave # 302.

Lillie was the wife of Eugene Benjamin Tierce, Jr. and the mother of Donald Tierce and Rogene Tierce and the grandmother of Eugene Benjamin "B. J." Tierce the son of Ben Tierce all of whom are buried in Macedonia Cemetery.

In addition, Lillie was the mother of Corendene (June 19, 1928-September 23, 2015) Rushing, Cordelia Rushing (February 1, 1931-January 13, 2008) and Ophelia Harrison who is still living in 2023.

**Tierce, Mollie Snyder:** November 11, 1895-September 23, 1937. Grave # 49.

Mollie was the wife of Elliott A. (tombstone reads "Elliott") Tierce.

Elliott A. Tierce was the son of Elliott Lee

Tierce and Julia Frances Tierce.

Elliott Lee Tierce was the son of Elliott Catlett Tierce (tombstone reads "E.C. Tierce") and Frances Caroline Doss.

Elliott Catlett Tierce was the son of Benjamin Tucker Tierce and Susannah Clardy Tierce.

**Tierce, Nellie F.:** November 30, 1897-January 7, 1974

Grave # 193.

Nellie F. Tierce was the husband of Benjamin Collier Tierce (June 6, 1890-August 15, 1946) who was the son of Eugene Benjamin Tierce, Sr. and his first wife Veturia Scales.

Nellie Tierce was the mother of Elsie Tierce Guy, Evelyn Tierce, and Katherine Tierce, and the grandfather of Kay Guy Rice and Daniel Tierce.

**Tierce, Nora Lee:** November 21, 1908-February 22, 1993.

Grave # 51.

**Tierce, Pauline:** January 19, 1925-January 8, 2008

Grave # 117A

**Tierce, Rogene:** July 10, 1946-March 25, 2010

Grave # 321

Rogene was the son of Eugene Benjamin Tierce, Jr. and Lillie Snow Chastine Tierce.

Eugene Benjamin Tierce, Jr. was the son of Eugene Benjamin Tierce, Sr. and his second wife Lela Hyche Tierce.

Eugene Benjamin Tierce, Sr. was the son of Elliott Catlett Tierce and Frances Caroline Doss.

Elliott Catlett Tierce was the son of Benjamin Tucker Tierce and Susannah Clardy.

Rogene was a brother to Donald Tierce.

All the above are buried in Macedonia Cemetery.

**Tierce, Susannah:** June 13, 1787-April 27, 1862

Grave #195.

She was the wife of Benjamin Tucker Tierce (1785-February 18, 1869). Her grave carries the date of the oldest tombstone in the cemetery. She was the mother of Elliott Catlett Tierce (December 17, 1827-March 21, 1906) and Eugene Benjamin Tierce, Sr. (May 15, 1865-August 30, 1918).

**Tierce, Tiny Inf. of E. B. & Veturia:** 1889

Grave # 194

**Tierce, Veturia:** November 22, 1869-June 21, 1907

Grave # 201

Veturia was the first wife of Eugene Benjamin Tierce, Sr. (May 15, 1865-August 30, 1918) and the mother of Victor Tierce, Festus Tierce, Collier Tierce (married to Nellie F. Tierce), Memnon Tierce, Sr., Octavia Tierce Hagler (married to John Martin Hagler) and Hester _____.

All the above except Memnon and Hester are buried in Macedonia Cemetery.

**Tierce, Victor:** October 9, 1897-September 24, 1968

Grave # 115.

Victor was the son of Eugene Benjamin Tierce, Sr. (May 15, 1865-August 30, 1918) and Veturia Scales Tierce (November 22, 1869-June 21, 1907).

Eugene Benjamin Tierce, Sr. was the son of Elliott Catlett Tierce (tombstone reads "E.C. Tierce") and Frances Caroline Doss.

Elliott Catlett Tierce was the son of Benjamin Tucker Tierce and Susannah Clary Tierce.

Victor Tierce was a brother to Festus Tierce, Memnon Tierce, Sr., Collier Tierce (married to Nellie F. Tierce), Octavia Tierce Hagler (married to John Martin Hagler) and Hester _____.

Victor was a half-brother to Louise Tierce Mathis and Eugene Benjamin Tierce, Jr.

All but Memnon and Hester are buried in Macedonia Cemetery.

**Tierce, Willie A.:** January 3, 1894-October 11, 1926

Grave #52

**Tucker, Donie:** March 2, 1899-November 4, 1990

Grave # 291

**Tucker, Percy:** October 4, 1899-February 15,

1975

Grave # 290

**Turner, James Clifton**: March 15, 1921-August 5, 2009

Grave # 318

Clifton was the husband of Martha Shirley.

Martha Shirley was the daughter of Byrdie "Byrd" Franklin Shirley and Matilda Ann Smith Shirley.

Martha Shirley Turner was a sister to John Ester Shirley (married to Annie Snow Rushing), Lonnie Lee Shirley (married to Estelle Wedgeworth), Grady Edward Shirley (married to Margaret Watkins), Fannie Lou Shirley Hamner (married to Edward Bruce Hamner), B. F. Shirley (married to Mary Alice Turner), Ruby Alene Shirley Mills (married to Erman Mills) and Emma Frances Shirley Hamner (married to Oll Dee Hamner).

All the above are buried in Macedonia Cemetery.

She was also a sister to Sue Lake and Joan Davis who are not buried in Macedonia Cemetery.

**Turner, John Louis**: June 19, 1910-July 16, 1943

Grave #91

John Louise was married to Vina Cordelia Smith, sister of Matilda Smith Shirley, wife of Byrd Shirley.

**Obit for John Louis Turner:**

John Lewis Turner, 32, known to his friends as "Lou" died Friday night at his home in Bessemer. Funeral services will be held today at 2:30 o'clock from the Macedonia Methodist Church nine miles north of Tuscaloosa on the Crabbe Road with the Rev. J. C. Maske officiating. Burial will be in the church cemetery by Jones and Seigner.

Serving Mr. Turner are his widow, Mrs. Wille Dean Franklin Turner and two children, Ann, aged 4 and Wayne, aged 2; four brothers, Cleo Turner and Fred Turner of Peterson in this county; Sam and George Turner of the US Army; one sister, Miss Maude Turner of Bessemer

Pallbearers for the funeral will be John Hagler, Frank Lafoy, Harwood Hamner, Nathan Chism, Roy Rushing and Eugene Tierce.

**Turner, John Johnson**: December 7, 1885-December 22, 1941

Grave # 92.

**Turner, Martha**: September 24, 1926-March 28, 2007

Grave #318A

Martha was the wife of James Clifton Turner and the daughter of Byrdie "Byrd" Franklin Shirley (March 17, 1880-November 17, 1932) and Matilda Ann Shirley (September 9, 1884-January 6, 1957).

Martha Shirley Turner was a sister to John Ester Shirley (married to Annie Snow Rushing), Lonnie Lee Shirley (married to Estelle Wedgeworth), Grady Edward Shirley (married to Margaret Watkins), Fannie Lou Shirley Hamner (married to Edward Bruce Hamner), B. F. Shirley (married to Mary Alice Turner), Ruby Alene Shirley Mills (married to Erman Mills), and Emma Frances Shirley Hamner (married to Oll Dee Hamner).

All the above are buried in Macedonia Cemetery.

She was also a sister to Joan Davis and Sue Lake who are not buried in Macedonia Cemetery.

**Turner, Mattie K.**: January 20, 1925-March 24, 1978

Grave # 293)

**Turner, Sam T.**: May 26, 1923-August 12, 1985

Grave # 292)

**Turner, Vina Cordelia**: October 18, 1887-October 18, 1932

Grave # 93

Vina was a sister to Matilda Smith Shirley (wife of Byrd Shirley). Vina was the wife of John L. Turner.

**Utley, Netta Ann**: November 12, 1935-October 28, 1937

# MACEDONIA CEMETERY

Grave # 123

Netta Ann was the daughter of Clyde Buel Utley and Clara Bell "Jim" Rushing.

Clara Bell "Jim" Rushing was the daughter of Thomas Hillman "Jack" Rushing and Annie Brazile Hamner.

Thomas Hillman "Jack" Rushing and Anne Brazeal Hamner Rushing are buried in Macedonia Cemetery. Netta Ann's parents are buried in Tuscaloosa Memorial Park.

**Obit for Netta Ann Utley:**

A *Tuscaloosa News* article of October 29, 1937 reads, "Netta Ann Utley, daughter of Mr. and Mrs. Clyde B. Utley of Northport died at her home last night following a short illness. Funeral services were to be held at 2:30 p. m. this afternoon from the Macedonia Church with the Reverend Trim Powell officiating. Jones and Spigener will direct interment in the church cemetery.

Active pallbearers will be Dawson Chism, James Rushing, Chester Utley, Harwood Hamner, Buddy Mayfield, and Jimmy Maxwell.

Honorary pallbearers will include Albert Holman, John Cole, Fayette Shamblin, Leon T. Chism, Hamner Dunn, and Dr. W. D. Partlow."

**Utley, Oleta Lee**: no date

Grave # 139

There is no date on her tombstone. Her obit in the January 23, 1938 *Tuscaloosa News* reads, "Funeral services for Mrs. Herman Utley, 24, were held at 3:00 o'clock Sunday afternoon from the residence of G. H. Utley of Northport followed by burial in Macedonia Cemetery by Jones and Seigner. Mrs. Utley died Saturday at the home of her parents at Havana after a long illness.

Surviving beside her parents and husband is one sister.

**David Walker**: October 22, 1938-September 3, 2005

Grave #159A

**Walker, Inf. son of Lewis B. & Mary Walker**: May 27, 1928

Grave # 177

**Walker, J. L.**: April 19, 1875-May 13, 1927

Grave # 174

**Walker, John**: February 23, 1933.

Grave # 178. He was the infant son of L. B. and Mary Walker.

**Walker, Mary Jane**: August 14, 1911-October 15, 1981

Grave # 158.

She was the wife of Lewis B. Walker

**Walker, Lewis B.**: February 24, 1906-February 17, 1975. Grave # 157. He was the husband of Mary Jane Walker.

**Walker, Samuel A.**: January 30, 1912-August 22, 1925

Grave # 175.

**Walker, Samuel P. Jr.**: April 22, 1973-December 16, 1991

Grave # 159.

**Whatley, Eugenie F.**: July 23, 1878-January 19, 1934

Grave # 186

**Whatley, Thomas A.**: 1874-1942

Grave # 186A

**Obit for Thomas Whatley dated March 9, 1942**

Last rites for Thomas Whatley, 86, who died Monday at his home on the Byler Road will be held at 4:00 p.m. today from Macedonia Methodist Church on the Crabbe Road with internment in the church cemetery by Jones and Spigener. The Rev. Ralph Taylor of Canton, Mississippi will officiate at the rites.

Mr. Whaley had been in ill health for only a short time. He was a lifelong resident of this county.

Surviving are two sons, Paul and Bernice Whatley of Tuscaloosa, and a daughter Mrs. Mattie Sue Taylor of Northport.

Active pallbearers for the rites will be Lark Hamner, Newt Hamner, James S. Clements, T. D. LaFoy, Charlie Newman and Mr. Rushing.

**Woodall, Ronnie**: July 4, 1959-September

15, 1969
 Grave # 233

March 3, 1981
 Grave # 282

**Worrell, Stella Stamps**: January 6, 1903-

CHAPTER 4

# Churches

## MACEDONIA METHODIST CHURCH

According to available information, the first gathering of people that would constitute Macedonia Methodist Church occurred in the late 1880s in a small windowless wood shed near the north end of Macedonia Cemetery. The cemetery had been established as a burial ground at least twenty years earlier. The history of the cemetery is given in a separate chapter.

Unfortunately, no organized history of the church has been preserved. Written copies of the church membership roll for certain years are available, but are sorely lacking in completeness. Moreover, the cursive penmanship is difficult to read. It is from those tattered and torn church records that I write the history of the church prior to the 1940s. I also draw from the wealth of material that is available in the family archives of the Rushing, Shirley, Tierce, LaFoy, Boyd, and Hagler families.

The material written on Macedonia history during the 1940s and 1950s comes primarily from my personal involvement in the church.

From its beginning, the Macedonia congregation was associated with the Northport Circuit of the Tuscaloosa District of the North Alabama Conference of the Methodist Episcopal Church South. The following ministers served the church.

E. P. Craddock, 1886
W. L. Miles, 1889
W. S. Gregory, 1890
P. A. Doss, 1891
E. S. Emerson, 1892
_____ Jennings, 1894
R. L. Abernathy, 1895
Leslie Hartee, 1896
J. M. McColeskey, 1897
Robert Erbole, 1898
H.V. Emerson, 1889
H.F. Crim, 1900
W.T. Hamby, 1901
P. A. Doss, 1902
_____ Barnes, 1903
_____ Knowles, 1904
P. V. McCoy, 1905-1906
P. A. Doss, 1907-1909
C. L. Ellis, 1920
J. L. Powell, 1924-1927
J. K. McKnight, 1928
F. L. Gillespi, 1930
J. F. Puer, 1931-1934
J. L. Salman, 1936-1938
C. L. Hollis, 1939
J.C. Crim, 1940
Guy Smith, 1941
J. C. Maske, 1942-1946
E.S. Jackson, 1947
H. B. Holt, 1948-1949
F. L. Thornbury, 1950-1951
Wayne Graham, 1950-1953

George King, 1953-1954
W. J. Hurst, 1954-1955
T. H. Wilson, 1955-1957

**Infant baptisms**
Alley L. Hamner, September 25, 1892,
Robin F. Hamner, September 25, 1892
W. T. Hamner, September 25, 1892
E. A. Hamner, September 25, 1892
Frances E. Tierce, September 25, 1892
Susie L. Tierce, September 25, 1892
Elyot A. Tierce, September 25, 1892
E. l. Tierce, September 25, 1892
J. T. Tierce, September 25, 1892

**Register of adult baptisms**
Jennie Hamner, September 3, 1893
Martha J. Lesley, September 3, 1893
Sarah A. Sexton, September 3, 1893
Benjamin Hamner, September 3, 1893
Zimri Hardin, November 3, 1889

**Register of marriages**
Eugene Benjaman Tierce, Sr. to Veturia Scales on January 15, 1889
E. L. Tierce to Verona Bedford on February 16, 1906

**Early Macedonia Church members**
The following people are listed on early church membership rolls. To present the entire list is a task too difficult. I have selected a few that represent members of families that lived in the community during the early years of the church's existence.
Frances C. Tierce
Etta Tierce
Mrs. Polly Anne Sexton
Robert Deason
James Deason
Tomie Deason
Susie Tierce
Dollie Stine
Jack Rushing, 1904

Macedonia Church shown in 1902

Byrd Shirley, 1904
Goldman Rushing, 1904
Josh Rushing, 1904
Jack Clements, 1904
Tom Cooper, 1904
Elliott Tierce, 1904
Memnon Tierce, 1904
Bennie House, 1904
Bascom Chism 1904
Collier Tierce
Victor Tierce
Author Stine
William Elmore
Brizzie Rushing
Fannie Rushing Snider
Janie Gay
Sarah Hamner Stines
Pearl Lloyd
Connie Smith Turner
Matilda Smith Shirley
Fannie Tierce
Viola Hamner
Emma Clements
Octavia Tierce Hagler
Tom LaFoy
Addie LaFoy
Lizzie LaFoy
Donia House
Verona Tierce, 1905
N. J. Hamner, 1906

# CHURCHES

Maggie Turner Booth, 1906
May Stines Poe, 1906
Eula Stines Sutton, 1906
Nellia Stines Sumer 1906
N. L. House, 1904
Earley Monroe Hyche, 1907
Lenora Belle "Lou" Rushing Hyche, 1907
Robert Rushing, 1907
Robert Gay, 1907
Pastor P. A. Doss, 1907
S. F. Eads, 1907
M. J. Gay, 1907
Mr. and Mrs. M. H. Turner, 1907
Mrs. J. E. Gay, 1907
David Yates, 1907
Gene Logan Hamner, 1907
W. T. Osborn, 1907
Mrs. Lela Tierce, 1907
Geoge Clements, 1908
Edna Thomas Watkins, 1907
Lula Evans, 1907
Emma House, 1907
Pearl Turner, 1907
J. King, 1907
Travis Doss, 1907
Mrs. Fannie King, 1907
Mrs. Myrtie Rushing Thomas, 1907
Samson Clements pastor, 1907
Hewett Rushing, 1907
Herman Thomas, 1907
Festus Shirley
N. J. Eads
W. A. Boyd, Aney Beck Boyd — husband and wife
Boyd children: Lillie Boyd, Lee Boyd, Early Boyd 1918
Clara Bell Rushing
Rob Tierce
May Lee LaFoy
Essie Queen Hamner LaFoy
Mary Lee LaFoy
Pastor C. L. Ellis
Mrs. Nellie Tierce, 1916
Trimm W. Hamner, 1920

Nannie Bell LaFoy, 1920
Lillian Cook Grady, 1920
Mae Bell Hamner, 1920
Vera Clements, 1920
Curtis Hamner, 1920
Lonnie Shirley, 1920
Eugene B. Tierce, Jr., 1920
Cora King Cannon, 1920
Jeff Sanders, 1920
Nora Turner Rushing, 1920
Azilee Rushing, 1920
Tommie M. Clements, 1920
Mrs. Jenie Turner, 1920
Mrs. Ida Shirley, 1920
Pastor J. T. Powell, 1920
David Rushing, 1920
Lula Hall Smith, 1920
Wayland Hyche, 1920
Thelma Rushing Cooper, 1920
Pastor C. L. Ellis, 1920
Louise Tierce, 1920
J. M. Thomas, 1920
R.E. Smith, 1920
Annie Bell Willard, 1920
\_\_\_\_\_ Rigsby, 1920
George Smalley
Martha Smalley Taylor
Mirtie Sexton
Andrew Sexton
Mrs. \_\_\_\_\_ Criswell
Mrs. Odessa Lewis
Henry Watkins
Minnie L. Hagler Taylor
John M. Hagler
Lizzie Hagler
Jennie Whatley
Marion Mackey
Albert Taylor
Lester Taylor
Martha Hamner
Sam Hamner
Jessie Allen
Leon Chism
Verner LaFoy

Macedonia Church First Sunday in May dinner on the ground

James Willie "Will" Rushing
Fannie Gay Rushing
Clara Shirley
Pricie Shirley
Ida Clements
Della Harkey
Gladys Hagler
Albert Hagler
Annie Turner
Susie Turner

## MACEDONIA UNITED METHODIST CHURCH, 2024

After meeting in the small building at the north end of the cemetery for the first few years after its formation, in 1902 the church erected a permanent building right beside the Crabbe Road adjacent to the south end of the cemetery. This building served as the meeting house both for preaching and Sunday School until it was damaged beyond repair by a tornado in the spring of 1945. I have vivid recall of that building.

The 1902 structure had only one room and could seat approximately 100 people. Homemade sheets made of cottonseed sacks were used to divide the large room into two rooms where Sunday School classes met—one for children under age twelve and one for teenagers. Adults met in the area not partitioned off. The pews were old, uncomfortable, and must have been original to the building.

A 1945 spring tornado dislodged the building from its pillars. No damage was done to the pulpit, pulpit chair, and piano. These three items were stored in the large center hallway in our home until a new building could be built. The new building was located between the 1902 church building and the cemetery.

The first task was to bulldoze a hole for the basement. The Tuscaloosa County Road Commission which was under my father's supervision provided a bulldozer and other equipment at no cost to the church to excavate the basement. Church member Grady Shirley brought his construction crew and erected the new building. Within a couple of months, the building was ready for occupancy. As it was late spring and early summer, Sunday School was held outdoors during construction. We children thought that was really neat. Lumber for the building was sawed and planed by another church member,

# CHURCHES

Collier Tierce, whose mill was one mile north of the church. Sadly, Mr. Tierce's funeral was the first to be held in the new church. He was killed in a sawmill accident on August 15, 1946.

**December 8, 1932 *The Tuscaloosa News* page 2**
Miss Mabel Hamner was hostess Saturday night at her home when the cabinet members of Macedonia Church Epworth league held their monthly business meeting.

Glyndon Newman, president, presided with Annie Snow Rushing leading the devotional. Waylon Hyche talked on "Faults of the League" and plans for raising money for the league were discussed and a finance committee appointed. Miss Hamner, assisted by Misses Nell and Azilee Rushing led the devotional.

The regular meeting of the League will take place Sunday evening at 6 o'clock with an interesting program and Curtis Hamner leading the devotional.

**January 29, 1934, *The Tuscaloosa News***
Many friends in this community attended services held last week in Macedonia Methodist Church for Will Rushing who died following several months of illness which confined him to his home. The Rev. Trimm Powell, the Rev. M. R. Smith, and the Rev. C. R. Manderson jointly conducted the services with burial in the church cemetery. Mr. Rushing is survived by his widow, Mrs. Fanny Rushing, and two daughters, Azilee and Annie Snow Rushing and other relatives. His passing is widely mourned in Lafoy by friends and family members.

**March 3, 1938 *The Tuscaloosa News*, page 3**
The Patterson Chapel League met recently in the home of Mrs. Jack Mills for a business session. A large crowd of young people attended the meeting. An interesting program was presented.

Lester Rigsby was a recent visitor in the home of Sim Patterson.

Jack Rigsby was a recent visitor of Lester Rigsby.

Mrs. Collier Tierce and Miss Maude Turner were recent guests in the home of Miss Edna Rigsby.

Mrs. L. Dunn of Patterson Chapel, Miss Margaret Tatum, Ollie Mae Clements, and Miss Edna Sullivan of Windham Springs were recent guests of Mr. and Mrs. Sellers and children. Dick Hagler and family of Northport Route 1 were recent guests of J. Albert Taylor.

**March 27, 1938 *The Tuscaloosa News* page 8**
**Patterson Chapel Church**
Sunday School will be held at 10 o'clock Sunday morning at Patterson Chapel Church. Prayer meeting is held at the church each Sunday at 7:00 p.m.

The public is invited to attend the services.

**Growing up in Macedonia Church**
One of my favorite proverbs comes from the early 18th century: "As the twig is bent, so grows the tree." Indeed, early in life influences have a permanent effect. That is certainly true of my growing up years at Macedonia.

My Sunday School teachers while I was in grade school included Mrs. John Shirley and Mrs. Roy Rushing who later in life would become my mother-in-law. As a youth, Mrs. John Hangler and Mrs. Mary Alice Shirley were my teachers. Mrs. Grady Shirley worked with us in MYF activities. In actuality, the entire small congregation of 50-60 people all had a strong positive influence on me.

Prior to the early 1950s, the only heat was supplied by a single pot-bellied wood-burning stove near the front of the church. Mr. John Hagler arrived about thirty minutes prior to Sunday School to get a fire roaring in the stove, but even so, the sanctuary was still cold two hours later when the preaching service ended at noon. The basement had no heat unless one of the teachers brought a small electric heater from home. In those days, people wore very heavy clothing in the winter to keep warm. In the early 1950s, four butane gas space heaters were installed in the sanctuary and one in each of the Sunday School rooms downstairs.

Separate outdoor privies for men and women were in the woods behind the church. The sanctuary windowpanes were clear glass. This allowed members to glance outside from time to time and watch butterflies, squirrels, and birds if one got tired of listening to the preacher.

A kitchen and eating area were added to the south side of the basement in the late 1950s. It was a one-story structure with a flat roof that from the outside was level with the windows in the sanctuary.

The old sanctuary will always have a special place in my heart for it was there that Peggy and I married on June 2, 1962.

In the early 1960s, a new sanctuary was built along with new Sunday School rooms. The old basement and kitchen area were turned into a beautiful fellowship hall and all kitchen appliances replaced with new ones. Frequent fellowship luncheons were thoroughly enjoyed by all.

**Special preachers**

**Reverend H. B. Holt**
Reverend H. B. Holt served as pastor 1948-1949. At the annual revival in August of 1948, I went forward at the time of invitation at the close of the service and accepted Christ as my Lord and Savior. I will never forget the wonderful expression on his face as I looked into his eyes and told him my intent.

**Reverend J. C. Maske,**
Reverend J. C. Maske served as pastor 1942-1946. Macedonia was on a circuit with three other churches—Patterson's Chapel, Union Chapel, and Jennings Chapel. As a result, Macedonia had a preaching service only twice a month—on the first Sunday morning and the

Macedonia Church building built in the early 1970s

third Sunday night. On the first Sunday night, he preached at Patterson's Chapel which was about three miles north of our house.

Our family was one of two or three families that provided Sunday lunch to the preacher and his wife each Sunday they were at Macedonia. Preacher Maske enjoyed raising a few animals including sheep. One Sunday the talk around our dining room table involved a discussion of sheep. We had never had a sheep.

One thing led to another including a bartering session. The outcome was that after Sunday lunch he would return to the parsonage at Jennings Chapel, take a nap, feed the animals, and load one sheep in the trunk of his car. That night he would drive right in front of our house on his way to Patterson's Chapel. He would release the sheep from the car and put it in the pasture in front of our house. He then drove on to Patterson's Chapel and preached the night sermon. On his way back home after the preaching service, he would retrieve one of Mother's prize roosters which she had put in our mailbox. I never forgot the strange way we swapped a rooster for a sheep. Mary, the sheep, became a real pet.

**Reverend T. H. Wilson**
Reverend T. H. Wilson served as pastor 1955-1957. He was an elderly retired preacher but came back into the ministry to serve as our pas-

tor.

The most important influence he had on my life was that he rejuvenated our youth program, the MYF. During my lifetime, up to 1957 Macedonia had no youth program although it was very active in the 1930s and 1940s. I became a leader in the youth group and several adults served as chaperones. One of the biggest events of the year was summer camp that was held at Camp Sumatanga at Gallant, Alabama.

**Recent years**

As has been experienced in most rural Methodist churches over the past fifty years, attendance and membership at Macedonia has dropped drastically. Today, there remains a handful of faithful members who struggle to carry on. They are a wonderful group of Christians. Only God knows what the future holds for Macedonia Church.

## CARROLLS CREEK BAPTIST CHURCH

No records have been found that tell the exact site of Carrolls Creek Baptist Church when it first met in 1842 on land owned by John H. Carrolls. Carrolls Creek is named for Mr. Carrolls.

From 1842 until the 1870s, little of the church's activities is available. It is not known how often the church met but it is likely that traveling preachers preached to the small congregation from time to time. prior to the church calling its first pastor in 1879. The church was constituted in 1877 and was accepted into fellowship with the Tuscaloosa County Baptist Association in September 1878. On April 3, 1879, the church called its first pastor, Joseph W. Hosmer. Hosmer was married to John Carrolls' daughter.

Sometime after 1867, a building known as the Grange Building was constructed at what today is the intersection of the Martin Road and the Crabbe Road. The Grange Building was built by local farmers as a place where they could meet and discuss community affairs. The building consisted of one large room that had three windows on each side, two front doors, and a back door.

The Grange building served as the church meeting house until March 29, 1942 at which time it caught fire and burned. For a while, services were held at Union Chapel Methodist Church on the two Sundays that the Methodist did not meet.

The Lafoy School had closed in 1941, and in 1942 Carrolls Creek Baptist Church bought the old vacant school house and held church there until a new building could be built across the Crabbe Road. The new church was completed in 1952.

## NEWSPAPER ARTICLES REGARDING CRABBE ROAD CHURCHES

**April 2, 1913, *The Breeze***
**Carrolls Creek Baptist**
We are always glad to get the *Breeze*.

Farmers are still trying to farm a little on Carrolls Creek and North River, but things look gloomy since the storm on the 10th which did much damage here. Much damage was done to Mr. James Clements and Mr. Bill Aaron, but worst of all, it nearly ruined Lafoy School house. The old one was blown several hundred yards away, and the new one was picked up by the wind and stove into the ground. We are thankful though that no one was killed. We earnestly hope that we will not have any more like that soon. The wind damaged Mr. J. E. Hamner about $100. I am sorry for him, but it could have been worse. We will have to pray more and work harder.

Everybody looked good at Sunday School after the storm.

We had a fine Sunday School at Carrolls Creek last Sunday. Fifty pupils enrolled.

Miss Pearl and Mr. Hall are all smiles.

Mr. Hall of Bessemer was with us last Sunday. We are glad to have him with us and remember

# A ROAD, A CEMETERY, A PEOPLE

The picture is erroneously labeled "Lafoy School." Rather, it is Carrolls Creek Baptist Church. The building is the Grange building.

the good work he did with us at Carrolls Creek.

Our church looks so much better since it was painted. We are going to have a rally day before long, and I know the folks will be there then, but that is all right. We will put the chicken to them that day. We want everybody to come.

Miss Corine looks like she is just about ready to say "yes."

Mr. Sam Gay is still hitching his mule at Mrs. Thomas'.

Our school teacher has gone home and Richard Gay looks very sad.

We are looking and praying to meet our pastor before long to tell us how we are living. Good wishes to all.

**March 20, 1919** *The Tuscaloosa News*
Lafoy School is progressing, and we are delighted with our teachers, Miss Anabel McElroy and Miss Annabel Beaver, both of Cuba, Alabama. We believe they are trying to do the right thing for the children.

Health is good in our community.

Mr. Bernice Whatley has purchased a new motor car.

There will be preaching at Carrolls Creek Baptist Church next Sunday.

We have good singings at Lafoy school house every Sunday afternoon.

Miss Bertice Rushing is spending the week in Northport with her cousin, Miss Thelma Rushing.

Mrs. Myrtie Thomas is spending a week with her daughter Mrs. Curtis Watkins at Buhl, Alabama.

**April 13, 1924** *The Tuscaloosa News*
J. C. Clements came home Wednesday night after sawmilling for a few days on the Watermelon Road for Fred Hilliard of Tuscaloosa.

There will be a singing at Lafoy school house Sunday afternoon at 1:30 o'clock, which will be conducted by Mr. Leon T. Chism and other good singers of the county. Everybody is invited to come.

**November 29, 1927** *The Tuscaloosa News*
Rev. McWright will preach at Macedonia Methodist Church on December 4 at 11:00 a.m. Everybody is invited.

There will be preaching services at Carrolls Creek Baptist Church on Sunday at 11:00 a.m. December 27 with Reverend Manderson preaching. Everybody is urged to attend.

**December 7, 1927** *The Tuscaloosa News*
Preaching at Macedonia Methodist Church will take place this Sunday at 11:00 a.m. The new pastor, Rev. McWright, will preach his first sermon for this church. Everybody has a hearty invitation to attend this service, and a royal welcome is extended the new pastor.

Sunday School is held at Lafoy school house every Sunday afternoon at 2:30 p.m. Goldman Rushing, member of Macedonia, is superintendent. You are extended a good invitation by this Sunday School. Come! God has need of you and is depending on you, for his harvest truly is great and his laborers are few. So, come for your Master while He has need of you.

Preaching services are held at Carrolls Creek Baptist Church every fourth Sunday both in the morning and in the evening. Reverend Manderson is pastor. He always has a spiritual message for his hearers.

At Lafoy school house on next Saturday night, December 10, there will be a social entertainment, box supper, and many nice things will be on exhibit for sale. Chicken pie is a leader. The public is cordially invited to come and dine. The proceeds are to be used for the filling of two boxes that will be sent to two orphanages: one at Selma (Methodist) and one at Troy (Baptist). Come and help us act Santa for these precious little ones whom the Sunday School has adopted for the Yuletide.

**August 12, 1928** *The Tuscaloosa News*
The Reverend Manderson pastor of Carrolls Creek Baptist Church will conduct preaching every fourth Sunday at 11:00 a.m. Hear him for he always produces a wonderful message for his congregation.

Sunday School is held at the Lafoy school house every Sunday afternoon at 2:30. Goldman Rushing, member of Macedonia, is superintendent. You are heartedly welcomed, so come. We need you and God is depending on you. So, fill the place God so sweetly calls you. Hear and do your best to help make this school a school for Christ.

**August 23, 1928** *The Tuscaloosa News*
Macedonia will hold preaching services every second Sunday, both morning and evening with the pastor, Reverend McKnight of Booneville. The Rev. Mr. Fitts and Rev. McKnight have closed a series of meeting. Thirteen new members were added to the church.

Carrolls Creek Baptist Church has preaching every fourth Sunday at 11:00 o'clock by the Rev. Mr. Manderson. All are invited to church and to Sunday school every Sunday afternoon at 2:30 at Lafoy school house.

In conclusion, in 2024 Carrolls Creek Baptist Church is a very active and growing church.

# A ROAD, A CEMETERY, A PEOPLE

CHAPTER 5

# Crabbe Road, First Settlers

Descendants of William Taylor Hamner, Sr. have been and remain richly entwined in my life. We are neighbors. For decades, we have worshiped together. During my childhood and youth years, members of the Hamner family were classmates at Northport Elementary School and Tuscaloosa County High School. We rode the same school bus, attended church together, and stood beside one another as our loved ones were lowered into graves in Macedonia Cemetery. It was my privilege to serve as family physician for several many members of the family. My wife, Peggy Rushing Boyd, is a great, great granddaughter of William Taylor Hamner, Sr., patriarch of the local Hamner clan. Peggy is an avid scrapbook collector. Her collection contains a lot of Hamner family material much of which I include in this memoir.

**THE TAYLOR HAMNER, SR., FAMILY**

William Taylor Hamner, Sr., arrived in Tuscaloosa County, Alabama circa late 1820s and acquired land in an area six miles north of Northport on the Crabbe Road near North River. The community became known as the Lafoy Community, named after another family of early arrivals to the area.

In 1981, Geneal Hamner Black and Mary Clark Ryan, descendants of William Taylor Hamner Sr., published *Hamner Heritage—Beginning Without End,* a history of the Hamner family. In pulling together material for this memoir, *Hamner Heritage Beginning Without End* has proven invaluable. Rather than using standard footnotes when citing material taken from *Hamner Heritage Beginning Without End,* I insert the page number in *Hamner Heritage Beginning Without End* at the end of the paragraph.

William Taylor Hamner, Sr. was born in Oglethorpe, Georgia, circa 1814, possibly as late as 1817. He died July 10, 1889, and is buried in grave # 2 in Macedonia Cemetery. Within the last few decades, an unidentified person has placed a marker at his grave with the wording, "1814-1889 Co. G 3 Ala Reg CSA." The marker acknowledges that he was a member of the Confederate Army during the Civil War. However, according to *Hamner Heritage—Beginning Without End*, he was in the Confederate reserves. He never served in active duty.

According to family tradition, William Taylor Hamner, Sr. acquired approximately 1,000 acres of land on the Crabbe Road near its juncture with North River. After clearing the land of trees, Hamner began to farm. The soil was fertile and ideal for growing cotton, corn, fruits, and vegetables. He also operated a sawmill and used lumber made from the virgin forest to construct his first home, a two-room log cabin with a wide dogtrot separating the two rooms. A wide porch extended across the front of the log cabin. Much later a large kitchen was added to the rear of the cabin. As his family grew to include sixteen children born by three of his four wives, several small lean-to rooms were added. There is no evidence he ever owned slaves. The farm work was done by his children and hired help.

William T. Hamner, Sr. was married four times. Three wives died leaving him a widower and one marriage ended in divorce. Two children were born by his first wife. Her name is not known. Thirteen children were born by his second wife, Permelia Chism. He divorced his third wife, Ella Hester Johns Stanley, by whom he had no children. He had one child by his fourth wife, Eglantine Ellen "Tiny" Stanley. (*Hamner Heritage,* pages 126-128).

**William Taylor Hamner, Sr.'s 1st marriage**
**Two children**
The name of William Taylor Hamner, Sr.'s first wife is not known nor is the date of her death known. However, her death was prior to 1845 because in 1845 William T. Taylor, Sr. had married a second time, to Permelia Chism, and the first child of that marriage, John Pruett Hamner, was born October 4, 1845. William T. Taylor, Sr.'s first wife is buried beside him in Macedonia Cemetery. The headstone is a simple rock without an inscription.

William Taylor Hamner Sr.'s first marriage produced two children: George Harrison Hamner and Thomas Wingfield Hamner.

George Harrison Hamner was born March 12, 1837, and died February 13, 1901. George Harrison married Sarah "Sally" McGee. George and Sally are buried in Macedonia Cemetery (*Hamner Heritage,* page 155.)

Thomas Wingfield Hamner's date of birth is not certain. He was married twice and lived, died, and is buried in Fayette County (*Hamner Heritage,* page 172).

**William Taylor Hamner, Sr.'s 2nd marriage**
**Permelia Chism**
**Thirteen children**
William Taylor Hamner, Sr.'s second marriage was to Permelia Chism. She was born circa 1825 and died August 10, 1874. The date of their marriage is not known. Their first child, John Pruett Hamner, was born October 4, 1845. Both William Taylor Hamner, Sr. and Permelia Chism Hamner are buried in Macedonia Cemetery next to his first wife (*Hamner Heritage,* page 126). The marriage to Permelia produced thirteen children.

John Pruitt Hamner
James T. Hamner
William Taylor Hamner, Jr.
Louis Alfred Hamner
Marshall Dee Hamner
Ezekiel Anders Hamner
Frances Louisa "Fannie" Hamner
Dovy Ann Hamner
Martha Elizabeth "Matt" Hamner
Louise J. "Lucy" Hamner
Sally Ann Hamner
Arminta "Minta" Hamner
Alabama B. Hamner

**William Taylor Hamner, Sr.'s 3rd marriage**
**Ella Hester Johns Stanley**
**No children, marriage ended in divorce**
When William Taylor Hamner, Sr.'s second wife, Permelia Chism, died on August 10, 1874, he was left with several small children to rear. He needed a wife.

On November 25, 1874, three months after his second wife's death, he married a third wife, Ella Hester Johns Stanley. Ella was the widow of John W. Stanley. Ella had six children by John Stanley. Ella Hester and William Taylor Hamner, Sr. had no children. They divorced after a short marriage. She moved to Texas to be near family. Hamner called her "Madam Run-a-way." (*Hamner Heritage,* page 339.)

## William Taylor Hamner, Sr. 4th marriage Eglantine Ellen "Tiny" Brittain
**One child**

William Taylor Hamner, Sr. married a 4th time on March 31, 1881 to twenty-one-year-old Eglantine Ellen "Tiny" Brittain. On January 15, 1887, Eglantine Ellen gave birth to Mary Ann Matilda Hamner. William Taylor Hamner, Sr. was seventy-three-years-old at the time. Leaving a two-year-old daughter, William Taylor Hamner, Sr. died July 10, 1889. Ellen died June 15, 1932. She is buried in Mt. Olive Baptist Church Cemetery (*Hamner Heritage*, page 339).

## Children of William Taylor Hamner, Sr. and Permelia Chism and their spouses

It is far beyond my ability and desire to include in this memoir a summary of all of William Taylor Hamner, Sr.'s family. That work is already available in *Hamner Heritage*. My goal here is to limit comments to just a few personal memories of several Hamner family members.

As noted earlier, my wife, Peggy Rushing Boyd, is a great, great, granddaughter of William Taylor Hamner, Sr. Her paternal family, the Rushing family, descends from Joseph Enoch Rushing, another early-arrival in the Lafoy Community. Four marriages occurred between the Hamner and Rushing families to which I give attention.

## Marriages and site of burial of William Taylor Hamner, Sr. and Permelia Chism's Thirteen children

Thirteen children were born to William T. Hamner, Sr. and Permelia Chism, his second wife.

**Child one:**
**John Pruitt Hamner** was born on October 4, 1845, and died on December 18, 1905. John Pruitt married Annie Margaret Hall on April 2, 1866. Both are buried in Macedonia Cemetery (*Hamner Heritage*, page 182).

**Child two:**
**James T. Hamner** was born circa 1846, and died before 1860. Little is known of him (*Hamner Heritage*, page 236).

**Child three:**
**William Taylor Hamner, Jr.** was born on April 2, 1847, and died on December 28, 1928. He married Emma Alabama Shirley. He is buried in Bethel Cemetery. He taught school in Lafoy School (*Hamner Heritage*, page 236).

**Child four:**
**Louis Alfred Hamner** was born on March 9, 1851. The date of his death is not known. He married Penina Wilson Clements. Both are buried in the old Alberta City Methodist Cemetery in Tuscaloosa (*Hamner Heritage*, page 247).

**Child five:**
**Marshall Dee Hamner** was born in February 1852, and died on May 11, 1904. He never married. His will was probated on June 15, 1904, and it is very interesting to read (*Hamner Heritage*, page 267).

**Child six:**
**Ezekiel Anders Hamner** was born in March 1854, and died in October 1899. He married Mary Jane McGee. Both are buried in Bethel Cemetery (*Hamner Heritage*, page 272).

**Child seven: Frances Louisa "Fannie" Hamner** was born on April 9, 1855, and died on October 15, 1938. She was married three times and is buried in Texas. (*Hamner Heritage*, page 299).

**Child eight:**
**Dovy Ann Hamner** was born in October 1856, and died between 1901-1903. She married George Washington Chism. They are buried in Macedonia Cemetery (*Hamner Heritage*, page 304). Dovy Ann married a second time to Nicholas "Nick" House (*Hamner Heritage*, page 309). He is buried in Macedonia Cemetery.

**Child nine:**
**Martha Elizabeth "Matt" Hamner** was born on February 7, 1858, and died on August 18, 1934. She married William Samuel Brittian. They are buried in Mt. Olive Baptist Church Cemetery (*Hamner Heritage*, page 312).

**Child ten:**
**Louise J. "Lucy" Hamner** was born circa 1863, and died in 1938. She was married twice. She moved to Texas but later moved back to Talladega, Alabama where she is buried (*Hamner Heritage*, page 319).

**Child eleven: Sally Ann Hamner** was born on April 20, 1862, and died on October 29, 1942. She married Ozzie "Sonny" Sanders. They are buried in Mt. Olive Baptist Church Cemetery (*Hamner Heritage*, page 325).

**Child twelve:**
**Arminta "Minta" Hamner** was born in December 1868. She was blind or near-blind. She never married and is buried in Macedonia Cemetery (*Hamner Heritage*, page 335).

**Child thirteen:**
**Alabama B. Hamner** was born on May 16, 1871, and died on September 17, 1917. She married William Zebulon Watkins. They are buried in Evergreen Cemetery in Tuscaloosa. (*Hamner Heritage*, page 337).

## THE JOHN PRUETT HAMNER FAMILY

### John Pruitt Hamner

John Pruett Hamner was the third child of William T. Hamner, Sr. and Permelia Chism and the first child to live to adulthood.

Of the thirteen children born to William T. Hamner, Sr. and Permelia Chism, I am most familiar with the family members of their third child, John Pruitt Hamner and his wife Annie Margaret Hall. This is partially explained by the fact that four of my wife's cousins married members of the John Pruitt Hamner family.

John Pruitt Hamner was born on October 4, 1845, and died on December 18, 1905. On April 22, 1866, he married Annie Margaret Hall who was born on January 10, 1846, and died on January 2, 1931. Both John Pruitt and Annie Margaret are buried in Macedonia Cemetery. John Pruitt Hamner sired thirteen children by Annie Margaret Hall (*Hamner Heritage,* page 182).

### The thirteen children of John Pruitt Hamner and Annie Margaret Hall

The thirteen children of John Pruitt Hamner and Annie Margaret Hall include the following: (*Hamner Heritage*, page 186).

An infant daughter was born and died on June 8, 1876. She is buried Macedonia Cemetery.

Mary Ulalah Virginia Hamner was born on December 14, 1868, and died on January 29, 1869. She is buried in Macedonia Cemetery.

Oliver Jackson Hamner was born on September 1, 1871, and died on October 11, 1938. He is buried in Macedonia Cemetery.

John Earley Hamner was born on September 21, 1873 and died on November 7, 1952. He is buried in Macedonia Cemetery. (*Hamner Heritage*, page 200).

Edward Powell Hamner was born on April 21, 1875, and died on December 29, 1936. He is buried in Macedonia Cemetery (*Hamner Heritage*, page 211).

Beuna Vista Hamner was born on January 27, 1877 and died on February 11, 1965. She is buried in Macedonia Cemetery (*Hamner Heritage*, page 212).

Larkin Rogers Hamner was born on February 2, 1879, and died on April 19, 1955 and is buried in Macedonia Cemetery (*Hamner Heritage*, page 214).

Gillie Pruitt Hamner was born on November 22, 1880, and died on October 19, 1960. He is buried in Tuscaloosa Memorial Park Cemetery (*Hamner Heritage*, page 220)

Annie Brazeal Hamner was born on April 10, 1882, and died on May 21, 1927. She is buried in Macedonia Cemetery (*Hamner Heritage*, page 222).

Permelia Alma Hamner was born on January 15, 1884, and died on February 3, 1970. She is buried in Macedonia Cemetery (*Hamner Heritage*, page 225).

Jacob Cullen Hamner, was born on March 20, 1885, and died on April 23, 1969. He is buried in Tuscaloosa Memorial Park (*Hamner Heritage*, page 229.)

Ozella Judson Hamner was born on October 4, 1887, and died on July 2, 1973. She is buried in Macedonia Cemetery (*Hamner Heritage, 229*).

Ulla Mae Hamner was born on May 2, 1889, and died on July 5, 1936. She is buried in Macedonia Cemetery (*Hamner Heritage*, page 233).

## THE OLIVER "OLLIE" JACKSON HAMNER FAMILY

### Third child of John Pruitt Hamner and Annie Margaret Hall

Oliver "Ollie" Jackson Hamner was born on September 1, 1871, and died on October 11, 1938 (*Hamner Heritage,* page 186). Ollie married Louise Rigsby who was born on February 7, 1875, and died on March 30, 1954. The Rigsby family was another early arrival in the Lafoy Community.

### Ollie Hamner and Louise Rigsby had eight children:

(1) First child: Jesse Pruitt Hamner

Jesse Pruitt Hamner was born on February 28, 1895, and died on December 28, 1968. On September 18, 1919, Pruitt married Ruby Pearson who was born on April 29, 1900, and died on May 4, 1984. Both are buried in Carrolls Creek Baptist Church Cemetery. Pruitt and Ruby had no children. (*Hamner Heritage*, page 190).

(2) Second child: James Webster "Jay" Hamner

James Webster "Jay" Hamner was born on March 21, 1898, and died on March 15, 1970. On December 19, 1920, Jay married Essie Queen Lafoy who was born on August 2, 1903, and died on January 2, 1990. The Lafoy family was another early-arrival family in the community. In fact, the area became known as the Lafoy Community. A rural two-room school near the Lafoy farm carried the name Lafoy School. Jay and Queen are buried in Carrolls Creek Baptist Church Cemetery (*Hamner Heritage*, page 190).

Jay and Queen had two children: (1) J. D. Hamner; (2) Essie Claudine Hamner.

(3) Third child: Loubelle Hamner

Loubelle Hamner was born on December 5, 1899, and died on October 3,1979. On February 11, 1923, Loubelle married Robert Edward Lee Rushing, a son of Joseph Enoch Rushing. Robert Rushing, was born on May 15, 1895, and died on March 16, 1992. This was the first of four marriages between the Rushing and Hamner families. Robert and Loubelle are buried in Macedonia Cemetery. (*Hamner Heritage*, page 192).

Robert Rushing and Loubelle had five daughters: (1) Wilma Maurine Rushing; (2) Margaret Louise Rushing; (3) Melba Lee Rushing; (4) Mary Evelyn "Cricket" Rushing; (5) Mildred Denese Rushing. Mary Evelyn "Cricket" is the only offspring of Loubelle are Robert buried in Macedonia Cemetery.

(4) Fourth child: Edward Bruce Hamner

Edward Bruce Hamer was born on August 25, 1901, and died on February 12, 1986. On February 14, 1926, Bruce married Fannie Lou Shirley, daughter of Byrd Franklin Shirley, Sr., and Matilda Smith Shirley. The Byrd Shirley family was another early-arrival Lafoy Community family. Fannie Lou was born on April 30, 1908, and died on August 17, 1988. Bruce and Fannie Lou are buried in Macedonia Cemetery.

When Bruce and Fannie Lou married, they moved into the kitchen area of the original William Taylor Hamner, Sr. plantation log house. Originally a two-room dogtrot cabin, the house had increased in size as lean-tos and a large kitchen had been added over the years to accommodate William T. Hamner, Sr.'s large family of sixteen children, all of whom were born in the old cabin. The first three of Bruce and Fannie Lou's four children were born while they lived in William T. Hamner, Sr.'s old house. (*Hamner Heritage*, page 194).

Bruce and Fannie Lou's four children include:

(1) Ollie Bruce "Doc" Hamner. He and his wife, Emma Louise Estes Hamner, are buried in Macedonia Cemetery. Ollie and Emma had four children. One of their children, Richard Bruce Hamner was born December 31, 1953, and died as a child on January 12, 1955. He is buried in Macedonia Cemetery; (2) Alvin Franklin Hamner married Eva Mae Guy. They are buried in Memory Hills Memorial Gardens in Tuscaloosa. Alvin and Eva Mae had three daughters; (3) Mary Geneal Hamner married Marion Devaughn Black. They are buried in Macedonia Cemetery. They had two children, a son, and a daughter; (4) Glenda Sheryl Hamner married John Howard Hewitt. They had two sons. The first son, John Howard Hewitt, Jr. was born on April 25, 1961, and died in April 1983. He is buried in Macedonia Cemetery. In 2023, Glenda resides in a local nursing home.

(5) Fifth child: Vera May Hamner

Vera Mae Hamner was born on December 29, 1905, and died on January 27, 1911 from complications of an abscessed tooth. She is buried in Macedonia Methodist Cemetery.

6. Sixth child: Ollie Lee Hamner

Ollie Lee Hamner was born on April 25, 1906, and died on January 4, 1907. He is buried in Macedonia Methodist Cemetery.

7. Seventh child: Oll Dee Hamner

Oll Dee Hamner, the 7th child of Oliver "Ollie" Jackson Hamner and Mary Louise Rigsby, was born on November 6, 1907, and died on September 8, 1993. On December 24, 1938, Oll Dee married Emma Frances Shirley who was born on June 9, 1913, and died on March 10, 2008. Emma Frances was a sister to Fanny Lou Shirley Hamner, the wife of Bruce Hamner. Oll Dee and Emma Frances are buried in Macedonia Cemetery. Following their marriage, they lived in the house Oll Dee's father Oliver "Ollie" Hamner had built as a new home in 1901. In the 1950s, that house was torn down and a new house built on the site. Oll Dee and Frances had one child, Emma Jean Hamner (*Hamner Heritage*, page 197).

8. Eighth child: Hollis Harwood Hamner

Hollis Harwood Hamner was the 8th child of Oliver "Ollie" Jackson Hamner and Mary Louise Rigsby. Harwood was born on March 2, 1910, and was killed in a deer hunting accident on December 12, 1953 (*Hamner Heritage*, page 198). He married Elsie Yow who was born on January 20, 1916, and died on September 10, 1990. Both are buried in Carrolls Creek Baptist Church Cemetery. They had no children.

## THE JOHN EARLEY HAMNER FAMILY

### The fourth child of John Pruitt Hamner and Annie Margaret Hall

John Earley Hamner was the fourth child of John Pruitt Hamner and Annie Margaret Hall. He was born on September 21, 1873, and died on November 7, 1952. He married Rose Anie Viella "Ella" Rigsby on May 26, 1897 *(Hamner Heritage*, page 205). John Earley Hamner and Rose Anie Viella Rigsby are buried in Macedonia Cemetery.

Prior to 1920, John Earley and his brother Oliver "Ollie" Jackson Hamner were in partnership in farming most of the original William Taylor Hamner, Sr.'s plantation on the Crabbe Road near North River. In 1920, the brothers' partnership was dissolved and John Earley and his family moved to Northport where he bought and operated a grocery store.

John Earley and Rose Anie Viella Hamner had seven children: (1) Asa Hamner was born on December 10, 1898; (2) William Claude Hamner was on born March 29, 1900 (3) Houston Augustus Hamner was born on January 13, 1902; (4) Maude Etta Hamner, was born on June 4, 1904; (5) Early Bradford Hamner, was born on August 13, 1906;(6) Nannie Marie Hamner was born on October 18, 1909; (7) Margaret Louise Hamner, was born on April 11, 1920.

## THE EDWARD POWELL "DICK" HAMNER FAMILY

### The fifth child of John Pruitt Hamner and Annie Margaret Hall

Edward Powell "Dick" Hamner was the fifth child of John Pruitt Hamner and Annie Margaret Hall (*Hamner Heritage,* page 211). He was born on April 21, 1875, and married Fannie Maybelle Duncan on December 4, 1905. "Dick" died on December 29, 1936, in Plainview, Texas. His body was brought back and buried in Macedonia Cemetery. Fannie died on September 6, 1946 and is buried in Texas.

Edward Powell "Dick" and Fannie Hamner had four children: (1) Lottie Ester Hamner was born on September 6, 1906; (2) Martha Lee Hamner was born on March 9, 1908; (3) Viola Vee Hamner was born on December 2, 1909; (4) James Foster Hamner. was born on August 11, 1911.

## THE BEUNA VISTA HAMNER FAMILY

### The sixth child of John Pruitt Hamner and Annie Margaret Hall

Buena Vista Hamner was the sixth child of John Pruitt Hamner and Annie Margaret Hall (*Hamner Heritage*, page 212). She was born on January 27, 1877, and died February 11, 1965.

Buena Vista first married John Monroe House on September 9, 1894. They had a son, John Monroe House, Jr., who was born on July 9, 1895. The date of death of John Monroe House, Sr. is not known but it was prior to June 1900 at which time Beuna Vista had remarried. John Monroe House, Sr. is buried in Macedonia Cemetery.

Beuna Vista Hamner House married a second time to her first cousin Arch George Chism on June 14, 1900. Arch George Chism was born on September 18, 1878, and died in 1949. (*Hamner Heritage*, page 212). Arch George Chism and Buena Vista are buried next to each other in Macedonia Cemetery.

Arch George and Buena Vista Chism had five children; (1) Maggie Lee Chism was born on December 27, 1900; (2) Ursula Judson Chism was born on April 15, 1906; (3) Ida Bell Chism, was born on December 1910; (4) Margaret Elizabeth Chism, was born on September 25, 1913; (5) Lewis Arch Chism was born circa 1915. Lewis Arch is buried in Macedonia Cemetery.

## THE LARKIN "LARK" ROGERS HAMNER FAMILY

### The seventh child of John Pruitt Hamner and Annie Margaret Hall

Larkin "Lark" Rogers Hamner was the seventh child of John Pruitt Hamner and Annie Margaret Hall. Lark was born on February 2, 1879, and died on April 19, 1955. He is buried in Macedonia Cemetery. His grave was the first grave in the new addition to the old cemetery. I was present for his burial. At the time, the area that would become the new addition to Macedonia Cemetery was still uncleared of trees and bushes except for the grave site for Lark.

Lark married Beatrice Josephine "Jo" Smith on May 16, 1926. "Jo" was born on December 23, 1884, and died on January 18, 1976. She is buried next to Lark in Macedonia Cemetery. (*Hamner Heritage,* page 214).

Lark and Jo had four children:

1.: First child: William Trimm Hamner

William Trimm Hamner was born on November 19, 1905, and died on April 20, 1962. Trimm married Annie Velma Rice who was born on January 7, 1903, and died on January 1, 1985. She was a school teacher for many years and was active in library work at Lafoy school.

Trimm and Annie Velma are buried in Carrolls Creek Baptist Church Cemetery. They had eight children: (1) Thelma Max Hamner was born on February 18, 1929; (2) Donald Rice Hamner was born on December 17, 1930; (3) Ramona Nell Hamner, was born on February 25,

1932; (4) Alton Rogers Hamner was born on September 6, 1933; (5) Carol Kay Hamner was born on February 22, 1937; (6) William Wayne Hamner was born on November 8, 1938: (7) Annie Wanita Hamner was born on February 16, 1941; (8) Carl Hoyt Hamner was born on February 20, 1944.

2. Second child: Annie Mable Hamner

Annie Mable Hamner was born on April 7, 1907, and died on May 18, 1988. She never married and lived at home with her parents and cared for them as their health deteriorated. She is buried in Macedonia next to her parents. (*Hamner Heritage,* page 218).

3. Third child: John Curtis Hamner

John Curtis Hamner was born on September 11, 1908. He married Louise Elizabeth Earnest. They had two children. Curtis was in the logging business. He and Louise later moved to Hueytown and the site of their burial is unknown.

4. Fourth child: James Lando "Kid" Hamner

Kid Hamner was born on February 18, 1911. He married Janie Myrtle Earnest. *Hamner Heritage,* page 219, gives the site of their burial as Arbor Springs Baptist Church Cemetery but does not give their death dates. They had two children: James Aubrey Hamner and Gene Autry Hamner.

## THE GILLIE PRUITT HAMNER FAMILY

### The eighth child of John Pruitt Hamner and Annie Margaret Hall

Gillie Pruitt Hamner was the eighth child of John Pruitt Hamner and Annie Margaret Hall (*Hamner Heritage*, page 220). He was born on November 22, 1880, and died on October 19, 1960. On December 22, 1905, he married Hassie Lou Lewis. Gillie operated a grocery store in Northport for several years. He also was a rural mail carrier for the U.S. Postal Service and served as the mail carrier to residents of the Crabbe Road. Gillie and Hassie Lou are buried in Tuscaloosa Memorial Park Cemetery.

Gillie Pruitt and Hassie Lou had eight children: (1) Jewel Clyde Hamner was born on October 31, 1908; (2) Ethyl Lou Hamner was born on March 9, 1910; (3) Lewis Melvin Hamner was born on December 25, 1911; (4) Rubel Park Hamner was born on January 9, 1918; (5) Ralph Clark Hamner was born on March 20, 1922; (6) Gillie Pruitt Hamner, Jr. was born on March 24, 1925; (7) Carolos Patton Hamner was born on June 18, 1928; (8) Dorla Dean Hamner was born on May 10, 1930.

## THE ANNIE BRAZEAL HAMNER FAMILY

### The ninth child of John Pruitt Hamner and Annie Margaret Hall
### A marriage joining the Hamner and Rushing families

Annie Brazeal Hamner was born on October 10, 1882, and died on May 21, 1927. She married Thomas Hillman "Jack" Rushing on October 15, 1902. Thomas Hillman was born October 15, 1876, and died on November 9, 1942. Both are buried in Macedonia Cemetery.

Annie Brazeal and Thomas Hillman had ten children:

1. Ozella Bertice "Bert" Rushing was born on February 21, 1904, and died on April 9, 1994. She married Herman Payne Thomas. They had no children. Both buried Tuscaloosa Memorial Park.

2. Clara Bell "Jim" Utley was born on December 26, 1906, and died on February 13, 1985. She married Clyde Buel Utley. They had one child, Nita Anne Utley, who was born on November 12, 1932, and died on October 28, 1937. Nita Anne is buried in Macedonia Cemetery. Clyde and Clara Bell are buried in Tuscaloosa Memorial Park.

3. Edward Nathan Rushing was born on July 2, 1908, and died on July 4, 1908. He is buried in Macedonia Cemetery.

4. Joseph Howard Rushing was born on March 4, 1909, and died on May 17, 1997. Late in life, he was married for a short time but then

divorced. He had no children. He is buried in Tuscaloosa Memorial Park.

5. Temperance "Temp" Hagler Rushing was born on January 17, 1911, and died on November 1, 1983. She married Floyd Alton Maughn. They had no children. They are buried in Tuscaloosa Memorial Park.

6. Roy Marshall Rushing was born on September 11, 1912, and died May 1, 2001. On July 2, 1938, Roy married Faith Vivian Ramsey who was born on December 21, 1918, and died on May 20, 2007. Both Roy and Faith are buried in Macedonia Cemetery.

Roy and Faith had four children: (1) Peggy Ann Rushing was born January 13, 1940. Peggy married David Hayse Boyd. Peggy and Hayse had three children: Tara Ann, Cinda Leigh, and Denson Hayse; (2) Larry Thomas Rushing was born on October 8, 1941, and died on July 6, 2020. He is buried in Memory Hills Gardens. Larry married Patricia Ann Pinion. Larry and Pat had two children: Stephen Lance Rushing and Jason Todd Rushing; (3) Linda Sue Rushing was born on April 8, 1945. Linda married Ronald William Harding. Ronald and Linda had two children: Shannon Sue Harding and Jill Suzanne Harding; (4) James Randall "Randy" Rushing was born on February 22, 1948. Randy married Sherry Wynette Harland. Randy and Sherry had three children: Kerry Michelle Rushing, Christopher Shane Rushing, and Jennifer Suzanne Rushing.

7. Nell Irene Rushing was born on December 22, 1914, and died on March 22, 2010. On April 27, 1940, she married Edwin George Owens who was born on December 23. 1914, and died on November 5, 2010. They are buried in Owens Cemetery in Repton, Alabama. Nell and Ed had two children: Edwina Lanell Owens and Susan Diane Owens.

8. Truman Hillman "Buck" Rushing was born on October 1, 1916, and died on October 3, 1990. On February 14, 1948, he married Corendene Tierce who was born on June 19, 1928 and died on September 23, 2015. They had two children: Rebecca Kay Rushing and Cindy Anita Rushing. Cindy was born on February 22, 1961, and died October 7, 2018. She is buried in Tuscaloosa Memorial Park.

9. Angela Gladys Rushing was born on December 30, 1918, and died October 7, 2013. She married Robert James Romaine who was born on September 12, 1918, and died on January 29, 1986. They had two children: Sherry Angela Romaine and Robert James Romaine, Jr.

10. Anthony Leon Rushing was born on March 9, 1921 and died on January 12, 1922. He is buried in Macedonia Cemetery (*Hamner Heritage*, page 224).

## THE PERMELIA ALMA HAMNER FAMILY

**The 10th child of John Pruitt Hamner and Annie Margaret Hall**
**A marriage joining the Hamner and Rushing families**

Permelia Alma Hamner was the tenth child of John Pruitt Hamner and Annie Margaret Hall (*Hamner-Heritage*, page 225). Permelia Alma was born on January 1, 1884, and died on February 3, 1970. On March 16, 1903, she married Joseph David "Gin" Rushing, born on October 15, 1876 and died on April 22, 1943. Both are buried in Macedonia Cemetery.

Joseph David "Gin" Rushing was a twin brother to Thomas Hillman "Jack" Rushing. Thomas Hillman "Jack" Rushing was married to Annie Brazeal "Brizzie" "Peggy" Hamner. Twin Rushing brothers (Thomas Hillman "Jack" and Joseph David "Gin") married Hamner sisters (Annie Brazeal and Permelia Alma).

At the time of Permelia Alma Hamner and Joseph David "Gin" Rushing's wedding, a popular hotel was located on the Crabbe Road near a series of warm sulfa springs ten miles north of the Hamner farm. Prior to the Civil War, the Windham Springs Hotel and Grounds were built to draw tourist to the area. The hotel prospered for decades. Permelia and Gin traveled by buggy to the hotel where they enjoyed a brief honeymoon. (The subject of the Windham Springs Hotel is the topic of another chapter.)

After the wedding trip, Permelia Alma and Joseph "Gin" returned to a house Gin had built on Rushing land near Carrolls Creek that was just two miles south of William Taylor Hamner, Sr.'s original house site. The lumber for Gin's house had been cut from virgin timber on the Rushing farm.

Permelia Alma and Gin had six children:

1. First child: John David Rushing.

John David Rushing was born on December 21, 1904. He first married Thelma Bell Utley who was born on March 1, 1905. John David and Thelma had three children and then divorced. The children were: (1) Dalton David Rushing was born on September 22, 1924; (2) Nina Loyle Rushing was born on January 10, 1927; (3) Dottie Sue Rushing was born on November 13, 1930.

John David Rushing married a second time to Gladys Ruth Smith who was born on August 3, 1914 They had one child: Richard Fred Rushing. John David and Gladys Ruth divorced.

John David Rushing married a third time to Stella Irene Connell. They had no children (*Hamner Heritage*, page 226).

2. Second child: Etta Alma Rushing.

Etta Alma Rushing was born on May 17, 1906, and was married on July 4, 1924 to Houston Lonzo Thomas who was born on February 14, 1908. They had no children. Both are buried in Macedonia Cemetery.

3. Theo Mae Rushing.

Theo Mae Rushing was born on October 4, 1907, and died on May 22, 1995. On July 4, 1924, she married Wiley Pruitt Hagler who was born on August 25, 1904 and died on July 7, 1976. The sisters, Etta Alma Rushing Thomas, and Theo Mae Rushing Hagler, were married on the same day, July 4, 1924. Theo and Wiley are buried in Macedonia Cemetery next to Etta Alma and Houston Thomas.

Theo and Wiley had two children: (1) Nellene Hagler was born on October 20, 1926; (2) Myra Joyce Hagler was born on October 2, 1938. Myra Joyce married her cousin William David Hamner, son of Alfred David "A. D." Hamner (*Hamner Heritage*, pages 58 and 227).

4. Margaret Lucille Rushing

Margaret Lucille Rushing was born on January 6, 1910, and died on December 2, 1934. Margaret married Walter Lee Speed. According to family tradition, her death at age twenty-four has been suspect to foul play. She is buried in Macedonia Cemetery, but her husband is not. They had no children.

5: Woodrow Clanton Rushing

Woodrow Clanton Rushing was born on June 23, 1912, and died on May 14, 2004. He married Margaret Janet Franklin. They are buried in Tuscaloosa Memorial Park Cemetery. They had two children: (1) Jacqueline Avaline; (2) Ravan Warren.

6. James Cleveland Rushing

James Cleveland Rushing was born on June 24, 1916. He married Marie Wilma Christian Guin on August 18, 1956. They had one son, Mickey Cleveland Rushing. Marie had previously been married to Byron Timothy Guin by whom she had two children: (1) Robert Jay Guin; (2) Virginia Elaine Guin. James Cleveland and Marie are buried in Sunset Cemetery in Northport.

**THE JOHN CULLEN HAMNER FAMILY**

**The 11th child of John Pruitt Hamner and Annie Margaret Hall**

Jacob Cullen Hamner was the eleventh child of John Pruitt Hamner and Annie Margaret Hall. John Cullen was born on March 20, 1885, and died on April 23, 1969 (*Hamner Heritage*, page 228). On September 16, 1906, he married Jesse Florence Lewis who was born on September 20, 1892, and died on November 22, 1964. They had six children.

1. An infant twin who died at birth on November 19, 1907.

2. An infant twin who died at birth on November 19, 1907. Both infants are buried in Macedonia Cemetery in graves marked only by rocks with no engravement in the rocks.

3. Edward Cullen Hamner

Edward Cullen Hamner was born on September 19, 1910. He married Notie Swindle on February 15, 1942. They had no children and are buried in Tuscaloosa Memorial Park.

4. Willie August Hamner

Willie Augusta Hamner was born on June 23, 1915. On Augus 23, 1940, she married James M. Marchant who was born October 5, 1917. They had no children.

5. William Perry Hamner

William Perry Hamner was born December 27, 1928. On September 2, 1942, he married Margaret Clark. They had two children.

6. Lewis Daniel Hamner

Lewis Daniel Hamner was born on December 10, 1920. He died on May 4, 1924.

A few months after his first wife died Jacob Cullen Hamner married a second time in April 1965 to Alda Kimball Rogers Wyjack. No children were born to this marriage.

No descendants of Jacob Cullen Hamner except for the twins who died at birth on November 19, 1907 are buried in Macedonia Cemetery.

**THE OZELLA JUDSON HAMNER FAMILY**

**The 12th child of John Pruitt Hamner and Annie Margaret Hall**

Ozella Judson Hamner was born on October 4, 1887, the twelfth child of John Pruitt Hamner and Annie Margaret Hall and died July 2, 1973 (*Hamner Heritage*, page 229). On December 20, 1905, Ozella Judson married Marvin Goldman Rushing. The marriage was the third marriage between children of John Pruitt Hamner and Annie Margaret Hall's children and the children of Joseph Enoch Rushing and his wife Samantha Lenora Deason. Ozella's sister Permelia Alma Hamner married Marvin Goldman Rushing and another sister, Annie Brazeal Hamner, had married Thomas Hillman "Jack" Rushing.

Marvin Goldman Rushing was born on October 8, 1884, and died on February 17, 1947. Ozella "Judie" and Goldman are buried in Macedonia Cemetery. Marvin Goldman and Ozella Rushing had eight children.

1. Thelma Ann Rushing

Thelma Ann Rushing was born on September 29, 1906, and died on December 8, 1932. On August 13, 1927, Thelma Ann married William Morgan Cooper who was born on August 23, 1906, and died on March 30, 1984. Morgan is buried in Piney Woods Cemetery and Thelma is buried in Macedonia Cemetery next to her parents.

Thelma and Morgan Cooper had two children: (1) Wilhelmina June Cooper was born on November 29, 1927 and died on October 6, 2019. She is buried in Sunset Cemetery. Her grave marker reads, "Wilhelmina June Cooper Sexton"; (2) Lester Lamar Cooper was born June 11, 1932, and died on April 11, 2007. He is buried in Sunset Memorial Park Cemetery.

2. Lottie Snow Rushing

Lottie Snow Rushing was born October 5, 1908 and died as a young child in 1909. She is buried in Macedonia Cemetery.

3. Marvin Barnard Rushing

Marvin Barnard Rushing was born on July 3, 1911 and died three years later in 1915. He is buried in Macedonia Cemetery.

4. Alda Judson Rushing

Alda Judson Rushing was born on June 7, 1914, and died on May12, 1995. On December 8, 1934, she married Willie Roy Hutchins who was born on May 16, 1913, and died on May 15, 1999. They are buried in Memory Hill Gardens. Alda and Roy had five children.

Mary Lenora "Nona" Rushing was born September 24, 1916 died on December 17, 2002.

On March 12, 1936, she married William Johnson Hutchins. They had two children.

Beuna Ettleline "Dick" Rushing was born on March 21, 1920, and died on February 10, 1989. On February 19, 1939, Ettleline married Cecil Wayne Skelton. Ettleline and Cecil had one child.

Charles Preston Rushing was born on September 24, 1922, and died September 26, 1994. He married Cordelia Kathryn Tierce who was born February 1, 1931, and died January 13, 2008. They are buried in Memory Hills Gardens. They had three children.

Billy Gean Rushing was born on May 15, 1926, and died on June 17, 2014. He married Betty Eldon Boyd, born August 24, 1928 and died August 9, 2023. They are buried in Tuscaloosa Memorial Park. They had two children.

**THE ULLIE MAE HAMNER FAMILY**

**The 13th child of John Pruitt Hamner and Annie Margaret Hall**

Ullie Mae Hamner was the thirteenth child of John Prewitt Hamner and Annie Margaret Hall. She was born on May 25, 1889, and died on July 5, 1936 (*Hamner Heritage,* page 233). On November 15, 1908, Ullie Mae married her first cousin Harvey Morgan Chism. Harvey Morgan was born on December 26, 1885, and died on July 8, 1924. They are buried in in Macedonia Cemetery.

Harvey Morgan was called 'Harve" and was a farmer and in the sawmill business. Harve and Ullie Mae lived at the intersection of Rice Mine Road and Bridge Avenue in Northport. All six of their children were born there.

(1) Clarence Hagler Chism was born on August 19, 1909, and died on September 30, 1910. He is buried in Macedonia Cemetery. His grave is marked only by a rock with no inscription.

(2) George Nathan Chism was born on October 7, 1910, and died on May 8, 1980. On September 3, 1938, he married Julia Elizabeth Broughton who was born on March 8, 1915 and died July 7, 1999. Julia and Nathan had two sons –James "Jimmy" Morgan Chism and George Nathan Chism, Jr. (*Hamner Heritage,* page 233).

(3) Virda Mae Chism was born July 7, 1912, and died June 12, 1921. She is buried in Macedonia Cemetery.

4. Harvey Dawson Chism was born February 7, 1914, and died on June 17, 1985. On September 2, 1939, he married Mildred Alene Carnathan who was born on April 22, 1920, and died on March 15, 2010. Dawson and Alene had two children—Harvey Dawson Chism, Jr. and Margaret Jureda Chism.

5. Annie Ruth Chism was born on July 8, 1916, and died on May 2, 2002. On February 2, 1940, she married Henry Isaac Morrison who was born on May 7, 1914, and died November 21, 1997. They have two children: Mary and Henry Isaac.

6. John Autry Chism was born on January 13, 1919, and died on April 8, 1944 while in action during World War II in Germany. He married Ola Margaret Booth. They had no children.

After Harvey Morgan Chism died, Ullie Mae married Oscar Junkin. They had no children. She is buried in Macedonia Cemetery and her grave marker reads, "Ullie Mae Hamner Chism Junkin."

**Cummings-Hamner-Chism Grocery Store**

In 1920, John Earley and his family moved to Northport and bought thirty-one acres of land on 20th Avenue which at the time was the Crabbe Road and 24th Street. Soon thereafter, he donated five acres of the land on which a new school, the original Tuscaloosa County High School, was built. He also bought a grocery store on the property from Mr. Hull Cummings. In 1932, John Early sold the store to his twenty-two-year-old nephew Nathan Chism who, along with Nathan's brother, Dawson Chism, operated Chism's Store there for about eighteen years. It would not be an exaggeration to say that Chism's store was the

# CRABBE ROAD, FIRST SETTLERS

grocery store used by many Lafoy Community citizens during its years of operation. Operating a grocery store during the depression years of the 1930s was difficult. Nathan provided groceries to many famers and told them, many of whom were kinfolks, "pay when the crops came in," meaning the farmers would settle their accounts with him when the cotton they grew was harvested and sold in the fall. Only then would the customers have cash.

In the 1940s, Nathan sold the store to his brother Dawson who had worked for Nathan earlier. Nathan became a deputy sheriff for Tuscaloosa County. He ran for Circuit Clerk of Tuscaloosa County in 1950 and won a spot in the two-man runoff. However, he withdrew and continued to serve as Chief Deputy Sheriff under his cousin Sheriff Leon T. Chism.

In 1951, Sheriff Leon T. Chism decided not to seek reelection at the next election in 1954. He urged Nathan to run for the office. On May 5, 1954, Nathan was elected sheriff of Tuscaloosa County and in subsequent years was reelected until he was defeated 1970.

In retirement, Nathan and Julia lived on the Crabbe Road on land that once belonged to John Pruitt Hamner.

Nathan and Julia had two sons: (1) James Morgan "Jimmy" Chism, born April 29, 1940, and died November 21, 2018; (2) George Nathan Chism, born June 17, 1946, and died on September 28, 2022.

# A ROAD, A CEMETERY, A PEOPLE

CHAPTER 6

# The Lafoy School

Topics discussed in this chapter:
  The LaFoy family
  Reference sources
  School activities
  Tuscaloosa County teachers 1928
  Schools close 1932 due to lack of funding
  Community singings
  Carrolls Creek Baptist Church buys old school

**Lafoy School opened circa 1910**
Lafoy School was located on the Crabbe Road eight miles north of Northport across the highway from the current site of Carrolls Creek Baptist Church.

The earliest newspaper article I have found relating to the school is found in the February 11, 1911 *Northport Gazette.* Based on material in that article, it can be assumed that the school opened circa early 1900s.

The school was named for the LaFoy family, a family who arrived in this community circa 1900. According to LaFoy family records, soon after the LaFoy family arrived, Thomas "Tom" Daniel LaFoy and his wife Addie Elizabeth Broughton cleared a narrow little dirt road through the woods from the Crabbe Road to the place where they built a house on what today is Fire Station Road just off the Lary Lake Road. They cleared the ground of trees and bushes and planted a garden and a field of corn. They also planted a few acres of cotton and harvested it as a cash crop. Tom worked the land and sold virgin timber from the property to provide funds to rear a family of nine children. Circa early 1900s, the LaFoy family donated a couple of acres of land from their farm for a school which was named LaFoy School.

The spelling of "LaFoy" has taken two forms. The family spells the name with the "F" in upper case (LaFoy). Newspapers and other research papers have the "f" in lower case (Lafoy). When I refer to the family, I use the spelling "LaFoy." Otherwise, I use the spelling "Lafoy."

Brenda LaFoy, a member of the LaFoy family, has engaged in extensive genealogy research on her family and other families in the community. She shared her data with me. I am deeply grateful. Brenda is not only a dear friend; she is a cousin to my wife. An entire chapter about the LaFoy family is found elsewhere in *A Road, A Cemetery A People.*

**Sources for research material**
Resource material for this story comes from five major sources: (1) newspaper articles—the *Northport Gazette,* the *Tuscaloosa Breeze,* and the *Tuscaloosa News*; (2) Brenda LaFoy's family history archives; (3) my personal experiences; (4) the Joseph Enoch Rushing family history composed by my wife, Peggy Rushing Boyd; (5) interviews with the late Dr. Joseph Shipp, a former student

at Lafoy School.

I was in the old Lafoy School building many times in the late 1940s and early 1950s. It is a pleasure to share a few of those experiences.

In 1942, Lafoy School closed and Lafoy Community students were bused to Northport Elementary School or to Tuscaloosa County High School. That year Carrolls Creek Baptist Church purchased the vacant Lafoy School building and property and used it for church purposes until the early 1950s when the church built a new building across Crabbe Road from the school. The original Carrolls Creek Baptist Church was located on Martin Road at its intersection with the Crabbe Road. It had been destroyed by fire in 1942. The story of Carrolls Creek Baptist Church is told in the chapter, "Crabbe Road Churches."

Lafoy School, circa 1940

**Personal involvement**
Our family attended Macedonia Methodist Church located a quarter mile north of Lafoy school. Our church did not have a fulltime pastor during my childhood years. Macedonia shared its pastor with three other area Methodist churches —Patterson Chapel Methodist Church, Union Chapel Methodist Church, and Jennings Chapel Methodist Church. Macedonia held Sunday School each Sunday, but we had a morning preaching service only on the first Sunday in the month and an evening preaching service on the third Sunday night of the month. On the first, second, and fourth Sunday nights, my family often attended the night services at Carrolls Creek Baptist Church.

Brother J. E. Horton was pastor of Carrolls Creek Baptist from 1951-1954. He lived in Fayette and commuted to Carrolls Creek on Sundays. My mother's people, the Farquhar family, also lived in Fayette and were good friends with the Horton family. This was an extra incentive for us to attend the Sunday night services there.

As an inquisitive kid, I came to know every crook and cranny of the old schoolhouse building while attending worship there. I especially was intrigued by a wood wall that could be slid back and forth on metal rollers configuring the interior of the building into either one large room or two smaller rooms. It was original to the structure and allowed students to be separated by age and grade. Grades first through third were in one room and grades four and up in the other room.

The building also served as the Lafoy Community Center where school plays were performed, square dances and community singings held, and civic events and political rallies scheduled. To accommodate large crowds, the sliding wall was rolled back to create a single big room.

**The Rushing family scrapbook**
My wife, Peggy Rushing Boyd, has spent almost two decades composing a pictural and genealogical scrapbook of her paternal family, the Joseph Enoch Rushing family. The first members of the Rushing family arrived in Lafoy in the late 1800s. Their land was on the Crabbe Road a mile south of Lafoy School. Joseph Enoch Rushing and his wife Samantha Lenora Deason Rushing sired ten boys and one girl. The Rushing children attended

# THE LAFOY SCHOOL

Lafoy School in the 1910s and 1920s, including Peggy's father, Roy Marshall Rushing.

Joseph Enoch Rushing died on August 5, 1911, and in his obituary, it is stated that he was a trustee of Lafoy School and active in school affairs.

**News article February 17, 1911**
A February 17, 1911, *Northport Gazette* article reads: "Friday, February 11, 1911, was temperance day and it was a red-letter day for Lafoy School as our teacher, Prof. L. A. White, had a well arranged and prepared program. He had the able assistance of Miss Flora Justin of Tuscaloosa, the efficient teacher for Turner District, who brought some students from her school and took part in the program. As the scribe has no copy of Miss Justin's program, I will only give Prof. White's song "White Ribbons," school recitations on temperance and an acrostic poem "Three little boys and seven little girls."

    Reading: Dragon ——— Valdior House
    Exercise: Alcohol Curse ——— Fifth grade
    Recitation: Cold Water Man ——— Pearl Gay
    Exercise: Why and Because ——— Irene Shirley, Ward Williams, Richard Eads, Asa Hamner
    Song: Sparkling and Bright ——— Buna Gay
    Recitation: Little Drops ——— Mattie Sue Whatley
    Recitation: Open Case ——— Irene Shirley
    Song: Four Leaf Clover ——— School
    Recitation: One More ——— Irene Shirley
    Exercise: Quotation ——— Fourth Grade
    Recitation: What Shall We Do with the Apples ——— Valda House
    Song: Alabama Score ——— Two School Girls."

**Boyd comment:**
Most Lafoy Community residents were teetotalers and regarded alcohol, especially drunkenness, as a wicked vice. It is not surprising that the teachers presented a drama supporting temperance. None the less, illegal moonshine whiskey stills were scattered among the hollows of the North River area on the Crabbe Road. Bootlegging was commonly practiced in the area until the 1950s. A separate chapter is devoted to the topic.

**News article April 2, 1911**
The April 2, 1911 issue of the *Tuscaloosa Breeze* reads: "We are always glad to get the *Breeze*. Farmers are still trying to farm a little on Carrolls Creek and North River but things look gloomy since the storm on the 10th which did much damage here. Much damage was done to Mr. James Clements and Mr. Bill Aaron, but worst of all it nearly ruined Lafoy School house. The old one was blown several hundred yards away and the new one was picked up by the wind and stove into the ground. We are thankful though that no one was killed. We earnestly hope that we will not have any more like that soon. The wind damaged Mr. J. E. Hamner about $100. I am sorry for him, but it could have been worse. We will have to pray more and work harder.

***The Tuscaloosa Breeze*, August 1, 1912**
Superintendent of Education Mr. Perry B. Hughes and Mr. Thomas B. Ward went out to Lafoy schoolhouse Tuesday night where they addressed the patrons of that school district concerning the possibility of state-aid funding to build a schoolhouse. It was the intention of the patrons of this neighborhood to go ahead and erect a building from their own funds, but after the meeting on Tuesday, they decided to apply for state aid in erecting a comfortable building. Yesterday, they filed their application need.

**Boyd comment:**
The source of funding to build the school noted in the 1911 *Northport Gazette* article can be assumed to be monies given by community citizens who desired to provide for the educational needs of their children. They were willing

to sacrifice in order to have a good school. However, after hearing that state funds might be available, the school board applied for outside financial help.

**The Tuscaloosa Breeze, March 13, 1913**
**Lafoy School House**
We are having some pleasant weather, and Carrolls Creek folks are getting along fine and burning over stalks, cleaning off fence rows, and doing other farm work. Our school will soon close for the summer. We feel sad to part with our teacher, Miss Temperance McCalley. We hope to have her back next year. School closes Friday night, March 14. The following program will be presented:
  Song: Greeting — all school students
  Recitation, opening — Ward Williams
  Recitation: A Little Speech — Estelle Shirley
  Dialogue: A Quarrel — Two little girls
  Song: Tiny Flakes — Little folks
  Recitation: A Boy's Opinion — Sellers Aaron
  Dialogue: What Ailed Maudie? — Five characters
  Recitation: Bessie Letter — Queen Lafoy
  Recitation: Moving — Mary LaFoy
  Song: Summer Is Passing Away — all school students
  Dialogue: Tom's Practical — Three characters
  Dialogue: The Way to Windham — Two boys
  Recitation: Writing to Grandma — Clara Rushing
  Dialogue: An Interrupted Proposal — Several characters
  Recitation: A Little Seam of _____ — Connie House
  Recitation: Be Polite — Claude Hamner
  Dialogue: The 10¢ Dude — Irene Shirley, Gus Hamner
  Drill: Come and Play — Six boys and six girls
  Dialogue: Arabella's Poor Relatives — Four classmates
  Monologue: $1 and I — Irene Shirley
  Recitation: Neberkenezer——Herman Thomas
  Dialogue: Sweet Family, "Ma Sweet" and her seven accomplished daughters
  Dialogue: A Negro Celebration — three classmates
  Magic: Miss Edna Thomas — Messers Jesse and William Hyche
  Everybody is cordially invited.

**Boyd comment:**
The Lafoy Community was a farming community. "Burning over stalks" refers to a controlled burn of a field of last year's corn stalks. Setting fire to an old field in late winter was thought to help control corn and cotton insect pests during the approaching crop season.

Miss Temperance McCalley was well liked. It was hoped she would teach in the fall term. Many teachers were young ladies not yet married. Often, after teaching for a year or so, they married and moved away to be with their new husbands. This led to a high turnover of teachers.

School terms were usually five months—November through March. This allowed farm kids to work in the fields from the time of spring planting until harvest ended. To survive, all members of the family were needed as laborers.

**The Tuscaloosa Breeze, April 2, 1913**
**Carrolls Creek**
We are always glad to get the *Tuscaloosa Breeze*.

Farmers are still trying to farm a little on Carrolls Creek and North River, but things look gloomy since the storm on the 10th which did much damage here. Much damage was done to Mr. James Clements and Mr. Bill Aaron, but worst of all, it nearly ruined Lafoy schoolhouse. The old one was blown several hundred yards away, and the new one was picked up by the wind and stove into the ground. We are thankful though that no one was killed. We earnestly hope that we will not have any more like that soon. The wind damaged Mr. J. E. Hamner about $100. I am sorry for him, but it could have been worse. We will have to pray more and work harder.

**Boyd comment:**

The reference to "The old schoolhouse" is to the original building noted in the 1911 *Northport Gazette* article. We may assume that the "new one" was built with state funds as noted in the August 1, 1912, *The Tuscaloosa News* article.

*The Tuscaloosa Breeze*
**August 10, 1913**
A second article from the *Tuscaloosa Breeze* dated August 10, 1913 gives additional information regarding the damage done to the Lafoy School noted in the April 2, 1911 news article. R. H. Cochrane was re-elected treasurer of the Tuscaloosa County Board of Education for the ensuing scholastic year on Saturday morning.

The Board also received three requests from school districts for state aid. Two requests were passed on favorably. District 31, the Lafoy School, received $110 for repairing the building which was blown over by a storm last year, and district 61, Slum, received $200 for the erection of a building. Action on the other request of district 59, Griffin, was postponed till the next meeting of the board."

**Boyd comment:**

Courthouse business and board of education business in rural farming counites such as Tuscaloosa County was usually done on Saturdays. This allowed farmers who went to town only once a week to be present.

*The Tuscaloosa News*, **Sept. 14, 1915**
**Tuscaloosa County Stirs to New Educational Impulse**
In school improvement and equipment, Tuscaloosa ranks second in the state according to State Department of Education. Jefferson County alone stands ahead of this county. In every list, there has been a remarkable advance in rural education in this county in the last five years. New school houses have been built; old ones have been repaired and painted; new equipment has been added and the number of teachers has increased. Tuscaloosa County is stirring to the new impulse.

In District 31, Lafoy, the school has a new state schoolhouse and library.

**Boyd Comment:**

This article confirms state funds were used in the construction of the second school building.

*The Tuscaloosa News*, **August 6, 1916**
**Lafoy Was Scene**
**School Meeting Held Last Night**
**Prominent Tuscaloosans Attended Meeting and Made Addresses**
A school meeting was held last night at Lafoy schoolhouse in the northern part of the county. Several Tuscaloosans were present and made addresses. Among the number were Judge W. W. Brandon, Professor J. H. Foster, County Superintendent of Education Perry B. Hughes, and the Honorable E. L. Dawson. The meeting was in the interest of the amendment to the constitution to allow counties to vote the 3-mill tax.

**Boyd comment:**

W. W. Brandon served as Probate Judge of Tuscaloosa County 1911-1923. In 1922, he was elected governor of Alabama.

*The Tuscaloosa News*, **July 15, 1917**
**80-Year-Old-Pupil Attends Adult School**
Miss Esther Foster, Professor L. K. Benson, and Superintendent P. B. Hughes went to Peterson Thursday where they held an enthusiastic meeting and organized an adult school with twelve pupils.

On Friday night, they went to Lafoy where a similar school was organized. The oldest pupil at the Lafoy School is 80 years old.

**Boyd comment:**

It is regrettable the identity of this elderly man was not given. It is noteworthy that Lafoy School offered this unique program.

*The Tuscaloosa News*, November 2, 1917
**Box Supper at Lafoy School**
There was a box supper at the Lafoy School where Miss Ruby Porter is principal last week. The receipts, together with voluntary subscriptions, amounted to about $90. Lafoy is fast becoming one the liveliest communities in the county.

**Boyd comment:**

Thus far in our story, we have been introduced to several Lafoy School teachers: Professor L. A. White, 1911; Temperance McCalley, 1913; Ruby Porter, 1917.

*The Tuscaloosa News*, March 20, 1919
**Carrolls Creek**
Lafoy School is progressing, and we are delighted with our teachers, Miss Anabel McElroy, and Miss Annabel Beaver, both of Cuba, Alabama. We believe they are trying to do the right thing for the children.

Health is good in our community.

Mr. Bernice Whatley has purchased a new motor car.

There will be preaching at Carrolls Creek Church next Sunday.

We have good singing at Lafoy school house every Sunday afternoon.

Miss Bertice Rushing is spending the week in Northport with her cousin, Miss Thelma Rushing.

Mrs. Myrtie Thomas is spending a week with her daughter Mrs. Curtis Watkins at Buhl, Alabama.

**Boyd comment:**

The notation that Bernice Whatley purchased a new car is thought-provoking. In 1919, few people in the Lafoy Community could afford an automobile. Wagons or buggies, along with riding muleback or horseback, were the usual means of transportation. Lafoy School students walked to school, some walking as far as three or four miles regardless of the weather.

The article does not state the brand of Mrs.

The above photo is from the Joel Thomas Shirley family collection. The sailor is not identified. The setting is in the Lafoy Community. The dirt on the car and the tires comes from driving on the dry dusty Crabbe Road and/or in the slippery mud during rainy weather.

Whatley's new car. I find it interesting that records show Ford Motor Company produced 498,342 Motel Ts in 1919 at a cost to the customer of $500, a price far above the means of most people in Lafoy Community.

*The Tuscaloosa News*, October 7, 1923
Northport News, by Lucille Curry

Miss Gladys Kilgore left Sunday for Lafoy where she will be teaching this winter.

**Boyd comment:**

As noted earlier, there was a rapid turnover of teachers at Lafoy largely due to the young ladies getting married and moving away. Here we are introduced to yet another new teacher.

*The Tuscaloosa News*, October 23, 1925
**Lafoy School Will Have Plate Supper**
There will be a plate supper at the Lafoy School on the Crabbe Road on Friday night, October 30, given for the benefit of the school. A play will be given free, and everybody is invited.

**Boyd comment:**

Fund raising events such as this occurred frequently.

# THE LAFOY SCHOOL

*The Tuscaloosa News*, October 6, 1926
**School curriculum**
As noted earlier, the academic school year was usually only five months in preceding years. By 1927, the school year had been extended and did not end until the end of April.

*The Tuscaloosa News*, November 29, 1927
**Lafoy News**
Rev. McWright will preach at Macedonia Church on December 4 at 11:00 a.m. Everyone is invited.

There will be a preaching service at Carrolls Creek Baptist Church on Sunday, December 27 at 11:00 a.m. Reverend Manderson will preach. Everybody is urged to attend.

School Activities:
The attendance at Lafoy School is very good. There are 42 pupils enrolled. In the very near future, the school expects to put on a play entitled "Mammy's Little Rose."

The pupils are delighted to have two days off for the Thanksgiving holiday.

**Boyd comment:**
As noted earlier, neither Macedonia nor Carrolls Creek Baptist Church held a preaching service every Sunday. However, each had Sunday School every Sunday.

*The Tuscaloosa News*, December 7, 1927
The efficient Mrs. Trimm Hamner has charge of the Lafoy School library, succeeding Miss Artie Stapler whose marriage to Mr. Pat Snow of Flat Creek was solemnized in Tuscaloosa prudently.

**Boyd comment:**
Again, we have an example of a young school teacher marrying and moving away from Lafoy.

Mr. and Mrs. Trimm Hamner were pillars in the Lafoy Community in the 20th century and dear friends of the Boyd family.

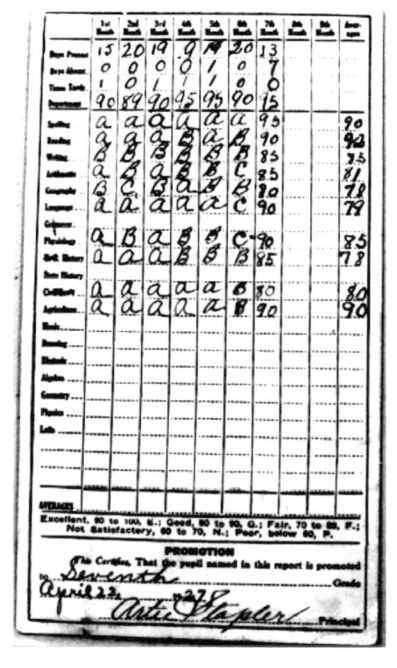

This is a copy of a Lafoy School report card dated April 22, 1927. For the sake of privacy, the identity of the student is omitted. The inclusion of the report card is to acknowledge the variety of subjects offered — spelling, arithmetic, geography, grammar, physiology, and U.S. history. Students at Lafoy received an excellent education.

*The Tuscaloosa News*, September 2, 1928
**Long-term schools open the year Monday with 192 teachers Supt. Sellers lists county faculty for 1928-1929**
With the long-term schools of the Tuscaloosa County School System opening Monday, September 3, Supt. James Sellers of the county schools, announced Saturday a list of 192 teachers who will be employed in Tuscaloosa County white schools in the 1928-1929 term.

In some instances, the faculties of various schools are incomplete, but those for the most part are short-term schools, and it will not be necessary to have those positions filled until October. Supt. Sellers will fill those positions in plenty of time for the opening of the short-term schools.

Everything is in readiness for the opening of the long-term schools. Preliminary to the beginning of the term, all county teachers whose schools open Monday met at the courthouse on Saturday. Despite the inclement weather, there was practically 100 percent attendance. Instructions regarding filling out school registers, subjects to be stressed and other phases of teaching were given out by the county superintendent.

The list of teachers for Tuscaloosa County follows:

Alberta City... principal and 7 teachers
Cottondale...principal and 2 teachers

Holt…principal and 15 teachers

Peterson…principal and [the line for teachers is unreadable]

Taylorville…principal and 3 teachers

Trye…1 teacher

Sterling…1 teacher

Sandtown…1 teacher

Echola…principal and 3 teachers

Fosters…principal and 1 teacher

Sylvan…1 teacher

Warrior Chapel…incomplete

Romulus…principal and 3 teachers

Sipsey Valley…1 teacher

Samantha…principal and 4 teachers

Deal…incomplete

Turner…1 teacher

Moore's Bridge…principal and 2 teachers

Brownville…principal and 2 teachers

McConnell's'…incomplete

Pine Bluff…1 teacher

Tierce…incomplete [This school was located in Reed's Spring, an area near the current Northside High School in northern Tuscaloosa County. It was named after William Coplin Tierce.]

Kemp…1 teacher

Etteca…principal and 3 teachers

Bethel…1 teacher

Flatwoods…2 teachers

Lafoy…1 teacher, Mrs. Floyd Robertson

White's…1 teacher

Copperas…principal and 1 teacher

Spencer Hill…incomplete

Antioch…1 teacher

Barbee…principal and 2 teachers

Mount Olive…principal and 2 teachers

Northport…principal, Miss Bessie Cleveland.

The remaining part of the news article is cut off.

**Boyd comment:**

Tuscaloosa County school terms operated at variable lengths during much of the 1920s and 1930s, depending upon availability of funding. A later article in this chapter dated March 2, 1938, gives additional information on the topic.

With the passage of time, most small rural elementary schools with only one or two teachers closed. However, one school near Lafoy, Bethel School on the Watermelon Road, remained open as an elementary school until the late 1940s.

*The Tuscaloosa News*, **December 8, 1932**
**Over 8,000 students will get early vacations**
**But, 14 white schools in the county system are able to keep open after Friday, Dr. Dowling reports**
**Resumption of term remains indefinite**
**Lack of funds from State is the cause for closing**
**Some try to continue on fee basis or other plans**
**Figures Cited**

Ninety-six schools in rural Tuscaloosa County with total enrollments exceeding 8,000 pupils will close their doors upon the backs of their young chargers Friday afternoon for an indefinite vacation period caused by the failure of the county schools to receive funds from the state treasury, Supt. H. G. Dowling announced today. The school closing will include all but 14 white schools in the county system.

The institutions closing school tomorrow afternoon number 48 white schools with a daily attendance of 5,350, and 47 Negro schools with a daily attendance of 2,589. The total enrollments number somewhat in excess of these figure although students have established records for promptness and attendance throughout the shortened term.

The present term began September 5 and with the closing Friday, the county school system is cut to about three months as compared with the standard of seven and one-half or eight months for grammar schools in previous years. Closing for county schools "as soon as all assured county and local funds are exhausted" was ordered by the County Board of Education two weeks ago after a mass meeting of teachers had decided that the majority of the instructors would be unable to continue schools without re-

# THE LAFOY SCHOOL

ceiving their salaries.

Many of the teachers are yet unpaid for a month or more of the term which ended last spring, and only a small partial payroll has been met this session. There is no indication as to when the state funds will be available for reopening the county schools, Mr. Dowling announced today. The patrons and the teachers will be kept informed through the press of any developments in the situation. Schools will be reopened when there is assurance that a substantial payment can be secured to assure an extension of the term.

The 14 schools that will remain open for an indefinite period have enrollment of 2,225. Extensions of their term is made possible by local tax districts, donations from individuals and firms, collecting of incidental or tuition fees, sacrifice of teachers and truck drivers who are in many cases serving without sufficient pay to cover their expenses. People of the various committees have "rallied magnificently" in their efforts to prevent a cessation of classroom activities. Similar sacrifices were made last spring to extend the term two weeks, or a month, in many cases.

County white schools remaining open for an indefinite period with the number attending are:

Note: the list is shortened to include only those relating to the Crabbe Road.

Tuscaloosa County High 469
Northport Grammar 337

County white schools remaining closed for an indefinite period with the number attending are:

[Note: the list is shortened to include only those relating to the Crabbe Road.]

Sterling 26
Gorgas 359
Windham Springs 229
Bethel 51
Lafoy 83

**Boyd comment:**

One of the most devastating consequences of the Great Depression was the closure of many schools. Even in areas where the schools remained opened, many farm children had to drop out of school and work on the farm in order to help the family survive.

Lafoy's enrollment of 83 students verifies the fact that the community population was probably in the neighborhood of two hundred people, many of whom were blood relatives through intermarriages of the Shirley, Hamner, Clements, Rushing LaFoy, Hagler, Gay, and Tierce families.

*The Tuscaloosa News*, **December 8, 1932 page 2**

**P.T.A. at Lafoy enjoys meetings**

The Negro minstrel given recently by the Lafoy P.T.A. was attended by a large and appreciative audience, and a nice sum of money was raised which will be used in the school's interest.

The P.T.A. plans for other entertainments during the school recess and Christmas holidays which begin Friday.

Alabama Day (December 14, 1819, the date of Alabama statehood) and Christmas programs have been arranged by the school's pupils with family and friends invited to attend. Plans are being formulated for covering and painting the school building during the holidays. Students with 100 percent attendance during November were Rachael Grammer, Myrtle Ester Hamner, James Rushing, Maurine Rushing, J. D. Hamner, Frances Rushing and Joe Rushing.

Singing

The community singing will be held at Lafoy School at 2:30 o'clock. Herman Thomas, the newly elected president, will preside. The public is invited to attend.

**Boyd comment:**

Gospel singings using shaped-note music were favorite events in Lafoy. The most beloved one was held at Macedonia Methodist Church on the first Sunday in May. It was also known as Homecoming Day or Decoration Day. Activities included placing flowers on the graves of family members and an all-day singing with "dinner on the ground." An entire chapter in *A Road, A Cemetery, A People* is devoted to that topic.

Alabama primary public elections were held on the first Tuesday in May. As a result, the activities at Macedonia's homecoming two days prior to the election always attracted politicians who were seeking votes.

*The Tuscaloosa News* **January 8, 1933 page 3**
**Elrod school to open on subscription basis**
**Children to assume their studies Monday morning:**
The Elrod School will open Monday morning on a subscription basis with all children of the community allowed to enter and will be financed by patrons and friends, Mrs. Irene Abernathy, principal, announced Saturday through the office of the County Board of Education.

It was stated that the institution would continue until the completion of the 9-month term due to the liberal support of parents and friends in the community.

**Boyd comment:**
The community of Elrod is located ten miles west of Northport on the Columbus Road. In 1933, it was a mill town, home of Pioneer Lumber Company. Due to lack of state education money, Elrod School, like other schools, was financed by private individuals. In my research, I have seen no evidence that Lafoy School ever closed during those hard times of the Great Depression nor was tuition ever required.

Mrs. Irene Abernathy was a member of the faculty at Tuscaloosa County High School during the 1940s and 1950s. She was my eighth-grade English teacher.

*The Tuscaloosa News*, **January 10, 1933, front page**
**Classes resume at Tuscaloosa County High on Monday**
**Private instruction will be given for $5 monthly**
**Registration begun:**
Tuscaloosa County High School will reopen as a "private school" next Monday at the regular hour to begin the second session of the 1932-1933 term with plans to carry the term through to its completion in all courses of school work, it was announced today by J. S. Rice, Chairman of the Citizens Committee which has perfected plans for the school's reopening.

Attendance will be on a tuition basis with all students paying $5 each month, in advance, throughout the session. These payments are necessary to provide teachers for the term, it was announced.

Revenue anticipated from the revenue fees will not be sufficient to finance any form of transportation through the school itself, Mr. Rice added. Associates with him on the committee are: Rev. B. F. Adkins; Rev. O. R. Burns; L. F. Barnes, Sam Faucett; S. T. McKee; John James; Tom Koster; Howard Maxwell; Mayor H. G. Shepherd; Mrs. Sam Fields; Bill Shepherd.

Employment of teachers will begin at once, but the number on the faculty will eventually be decided by the registration of the students. All who desire to register for the instructors are to call at the school building this week.

**Boyd comment:**
Lack of funding caused by the Great Depression forced Tuscaloosa County High School to become a "private school" with a $5 per month per child registration fee. I have been unable to document the length of time the school required tuition. The individuals noted were leading citizens of Northport and among the most affluent.

**October 15, 1933**
**(This article comes from a scrapbook assembled by Etta Rushing Thomas)**
The Lafoy Public School opened Monday for the 1933-1934 regular session with appropriate exercises. Pupils and patrons were gratified with the improved appearance of the remodeled school building which had been painted throughout and recovered and equipped with a new stage.

Professor Houston Cole, principal of the Northport schools, delivered the main address.

# THE LAFOY SCHOOL

Other patrons and friends of the school spoke and special music was enjoyed. Mrs. Jack Deason and Miss Lola Thompson of the teaching staff outlined their plans for the year and expressed appreciation for the cooperation of the Parent Teacher Association of the community. Jack Rushing and J. Hamner, trustees of the school, expressed their appreciation for the support of the community.

A resolution protesting the recent crime wave in the community was passed by patrons of the school and cooperation and support of all law enforcement agencies were assured.

**Boyd comment:**

During the Great Depression, the Lafoy Community continued to support and keep open their two-teacher school. Jack Rushing and J. Hamner were farmers whose income was quite limited. Yet, they sacrificed so that Lafoy School remained open.

Jack Rushing (Thomas Hillman Rushing) was the paternal grandfather of my wife and a leader in both community affairs and at Macedonia Methodist Church.

### *The Tuscaloosa News*, October 25, 1933

A Halloween party will be given a the Lafoy School Saturday.

### *The Tuscaloosa News*, December 7, 1933

The Lafoy School Parent-Teacher Association will sponsor a fiddlers' convention and Christmas playlet, a short and entertaining play, in the school Friday night, December 22 at 7:30 o'clock. A contest will be held to decide the ugliest man and woman. Proceeds from the entertainment will be used for school equipment. All fiddlers and the public are invited.

**Boyd comment:**

Several members of the Lafoy Community were musically talented. Fiddling contests occurred frequently. Lafoy had its own renown band, the Lafoy String Band. As a young man, Oli Dee Hamner, son of Oliver "Ollie" Jackson Hamner and Mary Louise Rigsby, and his brothers Hollis Harwood and John O'Neil, along with their friend Richard Patrick, formed a band that played widely at square dances, political rallies, community gatherings and fiddlers' conventions.

### *The Tuscaloosa News*, December 24, 1933
**Large crowd attends Lafoy fiddlers' match**

A large crowd enjoyed the fiddlers' convention and a playlet presented Friday night by the Lafoy Parent Teacher Association at the school. Herman Purdue of the First National Bank personnel presided as master of ceremonies.

John W. Hamner won first prize with Artamus K. Callahan second, and Bill Johnson of Cottondale third. Special selections were given by the Lafoy String Band with Dee Hamner playing the violin and Harwood Hamner handling guitars.

A short play "A Saturday Night Social" was directed by Miss Lenora Hyche. It was a blackface minstrel production which caused much merriment.

Last Wednesday, as a closing exercise for the holidays, the Lafoy School gave a community Christmas tree ceremony that was attended by many patrons.

**Boyd comment:**

Lenora Hyche was the daughter of Lenora Bell "Lou" Rushing Hyche. She later married Ed Earnest. Her name appears often in news articles about Lafoy Community. She was my wife's cousin.

### *The Tuscaloosa News*, February 27, 1934 page three
**Plans mock trial and rally**

An interesting program was held by Lafoy P. T. A. recently with reports given by those who attended the Tuscaloosa County Council meeting. Plans were made for a mock trial, supper, and political rally at the Lafoy School, Saturday night.

All candidates are invited to attend and speak. For the mock trial, Chester Walker will be the judge. Local attorneys Henry Mayfield, Billy Partlow, Jack McGuire, Charles W. Gross, Henry Snow, Charles LaFrance, and George H. Denny, Jr. will be present to offer advice to the school students as the trial unfolds.

The Lafoy P.T.A. met last Saturday to plant shrubbery and otherwise beautify the school grounds. The floors were also oiled. Several shrubbery plants and flowers were donated by Mesdames Ezra Jonah Shipp, Bruce Hamner, Jay Hamner, Tom Morrison, Therman LaFoy, Lonnie Montgomery, Steve Bevels, O. J. Hamner, J. S. Clements, Jack Deason, and the Misses Frances Shirley, Ruby Shirley, Joan Shirley, Lola Thomson, and the following boys, D. Hamner, Thurman Rigsby, Bernard Rushing and Mr. Loper.

**Boyd comment:**

The names of the local attorneys have little meaning to the reader in 2024, ninety years after the event. However, I remember them well. They were solid citizens who excelled in their professional lives and were dear friends of my parents. Charles Gross's daughter, Mary Alice, married my first cousin Bobby Joe Kemp. Mr. Gross served with my father on the Tuscaloosa County Selective Service Committee in the early 1950s. I talked with him often.

Chester Walker served as judge of probate for Tuscaloosa County for many years during which my father was a member of the Tuscaloosa County Board of Revenue.

Decades after this article was written, I had the privilege of being Bernard Rushing's family doctor.

*The Tuscaloosa News*, **March 7, 1934 page five**
An outstanding event of the past week was the mock trial, pie supper and political rally sponsored by the P. T. A.

Lafoy School students Miss Lola Thompson sued Curtis Hammer for breach of promise.

At the political rally, fifteen or more candidates spoke and others sent representatives and contributions. The P.T.A. and the community appreciate the interest shown.

The next meeting of the P.T. A. will be held Tuesday afternoon instead of the regular time on account of the teachers attending a demonstration.

People of Lafoy are urged to make an extra special effort to keep their children in school for the next two months. It is only through federal aid that the schools are being extended. Parents are being urged to show their appreciation for the extension by sending their children every school day.

Bird Day was observed at Lafoy School with a program being given by Joan Shirley, Frances Rushing, J. D. Hamner Bernard Rushing, B. F. Shirley, and Mrs. Deason.

**Boyd comment:**

The idea of having the students serve in a mock trial allowed them insight into the real world of civil trials. It was fun for the students to assume the rolls of judges, lawyers, and jury members. It is interesting to speculate regarding the breach of promise Curtis Hamner broke to Lola Thompson. Perhaps he had promised to marry her, but reneged.

Times were hard. Here, we see a plea to parents to keep kids in school not only for the benefit of their education but also because federal and state funding was determined by school attendance records. Sadly, when children reached the age or ten or eleven, they often had to drop out of school and work on the farm in order for the family to survive. That was the case with Peggy's father, Roy Rushing.

*The Tuscaloosa News*, **March 14, 1934**
A fiddlers' convention will be held Friday night at Lafoy school which is located eight miles from Tuscaloosa on the Crabbe Road. Sandwiches, Eskimo Pie, and a pretty-girl cake will be sold. All fiddlers and candidates are invited.

# THE LAFOY SCHOOL

*The Tuscaloosa News*, March 2, 1938 front page
**County School Terms Listed**
**All in state operate seven months unless taxation under limit**
**Montgomery, Al.**
All Alabama counties have budgeted elementary schools to operate seven months or more, except in districts not leveling full educational taxes. However, high schools are scheduled to operate less than nine months in 15 counties.

Most cities plan to operate both elementary and high school grades for nine-month terms, and none will be short of seven months.

This was revealed today by the State Department of Education whose figures, it said, were based upon budgets submitted by county school superintendents for the 1937-1938 period.

Dr. R. L. Johns, Chief of the Department of Administration and Finance, said the following counties would operate elementary school terms of less than seven months in districts not levying all taxes permitted under the constitution:

Choctaw, 6 months; Coffee, 5 months; Coosa, 6 months; Henry, 6 months; Lawrence, 5 months; Pike, 5 months; Russell, 6 months; Tuscaloosa, 6 ¾ months; Barbour, 6 ¾ months.

High schools are budgeted to operate nine months, Johns said, except in the following county systems:

Chambers, 8 ¼ months; Choctaw, 8 months; Dallas, 8 months; Greene, 7 months; Henry, 8 months; Jefferson, 8 months; Lamar, 8 and 4/10 months; Marengo, 8 months; Marion, 8 months; Marshall, 8 months; Morgan, 8 ½ months; Russell, 7 months; Tallapoosa, 8.3 months; Wilcox, 8 months.

The following counites, instead of operating high schools nine months and elementary grades nine months, are opening both for eight months:

Dallas; Jefferson; Marengo; Wilcox.

Short term high school budgets were necessary in the following counties, Jones said, because of their failure to levy all taxes permitted:

Dallas; Greene; Henry; Dallas; Russell; Wilcox.

The following counties were unable to budget high schools because of debt occurred in prior years:

Dale; Tallapoosa; Winston.

Negro high schools in county systems generally operate seven to eight months, with elementary grades running seven months in districts levying full taxes. In areas not collecting all taxes permissible, the term averages about five months.

**Boyd comment:**
The year is 1938. The ravages of financial despair from the Great Depression still linger. Full nine-month school terms were the exception, not the rule.

Not to be overlooked is the fact the funding for Negro schools lagged that for white schools.

*The Tuscaloosa News*, March 27, 1938, front page
**Teachers ask higher salaries and longer term**
**Birmingham, Alabama meeting of the Alabama Education Association**
A legislative program to provide a minimum school term of eight months, an increase in teachers' salaries and a retirement pay plan was adopted today by the Alabama Education Association at its closing session.

The resolution fixing the eight-month term stated that the AEA advocated a nine-month term, and proposed the eight-month term as the next step to that end. A seven-month term is in effect in all the counties which levy minimum local taxes.

*The Tuscaloosa News*, November 27, 1938 page two
**Lafoy News**
The third monthly meeting of the Lafoy P. T. A was held recently in the school auditorium with a representative number of interested patrons and parents attending.

Mrs. John Rushing, president, called the

meeting to order and presented Mrs. Conn Bolton, who directed the opening chorus in singing. Mrs. H. G Mullens led a brief devotional. Miss Frances Shirley read the minutes which were approved. A brief business session was transacted.

Professor N. F. Nunnally and Mrs. Luttrell McCall of the Holt High School spoke on the theme for the evening, "Training for Citizenship." E. J. Shipp read the president's message.

At the conclusion of the meeting, the P.T.A. served delicious refreshments consisting of homemade cake and coffee.

**Later in the above article, the following additional information is given.**
Fiddlers' convention

An old-time fiddlers' convention was held at Lafoy School recently under the auspices of the Parent Teacher Associator. A large crowd attended. Herman Perdue of the First National Bank was master of ceremonies. Aaron Gray, Comer Montgomery, and John O. Hamner won prizes for the best fiddling.

Miss Maurine Rushing won the prize for the prettiest girl and was presented a cake. A considerable sum was realized from the entertainment which will go to buy equipment for the school.

Thanksgiving

A delightful Thanksgiving program was rendered by pupils of the Lafoy school at the school building recently. Mrs. Frances Simpson led a beautiful devotional with Mrs. Conn Bolton leading in prayer with a song. Several appropriate Thanksgiving songs were sung by the group. Mrs. H. C. Mullins read stories of the Pilgrims and the first "Thanksgiving basket."

A short playlet was presented entitled "First Thanksgiving." The cast was composed of Mattie Sue Shirley, Howard Montgomery, Clara Yow, Jack Smelley, Melba Rushing and Irene Naramore.

**Boyd comment:**
Lafoy School was blessed with great teachers who not only stimulated their students to increase in knowledge, but they also offered programs that brought fun and laugher to the classroom.

**The *Tuscaloosa News*, August 17, 1947, front page**
**45 School Bus Drivers to get Lions Safety Awards**

45 school bus drivers in the Tuscaloosa County School System, adjudged "best all-round drivers" for the 1946-1947 school year will be honored Monday night by the Lions Club which will present "safe-driver" award certificates to the group. Among those chosen is Ause Sellers of the Crabbe Road.

**Boyd comment:**
In the 1940s and early 1950s, Mr. Sellers drove bus # 20, the bus that picked up all students who lived on the Crabbe Road from Turkey Creek to Two Mile Creek in Northport. The bus was very crowded with some students having to standup for lack of seats.

Eleventh and twelfth grade students were allowed to drive school buses in the 1950s and my brother Herman and I each drove bus # 20 when we were juniors and seniors in high school. My pay was $30 per month.

**Interviews with Dr. Jospeh Shipp, a former student**

When I began research for this memoir several years ago, the only living alumnus of Lafoy school was Dr. Joseph Shipp. We shared many conversations about his experiences at the school. Sadly, he died in 2021 at the age of ninety-five.

Young Shipp entered Lafoy school as a first grader in 1933 and remained a student there until 1940 when he entered Tuscaloosa County High School as a seventh grader.

It is interesting that pupils were not assigned a grade level at Lafoy. Rather, upon entering school at age six, the student was given a *Beginner's Primer* for reading and writing. When the

# THE LAFOY SCHOOL

student completed the beginner's primer, he or she advanced to the next level. Other subjects such as arithmetic were added along the way.

In the early 1920s, Ezra Jonah Shipp and Nora Earnest Shipp, Dr. Shipp's parents, bought a 100-acre farm across the Crabbe Road from Macedonia Methodist Church and built a home.

Joe tells of walking to school on a muddy road with the temperature below freezing. In dry weather, the road was dusty and his feet became sore from walking on the rocky roadbed. The one-mile trip took about fifteen minutes, longer if he stopped along the way to play. He did not have to take his lunch as the school had a good kitchen where hot meals were served each day.

Joe had a brilliant mind and achieved world renown as la physician who served as dean of two medical schools. He had glowing praise for the education he received at Lafoy School and stated his years there laid a solid academic basis for his subsequent ascent to lofty heights in academia. His favorite teacher was a retired professor from the University of Alabama.

His parents were very involved in school affairs. Mr. Shipp served as chairman of the board of directors and Mrs. Shipp served the school in several ways.

An entire chapter in this memoir is devoted to the Shipp family.

**Student enrollment at Lafoy School**
School terms in many areas in the rural South in the 1910s, 1920s, 1930s, and extending in some areas until the 1940s were five, or no more, than six months in length—November through March. This allowed children above the age of ten or eleven to be available to work on family farms and take day-labor jobs. Without the help of children, many families would not have survived in the economically deprived South in those years.

Tuscaloosa County School Superintendent James Sellers, in an article in the September 2, 1928 the *Tuscaloosa News*, urged parents to please keep their children enrolled in school. The article listed the faculty for Tuscaloosa County schools. Lafoy School's sole teacher for the 1928-1929 school year was Mrs. Floyd Robertson. However, by 1932 enrollment had increased to eighty-three students according to an article in the December 8, 1932 edition of *The Tuscaloosa News*. Lafoy School then had a faculty of two. The rapid turnover in teachers at Lafoy School is largely due to the fact many of the teachers were young single women, and when they married, they moved to other areas with their husbands.

**Methodology used in composing this story**
As noted, newspaper articles about Lafoy School provide much of the material that I use. In some instances, I offer commentary to personalize the story. Most of articles have been typed from *The Tuscaloosa News* as they appear on-line in the archives of *The Tuscaloosa News*. In general, the material is unaltered, including punctuation. In a few instances, part of an on-line article is smudged and unreadable. In those instances, notation of the fact is given.

**Boyd comment:**
As the storyline unfolds, the reader will discover the citizens of Lafoy, a small farming community made up of common folk many of whom did not have the opportunity to secure a formal education, supported Lafoy School even to the point of self-denial during the trying years of the Great Depression. The two-teacher school attracted dedicated men and women who loved their students and provided them with a good education.

**First public schools in rural Tuscaloosa County**
Free public education did not come to Northport and to rural areas of Tuscaloosa County until the beginning of the 20$^{th}$ century. The first truly public school in Northport, the Laycock School, was established by the City of Northport in 1901 and was located at the intersection of 9$^{th}$ Street and Main Avenue in downtown Northport. Initially,

the Laycock School included only grades one and two. Within the next few years, additional grades were added. A new two-story, brick school was built four blocks north on Main Avenue that included grades one through eleven, but no twelfth grade. The only high school in Tuscaloosa County that offered the twelfth grade prior to 1926 was Tuscaloosa High School.

In 1920, the Northport schools were incorporated into the Tuscaloosa County School System. In 1926, a new high school, Tuscaloosa County High School, was built at the intersection of 24th Street and 22nd Avenue. The former Northport High School became Northport Elementary School.

It is a lasting tribute to the people of Lafoy Community that it established a free community school in the first decade of the twentieth century.

In addition to Lafoy School, it is thought two other small schools were in the Lafoy Community. That history is now lost, but members of the Byrd Shirley family remember from their childhood in the 1950s there was a rock chimney on their property near Lary Lake Road that once was part of a small school. In the second instance, my father told me on multiple occasions that in the 1910s, he attended a small school on the Crabbe Road located on the bluff overlooking North River at its bridge. His teacher was Mrs. Octavia Tierce Hagler.

**Oldest known picture of Lafoy School**
The picture shown at the beginning of the chapter is circa 1940. This 1921 photo (on this page) of Thelma Rushing and Pricey "Ted" Shirley comes from the Joel Thomas "Tom" and Ida Curry Shirley family album. "Ted" was the daughter of Tom and Ida and was eighteen years old at the time. Thelma, daughter of Goldman and Ozella Hamner Rushing, was sixteen years old at the time. They are standing on the side steps of Lafoy School. This is the oldest known photo of the school. (In 1933, Pricey "Ted"

Thelma Rushing and Pricey "Ted" Shirley, Lafoy School 1921

Shirley was murdered by her husband Joe Dawson White. (A separate chapter in the memoir is devoted to that topic.)

As can be seen from the photo, the building was constructed in a "L" configuration consisting of two large open rooms. As noted earlier, the two rooms were laid out at 90 degrees to the other. A sliding section of wall was anchored on rollers and could be rolled on a track to create an "open" or "closed" setting. In the "closed" position, two separate classrooms were created allowing students to be divided into two classes. In its "open" position, the two wings of the building became one. This arrangement provided adequate space to accommodate square dancing, concerts, polit-

# THE LAFOY SCHOOL

ical rallies, and other community gatherings that might have an attendance of 200 people.

Drinking water came from a spring just north of the building. Outhouses for boys and girls were out back away from the school. During the years the school operated, electricity had not come to the Lafoy Community. That happened in 1941.

Research has produced no photo of the building built in 1911. That building was destroyed by wind in 1913. An article earlier in the chapter from the April 12, 1913, *Tuscaloosa News* tells the story. The rebuilt building shown at the beginning of the chapter remained essentially unchanged until it closed in 1941 except for periodic repairs including a new roof and repainting. When the Tuscaloosa County Board of Education sold the old building to Carrolls Creek Baptist Church in 1942, a few changes were made. The old school stage at the front of the room was renovated to accommodate a pulpit/choir area. Petitions were added to create Sunday School rooms. Electric power was available for the first time.

Members of the church were gracious to allow community events such as singings, political rallies, quilting parties, and over community civic events to continue to be held in the building until the early 1950s. I attended many political rallies there.

**Carrolls Creek Baptist Church**
A separate chapter is devoted to the churches of the Crabbe Road including Carrolls Creek Baptist. For the sake of continuity, I offer here the following comments on Carrolls Creek Church.

In the mid-1800s, John H. Carrolls, according to land records of Tuscaloosa County, purchased land a few miles north of Northport on the east side of the Crabbe Road. A creek ran through the property and it became known as Carrolls Creek. Mr. Carrolls died in 1873.

Asa Hamner and Pricey "Ted" Shirley, circa 1932

Carrolls Creek Baptist Church was founded in 1842. John H. Hamner and Samuel W. Hassell were faithful leaders in the church. However, the church was not constituted until 1877. Around 1867, a building, the Grange Building, was built on the Martin Road at its intersection with the Crabbe Road. The Grange was built by local famers as a site for community events. The structure had four large windows on each side and three doors, two on the front and one in the back. The Grange became the home of Carrolls Creek Baptist Church. The church had an excellent Sunday School and preaching was held after Sunday School twice a month. In 1942, the building burned. It was at this time that the church began meeting in the old Lafoy School building.

**Carrolls Creek Baptist Church (the Grange Building)**
The photo (above) of Thelma Rushing and Pricey "Ted" Shirley made in 1921 was made on the steps of Lafoy School. The 1932 photo (on page 126) was made in front of the Grange Building which served as the home for Carrolls Creek Baptist Church one year prior to Ted's murder.

The photograph on this page shows members of Carrolls Creek Baptist Church standing in front of the Grange building. Identification of individuals is not available. The age group span is from very young children to adults. Everyone is dressed in their Sunday best.

# A ROAD, A CEMETERY, A PEOPLE

*The Tuscaloosa News*, August 3, 1964
**Mrs. A. J. Deason, dies, retired school teacher**

Mrs. A. J. Deason of 1114 Main Ave., Northport died early Sunday morning at Druid City Hospital following a lengthy illness.

While a teacher in Tuscaloosa County for more than 30 years, she taught at Northport Elementary School, Lafoy School and was principal of Taylorville Elementary School.

Carrolls Creek Baptist Church members, circa 1930s

CHAPTER 7

# Growing up on a Cotton Farm

Topics presented in this chapter:
Introduction
Life on the Boyd farm
Sharecropping
Small acreage farms
Boll weevil control
Federal government incentives for not planting cotton
Local cotton gins
Two mules die when they fall in an abandoned well
4-H Clubs

**Introduction**
During the first half of the 20th century, like most rural areas in the South, many Lafoy Community families planted five or so acres of cotton for a source of cash. If at the end of the years, they netted $1,000 to $2,000 it was a good year. To supplement income earned from growing cotton and corn, the farmer might hire out and work in sawmills, cut timber, drive log trucks, dig coal, and work in construction.

Starting in 1901 with the opening of Central Foundry followed by the opening of Gulf States Paper Corporation in 1929 and Reichold Chemical in 1942, many Lafoy men found employment in local industries and depended less and less on growing cotton as the means of making a living. Still others worked at the Tuscaloosa Veterans Hospital or Bryce Hospital. In 1946, B. F. Goodrich opened a tire manufacturing plant in Tuscaloosa, and many returning soldiers from World War II found good paying jobs there.

Most families had large gardens in which they grew much of the food they ate—vegetables, fruits, molasses, and corn. The family cow produced needed dairy products. A flock of chickens provided eggs and was a major source of meat. Few things taste better than fried chicken and gravy on a hot biscuit! One or two hogs were slaughtered in early winter that provided tasty ham, bacon, and sausage. Life was a struggle, especially during the Great Depression of the 1930s, but no one in the community starved or lacked clothing and housing.

Land ownership was divided into two groups—family-owned farms of 100 acres or so that had been in the family for years and large-acreage farms owned by Northport merchants including the Rice, Christian, Faucett, Barnes, Holman, and other families. Their lands were leased out to tenant farmers.

My objective in this chapter is to describe the life I experienced growing up on a 120-acre farm that included five tenant farm families. In addition, I insert articles from the *Tuscaloosa News* from the 1930s and 1940s that are relevant.

**Life on the Boyd farm**
In the chapter "The Boyds of the Crabbe Road," it is noted that in 1940 my parents purchased a

# A ROAD, A CEMETERY, A PEOPLE

The Latham Barnes tenant house
The photo was made in 1974.

one-hundred-twenty-acre farm from Mrs. Lela Hyche Tierce Clements, the widow of Eugene B. Tierce, Sr. Included in the purchase was the Tierce house, an eight-room, four-porch lovely home built in 1896.

My father was not a farmer. He was a business man, a salesman at the local Ford agency, Tucker Motor Company. Daddy oversaw all farm activities performed by five tenant farm families who were also known as sharecroppers.

The US Department of Agriculture determined cotton allotment acreage for all farmers in the 1930s and 1940s. The allotment for our farm was thirty acres of cotton. Each of the five tenant houses were clustered within a hundred-yard radius of our home. The one shown here is the house occupied by the Latham Barnes family. It sat within forty feet of the Crabbe Road. It is the site where our current driveway exits the Crabbe Road.

Three of the tenant houses had a well in the yard, but the water in the wells were not safe to drink. It was suitable for washing clothes and dishes, bathing, and scrubbing floors. To secure drinking water, tenants had to walk to our house and fill up large buckets from a spigot in our yard and then trudge back home carrying those heavy jugs. I always felt sorry for the families, but I was helpless to do anything about the problem.

## Economics of sharecropping

The economics of sharecropping can be summed up in this manner. The land owner provides all the money and land needed to grow a crop of cotton. The sharecropper provides all the labor. When the cotton is sold at the end of the year, monies generated from the sale of the cotton is split between the land owner and the sharecropper, usually on a half and half ratio.

Daddy provided the land, a Ford tractor, three mules (Atta, Emma, and George), feed for the mules and diesel fuel for the tractor, fertilizer, seed, shoeing for the mules, veterinary bills, and insect control for boll weevils.

Throughout the year, Daddy provided a weekly cash advance to the sharecroppers to be used to buy groceries, staples, clothes, and other needed items including medical expenses. Mother kept a record of all financial transactions. Unlike some merchants in Northport, Daddy never charged interest on the money that he advanced to the sharecroppers during the year.

The sharecroppers provided all the labor including cutting and burning dead cotton and corn stalks from the prior year's crop, tilling the ground in preparation for planting, establishing a system of rows and terraces in the fields, planting the seeds, plowing, hoeing, "laying by" the field in July, and waiting for cotton picking time in late summer and early fall.

In December, the cotton was sold. The landowner and tenant farmer "settled up." The tenant paid back the money Daddy had advanced during the year. All leftover cash was split between Daddy and the tenant on a pre-agreed percentage. Any money the sharecropper had left over was his to keep, usually about $1,000.

Sharecropping never was a good system. A major problem was the matter of unpredictable weather. Floods or droughts could lead to total crop failure. Most sharecroppers, white and black, had little education, produced large families, and had few opportunities to secure public work, especially during the Great Depression years of the 1930s. However, the system did allow them to survive and keep food on the table. If a crop year was bad, Daddy wrote off the tenant's debt. He never forced a family to become homeless, go without food, or lose access to medical care. An example is seen in the instance of Jim Bonner, one of our tenants. Jim was an insulin-dependent diabetic, but Daddy always saw that he received his insulin and was taken to the doctor when necessary.

Spraying poison over a cotton field to kill boll weevils

## The perils of cotton farming for small land owners

Unlike my family, small land owners provided their own labor and had no sharecroppers. They often had to borrow money from Northport merchants at the beginning of the year to purchase seed, fertilizer, and other necessary items on which to live until the cotton was sold in December. They used a line of credit in which their farm served as collateral. At the end of the year when the cotton was sold, the farmer repaid the merchant who often charged interest on the loaned money. If there was a crop failure, the merchant foreclosed on the loan and the farmer lost his land. Unfortunately, this tragedy happened on many occasions in Tuscaloosa County. This allowed wealthy owners of large tracts of land to further increase their land holdings.

Poor business judgement on the part of one farmer resulted in the loss of all his property and other assets. The dear hardworking cotton farmer listened to bad advice given by his son-in-law. The son-in-law convinced the farmer to purchase a water sprinkler irrigation system to irrigate his fields. The water was pumped from nearby Carrolls Creek. The project was a failure, and the bank foreclosed on the loan. The elderly gentleman and his wife lost their home and farm and spent the rest of their lives living in vacant houses that belonged to family members.

## Spraying cotton for boll weevils

One of the most fascinating events of my summers on our farm was watching a small airplane spray boll weevil control dust over our fields. On a certain morning, Daddy would tell me, "Hayse, an airplane is going to spray the cotton today. Be on the lookout but stay a safe distance from the edge of the field."

I would spend the morning in the back yard waiting. Suddenly, I would hear the roar of a plane coming in the distance. As soon as the plane cleared the tree line of the field, the pilot would divebomb the plane until it was just a few feet above the ground. He would then pull a lever releasing thick dust as he flew over the ten-acre field. Just before the plane reached the tree line at the other end of the field, the plane would make a steep climb back into the sky. The plane was flying so fast the entire sweep lasted less than a minute. Then, the pilot would spray the field twice again before going to the next field. I held my breath for fear the pilot would crash.

The back of our house was less than a hundred feet from the field. The house was not air-conditioned so the windows remained open all summer. For several hours after a crop dusting, the odor and dust from the cotton poison dust extended all through the house.

**Earning money by not planting cotton**
The law of Supply and Demand is a basic economic principle that applies to all areas of economics, and it certainly influenced cotton farmers in our community during the 1930-1950 era. The US Federal Government offered incentives to farmers to reduce the amount of cotton they produced, either by not planting or plowing under cotton already planted. I remember Daddy discussing the matter with me and that he participated in the program. The following *Tuscaloosa News* articles discuss the program.

**September 24, 1933, *The Tuscaloosa News*, page 2**
**Curtis Hamner gets first cotton check**
Curtis Hamner, a young farmer living on Route 1, Northport (Watermelon Road), was happy Saturday as he received the first share of money in Tuscaloosa from the federal government's cotton reduction campaign.

Mr. Hamner, one among 120 for whom checks arrived Friday, called at the farm office in the post office building immediately after receiving an official notice that his money was available. Many others followed, and all checks in the initial group were expected to be delivered by early in the week.

Checks for the great majority of Tuscaloosa County farmers who plowed under their cotton have not yet been received. In fact, 2,326 are yet to be received. For that reason, the office urges farmers not to apply for the money until official notices have been sent to them, and all such notices for those in the first group were mailed Friday. The first checks represented $7,238 out of approximately $130,000 to be distributed in the county.

**September 26, 1933, *The Tuscaloosa News*, front page**
**Less than 50 ask for their cotton checks**
**To be returned unless owners apply in 15 days**
What's wrong?

This question was directed today to those 80 or more Tuscaloosa County cotton-growers who have not called for their checks at farm headquarters in the downtown post office.

Checks for 128 persons who plowed under their cotton during the crop-reduction arrived last Friday, and today less than 50 growers have called for their money, even though notified by special cards.

The office has received instructions to return checks to Washington if they have not been delivered by 15 days after receipt, which means October 6.

Do not call for the money however unless notified by card. These cards will be mailed out immediately upon the arrival of each group of checks.

**October 1, 1933, *Tuscaloosa News*, front page**
**Fourth group of checks arrive for county**
**96 received Saturday, total now stands at $37,642**
Cotton farmers of Tuscaloosa County saw a big day Saturday when scores of them received their money in the federal government crop reduction campaign and another group of 98 checks, the fourth for the county, arrived here for distribution.

The latest checks that amount to $6,034 proved the third batch in as many days. G. W. Ray said the post office headquarters moved steadily forward with the distribution of the money in all parts of the country.

Except for half a dozen, the first group of 128 checks received September 23 had been given out Saturday. On Thursday of this week, 284 checks were received and 174 on Friday. A number of these had been distributed Saturday afternoon.

The latest checks bring the total to $37,642 with 682 farmers to share in this money. When the last checks have been delivered, approximately $130,000 in money will have been given to 2,452 farmers.

Mr. Ray's office again stated that farmers must bring their cards with them in order to receive the money.

**The March 11, 1938 Friday**
**Cotton Farmers vote Saturday**
**Voting places open 9:00 a.m.**
**Auburn, Alabama**

Alabama cotton farmers will join other southern ruralists tomorrow in voting to determine whether marketing quotas shall be enforced on the 1938 crop under the new agriculture adjustment act.

Walter L. Randolph, state chief of the Agriculture Adjustment Administration, estimated that 282,000 Alabamians would be eligible to vote.

Randolph said that Covington and Geneva County growers would vote on tobacco quotas, estimating that only about 25 would be eligible to cast ballots. Alabama produces only flue-type tobacco.

To be eligible to vote on quotas, farmers must have produced either cotton or tobacco last year. Two-thirds must favor quotas if they are enforced.

Randolph said that 1300 polling places had been designated.

Balloting in Tuscaloosa County tomorrow will be held at the customary polling places in beats throughout the county. In some cases where there are usually two boxes in the beat, there will be one box however, said County Agent A. W. Jones.

The polls will open at 9:00 a.m. and remain open until 7:00 p.m. with committees of farmers serving as officials. Three members have been named for each committee.

**March 13, 1938 in which the following is found:**
**Overwhelming Farm Vote Approves Cotton Quota**
**Tally in This County Goes 4,410 to 82 for Quota Approval**

Tuscaloosa County voted approximately 55 to 1 for the cotton proposal according to totals announced late Saturday night by County Agent A. W. Jones. The county figure with all boxes reported was 4, 410 to 82.

Nine beats were reported giving the plan unanimous approval, including the Fosters precent where 274 votes were cast. The heaviest vote against the quota systems was at Brownville where 34 opposed it.

The count was quickly completed after polls closed at 7:00 p.m. and canvassing committees quickly brought their results to the courthouse.

The Tuscaloosa County ballot, by beat, follows.

|  | Yes | No |
|---|---|---|
| Windham Springs | 106 | 1 |
| New Lexington | 200 | 0 |
| Moore's Bridge | 131 | 0 |
| Gorgas | 318 | 7 |
| Kellerman | 28 | 0 |
| Hassells | 73 | 0 |
| Samantha | 163 | 4 |
| Elrod | 125 | 1 |
| Hughes | 72 | 0 |
| Northport | 502 | 4 |
| Brookwood | 70 | 1 |
| Abernant | 65 | 1 |
| Vance | 132 | 2 |
| Coaling | 106 | 1 |
| Cottondale/Holt | 50 | 1 |
| Tuscaloosa | 473 | 5 |

| | | |
|---|---|---|
| Ralph | 151 | 1 |
| Friersons | 215 | 1 |
| Duncanville | 129 | 0 |
| Echola | 88 | 7 |
| Romulus | 169 | 1 |
| Fosters | 274 | 0 |
| Mitchells | 97 | 4 |
| Brownsville | 127 | 34 |
| Whitson | 64 | 1 |
| Coker | 73 | 0 |
| Taylorville | 200 | 3 |
| Sterling | 52 | 1 |
| Buhl | 84 | 1 |
| Carrolls Creek | 29 | 0 |

(Lafoy Community is identified here as Carrolls Creek.)

### *Tuscaloosa News* Jan 1, 1940 cotton production

From the 10-year period from 1928-1937, Alabama ranked fourth across America in cotton production. Its production for this period averaged 1,203, 000 bales. Texas topped them all with 4,077,000. Mississippi came in second with an average of 1 596, 000 and Arkansas came in third with 1,273,000.

During the last and lamented crop year just quietly laid to rest, Alabama ranked sixth in cotton production with something like 660,000 bales of cotton. Texas as usual came in first and Mississippi held on to second as did Arkansas third. Georgia however took Alabama's fourth place and even South Carolina which usually produces 400, 000 less than Alabama took fifth. As a matter of fact, we were barely able to nose out Louisiana and our crop was less than twice the size of California which over the ten-year period has produced less than one-fourth of that of Alabama.

In the late 1940s, federal programs urging farmers to limit the production of cotton remained in effect. I recall Daddy discussing the subject with Mother. "How much of our allotted cotton acreage shall we not plant this year?"

Our 1949 Ford pickup looked just like this one.

### Picking cotton and getting it to the gin

All cotton on our farm was picked by hand. Commercial mechanical cotton pickers were not widely available until the 1950s. A good cotton picker could pick 250-300 pounds of raw cotton in a day. The average was 150 pounds per day. About 1,200 pounds of raw cotton were needed to result in a 450-500 bale of ginned cotton.

If hired helpers were brought in to help harvest the cotton, they were paid two cents per pound of cotton picked. They earned $2 to $3 each day. During August prior to the opening of school in September, I often picked cotton to earn a little spending money. I certainly did not get rich as I rarely picked 100 pounds or more.

Two gins were in Northport. Barnes and Norris Gin was at the south end of Main Street on the banks of the Black Warrior River. Rice Brothers Gin was on 10th Street adjacent to the old Northport L & N trains station. During harvest season, I often had the opportunity on Saturday to drive our 1949 Ford pickup loaded with 1,200 pounds of raw cotton to one of the two gins. I would leave the truck there and walk a few blocks to Faucett's Store on Main Avenue where I held a job on Saturdays. At the end of the day, I would drive the empty truck home and repeat the process the next Saturday.

The event recorded in the following news article did not happen in the Lafoy Community, but the related account of a near tragedy did hap-

# GROWING UP ON A COTTON FARM

A gin on the Byler Road near Northport 1930s
The two mules and wagon are representative of the mules and cotton wagon used on the Boyd farm.

Barnes and Norris Gin long after it closed

pen to me on the Boyd farm.

**December 24, 1933, *Tuscaloosa News* page 7**
**Two mules die when they fall into a well**
Two mules belonging to Johnnie Snider of Taylorville died when they fell into an abandoned well in the southwestern part of the city.

Snider's two boys had driven the wagon to town with a load of wood, and they later stopped at a friend's house

Unhitched, the mules were drawn to a patch of hay scattered over a set of old bedsprings in the yard. The springs had been used to cover an abandoned well, and as the mules stepped upon them, the springs gave way.

The mules dropped 25 feet into the well. Efforts to rescue them while still alive proved of no avail. Eventually, a wrecker was summoned from Canty's Garage and the machine, a new two-and-a-half-ton affair, lifted the mules out of the well.

The above story calls to mind a near tragedy in my own life. In 1977, Peggy and I moved back to the Boyd farm after having lived in Birmingham since 1961. One day I was tramping through the woods near the site where one of our tenant houses once stood. The house had long since rotted down. I had forgotten that there was an old dug well in the yard. Over the years, the wood casing outlining the covering to the well had rotted and the area was covered with pine straw, decaying leaves, and overgrowth. As I made my way through the vines, I suddenly stepped on a piece of the rotten board covering the well. As with the two mules in the news article, my leg began to slip down into the deep dark hole. I held on to a vine for dear life and was able to wriggle out of the well. This could have been a major disaster. The well was about twenty feet deep. Peggy had no idea where I was. I was so far from the house that no one could hear me hollering for help. I might not have been found for hours, or days! The next day I had a load of gravel dumped into the hole leaving no sign of the prior well.

**The race to have the first bale of cotton ginned August 23, 1947 *Tuscaloosa News* front page Partners pick 40 acres to win first-bale title Parham-Averette, also grocers take cotton prize in first try**

Two brothers-in-law partners in a grocery store who rented a cotton farm last March with the intention of ginning Tuscaloosa County's first bale of cotton of the 1947 crop won their race this week. It was won when Allie Averette, 24 and Adrian Parham, 27, brought in 1200 pounds of seed cotton at noon Tuesday produced a 425 bale of cotton.

"We had to spend a day and a half picking cotton over a 40-acre area with 15 workers helping to get that bale out" the modest partners admitted when asked how they managed to take first honors.

**Sells for $210.42**

Their first bale ginned at 1:00 p.m. Tuesday, August 19, brought them $210.42. This was $68.67 above normal spot cotton prices, a premium of about 17 cents per pound being paid by Rice Brothers Gin of Northport. Frank Rice who bid the cotton in at auction said he was buying it for Avondale Mills, a firm of Sylacauga that has bought more than half of Tuscaloosa County cotton for the past 20 years.

Aaron Christian, longtime friend of the two cotton growers, handled the auction gavel. In addition to their premium sale price, the Averette-Parham combination received a $10 first-bale prize presented by Hugo Freidman of the Friedman-Hansard Cotton Company.

Days of "watchful waiting" preceded "D-Day," the day an all-out assault began that yielded the first bale the partners agreed. When they decided early Monday that enough open cotton was in the field to make a bale, they started picking and stayed with it.

This prize-winning partnership developed last year when Parham returned from the US Navy where he had served for two years. The two young men decided to go into the grocery business together and opened the A. G. S. Grocery store in Southside.

Early this year they made plans to branch out their operations and rented the Edgar Tidmore farm at Hulls eight miles south of Tuscaloosa on the Greensboro Highway. They planted 90 acres in cotton and 25 acres in corn.

It was then they started "staying with it" as Adrian explained the operation.

**The *Tuscaloosa News*, date is missing**
**First open bolls**

On Wednesday, August 6, they brought to town the first reported open bolls of cotton in this county. They were quoted in *The News* as saying "Whoever get the first bale honors in Tuscaloosa County will have to beat us to the gun."

The partners kept right on "staying with it" despite the hardworking effects of boll weevils, and the recent attack of Army worms on the farms and gardens of that section. First bale honors on their first year of partnership is the result. Both men are experienced farmers although this was the first time they worked together.

Winning first-bale honors is nothing new for the Averette family although this was Allie's first cotton triumph. His dad, Ivin Averette, has copped honors in prior years. The father said he had brought in the first bale about six times in 23 years of cotton growing.

Allie and Adrian became related when Parham married Allie's sister, Miss Lois Averette.

Last year Frank Foster, Negro, produced Tuscaloosa County's first bale of cotton on the J. W. Parker place bringing in a 420-pounder on August 15. Back in 1945, Frank was the first in line with a 433-pound bale.

The preceding article made mention of army worms. I include the following *Tuscaloosa News* article on the subject.

**The Tuscaloosa News, August 7, 1947, page four**
**Army worms**
**Phenix City, Ala**

Russell County farmers were purchasing quantities of DDT today in a desperate bid to check a wave of small Army worms which were destroying corn, alfalfa, and sugarcane crops.

County Agent V. O. Deloney said the worms were attacking crops in all parts of the county and advised farmers to use DDT or cryolite in resisting them. The Army worm, he said, remains hidden during the day and attacks plants at night. Its presence is not usually suspected until the crop is almost destroyed.

Dichlorodiphenyltrichloroethane, commonly known as DDT, is a colorless, tasteless, and almost odorless crystalline chemical compound, an organochloride. Originally developed as an insecticide, it became infamous for its environmental impacts. DDT was first synthesized in 1874 by the Austrian chemist Othmar Zeidkcmical. It is now banned in the United States.

During the World War II years, 1941-1945, the United States Government placed many restrictions on civilians regarding items urgently needed by the military to fight a war. Restrictions applied to agriculture as well as is demonstrated in the following article.

**September 1, 1942**
**By O. N. Andrews, Assistant County Agent**
**4 H Club**

Boys who plan to take corn as the project for next year should start now. Due to the use of nitrate in the manufacturing of vital war material, we are advised not to expect any use of soda nitrate as a side dressing in the production of our crops. To produce profitable yields of corn on our lands in our county it is essential to use nitrogen. We can provide this nitrogen right on our farms by planting Australian winter peas or fetch.

The nitrogen produced on a good acre of Australian peas or fetch would save enough commercial nitrogen to produce one 500-pound bomb. So, select the area you expect to plant in corn next spring and then make plans for planting and producing a good crop of legumes. If you follow the following recommendations, you should produce a crop of legumes that under average conditions will increase your production of corn yield by 10-15 bushels per acre.

First select an area that produces average yields. If you plant on poor washed-away soil, you will be disappointed unless you use large amounts of phosphate fertilizer.

Second. Apply 200-300 pounds of sulfur phosphate or 300-400 pounds of basic slag.

Third, inoculate your seed. Dampen seed with sweeten water and mix them thoroughly with commercial inoculation. As much as possible, remove soil from an area that has produced a good crop of Australian winter peas or vetch equal to the amount you have of seed.

Fourth. Drill or broadcast 20-25 pounds of hairy vetch or Australia winter pea per acre between September 1 and October 15. Early planting allows you to turn your legumes earlier in the spring.

Cooperate with the war effort. 4 H club members of Tuscaloosa County and Alabama have made a great contribution to our victory program. They have increased their production projects to produce food for freedom. They have bought stamps and bonds and cooperated with agencies that sponsor this program. They have collected scrap iron, rubber, and paper. The harvest season is here. Invest as much of your earning as possible in war bonds and savings.

Let me insist you make another search of your farm and your neighbor's farms and collect up the rest of that scrap iron and paper. Everybody has a place in winning this war. Most of you are too young to join up but you can help provide equipment for your older brothers and friends by collecting scrap iron and rubber.

## July 1, 1946
### B.R. Holston takes over as farm agent

Beverley R. Holstun returned to his duties as Tuscaloosa County Farm agent after an absence of nearly four years which he spent in the US Army during World War II.

Holston had been granted a leave of absence by the county board of revenue. O. N. Andrews, former assistant county agent, who has been acting agent in Holston's absence, has been assigned to special duties in promoting livestock and dairy programs in Tuscaloosa County. John Weeks will continue to serve as assailant agent in charge of boys 4 H club work in the county.

## Community Programs Guide Lafoy to Better Living
### *The Tuscaloosa News*, January 1951

Members of the Lafoy Community located about eight miles north of Tuscaloosa on the Crabbe Road are leaving a trail of local improvement and development that reaches into every home and every part of this community.

Working through their community club which meets one night each month, they have for several years kept at the task of improving their surroundings. In 1947, and again in 1948, the club was awarded certificates for outstanding work done in community improvement. They are out to win another honor this year.

Mrs. T. S. Black, Chairman of the Community Improvement Committee, has set a good example by improving her own farm home. Others have followed Mrs. Black's example by adding clothes closets to bedrooms and constructing additional rooms to the house. Now that electric utility service is available in the community, electric water pumps are installed in wells. This allows for indoor running water and the addition of bathrooms. Gone are the smelly outhouses in back yards. For the first time, farm housewives are beginning to purchase electric kitchen stoves, refrigerators, deep freezers, washing machines and other electrical appliances.

At the regular monthly meetings, both educational and recreational programs are planned and carried out by the members. County Agent B. R. Holstum and his staff bring the latest information on farming and homemaking to an interested audience of 75 members.

Other projects that will improve farm living are studied and followed by Lafoy residents. Cotton production, corn production and pasture improvement are only a few of the subjects that receive attention by the progressive group.

All members of the group, old and young, join in the fun after the learning session. Three or four may bring along fiddles or guitars and play. Some of the children may put on a skit or they all join in an old-fashioned group singing. Whatever the attraction, everyone joins in whether it is work or play.

Members of the community believe they have close to a record on farm Bureau membership. Almost every adult in the community is a member.

Finally, the community projects show the interest they take in their community churches. They have spent $150 for shrubbery to landscape their three churches—Macedonia Methodist, Carrolls Creek Baptist, and Union Chapel Methodist. Members have also donated several hundred dollars to the building fund to build a new church building for Carrolls Creek Baptist.

The Lafoy community clubs have three guiding thoughts for better living on the farm and for a better farm community: (1) education on how to do the job; (2) cooperation to get the job done; (3) recreation to make the job seem easier.

CHAPTER 8

# Dock "Doc" Bigham (1869-1918)

Doc Bigham (often spelled "Dock"), a bootlegger in the Piney Woods Community seven miles north of my boyhood home on the Crabbe Road, shot and killed Tuscaloosa County Sheriff P. M. Watts on August 15, 1918, and injured sheriff deputies Verner Robertson and Nick Hamner, along with special revenue officers Smith and Draper when the law enforcement party raided Bigham's whiskey still.

My introduction to the tragic tale of Doc Bigham dates to childhood when I first stood at his grave in Macedonia Methodist Cemetery as my father related the sad story of this notorious outlaw. Doc's grave is just a few feet from the Boyd family plot which at the time contained only the earthly remains of my little brother John Howard Boyd. The Boyd plot would include my mother, in 1958, and my father, in 1964.

As noted in other chapters, each first Sunday in May is *Decoration and Homecoming Day* at Macedonia. Family members place flowers on the graves of loved ones and then enjoy an all-day singing in the church with dinner on the ground at lunch. No flowers were ever placed on Doc's grave. Every time I visited the cemetery and paused to look at his tombstone, the tragic story was refreshed in my mind.

I have a second personal connection to the Doc Bigham story. At the time of the killing, the closest telephone to the shooting site from which to call the sheriff's office asking for help was in our home. Until the early 1950s, public telephone service was not available in the Lafoy Community. However, back in the 1910s, E. B. Tierce and six other families in the community had had a private telephone system installed in their homes. In the Tierce home, the wall-mounted telephone was hung in the front hall of the house. When my parents bought the Tierce home and farm in 1940, the old phone remained in working order and was the phone people in the community used in times of emergency. It was from that phone that the call went forth to the sheriff's office in Tuscaloosa calling for help.

On many occasions, residents of the rural areas north of our home came to our house to use the phone to call for the law, a doctor, the coroner, or the undertaker when needs arose. That was much quicker than driving all the way to town to seek help.

The phone remains in pristine condition and is now mounted on the wall beside my computer. Each morning as I begin my day and look at the beautiful old phone, I ponder the messages that have passed through its wiring over the past 110-plus years. None were more poignant than the call of August 15, 1918.

**Doc Bigham, the man**

Doc Bigham was known as one of the most notorious criminals that ever lived in West Alabama. Born in the Piney Woods area in 1869, Bigham's conflict with the law began early in life. As a teenager, he had married and fathered two sons who followed the lifestyle set by their dad.

In 1893, twenty-five years prior to killing Sheriff Watts in 1918, Bigham was arrested on charges of the ambush murder of his uncle, E. Cooper, for which he was reportedly paid fifty dollars. He also was charged with killing a black man, Sonny Prewitt. Bigham bragged publicly that thirteen people had been put in jail for the murder of Prewitt but none had been convicted. He boasted that he was present and could, but would not, identify the murderer. Also, he was accused of being a part of the burning of several houses in the E. B. Tierce, Sr., neighborhood. He denied the charge but claimed he knew the identity of the guilty party.

Bigham was given a twenty-five-year sentence to the Alabama State Penitentiary in Wetumpka, the first state prison in Alabama whose construction was completed in 1841 at a cost of $84,889. The 208-cell prison was surrounded by a twenty-five-foot wall. During the 1920s, the facility was used exclusively for women. Male offenders were housed in Kilby Prison at Mt. Meigs an unincorporated community in Montgomery County.

Bigham could neither read nor write, but because he was such a likeable fellow, he gained the confidence of state prison keepers and was made a trusty. In 1914, despite the confining wall around the prison, he escaped and returned to Tuscaloosa County. For two months, he dodged capture by hiding in the woods. Common talk was that Dock's cronies continually notified him of each movement of the law allowing him to stay one step ahead of arrest.

**Hiding out following escape from prison — 1914**
Word got out that Dock and his sons were living in a tent on land owned by I. A. Robertson near the Warrior River twelve miles south of Tuscaloosa just off Foster's Ferry Road. As Tuscaloosa police officers Hertis Thomson and Bertram Ozment approached the tent, they were fired upon and got separated. Thomson thought Ozment had been killed. He sent word to Tuscaloosa asking for help. Tuscaloosa County Sheriff W. C. Palmer and several deputies and policemen, along with Coroner Rogers and several doctors hurried to the scene. Ozment was soon located unharmed as was Thomson. Judge H.B. Foster notified Governor Emmett O'Neal and the reward for the capture of Bigham was raised from $50 to $150.

Two days later on November 10, 1914, Bigham and his son, seventeen-year-old Dugs, were located on the bank of the Warrior River several miles below Foster's Ferry. As officers approached, Bigham and his son opened fire. The officers returned fire and both Bigham and son went down. Dugs rapidly bled to death from a severed artery in his leg. Doc was badly wounded. He was taken up the Warrior River to Tuscaloosa in a boat where he was treated at the Williamson Faulk infirmity in Tuscaloosa. Dr. J. H. Ward said he believed Doc would likely recover; he did.

Note: Macedonia Methodist Cemetery records show that Dugs was born May 15, 1897 and died November 10, 1914.

Area gossip soon spread that Doc begged the officers to take a gun and shoot him dead as he was so despondent over Dug's death. Bigham's second son, George Bigham, alias George Scales, was captured and placed in the Tuscaloosa County Jail. Doc was sent back to prison at Wetumpka, but in 1918 he escaped Wetumpka Prison a second time and returned to Piney Woods. By then, in his own mind, he was a greatly persecuted man. Like many others of the era, Bigham was of the mindset that he had a right to grow his own corn and to turn it into booze and it was no other man's business. He vowed he never would be taken alive again.

**The shootout at Piney Woods August 15, 1918**
On August 15, 1918, Tuscaloosa County Sheriff Palmer M. Watts armed with a rifle and a pistol and deputies Verner Robertson and Nick Ham-

# DOCK "DOC" BIGHAM (1869-1918)

ner, along with special revenue officers J. H. Smith and J. H. Draper raided two big whiskey stills in Piney Woods. They arrested two moonshiners and were on their way to a third still when a shotgun blast shattered the quietness of the woods. Robertson and Hamner rushed to the sheriff's body only to discover he was already dead. As Robertson was bending over Watt's body, he saw a man hiding behind whiskey barrels with a shotgun pointing straight toward him. The gun discharged severely wounding Robertson in the left arm and shoulder. Robertson called for Draper and Smith who had become separated from one another. Realizing the seriousness of his wounds and barely able to walk, Robertson began to make his way to the nearest house on the Crabbe Road a mile away to seek help not waiting for Smith and Draper.

In the meantime, and upon hearing the shots, Draper began walking toward the area. He saw Watt's body lying near a small stream, but at the moment, he thought the sheriff was hiding from the shooter. Upon reaching Watts, he realized he was dead. Looking around, he got a glance of a man crawling down the hill toward a ravine. The two men exchanged pistol fire as the moonshiner ran off in the woods. Later upon capture, it was discovered that Draper's shot had wounded one of Bigham's arms and had shot off one kneecap. Draper then made his way to the nearest house where he found Robertson's wound being attended. Office Smith arrived soon afterward.

Bob Kyle (1909-1990) was a *Tuscaloosa News* staff writer and organizer of local political rallies during the 1940s-1970s decades. His weekly column was probably the most-read article of any concerning local news. I looked forward to reading it each week. He is truly a legend of my generation. In his *Tuscaloosa News* article on April 28, 1957, recapturing the Doc Bigham story, he states that on August 15, 1918, Deputies Robertson and Hamner along with agents Smith and Draper and two captured moonshine prisoners stopped at the E. B. Tierce house, the house in which I grew up, to telephone word of what had happened and of their impending arrival.

### The capture of Bigham
W. C. Kyle was appointed acting sheriff following Sheriff Watts' death. Kyle served until B. B. Hughes was elected sheriff in 1919. Hughes served from 1919-1923. In 1922, W. C. Kyle was elected sheriff and served from 1923-1928.

Piney Woods was a tight community with little use for the law. Bootlegging was a way of life and protecting your neighbor was a matter of survival. But in this instance, the citizens of Tuscaloosa County were outraged over the killing of Watts and most viewed the bootleggers of Piney Woods as a gang of outlaws and desperados. Bloodhounds were brought in and a posse formed. When they reached the scene of the shootout, a relative of Doc Bigham reported that Bigham, a man who had twice escaped the Alabama State Penitentiary in Wetumpka where he was serving a twenty-five-year prison term for killing two men, along with other crimes, was indeed the man who killed Sheriff Watts.

Bigham managed to escape capture for three days. On the third night about nine-o'clock, Bigham was captured in the swamps of Turkey Creek about four miles from the site of the murder. He was unarmed and made no fight as the bloodhounds closed in on him. While in hiding, he had tried to doctor his wounds by running a string through the hole made in his knee by a bullet. He had dampened the string with kerosene oil and pulled the string to and fro in hopes of sterilizing the wound. Sixteen people were arrested, some for moonshine-related activities and others were detained as witnesses. Others were held for harboring the killer and aiding in his escape.

### The trial and appeal
On September 17, 1918, Bigham went before a jury in Tuscaloosa presided over by Judge H. B. Foster and was charged with the murder of Sher-

iff Watts. Tuscaloosa attorney F. F. Windham represented the defendant.

Bigham did not deny killing Watts, but he said it was in self-defense. However, the state presented evidence that when Watts' rifle had been removed from beneath his body, it had not been fired. Testimony from Piney Woods residents testified that Bigham knew the raid was coming and had said that he would kill the first g... d... officer that appeared at his still.

Note: the following is an excerpt from the Alabama Supreme Court records relating to Bigham's appeal. It affirms the truth of preceding paragraph:

When Pete Leonard was introduced as a witness [before the Supreme Court of Alabama] by the state, he testified that Kil Sellers and the defendant Doc Bigham were related by marriage and told of the occasion on the morning before the homicide when defendant came to Sellers' house at 4 o'clock and Bigham told Sellers that if "they" (identified elsewhere as Pete Leonard and a Mr. Barnett) would watch, he (Bigham) would 'go down there and run it (the moonshine) off and that the first man that came in there he would kill him if he was an officer.'

The Tuscaloosa County jury foreman was John Wesley Morrison. The trial lasted for three days. The jury debated for five hours. When the jury returned to the courtroom, Judge Foster asked if the jury had reached a verdict. Morrison replied, "Yes, your honor. We find the defendant guilty." Judge Foster passed a death sentence to be carried out by a public hanging on the grounds of the Tuscaloosa County jail on November 1, 1918.

Defending counsel appealed the verdict to the Alabama Supreme Court. The high court did not hear the appeal until May 15, 1919. It upheld the lower court ruling and set June 19, 1919 as execution date at which time Bigham "would be hung by the neck until dead." Attorney Windham sought a hearing and pardon from Governor Thomas B. Kilby both of which were denied.

**The interval between the September 17, 1918 trial and the hanging on June 19, 1919**

During this period, Bigham often was the only prisoner in the Tuscaloosa County jail. He was befriended by Dr. C. M. Boyd, pastor of the First Presbyterian Church of Tuscaloosa. The kindly preacher visited Bigham almost daily offering spiritual guidance. Bigham made a profession of faith in Jesus Christ. He related that he had never heard the real story of Christ and was now ready to meet his Creator. Dr. Boyd asked the sheriff if he would allow him to be arm-cuffed to Bigham and take him to church with two plain clothed officers in front and one behind and sit in the balcony. Boyd was granted his request.

Two months before his execution, Bigham reluctantly posed for his picture to be taken for the local newspaper *The West Alabama Breeze*. He said he did not want to talk any more about the case because every time he talked about it, he got mad. He did not like to get in that frame of mind. He requested to be buried in Macedonia Methodist Cemetery ten miles north of Tuscaloosa on the Crabbe Road near the grave of his son Dugs and other relatives. As noted earlier in the story, Dugs had been killed in a shootout with the law on November 10, 1914. Doc's wife had long previously divorced him.

**The hanging**

Between 9:00 and 10:00 a.m. on June 19, 1919, the sheriff and his deputies began fixing the rope and oiled the trap door hinges. Bigham asked and was granted permission to tie the hangman's knot to guarantee an instant break of his neck in the fall. He also asked that the sheriff not permit the hanging rope to be cut into bits and carried away as souvenirs as was sometimes done. The rope was arranged so that Doc's body would fall six feet giving sufficient momentum to give the proper jerk when the end of the rope was reached. The customary number of wraps were made around the rope so that the weight of Bigham's body would cause it to slip easily when the big knot at

# DOCK "DOC" BIGHAM (1869-1918)

the upper end of the hangman's neck would strike behind the ear, breaking his neck when the weight of the body jerked on the rope.

The crowd gathered early on the execution day. Many asked to see Doc but their requests were denied. The sheriff put a lock on the gate by the jail and posted guards including deputies Will Lee and W. F. Wright. Three physicians and Dr. C. M. Boyd, pastor of the First Presbyterian Church of Tuscaloosa and Bigham's spiritual mentor who had led him to faith in Jesus Christ, were there. Dr. Boyd had brought a new suit of clothing for Bigham to wear.

Sheriff Hughes and Dr. Boyd accompanied Bigham to the gallows shortly before 11:00 a.m. The crowd around the jail was made up of many of the grownups of Tuscaloosa County including rural farmers who had turned their mules to pasture and had come to town to watch the hanging. Everything was done orderly. Guards had been employed to hold back the curious. Many city folks had taken the day off. When the hour of 11:00 a.m. came, the crowd outside fell silent. Men took off their hats. Doc had requested that the trapdoor lever be pulled by Sheriff Perry B. Hughes' brother B. V. Hughes, a man Bigham felt to be "an honest man." At 11:02 a.m., Hughes pulled the lever. Doc's body fell through the hole and his neck was broken by the fall. The doctors recorded a pulse beat for a few minutes but thought he did not suffer. As the body hung, the crowd grew compassionate. A hat was passed around and $49 dollars were collected to see that Doc had a respectable burial which was conducted by Dr. Boyd at Macedonia Methodist Cemetery.

Doc Bigham was the last person legally hanged in Tuscaloosa County.

# A ROAD, A CEMETERY, A PEOPLE

CHAPTER 9

# Moonshining on the Crabbe Road

The Eighteenth Amendment to the US Constitution making the manufacture, transportation, and sale of alcohol illegal was passed by the U.S. Congress in 1917. In 1919, the amendment was ratified by three-quarters of the nation's states. This met the requirement to make it constitutional. On January 17, 1920, the entire United States went dry shutting down the country's fifth-largest industry. In November of 1932, Franklin Delano Roosevelt was elected president after campaigning, among other things, to end Prohibition. On December 5, 1933, the 21st Amendment to the US Constitution repealing nationwide prohibition in the United States was ratified.

As occurred throughout the nation, prohibition gave rise to the manufacture of moonshine whiskey. The term "moonshine" comes from the fact that illegal alcoholic drinks were made under the light of the moon. In every part of America, early moonshiners worked their stills at night to avoid detection from authorities and to avoid the taxes placed on alcohol spirits that began shortly after the American Revolution.

During the period of prohibition and continuing into the mid-1950s, moonshining was common along the Crabbe Road, particularly in the area between North River and Piney Woods.

The following articles from the *Tuscaloosa News* tell an intriguing story of local moonshining.

*The Tuscaloosa News*, **July 19, 1929**
**Still Raiders Find Dead Hog in 3,000 Gallon Plant as Officers Continue Countywide Cleanup**

Law breakers, liquor stills, mash, beer, and a dead hog were numbered among the confiscations of state and county law enforcement officers Wednesday as the cleanup of Tuscaloosa County continued. There were four arrests, two cars were confiscated, four stills were destroyed, beer poured out and a severely decayed body of a dead hog was found inside one still.

The raids were conducted by O. L. Lawrence, Jr., the Tuscaloosa County enforcer in cooperation with Pugh Haynes and W. H. Harrison of the State Law Enforcement Department under Chief W. C. McAdory. The big liquor hauls were reported made in the northern portion of the county in the North River swamps. Chief McAdory is expected here today to direct personally efforts to dry up this section.

The four stills destroyed included two with 3,000-gallon capacity, one 1,500-gallon capacity, and one 500-gallon capacity. One of the largest gave forth the dead hog with its skin slipping and hang-hug about the already rotting bones as the gruesome body tumbled from the still. Buzzards circled above and vermin beneath while green flies buzzed a sardonic flight overhead.

Officers were almost overcome by the odor and the repulsive site. They were forced to place

143

handkerchiefs over their noses to approach the still where the dead hog's body was plainly seen half in and half out in the slimy pool of moonshine beer.

When the moonshiner returns to his still, he will find sure evidence of the officers' visit. And the moonshiner will likely return to get his hat.

The hat found nearby by the officers is now perched on the skull of the drowned hog and the skull is hanging on a tree. If the moonshiner is smart, he will recognize this as a warning that his practice is imperiling lives in Tuscaloosa County, Officer Haynes said.

State enforcement men say that such slimy finds are not uncommon, but frequent in the moonshine raiding business. Snakes, dogs, cats, hogs, and other larger animals are frequently disgorged by destroying stills while the smaller insects and vermin are found at practically every site.

The four arrests Wednesday included three for violation of the prohibition law and one for carrying concealed weapons.

Wednesday's toll raised the five-week campaign to 47 stills destroyed with 41,000 gallons of beer and mash poured out.

*The Tuscaloosa News,* **July 21, 1929**
**11 More Stills Are Destroyed by Dry Forces**
**McAdory Personally Leads Attacks on Moonshiners**
Eleven more stills fell before the axes of state and county law enforcement officers on Thursday and Friday in their cleanup of Tuscaloosa County, but instead of the liquor plants disclosing the bodies of dead hogs, five swollen rats were yielded in one of the huge pools of mash poured out on the hills near Lock 17.

Chief W. K. McAdory, head of the state law enforcement department, directed the onslaught Friday with the total numbering seven stills for the day. He was assisted by state enforcers R. C. Linch, Pugh Haynes, W. H. Harrison, and county officer O. L. Lawrence, Jr.

A whiskey still

**All Large Plants**
Among the seven findings Friday, were four 1,200-gallon stills, two 1,000-gallon stills, and on giant plant with a capacity of 3,000 gallons. The contraband stuff poured out was 4,500 gallons of beer and mash.

Two men were found at one still, but apparently after being warned of the approach of officers, one tumbled down a 75-foot bluff and the other scurried into the dense forest leaving behind 21 empty cans and 30 gallons of manufactured liquor.

Officers state that these stills had been in operation for several years from information obtained from residents of the community. All were situated less than a mile from Lock 17 and smoke could be seen from the Warrior River when the plants were in operation. No arrests have been made but officers were said to be in possession of the names of persons connected with them.

*The Tuscaloosa News,* **July 25, 1929**
**Officers Raid the Biggest Moonshine Distillery Discovered in County**
**Haul near Windham Springs includes: Four Large Stills; 625 Tin Cans; One Ton of Sugar; 1,000 Pounds of Meal; 250 Gallons of Liquor; 4,000 Gallons of Beer.**
**Five Men Escape Officers; Secret Road Through Garage Discovered.**
County officers last night seized near Windham-

# MOONSHINING ON THE CRABBE ROAD

Drawing of how a whiskey still works

Springs on the Crabbe Road one of the most complete and best equipped liquor plants in the history of this county. Two trucks were required to haul in the contents comprising one hundred twenty-five 5-gallon cans, 500 one-gallon containers, two 1,500-gallon stills, two 2,000-gallon stills, one ton of sugar and 1,000 pounds of meal and shorts.

More than 250 gallons of liquor and 4,000 gallons of beer were poured out on the hillside in the raid.

Officers found five men at work at the stills, but they made good their escape after officers had surrounded the plant and fired sixteen shots to frighten them.

The four stills were less than "ten" feet apart and a 150-foot hose line had been laid to a creek to furnish water. A pump to provide an adequate flow of water to the still was taken in by the officers.

Officers of the raiding party included Deputies John Payne, C. L. Lawrence, Sr., Louis King, W. I. Huff, Will Kuykendall, and Will Wilcutt.

All the liquor found was stored in new tin cans and officers pointed out the danger of allowing it to remain in tin containers for any length of time. It is believed that it was being manufactured for sale in other counties. All the containers were packed ready for shipment.

The road to the still made a secret entrance through the garage of a man's house. The rear wall of the garage was converted into a door, and a road led from there through a cotton field to the stills. A car was usually left parked in the garage while the still was in operation to conceal the entrance to the road, said officers.

The contents of the modern outfit were brought here and thrown out near the city jail. Crowds congregated near the jail this morning and saw what officers say is the largest seizure of one night.

### *The Tuscaloosa News,* August 5, 1929
### Dry Officers Here Destroy $90,000 Property in Raids

A complete report of activities in Tuscaloosa County of state law enforcement officers was given out today by Pugh Haynes, member of the party of dry officers who have been conducting a seven-week campaign here. The report lists each still separately with the amount of sugar, beer, and liquor destroyed.

Figures show that the destroyed property of Tuscaloosa County moonshiners was valued at a retail price of $90,000. The price includes the estimated value of stills, market price of the distilled liquor, the beer poured out at the stills, and the estimated value of the sugar consumed.

The intensive cleanups have netted 71 stills, an average of ten each week. As high as seven have been destroyed in one day. The weekly average, if counting only active weeks, would amount to 12 stills. Only six weeks of active work have been carried out due to the absence of officers from this county due to the trial of slayer of Jack Hines, Eufaula mechanic. Chief Walter K. McAdory, head of the state law enforcement bureau sent the local officers to Eufaula to protect the suspect.

The total amount of beer poured out was 67,740 gallons which were made from sugar with a value estimated of $3,600. The liquor totaled 731 gallons. Twenty-one men have been hauled into court to answer charges of distilling and two automobiles have been confiscated.

Values placed on the stills were set at a total of $5,000 and mash containers, pipes, and other items necessary to the operation made up the balance of the $90,000 estimate.

**Boyd comment:**

The August 30, 1929, edition of *The Tuscaloosa News* has on page twelve a Piggly Wiggly advertisement that shows the price of ten pounds of sugar to be 55¢ with a limit of one per customer. One hundred pounds of sugar is advertised for $5.50 with a limit of one per customer. The Yellow Front stores advertised 17 pounds of sugar for 99¢. Due to the limit in quantity imposed by local grocery stores, the bootleggers who used sugar by the tons surely had access to "Black Market" sugar.

*The Tuscaloosa News*, **November 6, 1929**
**Man is wounded on the Crabbe Road**
**Argument with motorist is thought the cause of shot**
**Bigham is injured.**
George Bigham, 22, resident of the Crabbe Road, was shot in the abdomen and seriously wounded late Monday by an unidentified assailant. He was on a road near his home when the shot was fired from an automobile.

Bigham told county officers that he had been in an argument with the driver of an automobile shortly before being shot, and he could identify the suspected party.

The injured man was not taken to the hospital, but he was under the care of physicians at his home 18 miles north of city (Piney Woods), relatives said.

**Boyd comment:**
The story of George Bigham, his father, Doc Bigham, and his brother, Dugs, is told in the chapter "Doc Bigham." George Bigham was the son of Dock Bigham, a moonshiner and murderer. Dock Bigham killed his uncle, E. Cooper, in 1893, reportedly for $50. Bigham was sent to prison. A few years later, he escaped and hid out in Piney Woods and opened a new moonshine still. In 1918, he killed Tuscaloosa County sheriff B. M. Watts as the sheriff and other officers raided his still. He was found guilty of murder and was hanged on gallows at the Tuscaloosa County jail in 1919. George Bigham's brother, Dugs, was killed by gunfire during the arrest of Doc in the swamps of the Warrior River near Fosters. Doc and Dugs are buried in Macedonia Cemetery.

*The Tuscaloosa News*, **July 24, 1934**
**Mose Temerson Gets $500 Fine for Beer Case**
**Admits Possession of Large Quantity; Cases Against Brothers Not Pressed**
A plea of guilty and a $500 fine in Tuscaloosa Circuit Court today disposed of a prohibition violation against Mose Temerson, prominent local produce broker, who admitted possession of almost 2,000 cases of 3.2 beer seized on the premises of Charles Temerson & Sons establishment last August.

The case was disposed of today at the opening of criminal week in circuit court. Solicitor Ed deGraffenried recommended the maximum fine of $500 after Temerson had pleaded guilty. The fine was agreed to by Judge Henry B. Foster and officially approved by a circuit jury.

A similar case against Nelson Daniel, employee for the Temersons, was disposed of with a plea of guilty and a fine for $50 recommended by the solicitor.

Mr. deGraffenried recommended that the prohibition cases against Jacob and Abraham Temerson, brothers of Mose, be not pressed because the elder Temerson claimed full responsibility for the beer.

Several other beer trials were set for today. Two were postponed due to illness of the defenders.

The prohibition charges handled today resulted in a fine 10 times as heavy as that agreed to by the court ten days ago, before it was learned that the beer seized from the Temersons had been later secured by them by a local warehouse where it was stored by the sheriff. When Mose Temerson pleaded guilty ten days ago on the prohibition count, his fine was set at $50, but the court revoked that order when the disappearance of the beer was ascertained.

A searching investigation of the beer disappearance is expected to be made by a circuit grand jury which is due to be called at an early date.

**Boyd comment:**

The illicit moonshine business could not have flourished without the support of some members of the business community. This article speaks for itself.

### *The Tuscaloosa News*, August 27, 1934
### Huge Rattler Killed at Still

"Snakes and corn liquor go together," say some folks. Three Tuscaloosa County officers today were prepared to testify to the truth of that saying. They found a 12 pound 15-rattle rattlesnake Sunday afternoon a short distance from a 50-gallon still.

Both the snake and the still were destroyed by the officers who are deputies Foster Wright and Harley Holemon and constable Leon Chism of Northport. The snake measured 65 inches long and was exceptionally large in circumstance. Deputy Holemon plans to preserve the snake skin. The still raid was made about twelve miles from Tuscaloosa in the vicinity of the Crabbe Road. Owners of the still were not on the premises.

**Boyd comment:**

The location of this still was either on or near the Eugene B. Tierce, Sr. farm my parents purchased from Mr. Tierce's widow in 1940. During my childhood years, I frequently explored our farm walking over the terrain. I discovered four rusting remains of moonshine stills scattered among the hollows where year-round small streams of water flowed which would have been necessary to operate the stills.

### *The Tuscaloosa News*, August 19, 1947
### 2 men arrested at Whiskey Still

Two men were captured "red-handed" while distilling whisky at 8:30 a.m. about ten miles from Northport on the Crabbe Road by a Tuscaloosa County deputy sheriff and two A. T. U. investigators, Sheriff John Henry Suther announced.

The would-be whiskey makers Ed Smith and Howard Grammer of Tuscaloosa County were captured working a 400-gallon still, the sheriff said. They had just run off 11 gallons when the officers came out of the underbrush where they had been waiting two days and made the arrest, Suther said.

Both men are being held in the county jail pending court action. Grammer faces an earlier distilling charge that is still pending with the federal court, Suther said.

The whiskey still was wrecked beyond condition for further use by Dept. Sheriff Walker Snyder.

The officers had been lying in wait since early yesterday morning and were ready to make the arrest as soon as the two men arrived and began the operation.

**Boyd comment:**

I was eight years old at the time. The still was just a half-mile south of our home and both men were well known to our family. The subject of moonshine activity in our community was often discussed around our kitchen table. In this instance, Ed Smith (May 5, 1896-June 3, 1970) was fifty-one years old at the time of the arrest. I have stood at his grave in Macedonia Methodist Cemetery many times. Howard Grammer is buried in Bethel Cemetery.

# A ROAD, A CEMETERY, A PEOPLE

*The Tuscaloosa News*, **October 5, 1951**
**5 stills destroyed**

Five whiskey stills and a truck were seized by county and state officers in separate raids yesterday. A 1,200-gallon still and two 1,000-gallon outfits were seized twenty miles northwest of Tuscaloosa near the Fayette Highway. Two 2,000-gallon stills were destroyed and a truck was seized 22 miles north of here on the Crabbe Road. No arrests were made. Raiding officers were Deputy Walter Snyder and State officer C. H. Jenkins.

**Summation:**

The preceding articles from *The Tuscaloosa News* span the years 1929-1951. Some of the bootleggers were neighbors; some were patients in my medical practice. Some were strangers.

CHAPTER 10

# The Murder of Pricey Shirley White

Cemetery tombstones normally consist of the name of the person interred, dates of birth and death, and possibly a two or three-word epitaph. With the passing of time, information about that person's life is lost unless the story is written and saved. In composing *A Road, A Cemetery, A People*, I have written short bios on several people buried in Macedonia Cemetery. One of the most interesting and saddest accounts is that of Pricey Shirley Gibson White who is buried in grave # 179 in the north end of the cemetery. Her grave marker reads, "Shirley Pricey Gibson, 1903-1933." The marker fails to include her married name "White." The omission is intentional.

**The following obit comes from *The Tuscaloosa News*, September 24, 1933.**
Funeral services for Mrs. Pricey Gibson Shirley White were held at Macedonia Methodist Church with Rev. O. R. Burns and O. L. Manderson officiating on Sunday, September, 23, 1933. Foster Funeral Home directed internment.

Mrs. White is survived by her parents Mr. and Mrs. Joel Tom Shirley, and four sisters: Mrs. Irene Pierre, of Stone Mountain, Georgia; Mrs. Maude Saye of Chicago, Illinois; Mrs. Emil Snow and Mrs. Josh Rushing of Northport; one nephew, Joe Rushing; and one niece, Maxine Robertson. (An entire chapter in *A Road, A Cemetery, A People* is devoted to the Joel Tom Shirley family.)

Pallbearers were: Police Chief Hardin D. Billingsley; J. Verner Robertson, Jr.; Gary McGee; Roy Faucett; R. V. Elledge; and George D. Johnson, Tuscaloosa County Tax Assessor.

Mrs. White has resided in Akron, Ohio, for the last 11 years and recently received a five-year service pen from the Goodrich Rubber Company.

Many friends attended the last rites for Mrs. White and mourn her death greatly. She was laid to rest under a bower of many beautiful flowers.

***The Tuscaloosa News*, September 24, 1933**
Joe Dawson White, widely recognized "White hope" for the world heavyweight boxing championship, shot his estranged wife in the back as she walked into Woolworth Store on Broad Street on Saturday morning. He was then placed in jail where he talked to fellow prisoners about his exploits in the prize ring.

Meanwhile, the wounded woman, Mrs. Pricey Shirley White, battled for her life in Druid City Hospital. Late Saturday night, her condition was reported to be extremely critical. She suffered bullet wounds to the abdomen fired from a Spanish made .25 caliber automatic revolver. A single bullet pierced her in the side.

White, being severely demented and in a condition generally known as "punch drunk" due to blows received in boxing, was transferred to the county jail Saturday afternoon after being held in the city jail for several hours. He was docketed on a charge of assault with the attempt to commit murder. Sargent Zack Ryan of the police department signed the warrant. Officers Ingram and Carraway arrested White a moment after the shooting, being only a short distance from the scene when the two shots were fired.

The Spanish made .25 caliber automatic revolver and the exploding cartridge made little noise. One shot went wild off its mark, although a sister of Mrs. White was at first believed to be wounded but was not. The two women were entering the store from Broad Street, and several other persons were standing nearby but luckily escaped injury.

As Mrs. White fell to the floor, her husband quit firing and the arresting officers arrived a moment later. White is said to have told them that he shot his wife because "She was spending all my money." He is also to have said he wished he had shot her "seven times." Directly after the shooting, he asked, "Why can't I shoot her?"

Police said their investigation indicated that White had made several threats against his wife previously. She had been residing in Ohio for the last three years, being separated from her husband. She returned to Tuscaloosa a day or so ago to visit family relatives and White apparently searched for her until he saw her Saturday morning in downtown Tuscaloosa.

White, thirty-four years old, was born on Northport Route One, the Watermelon Road. His wife, the former Miss Pricey "Teddy" Shirley was a resident of the Crabbe Road about five miles from Northport. Both were widely known in this county.

For several years, White was prominently known in the fight game. He took on many of the topnotch heavyweights including Tommy Gibbons twice, W. L. Stribling, Angel Fritz, Fred Fulton, Harold Willis, and George Godfrey. For two years, he was a sparring partner with Willis and at one time was touted as a probable opponent for Jack Dempsey. He was known as the "Tuscaloosa Bearcat" and at one time as the "Mansfield White Hope" in Ohio.

Police said that he ahd been committed to an insane hospital on at least one occasion due to his demented condition, but it was not thought that he was in a dangerous state. The case will be presented to the grand jury which is already set to convene on October 9.

**Tuscaloosa News article
September 25, 1933**
Mrs. Pricey Gibson Shirley White, estranged wife of Joe White, erstwhile heavyweight boxing contender, died at Druid City Hospital at 6:00 o'clock this morning as the result of wounds in the stomach inflicted by a revolver bullet fried by White on Saturday morning.

Relatives said today that she had been separated from the former boxer for the last six years. She had not seen him for the last four years and had supported herself for the last ten years. Her father, J. T. Shirley declared that White's statement given the police as to Mrs. White "spending all my money" was wholly a fabrication and false in every word.

They further said that White had repeatedly made threats against his wife and on one occasion while residing in Akron, Ohio, he had been committed to an insane hospital because of brutal treatment to Mrs. White.

I close this sad story of the murder of one of Joel Tom and Sara Ida Shirley's daughters by noting that this fine family experienced losses of other family members at young ages. Early in their marriage in 1904 they lost an infant daughter who is buried in Backbone Cemetery in Elrod, near the Tuscaloosa County/Pickens County line.

In 1911, they lost another infant child to death, M. T. Ormand Shirley, who is buried in Macedonia Cemetery. His grave has no gravestone.

J. T. and Sara Ida were parents to five daughters who lived to adulthood. One, Estelle Shirley, was born on May 9, 1905 and died at age twenty-four on July 25, 1929. At age fourteen, she gave birth to an infant son, W. Brady Robertson. He is buried in grave #172 in Macedonia Cemetery beside his mother. His grave marker reads. "W. Brady Robertson, 1919." Shirley family history does not know what happed to Estelle's husband following her death other than "He departed for parts unknown."

None of the sisters of Estelle—Clara Barton Shirley Rushing, Emile Mae Shirley Snow, Maude Shirley Bobo, and Mary Irene Shirley Pierre—are buried in Macedonia Cemetery.

Headstone of one of Joel Tom and Sara Ida Shirley's infant daughters

# A ROAD, A CEMETERY, A PEOPLE

CHAPTER 11

# Politics along the Crabbe Road

The following stories of seven Tuscaloosa County politicians with connections to the Crabbe Road are told from firsthand experience except for one, Eugene B. Tierce, Sr. His bid for public office occurred prior to my birth. I include the stories of two politicians, Tuscaloosa Circuit Judge W. C. Warren and State Senator Hayse Tucker, who did not live on the Crabbe Road. However, *A Road, A Cemetery, A People* would be incomplete without the inclusion of these men whose public service benefited all who live on the Crabbe Road and who strongly influenced my life.

As always, articles from the *Tuscaloosa News* provide much of the resource material included here.

**Note regarding *The Tuscaloosa News*:**
Many Crabbe Road residents prior to 1950 could not afford to subscribe to the local newspaper even though the annual subscription cost was only $3.25 for residents of Tuscaloosa County. For those in rural areas, the paper was delivered via the US Postal Service R. F. D. The paper arrived in the mail the day after it was printed. If delivered outside Tuscaloosa County, the annual subscription rate was $9.00 per year. For residents in town, newspapers usually were delivered by paper boy carriers at a weekly rate of 20¢.

**Politics in the 1910s**
Eugene Benjamin Tierce, Sr. was the grandson of Benjamin Tucker Tierce, one of the first settlers on the Crabbe Road near North River. The Tierce family arrived circa 1830. In 1916, Eugene B. Tierce, Sr. ran for the office of Board of Revenue of Tuscaloosa County. In the 1910s, it was common for the office of County Board of Revenue to attract many candidates. This is seen in the following news article in which Mr. Tierce was one of ten candidates.

***Tuscaloosa Gazette*, January 26, 1916**
The *Gazette* is authorized to announce the following men are candidates for the board of revenue subject to the action of the Democratic primary: Mr. R. H. Hubbard of Beat 14; Mr. W. F. Chapman of Beat 15; Mr. R. Bob Patton of Kellerman, Beat 5:

Mr. L. N. Tutwiler of Beat 12; Mr. N. G. Holley of Northport; Mr. W. C. Hinton; Mr. A. P. Patton of Ralph; Mr. William Toxey of Beat 23; Mr. R. H. Williamson; Mr. E. B. Tierce of Crabbe Road.

**My father's love of politics**
My father was drawn into politics and first ran for public office, sheriff of Tuscaloosa County, at age thirty in 1938. I do not know the reason for the attraction. I can only speculate.

It is possible his race for sheriff in 1938 was

to have his name receive public recognition knowing that he likely would run for other offices in the future. Ten men were in the race for sheriff that year and included two very prominent citizens, Largus Barnes and Foster King, who previously had held public office. The other candidates were far more well-known than Daddy. He probably realized his chance of beating such opponents was slim.

The following is my father's political ad as it appeared in the newspaper. I think it is a good one.

### *The Tuscaloosa News,* May 1, 1938, page 8
### A young man for sheriff
### Political ad

I am not quite 30 years old. That may sound too young to some people, but it is a matter of record that among the best sheriffs West Alabama has known in recent years are two men who are younger than I, Howard Davis of Pickens County and Frank Lee of Greene County. They are recognized throughout the state as among the very best.

A sober young man with personal integrity and ambition has possibilities not possessed by older men. I know a great deal about the problems of youth, and it is from the youths of the land that a great majority of our criminals now come. I believe I can deal with the problems of young criminals in a way that may not only protect society but save many a boy or girl as well.

I do not wish to blow my own horn too loudly, but I do have the character, the physical energy, and the determination to make the kind of sheriff this fine old county deserves.

With consideration for all but special favors to none, I will do my duty as your sheriff all the time.

Your vote and influence will be greatly appreciated.

Herman C. Boyd

### *The Tuscaloosa News,* May 1, 1938, page 13
### Political ad

To the people of Tuscaloosa Cunty,

I wish to express my appreciation for the many compliments and kind expressions as well as the many promises of support for my son, Herman C. Boyd, during this campaign. The people of the county have been kind and courteous to me during the time I have been campaigning for my son. I shall always remember with pleasure the courteousness and help whether my son is elected sheriff or not.

I firmly believe from the numerous favorable reports that he will be in the run-off in the sheriff's race. He and I both will appreciate greatly anything you can do for him before election day and we will especially appreciate your vote on that day.

Sincerely, W. A. Boyd.

**The following news article gives the results of the 1938 sheriff's race.**

### May 4, 1938, *The Tuscaloosa News*, front page

The vote tally for sheriff is as follows. Robert Baker, a café proprietor, received 182 votes. Largus Barnes, a former Board of Revenue member, prominent farmer and large land owner who also owns a cotton gin in Northport, received 1,803 votes. Herman Boyd, an automobile salesman, received 350 votes. Henry Burks, a dairyman, received 1,284 votes. Aaron Christian, a furniture dealer, received 803 votes. Allan Hargrove, a highway patrolman, received 646 votes. Dr. W. A. Harris, a veterinarian, received 225 votes. Foster King, a former sheriff, received 1,624 votes. Murray Pate, a deputy sheriff, received 810 votes. Grady Tubb, an automobile salesman, received 152 votes.

In the runoff election held June 14, 1938, Foster King received 3,940 votes to defeat Largus Barnes who received 3,183 votes.

# POLITICS ALONG THE CRABBE ROAD

**The dream continues**

Following Daddy's unsuccessful race for sheriff in 1938 at the age of twenty-nine, political ambitions remained in his blood. He postponed his next bid for public office for six years. In 1944, he could resist the call to action no longer. He ran for a position on the Tuscaloosa County Board of Revenue.

The Board of Revenue was a three-man commission in 1944. Candidates ran for a seat at large, not for a specific commission seat. There was no limit to the number of candidates that could toss their hat into the ring. Usually, ten or so people filed qualifying papers. The primary election was held on the first Tuesday in May. The six men with the highest votes were placed in a runoff election six weeks later. The top three were declared elected and each man assigned to a specific district.

The following is one of Daddy's political ads in the 1944 bid for election.

**The Tuscaloosa News, March 1944**
**Tuscaloosa County Board of Revenue**
**A political ad**

I hereby announce my candidacy for membership on the Tuscaloosa County Board of Revenue, subject to the action of the Democratic Primaries of May 2 and 30.

I am a native of this county and am thoroughly familiar with the vast network of dirt roads, the upkeep of which is one of the important duties of every member of the County Board of Revenue.

I will bring to the job the will to accomplish something progressive, to build for the convenience, prosperity, and well-being of present as well as future generations.

It is my belief that 85 percent of a road commissioner's time should be devoted to the maintenance and upkeep of his roads. Rural people of Tuscaloosa County deserve better roads.

Your vote for me will be a vote for honest, conscientious, and fair administration of the trust you place in me. I want to serve as a member of the Board of Revenue. I will help build Tuscaloosa County, ever looking towards improvement of roads and all county institutions.

Sincerely,
Herman Boyd

Following the primary election of May 2 election in which Daddy did very well, a couple of very interesting articles about the election and my father appeared in *The Tuscaloosa News*.

**The Tuscaloosa News, May 3, 1944, Front page**
**Board of Revenue Close**
**Six Highest Will Face Runoff May 30**

Based on unofficial but complete returns from Tuscaloosa County's 58 boxes in Tuesday's Democratic Primary, a runoff election on May 30 to fill the three places on the County Board of Revenue appears certain today.

The unofficial results showed the six candidates running neck and neck in one of the closest contested races in Tuscaloosa County history. Only 450 votes separated the top and sixth man in this race.

Pat N. Lancaster, seeking reelection to a third term on the board, led the nine-man ticket with 2,454 votes followed in order by: Joe H. Boteler, 2,397; John E. Walker, 2,391; Herman Boyd, 2,235; Cliff Lindsey, 2,143; W. H. "Fats" Thomas, 2,004; T. E. Christian, 1,634; Cliff Atkinson, 1,564; M. C. Fitts, 1514.

Lancaster, Boteler, Walker, Boyd, Lindsey, and Thomas will be the candidates in the runoff.

The official canvass of the votes will begin Thursday at 9:30 a.m. in the county courthouse. This canvass will be made by the County Democratic Executive Committee of which James W. Mustin is chairman.

Approximately 6,103 votes were cast in the Board of Revenue Race while approximately 6,100 votes were polled in the US senatorial race which also turned out to be the most closely contested race in this county in several years. Four years ago, in an 8-man race for Board of Revenue, approximately 8,000 votes were polled, three men receiving a clear majority in the first primary to win without a runoff.

**Boyd is a surprise**

Herman Boyd, Tucker Motor Company employee and farmer, proved to be the surprise candidate in the nip and tuck Board of Revenue race. Boyd, a candidate for sheriff 6 years ago, led his opponents in 12 county boxes. They include: Moore's Bridge; Thompson Mill; Kellerman; Elrod; Hughes; Chism Store (Northport); Christian Store (Northport); Searles; Vance; Atlantic Oil; Courthouse box 17; Romulus.

Cliff Lindsey, proprietor of a local dry-cleaning establishment, led in 9 county boxes. It was Lindsey's first race for public office.

John Walker, seeking reelection to a second term of office, led in 8 county boxes.

Thomas, local insurance man seeking his first public office, received substantial support from all boxes in Beat 16, Tuscaloosa proper, and Beat 15 and 10, Northport. Taylor is serving the unexpired term of the late John B. Taylor by appointment of Governor Chauncey Sparks. He has been on the Board of Revenue since last August.

Mr. Christian, for 40 years a teacher in the Tuscaloosa County School system, was seeking his first public office. Mr. Atkinson, who at one time served on the Tuscaloosa City Commission, was making his second race for the Board of Revenue. Mr. Fitts, in the 1940 Democratic Primary in Tuscaloosa County, received 2,147 votes to place fifth in the eight-man race for the board.

***The Tuscaloosa News,* May 31, 1944, front page**
**Boyd, Lindsey, and Walker win Board of Revenue nominations**

Tuscaloosa County voters shuffled the cards convincingly in Tuscaloosa County's Democratic party runoff election, coming very close to turning up three new aces.

Youthful Herman Boyd, 36 years old, surprise candidate who ran fifth in the nine-man race for Board of Revenue on May 2, virtually set the woods afire in the pay-off battle to lead the ticket and win going away. Boyd polled a total vote of 3,522 based on unofficial returns gathered by *The News.*

Close on the heels of Boyd was Tuscaloosa's Cliff J. Lindsey who received 3,518 votes to place second. Boyd and Lindsey were the only two candidates in the six-man runoff to poll 3,000 votes or more.

New Lexington's John E. Walker, seeking reelection to a second term on the Board of Revenue, was the sole survivor of the old board. Walker was pushed in the stretch drive by Holt's Joe H. Boteler but emerged the victor by 23 votes in the unofficial tally to win the nomination to the third place. Walker received 2,878 to Boteler's 2,855 votes. In the May 2, primary, Walker nosed out Boteler by two votes to place second.

Walker gained 22 of the 23-vote-margin over Boteler in the latter's home beat in Holt.

Pat Lancaster, veteran campaigner who has served seven years on the Board of Revenue and twice led the campaign in convincing style, was dropped out of the running, along with Boteler and W. H. "Fats" Thomas, running for his first public office.

Four years ago, in an 8-man race for Board of Revenue, Lancaster polled 4,648 votes to lead the ticket and win nomination without a runoff. On May 2 in this race, again lead the ticket but by a smaller margin. In yesterday's election, Lancaster polled 2,380 votes to drop to fifth place in the runoff. Thomas received 2,213 votes to drop to sixth place in the runoff.

Based on unofficial tabulates, four men, Boyd, Lindsey, Walker, Boteler received a majority of votes cast.

Lancaster was the only candidate to receive less votes than on May 2. The unofficial tally showed he lost 74 votes.

Tuesday's voting was the lightest ever recorded in a Board of Revenue race in Tusca-

# POLITICS ALONG THE CRABBE ROAD

loosa County's history. The unofficial tally shows there were approximately 5,688 votes cast as compared to 6,100 in the May 2 election. The voting in Beat 16, Tuscaloosa proper, lagged more than in rural beats. Only about 800 absentee votes were cast as compared with about 500 in the May 2 election.

Boyd who turned out to be the hottest candidate in the race, led all his opponents in 26 of 58 boxes in the county. He tied with one or more candidates in 5 other boxes. Mr. Boyd was running his second political race. He was a candidate for sheriff in 1938. He is employed by Tucker Motor Company and operates a farm on the Crabbe Road near Northport.

Mr. Walker led all his opponents in 8 county boxes and tied in two others.

Mr. Lindsay who operates a dry-cleaning business, led all his opponents in 9 county boxes and tied for leadership in four other boxes.

After winning in the run-off, Daddy served as Commissioner for District One which was made up of the western part of Tuscaloosa County including Ralph, Fosters, Romulus, Buhl, Echola, Moore's Bridge, Northport, and Highway 69 North that laid south of North River. In 1947, a new system was instituted. Candidates ran for a specific district. This simplified the election process. It remains in effect today.

**The Tuscaloosa News, July 6, 1947, front page**
**New Revenue Board Election Plan Given**
**Proposal designates three places, district setup unchanged**

A new system of electing members of the Tuscaloosa County Board of Revenue is proposed in a bill which will be sponsored by the local delegation in the State Legislature and introduced in the present session at Montgomery.

The proposed legislative act, modeled along the lines of laws governing the selection of legislators, provides for the election of a three-member County Board of Revenue every four years, the places to be designated Place No. 1., Place No. 2. and Place No. 3.

Every candidate for the Board of Revenue shall designate in his announcement the number of the place he is seeking, and the ballots shall be numbered accordingly.

Under the proposed system of running for designated places, it would be possible for one or two members of the Board of Revenue not to have opposition while there might be a race for the other place or places.

The new system is designed to "get the three best men in the race" as one legislator expressed it.

Running for the County Board of Revenue has been a popular past-time with a lot of folks, it was explained. This has been one of the most popular offices from a candidate point of view which the people are called upon to fill. There was a time in Tuscaloosa County when 22 candidates went to bat for the three places on the board.

The current board is composed of Herman Boyd, Cliff Lindsey, and John E. Walker. They were elected out of a field of eight candidates three years ago. All are expected to seek re-election next year.

The bill as now composed should not be confused with an earlier proposal which would have created three separate districts in the county. This proposed measure was not introduced in the legislature.

Under conditions of the latest proposed act, the three members of the board will still have the right to carry on their work by districts as is now the case.

The present law makes the probate judge the presiding officer at meeting of the board. The bill setting up a new system of electing board members will not change this practice.

**1944-1952**

I was five years old when Daddy was elected to the Tuscaloosa County Board of Revenue in 1944. I have no memory of the election campaign, but as I matured over the next four years, I became aware of the aroma of politics that overshadowed our family. Discussing politics was part of our family's daily life. I enjoyed a front row seat to local politics. Daddy took me with him when he attended political rallies in schools, churches, and community centers throughout the county. This allowed me the rare opportunity to meet many officer holders. Occasionally I hung out in the Tuscaloosa County Courthouse when he was there conducting county business. He introduced me to many people who later became good friends. Years later, some of those people allowed me to serve as their family doctor.

Tuscaloosa County is the second largest geographical county in Alabama; Baldwin County is the largest. When I accompanied Daddy as he canvassed votes and attended political rallies all over the county, I became familiar with hundreds of miles of the Tuscaloosa County Road system including major paved roads along with little one-lane dirt roads. To this day, I can navigate the roads throughout the county without the aid of GPS. One of my favorite pastimes is to take rides over some of the back roads that I first traveled with him in childhood.

Unlike my father, I never developed an interest in politics and certainly never aspired to run for public office.

In 1948, the citizens of District One, the district he served, gave Daddy an overwhelming majority of votes in his district. One example of the support his constituents rendered is seen in the following political ad sponsored by our neighbors in Lafoy Community.

***The Tuscaloosa News*, Sunday, May 2, 1948, page 11**
**The citizens of Lafoy Community urge you to vote on May 4 for Herman C. Boyd Place Number 1, County Board of Revenue**
A political ad

The Lafoy Community on the Crabbe Road is where Herman Boyd lives. We are his friends and neighbors who have known him all his life.

He has served as Superintendent of Sunday School and a teacher of the adult class at Macedonia Methodist Church.

We know him to be in every way a Christian gentleman, a fine neighbor, a good public servant who has ably performed every duty placed upon him in the administration of county affairs and in supervision of the road district assigned to him.

Mrs. John Shirley
Harwood Hamner
J. P. Hamner
Frances Hamner
J. D. Hamner
Dee Hamner
James L. Hamner
Janie Myrtle Hamner
John E. Shirley
B. F. Shirley
William T. Hamner
N. J. Hamner
J. Bernard Rushing
Mrs. Reba V. Rushing
Mrs. Bruce Hamner
Bruce Hamner
Ollie B. Hamner
J. Hewitt Rushing
Grady E. Shirley
C.D. Newman
J. Polk Rushing
Josh M. Rushing
Mrs. Clara Rushing
Nathan Maddox
James Rushing
B. A. LeSueur
Vera LeSueur
L. L. Shirley
Mrs. L. L. Shirley
N. A. Wedgeworth
J. W. Hamner
F. Moody Fields
M. D. Black
G. M. Rushing

# POLITICS ALONG THE CRABBE ROAD

Tucker I. Mathis
N. J. Walters
T. J. Black
Hugh Spencer
Comer Montgomery
Robert Rushing
E. W. Earnest
Faith Rushing
Jack Hagler
Alex Colburn
Curtis T. Watkins

### *The Tuscaloosa News*, Sunday, May 2, 1948
### 14,000 set for primary race Tuesday

The stage is set in Tuscaloosa County for what most observers predict will be a whopping big county Democratic primary vote Tuesday. More than 3,000 new voters have been added to the county list since the last election. The total vote Tuesday is expected to exceed the county record of 10, 091 ballots cast in the three-man sheriff's race of 1946.

Polls at all voting places will open at 8:00 a.m. and close at 5:00 p.m. except for Beat 16, Tuscaloosa. Beat 16 will close at 6:00 p.m.

The published voting list contains more than 14,000 names, nearly 9,000 being in Tuscaloosa, Beat 16. Since the list was published, several hundred names have been added. Men with service connection may register Monday and vote Tuesday by displaying registration certification.

Candidates unopposed for local races whose names will not be on the ballot include Tax Assessor, Festus Shamblin, Circuit Judge Reuben Wright, and Coroner, S.T. Hardin. Under a new law, names of candidates who are unopposed may not be printed on the ballot.

Sample Ballot Vote for one
Board of Revenue Place 1
Herman C. Boyd
W. H. (Pat) Thomas
Board of Revenue Place 2
Frank S. Dockery
Pat N. Lancaster
Cliff J. Lindsay
Jake B. Yessick
Board of Revenue Place 3
Murry Fondren
George W. Rose
John E. Walker

The tally of votes in the May 2, 1948, election in District One is given in the following news article. It affirms Daddy's popularity and support by those whom he served. Each voting precent that is noted is in District One.

### *The Tuscaloosa News*, May 5, 1948,
### Herman Boyd 6,166 votes
### W. H. "Pat" Thomas 3,250 votes

In the district he served, these are the vote tallies

| Voting precinct | Boyd | Thomas |
| --- | --- | --- |
| Moore's Bridges | 53 | 16 |
| Elrod | 92 | 20 |
| Hughes | 32 | 10 |
| Northport #1 | 156 | 61 |
| Northport #2 | 223 | 31 |
| Northport #3 | 130 | 72 |
| Ralph | 84 | 22 |
| Echola | 57 | 12 |
| Romulus | 63 | 14 |
| Fosters | 59 | 6 |
| Buhl | 14 | 0 |

One of the major responsibilities of the Commissioners of the Tuscaloosa County Board of Revenue was to see that the roads in his district were maintained. In the 1940s and extending into the 1950s, more than half of the county roads were not paved. The dirt roads were scraped by road machines on a regular basis. It was Daddy's responsibility to drive over the district, inspect the roads, and to discuss problems with residents. In doing so, he personally met almost every resident and learned the names of their spouses and kids. During the summers, he frequently took me along.

An example of the love and appreciation his constituents had for Daddy is seen in another news article in which the wonderful people of

Romulus honored Daddy and the county work crew that maintained the roads in the area.

***The Tuscaloosa News*, Sunday, July 2, 1950**
**Feast in honor of Tuscaloosa County Board of Revenue Workers, District 1**
**They prepared the feast**
Famous for their fine cooking, the women of the Romulus Community prepared a delicious picnic spread that was served in honor of District 1, County Road Department, at the Romulus School on Thursday afternoon. The ladies include: Mrs. F. B. Browning; Mrs. A. N. Burroughts; Mrs. Gay Dorroh; Mrs. Cordie McCracken; Mrs. Marvin Dees; Mrs. Verner Booth; Mrs. J. C. Cork; Mrs. Cliff Burroughts; Mrs. Tim Leatherwood; Mrs. Harvis Faulkner; Mrs. W. A. Cork; Mrs. Ray Burroughts; Miss Ruth Leatherwood; Mrs. A. P. Burroughs, Jr.; Mrs. W. V. Burroughs, Jr.; Miss Sally B. Evans; Mrs. Nelson Burroughs.

**They did the road work**
The men who were the honored guests included:
"Preacher" Wilbourne; Tolly Wicker; Lonnie Shirley; Board of Revenue member, Herman Boyd; J. O. Allen; Jim Allen; Olen Booth; P. M. Beck; P. T. Pool; Early Grammar; Delmas Beck; Clyde Utley; Virgil Barton; James Hewett; County Engineer, Rayburn Moore; Dewey Fair; James Robertson.

**They did the speaking**
These county and community leaders were the principal speakers at the Romulus picnic Thursday to honor the county road crew of District 1 and Board of Revenue member Herman Boyd. Those speaking included Virgil Barton, community leader and Beat 21 committeeman; Herman Boyd; Gay Dorroh, community leader; Cliff Lindsey, Board of Revenue member for District 2; Probate Judge Chester Walker; Tax Assessor, James R. Maxwell; Tax collector, Festus Shamblin; Dr. A. W. Patton, dentist, served as

Herman Boyd, 1950

master of ceremonies.

As noted earlier, in discussing politics in *A Road, A Cemetery, A People*, I include two men, Circuit Judge W. C. Warren and Alabama State Senator Hayse Tucker that were not residents of the Crabbe Road. The memoir would be incomplete without the inclusion of their influence upon my life.

**Hayse Tucker**
Mr. Tucker's first bid for public office came in 1934. It was successful. He was elected to the Alabama State Senate in Montgomery.

Mr. Tucker owned the Tuscaloosa Ford dealership, Tucker Motor Company, the company for which my father began work as a salesman in the early 1930s. Daddy eventually became manager of the entire sales force, a position he held until his death in 1964. During my growing up years, I often hung out at the dealership and got to know Mr. Tucker quite well. He always asked about my school work and my plans for the future. I told him I wanted to be a doctor. He always gave encouraging words. As a state senator, he was very interested in medical affairs in the state and his interest was enhanced by the fact that his son-in-law was a surgeon in Montgomery. I am honored that my parents named me after such a distinguished man.

## The election of May 2, 1934

### *The Tuscaloosa News*, May 2, 1934, page two
### The results of the Democratic Primary held May 1, 1934 are given below.

Name  Vote in Lafoy County wide total

State Senator:
| | | |
|---|---|---|
| Hayse Tucker | 10 | 4,932 |
| Henry Mize | 15 | 3,115 |

Probate judge:
| | | |
|---|---|---|
| Wm. Brandon | 22 | 5,070 |
| John Pearson | 4 | 2,309 |

Inferior judge:
| | | |
|---|---|---|
| Herbert Findley | 23 | 4,071 |
| W.C. Warren | 3 | 3,292 |

Sheriff:
| | | |
|---|---|---|
| Foster King | 12 | 3,753 |
| Festus Shamblin | 14 | 4,717 |

Circuit solicitor:
| | | |
|---|---|---|
| John Beale | 14 | 2003 |
| Gordon Davis | 1 | 1314 |
| Ed deGraffenried | 1 | 1257 |
| Monroe Ward | 0 | 784 |

Governor:
| | | |
|---|---|---|
| Frank Dixon | 12 | 3,359 |
| Bibb Graves | 10 | 2,694 |
| Leon McCord | 4 | 1,913 |

At the time of the election, Mr. Tucker's opponent, Henry Mize, was in a business partnership with my grandfather, William Aaron Boyd, Jr. This placed my father in the awkward position of being employed by Hayse Tucker who was running against Daddy's business partner. Grandaddy Boyd and Mr. Mize operated, among other business ventures, an insurance agency with an office in the Alston Building, Room 405-406. The six-story building was located on the southeast corner of the intersection of Greensboro Avenue and 6th Street. It was the second tallest building in Tuscaloosa.

## The election of 1938

Political ads are written to entice voters to vote for a candidate. Frequently, the qualifications of the candidate as stated in the ad are exaggerated, embellished, or overtly untrue. Further, promises candidates make are unrealistic. In other instances, the opposite is true. An example of a political ad that is factual and without fraud is found in Hayse Tucker's ad of March 20, 1938 when he ran for reelection to the state senate.

### *The Tuscaloosa News*, page 2
### March 20, 1938
### A political ad

I will appreciate your support and vote for reelection to the State Senate from Tuscaloosa, Alabama

It has been my privilege and responsibility to serve this county as State Senator during the last three sessions of the State Legislature. With the date not far off when our citizens will again make their choice from a list of candidates, I sincerely wish that I had the time and opportunity to talk to each voter and attend all the political rallies.

As you will recall, the regular session in 1935 started in January and did not adjourn until August. There was also a special session in 1936 that lasted several months. In an effort to live up to my responsibility to the best of my ability, I not only attended every legislative day, I stayed in Montgomery every mid-week during the entire three sessions when committee sessions were held in order to study and learn more of the issues involved. This is a considerable sacrifice for a businessman with the heavy daily expenses of his own business to look after. As you know, the pay to a member of the Legislature is not sufficient to cover the expense of travel, hotel, and meals. This is not said to complain, but to keep the record straight. I served then and am asking to be permitted to serve again with the conviction that all of us have a "heavy" responsibility to pay back some of this obligation.

But as a result, this is my first spring in four years that I have been able to devote most of my time to my business. Because of these facts, I know that most fair-minded people of this community will understand why it is impossible for me to attend all the political meetings. Please know that my heart and spirit are with the sincere efforts working for better government as expressed by these meetings.

I have given much thought now, as I did four years ago, to the question of a platform. I have too high a respect for the patriotic and thinking people of Tuscaloosa to submit a list of good-sounding promises, some of which could not exist together, for no other purpose than to get votes. Events change so rapidly that what might be desirable today under today's known conditions might not be desirable next year when the Legislature will be in session and conditions may have changed.

As a matter of fact, overshadowing in importance in any possible platform, is the question of training, experience, ability, and character of the candidate. I am convinced that the citizens of this community feel that this is the prime obligation for them to decide as voters. With over 1,500 bills, many of them on vital issues, introduced in the regular session, it is easily apparent that promises on a few issues are not the assurance which the voters expect. They must be satisfied as to what principles their candidate will stand for under all circumstances and even under pressure.

Because of this, I feel the best platform I could possibly offer is my record itself, which is open information as shown in the official journal of the Senate. I can report to my community that my every act and vote was for clean government. I not only had no member of my family on the State payroll, neither asked for any friend as a "Pie-eater" due to my request. I am in the automobile business, and because the State is a big purchaser of trucks and cars, during the administration before my election as a member of the Senate, our company has always entered competitive bids for State purchases and secured some business. Many of my friends feel that I have leaned over backwards, but I have been so determined that my whole effort has been for clean government that on my oath taking of office, our company has entered no bids for State purchase. This is the real issue because vital as are the problems of education, health and all else, these programs cannot prosper unless the integrity of our state government cannot be first established.

I am mindful of the added responsibility of representing this county in the Legislature because of the presence of unexcelled institutions in our community.

The best platform that I know to offer is to promise to continue to work for the upbuilding of our State and remain faithful with all my heart and energy to the principles of good government.

I will sincerely appreciate your support and vote.

Sincerely,
Hayse Tucker

**The Tuscaloosa News, May 4, 1938, front page**
The results of the May 3, 1938, Democratic Party primary showed that Hayse Tucker won the election over two opponents by a margin of 910 votes. The official tally showed Luther Hearn, attorney, with 2,080 votes; Ed Long, labor leader with 1,385 votes; Hayse Tucker, current senator, with 4,375 votes.

The voting box on the Crabbe Road at Windom Springs gave Hearn 43 votes; Long 22 votes; Tucker 34 votes.

The voting box on the Crabbe Road at Carrolls Creek gave Hearn 26 votes; Long 31 votes; Tucker 11 votes.

# POLITICS ALONG THE CRABBE ROAD

## WILLIAM CHARLES WARREN

**Alabama State Senator and Circuit Judge of Tuscaloosa County William Charles Warren**
William Charles Warren, lovingly known as Charles by his friends, is the second elected public official I include in *A Road, A Cemetery, A People* who was not a resident of the Lafoy Community. The reason for his inclusion will become evident.

Charles Warren and his lovely wife Anabel Rice Warren became dear friends with my father in the early 1930s and that friendship ultimately led to a close bond between them and me.

Charles Warren was born August 7, 1887, in Sulfur Springs on Sand Mountain in North Alabama. On October 27, 1912, he married Anabel Rice and over the years they were parents to four lovely daughters.

Economic times were hard for the Warrer family on Sand Mountain. After graduating from high school in 1912, he did not have the money to enroll in college. He began saving every spare penny and in 1916 he moved his growing family to Tuscaloosa and enrolled in the University of Alabama. Working odd jobs when not in class, along with occasionally dropping out of school for a semester to work fulltime, he earned the necessary money to cover all college expenses and expenses incurred during his law school years at the University of Alabama School of Law. He received his LLB in 1925.

Warren's ambition from childhood was to become a lawyer and to enter politics hoping one day to serve as a judge. He wasted no time in getting into politics. In 1926, only one year after completing law school, Mr. Warren was elected to the Alabama State Senate. In 1934 after serving two terms, he became a candidate for Circuit Judge in Tuscaloosa County. He lost that election.

After losing the 1934 election, he continued to practice law in Tuscaloosa but his dream of becoming a judge grew stronger. The dream was realized in 1940 when he was elected Judge of the 6th Judicial Circuit of Alabama in Tuscaloosa. He served as judge for almost thirty years. He died at age 85 on February 2, 1973.

***The Tuscaloosa News*, May 8, 1940 Front page**
**Hughes, Warren Lead in County Court Races**
Tuscaloosa Count broke all election records for total voting in Tuesday's Democratic primary to nominate a three-man Board of Revenue from a field of eight candidates, chose two members of the Tuscaloosa County Board of Education, and returned a county majority for a home-county candidate [W.D. Partlow] for Representative of the Sixth Congressional District.

The total vote was approximately 8,200, with a high of 8,186 cast in the circuit judge's race. This was 200 more than cast in the previous record primary vote in 1938.

Two county races remain undecided based on unofficial returns from all 54 boxes in Tuscaloosa County. They are the circuit judge's contest where W. Charles Warren lacked 362 of a majority over Judge Herbert L Findley and the circuit clerk's race where young Perry Hughes, Jr. lacked 112 votes of a majority over L. N. Hobson, veteran clerk.

Pat N. Lancaster of Tuscaloosa and John B. Taylor of Ralph were reelected to Board of Revenue membership in that order, and John E. Walker of New Lexington, a newcomer in politics, staged a surprising race to win a clear majority as third man. Lancaster's majority was 615, Taylor's was 300 and Walker's was 293.

Unofficial totals
Circuit Judge:
| | |
|---|---|
| E.L. Dodson | 1,587 |
| Herbert L Findley | 2, 897 |
| W.C. Warren | 3,736 |
| Required for majority | 4,098 |

Circuit Clerk:
| | |
|---|---|
| Ike M. Boone, Jr. | 993 |
| L. N. Hobson | 3,182 |
| Perry Hughes, Jr. | 3,950 |

| | |
|---|---|
| Required for majority | 4,062 |
| Board of Revenue: | |
| Cliff Atkinson | 2,102 |
| Woolsey Finnell | 3,564 |
| Pat Lancaster | 4,645 |
| Neil Palmer | 1,743 |
| W. O. Reynolds | 1112 |
| John B. Taylor | 4,431 |
| John Walker | 4,424 |
| Required for majority | 4,031 |

**Run-off results**

A runoff election was held on June 4, 1940. The runoff election is given below. I include county-wide totals and totals for the Carrolls Creek voting precinct on the Crabbe Road.

***The Tuscaloosa News*, June 5, 1940, front page**

| Circuit Judge: | | |
|---|---|---|
| Name | Carrolls Creek | County wide |
| W. C. Warren | 20 | 4,737 |
| Herbert Findley | 10 | 3,396 |
| Circuit Clerk: | | |
| L. N. Hobson | 24 | 2,941 |
| Perry Hughes, Jr. | 6 | 5,189 |

## EDWARD ROBERTSON

Edward "Big Ed" Robertson was born October 16, 1930. He was reared in the Piney Woods community on the Crabbe Road in north Tuscaloosa County near Windham Springs. Ed married Sarah "Jean" Moore. They made their home in Northwood Lake in Northport. Always a country boy at heart, Ed retained ownership of a farm and fishing lake near Turkey Creek on the Fire Tower Road just off the Crabbe Road.

Ed was a large man in statue and in action. In childhood, he was never bashful. Public speaking came easy with him. On page 14 in a March 20, 1938, issue of *The Tuscaloosa News*, it is noted that Ed spoke at a weekly chapel meeting at Windham Springs School when he was only eight-years-old.

Ed's political aspirations began in childhood and reached fulfilment first in 1964 when he was elected to the Northport City Council. After serving as a councilman for three years, he was elected to fill the unexpired term of State Rep. Hugh Thomas who was killed in a 1967 car accident. He served as a representative for 11 years; he was re-elected twice.

In 1979, "Big Ed" won a seat in the state senate. In 1983, Alabama senate district geographic lines were rearranged. Ed's district was combined with another district represented by Charles Bishop. Robertson lost the election to Bishop and returned to city government in Northport. He was elected mayor of Northport in 1984 with 65 percent of the vote, but failed to win reelection four years later. He often was at odds with the city council.

Ed was a close friend. He and I never were at odds with one another. However, he could become a gruff and controversial politician. He had the reputation of speaking his mind regardless of the consequences.

"Big Ed" was one of the leading advocates for a hospital in Northport to "offer competition" to Druid City Hospital. He worked tirelessly for the project. Eventually, in July 1976, the hospital opened its doors for patient care for the first time. However, the road had been rocky and filled with frustration.

Jean and Ed were married for 53 years. When the legislature was in session, she would spend several days a week in Montgomery living in a hotel and assisting with his duties at the Capital and with constituents. She was an attractive outgoing lady who was a great help to her husband.

Ed loved to host fish fries with all the trimmings beside his lake at the farm. The annual event drew large crowds. I enjoyed sitting back and just listening as political issues were discussed, and argued!

Ed was a down to earth neighbor who often left baskets of vegetables from the farm on the porches of elderly neighbors in his neighborhood,

Robertson retired from Uniroyal Goodrich in 1985 after working nearly 36 years at the plant. He died on November 26, 2003 and is buried in Sunset Cemetery in Northport.

## GEORGE NATHAN CHISM

### Genealogy

Geroge Nathan Chism was born October 7, 1910, the son of Harvey Morgan Chism and Ullie May Hamner.

An entire chapter in *A Road, A Cemetery, A People* is devoted to the descendants of William Taylor Hamner, Sr. (1814-1889) the patriarch of the Hamner clan that settled on the Crabbe Road near North River in the late 1920s. Nathan Chism was the great grandson of William T. Hamner, Sr. Many Hamners are buried in Macedonia Cemetery. Nathan Chism is buried in Tuscaloosa Memorial Park Cemetery.

Nathan Chism's Hamner genealogy line through Ullie Mae is interesting. William T. Taylor, Sr. married four times and fathered 16 children by three of his four wives. All the children were born in the same house, a dogtrot log cabin one mile east of the Crabbe Road on what in 2023 is the Dee Hamner Road.

His second marriage was to Permelia Chisms, a marriage that produced thirteen children one of whom was John Pruitt Hamner.

John Pruitt Hamner married Annie Margaret Hall (January 10, 1846-January 3, 1905). They, too, were parents of thirteen children the last of whom was Ullie Mae Hamner (May 25, 1889-July 5, 1936).

Ullie Mae married her first cousin, Harvey Morgan Chism, on November 15, 1908. They were the parents of George Nathan Chism.

### Earning a living during the Great Depression

Nathan first worked for a short time as a clerk in the Northport Post Office. At the age of twenty-two (1932), he bought his Uncle Earl Hamner's grocery store in Northport. The store was on the Crabbe Road one block east of Tuscaloosa County High School. The relatively new school first opened for classes in 1926.

Times were tight; little money was available as the country struggled with the effects of the Great Depression. Nathan allowed customers, many of whom were relatives, to buy groceries on credit with the understanding repayment would be made as circumstances allowed. In the middle 1940s, Nathan sold the grocery store to his brother, Dawson Chism, and took a job as a Tuscaloosa County deputy sheriff working under Sheriff Leon T. Chism, his second cousin.

### Political office

In 1952, Nathan ran for Circuit Clerk of Tuscaloosa County. He won a spot in a two-man run-off election but withdrew his candidacy against Lowell Hardin. By that time, Nathan was chief deputy sheriff and rumors had it that Sheriff Leon did not plan to run for re-election in 1954. This set the stage for Nathan's campaign for sheriff two years later, a contest between him and my father.

My father had served as a member of the Tuscaloosa County Board of Revenue from 1944-1952. He lost his bid for reelection in 1952, but his love for politics remained. So, he became a candidate for sheriff in the 1954 election, twenty years after his first run for sheriff in 1934, a matter covered earlier in this chapter.

The May 4, 1954, Tuscaloosa County sheriff's race drew ten contenders. In a very large turnout, 17,320 people voted. In the primary on May 4, my father, Herman Boyd, Sr. won the most votes, 3,985; Nathan Chism came in second with 3,243 votes; third place went to Darrell Fitts with 2,594 votes; fourth place went to John Henry Suther, a former sheriff who gathered 1,638, votes; fifth place was Sam Dockery with 1,550 votes; sixth place went to S. E. Harless with 1,225 votes; seventh place went to Jack White with 1,073 votes; James Frazier, Jr. captured eighth place with 932 votes; ninth place went to James Nash with 682 votes; tenth place went to Jack Brewer with 558 votes. In the June 1, runoff election, Chism came out the winner. I have been unable to determine the exact vote as *The Tuscaloosa News* archives for that day are not available online.

Nathan Chism was the first sheriff to succeed himself in consecutive terms. He was reelected in 1958, 1962, and 1966. He lost his bid for a fifth term on May 5, 1970 to Beasor Walker by a vote of 15,322 to 9,437. Walker was a Tuscaloosa businessman who operated an oil distributing business in Tuscaloosa and had served for 30 years in the Alabama National Guard.

During his tenure as sheriff, Nathan rarely was armed with a gun. When he wore a pistol, he tried to keep it inconspicuous as possible. His wife Julia Broughton Chism, served as chief cook for at the county jail during part of his tenure.

Nathan and Julia lived on Chism Road just off the Crabbe Road six miles north of Northport on land that once belonged to his grandfather, John Pruitt Hamner. Nathan and Julia were the parents of two children, Jimmy Morgan Chism, married to Jo Walker Chism and George Nathan Chism, Jr., married to Eugena Brown Chism. In retirement, both sons and their spouses moved back to the family Chism property. Jimmy died on November 21, 2021. George died September 28, 2022., Jimmy's widow, Jo, and George's widow, Eugena, continue to live on the property.

**Political rallies in the Lafoy School building**
Prior to the 1970s, Tuscaloosa County, along with most of the southern states, was a one-party area; the Democratic Party ruled supreme. Primary elections in Alabama were held on the first Tuesday in May. If a runoff was necessary, it was held five or six weeks later. Winning in the May primary was tantamount to election in the general election held in November.

Campaigning began in March with political rallies scheduled at schools or community centers throughout the county. Lafoy School was the site for our community's political rallies. These events were well attended. Candidates, or their representatives, were expected to attend as many political rallies scattered throughout the county as possible. At the end of six weeks of attending rallies two or three nights each week, candidates were fatigued. Many gained a few pounds of weight because at each rally the women of the community served meals, mostly greasy, fried chicken, and its trimmings. Cakes, pies, homemade preserves, and other fattening but delicious foods were offered for sale as a means of raising money for the school or community center.

After the meal, each candidate was given three to five minutes to speak soliciting votes. The Master of Ceremonies served as timekeeper. Some candidates had to be "called down" for overextending their allotted speaking time. The situation could get quite "hot" as angry candidates waxed and waned on and on badmouthing their opponents.

The following article grants insight into the nature of political rallies in Lafoy.

*The Tuscaloosa News*, **March 22, 1938**
**Lafoy Rally Changed**
The chicken supper and candidates' rally at the Lafoy School which was scheduled for Tuesday night has been rescheduled for Monday night, March 28 because of a conflict with another school in the county. All candidates and the public are invited to attend. This is being sponsored by the school's PTA.

**Saturdays were a big day at the Tuscaloosa County Courthouse**
Prior to the 1950s, the county courthouse was the scene of much activity. Most of the offices were open for business. Many rural citizens who lived and worked on farms many miles from Tuscaloosa did not come to town except on Saturday. I cite one news article confirming the fact.

# POLITICS ALONG THE CRABBE ROAD

*The Tuscaloosa News* **May 30, 1943 Page 3**
**County Board of Revenue Meets**
Business of a routine nature was disposed of by the Tuscaloosa County Board of Revenue on Saturday at the Courthouse.

The Tuscaloosa Farmer's Curb Market was located on the sidewalk beside the courthouse and it was the scene of great activity as well. An entire chapter in *A Road, A Cemetery, A People* is devoted to the Curb Market.

**D. CUNNINGHAM**
(November 29, 1900-December 26, 1980)

No story about politics on the Crabbe Road and Lafoy Community would be complete without including remarks about D. Cunningham.

D. Cunningham was a man whose first name was simply "D." His tombstone in Yellow Creek Cemetery confirms the fact. Many articles in the newspaper over the years used that identification as did all who knew him.

D. was an interesting person, a man I knew well. His wife, Carrie Grammer Cunningham, was a cousin to my paternal grandmother, Aney Beck Boyd. I was in the Cunningham home on many occasions and often attended the annual political picnic held in their yard shortly before the Democratic primary in May each election year. I also served as D.'s physician and cared for him in the Northport Hospital during his final illness.

D. came from a humble background. However, he acquired large tracts of land in the Yellow Creek/Turkey Creek/ Piney Woods region. Coal and natural gas were discovered in the area and on his lands. As a result, he became very well off from mineral rights' royalties. However, he and Carrie continued to live in their modest small home, and they never displayed evidence of wealth, with one exception. D. purchased a top-of-the-line Cadillac about 1950. However, he never used it for transportation. He parked the car in the open central hallway of the barn next to his house where it sat uncovered until his death. I kidded him about this. He replied, "Doc, I just enjoy looking at it. It is too pretty to drive."

D. was prominently involved in county and state Democratic politics. He served on the Tuscaloosa County Democratic Executive Committee for several years. He influenced a lot of voters in his area of the county. Political candidates courted his friendship and influence. His only child, Curtis Cunningham, shared D.'s passion. At age nineteen, Curtis was elected a Democratic Beat Committeeman, a position he held for years. The following article appeared on page one in the May 9, 1952 issue of *The Tuscaloosa News*.

"D. Cunningham plans to contest Beat 6 returns"

Attorney E.M. Ford said today he is preparing papers for D. Cunningham of Beat 6 who will contest the nomination of G. W. Smith in the May 6 primary for Tuscaloosa County Democratic Executive Committee. He said the papers will be filed Monday or Tuesday with Leslie Dee, committee chairman.

Cunningham will allege there was misconduct on the part of an election official in Beat 6; that illegal votes were cast and that there were mistakes in counting.

Cunningham was defeated by Smith, the official count being 76 to 63."

The political picnics that D. hosted were set up in the yard of his home. The affair attracted one of the largest such crowds in Tuscaloosa County during election years. Long outdoor tables were set up in the shade under beautiful old oak trees. Almost every current office holder and any who held political ambitions attended, along with courthouse employees and other county employees and most members of the county bar association. It was not uncommon to see the governor, U. S. senators and state judges moving among the crowd. As a member of the Board of Revenue, my father, along with Mother and me, were always present.

Being a man of prominence, D.'s reputation

was widely known around the county for yet another reason. He was a cross-dresser. Most of the time he wore dresses. Being an inquisitive young boy, I asked Daddy why D. wore dresses. The rumor mill had it that D. cross-dressed to avoid arrest for operating moonshine stills.

That area of the county was known for its wildcat whiskey stills. The story went that if word got out the sheriff was looking for D. in connection with a raid on a still, when officers arrived at the Cunningham home, they were greeted by a "woman" who was D. dressed in a dress camouflaging him as a woman. Whether the story was true or not, D. routinely wore dresses. He must have enjoyed the feel of women's clothing, so it became a way of life even if he was not hiding from law officials. It never seemed to bother his wife. She was a dear, dear person.

As noted, D. was my patient. He wore dresses to the office. When he was in the hospital terminally ill, the nurses enjoyed taking care of him and found him a model patient. Peggy and I attended his wake in his home; he was laid out in the coffin in a beautiful pink dress. The yard was filled with cars.

## MAGARIA HAMNER BOBO

### Circuit Clerk

In 2023, a resident of the Crabbe Road, Magaria Hamner Bobo, serves as Circuit Clerk of Tuscaloosa. She, like Nathan Chism, is a descendant of William T. Hamner, Sr. and a cousin to Nathan Chism.

Magaria is the daughter of Alvin Franklin Hamner and Eva Mae Guy. Alvin Hamner was the son of Bruce and Fannie Lou Hamner, the grandson of Oliver "Ollie" Jackson Hamner, the great grandson John Pruitt Hamner and Annie Margaret Hall, the great, great grandson of William T. Hamner, Sr.

Magaria's father, Alvin Hamner, served in the US Army 1948-1954. In 1957, he was employed by the Tuscaloosa County sheriff's department. As a deputy sheriff, he received numerous honors including Law Officer of the Year in 1973 and 1979.

CHAPTER 12

# Recreation on the Crabbe Road

Recreational opportunities for country folks in the Lafoy Community during my growing up years centered around family get-to-gathers, church socials, gospel singings, political rallies, square dances, Lafoy School drama presentations, Sunday afternoon baseball games in cow pastures, Home Demonstration events, fiddler contests, swimming in North River or Carrolls Creek, and community picnics.

Men and boys, along with some females, enjoyed coon hunting, fox hunting, squirrel hunting, deer hunting, and fishing in North River and in private ponds in the area.

Recreation always occurred after farm chores were completed. Farm work began before sunrise and ended after dark. Milking cows and feeding hogs and mules had to be done before breakfast and again prior to supper. Field and garden work was toilsome and occupied the day except for a short break at lunch. Many farm houses had a large iron outdoor bell that was rung loudly at lunch to call the field workers to the house for a hearty meal of homegrown vegetables, meats, and iced tea or lemonade, along with homemade pies, custards, or cakes. On rainy days when it was too wet to work in the fields, fences were repaired, firewood was cut, new-ground was cleared, and corn from the crib was shucked and shelled and made ready to be taken to the gristmill in Northport to be ground into cornmeal. Repairs to barns and sheds were ongoing. Life was busy with little time for recreation.

By the end of the Great Depression in the late 1930s, many of the younger men in the community found they could no longer earn a living by farming. They sought employment in public jobs at Gulf States Paper Corporation, B. F. Goodrich Tire Company, the V.A. Hospital, Bryce Hospital, Reichold Chemical, Central Foundry, or other places of employment including the City of Tuscaloosa and Tuscaloosa County. Yet, they continued to tend gardens, raise livestock, and make repairs around the farm after they got home in the afternoons and on Saturdays.

Most women in the Lafoy community found their life calling as housewives and in motherhood. Unlike many city women, very few farm wives could afford household help such as maids and cooks. They had no outside help in washing dirty clothes, preparing meals, scrubbing floors, churning milk into butter, tending gardens, and canning or freezing vegetables and fruits grown on the farm. In cold weather, the only source of heat came from open fires in fireplaces which had to stoked throughout the day.

Unlike their counterparts in town, electric power service did not come to the Lafoy community until 1941. Even then, some poorer families could not afford electric service until after World War II ended in 1945. Public telephone service was not available until the early 1950s. Cooking

# A ROAD, A CEMETERY, A PEOPLE

was done on wood-burning iron stoves in the kitchen. Farm wives had no time to enjoy the pleasures of being in a bridge club or study club.

Nevertheless, the people of Lafoy found avenues of recreational pursuits that allowed them to enjoy a few hours of rest and fun. It is an intriguing story.

**Baseball**
Baseball has been called the American "national sport." From the 1930s until the late 1950s, baseball and softball were the favored sports in which the residents of the Lafoy Community participated on Saturday and Sunday afternoons. However, after 1957, the year Paul "Bear" Bryant became head football coach at the University of Alabama, "Alabama football" replaced baseball and softball as the most popular sport in the Lafoy community.

The Lafoy community baseball team was given the name "Carrolls Creek Nine" when it was organized in the early 1930s. In the preceding photograph, James Valentino Rushing is seen on the back row, far left. The following article about Rushing and the Carrolls Creek Nine comes from *The Tuscaloosa News*.

***The Tuscaloosa News*, June 11, 1933, page 9**
**Rushing Youth Hurls One-Hit Victory for Carrolls Creek Nine**
James Valentino Rushing, a sixteen-year-old pitcher, held the Windham Springs baseball team to a single hit Saturday and struck out eleven batters to give the Carrolls Creek Nine a ten to one victory. His first cousin, Roy Rushing, served as catcher.

Jones, Nelson, and Fields pitched for Windham Springs with Dunn on the receiver's end.

Carrolls Creek Nine baseball team, 1930s

**Boyd comment**:
The Rushing family was one of Lafoy Community's most prominent families. An entire chapter in *A Road, A Cemetery, A People* is devoted to the family. Joseph Enoch Rushing and his wife Samantha Lenora Deason Rushing arrived in the area in the late 1800s. They were the parents of ten sons and one daughter. Sixteen-year-old James Valentino Rushing was a grandson of Joseph Enoch and Samantah Lenora and the son of James Polk Rushing.

The Rushing property consisted of several hundred acres of land bounded on the east by Carrolls Creek and on the west by the Crabbe Road. The southern border began at the Crabbe Road bridge as it crossed over Carrolls Creek. The west border extended north along the Crabbe Road for about a mile and ended at what in 2024 is Rushing Loop Road.

James Valentino was exceptionally talented. He had the talent to be a professional baseball player. In fact, he entered a professional baseball training camp upon graduating from Tuscaloosa County High School, but after a few weeks, he decided professional baseball was not for him. He returned to the Rushing farm and worked on the farm. When World War II broke out in 1942, he joined the U.S. Military and served for the duration of the war. Following discharge, he was em-

170

ployed by B. F. Goodrich Tire Company and retired from that company after many years of service.

Like James Valentino Rushing, many Rushing relatives, both male and female, were very talented baseball and softball players including two of James' sisters, Frances Rushing Franklin, and Annette Rushing Mills. James' son Johnny and Johnny's son James Edward were great ballplayers as well. Another star softball player was my wife's aunt, Gladys "Dick" Rushing Romaine.

Roy Rushing is noted in the previous news article. He was my wife's father. Like other Rushings, he was a good player but limited his time playing baseball to an occasional impromptu game with neighbors on Sunday afternoon.

Indeed, rural life did not offer much leisure time to engage in sports except on Sunday afternoons. During the summertime, several members of the Lafoy community often gathered on Sunday afternoon in Robert Rushing's cow pasture for an impromptu baseball game. The land was flat and ideal for playing baseball. However, one had to be careful to avoid stepping into one of many cow patties scattered throughout the pasture.

Two team captains were selected. The captains alternated choosing the players for their team. Everybody knew who the best players were. So that the game was competitive, the captains made sure each team had some better players and some not so talented. Family members and friends gathered around sitting on the ground and enjoyed a wonderful afternoon. The game had to be over in time for the crowd to get back home, milk the cow, tend the animals, grab a bite of supper, and be ready to attend the Sunday night church service at 7:30 p.m.

## Softball

A softball team made up of Crabbe Road young women reached state-wide fame. They were called the "Mud Hens" softball team. The following articles from the *Tuscaloosa News* share interesting information about these talented ladies.

### March 27, 1938 page 6 *The Tuscaloosa News*
### Northport Mud Hens Pick Leaders

The Northport "Mud Hens" girls' softball team completed organization plans last week in the home of Mrs. E. W. Hagler. "Mud Hens" was chosen the official nickname with blue and white for colors.

Miss Gladys Rushing was chosen as captain with Oneto Fitts as alternate captain. Woodrow Rushing will serve as manager, and Alston Burroughts as alternate manager. Practice will be held on Tuesday and Thursday afternoons.

Following the business meeting, delicious refreshments were served to the following: Gladys Rushing; Oneto Fitts; Louise Rankin; Dorothy Hogg; Minnie Hagler; Mabel Powell; Janet Franklin; Mattie Harper; Etteline Rushing; Katherine Burroughs; Sarah Hayes, and Mrs. E. W. Hagler.

**Boyd comment:**

From the time of this article in 1938 until the early 1950s, a span of about fifteen years, the Mud Hens would go on to receive many softball awards and played in several states in the Southeast. The Rushing name appeared often.

The Mud Hens on occasion were known as the "Pullets."

### *The Tuscaloosa News*, May 18, 1950
### Mud Pullets play Epps here Saturday

The Sokol softball team will play Epps Jewelry Company of Birmingham here Saturday night at 8:30 o'clock at the Northport City Park. The Epps team is Birmingham's city championship team.

Coach Woodrow Rushing said he would send either Gladys Rushing Romaine or Bell Sanford to the mound for the Pullets.

In the first appearance of the season last week in Birmingham, the Pullets divided a twin bill with the Sokol team of Birmingham.

The girls of Lafoy community shared an enthusiasm and talent for softball that matched the love the boys had for baseball. The "Mud Hens" softball team competed on a regional basis.

**Pullets leave for Southern meet tonight:**

Northport's Sokol Pullets are St. Petersburg-bound for the Southern women's softball tournament after trouncing Sheffield's Pharmacy 18-0 in an exhibition game at Northport City Park last night. Manager Woodrow Rushing and his bevy of softball stars will leave for St. Petersburg tonight, going by auto. The Pullets meet South Carolina at 2:00 p.m. Sunday Eastern Standard Time in their first-round game.

Nell Sanford, the Pullets' star pitcher, fanned nine Sheffield batters in the four-ending game Saturday night. Only one visitor got on base, the result of walking. Seven pullets hit safely. Mary Edna Nelson homered. Boots Howard hit a double and triple. Elizabeth Beatty and Nell Sanford triples. Dot Rushing had three singles.

Manger Rushing today announced the following roster for the St. Petersburg trip.

Players making the trip will be Annett Rushing, Nell Sanders, Dot Rushing, Mrs. Jean Evans, Boots Howell, Betty Frazier, Jenet Rushing, Mrs. Gladys Rushing Romaine, Sue Walker, Lewis Booth, Jean Patterson, and Earline Hamner.

Three other players, Nina Rushing, June Cooper, and Betty Turner were unable to make the trip.

Three husbands of wives on the team will also make the trip. They are Troy Sanford, Arthur Lee Evans, and Robert Romaine. Traveling along with manager Woodrow Rushing will be his brother, James, and Howard Rushing, brother of Mrs. Romaine.

**Boyd comment:**

It was my pleasure to know most of these people. All of the Rushings noted in these articles were cousins of my wife, Peggy Rushing Boyd.

**The annual Lafoy community picnic**

Farm folks rarely had a break of complete rest and recreation. Looking after farm matters did not let up, but by August cotton and corn crops had been laid by and would require little work until harvest time. Delicious fruits and vegetables grown in local gardens had been gathered and housewives had worked long hours in hot kitchens canning and freezing the yield of their gardens and orchards. The pantries and food cellars were stocked with jars of canned goods that would provide food until the next growing season. With outdoor temperatures in the mid and high 90s, the heat created by the wood-burning kitchen stoves produced a room temperature of over one hundred degrees. Air-conditioned farm houses were a thing of the future.

August was the month for two big events. One was the annual Lafoy Community Farm Bureau picnic. The other was the annual revivals held at Macedonia Methodist Church and Carrolls Creek Baptist Church. The following news article describes a typical Lafoy summer picnic.

***The Tuscaloosa News*, August 7, 1947 front page**
**Long home runs, short talks**
**Big baskets, feature Lafoy Picnic**

The old men hit the longest home runs while their wives cheered them on. Probate Judge Chester Walker, as usual, ate more than anybody else, and everybody who attended the annual Lafoy Community Farm Bureau picnic Wednesday had a good time.

Some 200 folks gathered under the shade trees at Lafoy for the all-day affair. A speaking program was held first, but it did not last long. At noon, women of the community spread lunch on a plank table.

The spread of food on the table consisted of roasting ears, peas, snap beans, potato salad, blood red tomatoes, butterbeans, cucumber pickles, and oh yea, fried chicken and everything that goes with it.

Iced tea was made up in a washtub and everything was complete except for a gourd from

# RECREATION ON THE CRABBE ROAD

Carrolls Creek swimming hole

which to drink the delicious liquid. There was a jug of chocolate milk, other soft drinks, and a barrel of ice-cold water.

Folks who didn't listen to the speakers or who didn't enjoy swapping news with their neighbors, played softball. Even the women and girls joined in the game. My father, a member of the Tuscaloosa County Board of Revenue, served as umpire. He called all the folks who could vote "safe" even though they bunted.

Hugh Spencer, president of the Lafoy Farm Bureau, served as master of ceremonies. Speakers included Probate Judge Chester Walker, Assistant Farm Bureau Agents John Weeks and G. B. Pruitt, and Miss Edna Coyle, Assistant County Home Demonstration Agent.

County Farm Bureau agent Beverly Holston would have made a speech but he was held up by attending a conference on army worm visitation and got there late.

The Lafoy Farm Bureau is made up of 70 members. It is one of the most wide-awake farm bureau groups in the county.

Its officers are: Hugh Spencer, president; Spurgeon Black, vice-president; Mrs. Annie Rushing, secretary-treasurer. Robert Rushing was chairman of the committee on arrangements for the picnic.

**Boyd comment:**

The annual picnic was a highlight event in the community. Our family rarely missed attending. I find the comment about my father humorous.

During the first years of my memory in the mid-1940s, the annual picnic was held at the Carrolls Creek swimming hole located beside the narrow one-lane Crabbe Road bridge that passed over the creek. The property belonged to the Polk Rushing family.

The swimming area was about half the size of a football field. The water nearest the road was shallow and was ideal for wading and for young non-swimmers to play in. The water in the far side was deep. Older dare-devil boys would scale up the steep rock wall on the far side of the water and jump into the creek below.

A long picnic table made of wood planks supported on sawhorses was quickly assembled and soon was filled with delicious dishes of food as noted above. The men and boys played baseball while children enjoyed playing games and the women visited and caught up on local news.

In the early 1950s, the site for the annual picnic was moved from Carrolls Creek swimming hole to a large pasture beside North River on Mem Tierce's farm in what today is Four Winds subdivision. Mr. Tierce was gracious to allow the use of his property and the area was much larger and could accommodate more people. The activities of the day were the same as at the old Carrolls Creek location.

The picnic table was right beside the river so that adults could keep an eye on their children who were playing in the river. Most of us kids enjoyed splashing in the water and splashing water on one another. We made so much noise that we must have scared the water moccasins away. I never saw one. It was while attending those picnics at North River that I first learned to swim, i.e., "dogpaddle." The area had no outdoor privies or dressing rooms. When nature called, business was taken care of out of sight behind the trees. To change into and out of bathing suits, boys gathered behind bushes and girls hid themselves a few yards away behind another set of bushes.

The mere mention of the names noted in this August 7, 1947, news article brings fond memories. The Lafoy Community was a wonderful place in which to grow up. Although much has changed and most of my mentors are no longer living, it remains a great community today.

## Hunting

Hunting in modern days primarily is enjoyed as a form of recreation and is not a means of providing meat for the table, albeit, many deer hunters, quail hunters, duck hunters, and turkey hunters still enjoy eating nutritious and tasty meats that come from the wild. Many men and some women in Lafoy are avid hunters. Several interesting hunting stories about local people have appeared in *The Tuscaloosa News*. I present a few.

### *The Tuscaloosa News*, September 5, 1930, page 2
### Dog collar is missing, so is prized hound
### Black and tan hunting dog strays from Northport Harris home

A dog collar bearing the name of Fleetwood Harris, President of the Tuscaloosa City Commission, is missing. Attached to the collar is a black and tan female fox hound, one of the favorite hunting dogs of this entire community.

Commissioner Harris says the dog is a shy creature and likely will avoid attempt of anyone to catch her. He asks that anyone finding the animal to communicate with him immediately.

**Boyd comment:**
The charming choice of words "Attached to the collar is . . ." is typical of sentence structure of the era. News reporters in the past not only presented facts, they used colloquialism that allowed the reader to both gain information and to be entertained as they read.

### *The Tuscaloosa News*, October 5, 1939
### Alabama's fox hunting dogs

Alabama has some noted foxhunting areas and famous foxhounds and enthusiastic devotees of the chase. In Wilcox County, Bob Goode boasts that before he came to Montgomery as Commissioner of Agriculture, he had not missed a Saturday night foxhunt in several years. He also was never quite as happy as when listening to the baying of hounds through the woods or recounting the merits of his foxhounds. A bobcat will give the dogs just as good a run as the fox, but the bobcat will make a smaller circle. The hunter can sit under a tree for two or three hours and enjoy every minute of the chase.

**Boyd comment:**
When I read this article, I immediately identified with it. My father enjoyed foxhunting. Daddy often allowed me to go with him when he hunted.

Daddy owned several foxhounds. Most Saturday nights right after supper, he loaded his dogs into the trunk of his Ford automobile and drove to a hilltop in Mem Tierce's pasture about a half mile from our house. This was the accepted meeting site where he met fellow fox hunters Clyde Utley, Virgil Barton, Gay Dorroh, Dr. A. W. Patton, B. F. Shirley, and one or two others. Each hunter brought one of two hounds. This created a hunting pack of eight or ten dogs. During the chase that followed, each man swore that he recognized his own hound's bark from the rest of the pack. I was always suspicious of their claims. All the barks sounded the same to me.

As soon as the dogs were turned free, the entire pack went running off in search of a fox scent. Once a scent was found, the race was on with all dogs in hot pursuit of the fox. North River bordered most of the Tierce pasture in the area where the hunt occurred. Steep rock bluffs

# RECREATION ON THE CRABBE ROAD

made up the far side of the river. The river border on the near side of the river was that of a gentle slope without rock cliffs. The area was open pasture and farmland, a terrain perfect for foxhunting.

The object of the hunt was not for the dogs to catch and kill the fox even though that happened occasionally. The object was for the men to just sit and listen to the melodious barks of the hounds as they chased the fox. The fox ran in wide circles crossing and recrossing North River and climbing steep hills and bluffs. The rock bluffs had many crevices. After being chased for a couple of hours, the fox tired and squeezed himself into one of the rock crevices in a bluff where he was safe and out-of-reach of the dogs. All the dogs could do was paw at the opening of the crevice, but to no avail.

The race was over. It was time to call in the dogs and head for home. Each hunter had his own fox hound horn and each made a distinct sound. One by one the tired dogs returned to the hilltop where they had been released. They were panting, soaking wet from swimming across the river several times, and ready to call it a night.

The real fun of the evening for the men was to sit and listen to the howling of the dogs, each man claiming his dog was the lead dog. As they sat and listened to the hounds, the men discussed farming, politics, the weather, and other topics of interest as they drank hot coffee from thermos bottles. I learned a lot as I sat and listened. In fact, I discovered the joy of listening at an early age. There is a time for speaking, but more often, I find listening serves me better.

Joel T. Shirley and his hunting shotgun
Joel was renowned as a hunter.

Invariably, one or two dogs did not return to the cars. So, the next day on Sunday afternoon, Daddy and I would get in his car and drive along all the little dirt roads in the area stopping several times to blow his fox hound horn. We also would stop at the few houses in the sparsely populated area and ask if anyone had seen the missing dogs. Everybody knew Daddy, and often the people had already put his dog in a pen knowing that Daddy would be by on Sunday afternoon to get the dog. He never lost a dog permanently.

Attending fox hunting with Daddy were times of bonding between father and son for which I will forever be thankful.

### Coon hunting

Raccoon and opossum hunting is a stimulating sport to many people. I share the following news articles.

### *The Tuscaloosa News*, March 2, 1938, page 5
### Windham Springs
### Opossum hunt held

A large crowd of boys, members of the Windham Springs 4-H Club, recently went opossum hunting. Included in the crowd were James Fleenor, J. R. Fields, Eugene Hamilton, Louis Christian, Wilbur Hamilton, Heflin Christian, Albert Catham, Wilton Fields, and Professor Cecil Vaughn.

### Boyd comment:

The Windham Springs Community is ten miles north of North River on the Crabbe Road.

Opossums, like racoons, are nocturnal animals. Men, young and old, get a thrill in hunting these nighttime animals. Hunting is usually done with a dog. A good coon dog will chase the animal while it is on the ground. As soon as the hound is narrowing the distance between himself and his prey, the possum or coon climbs a nearby tree and perches itself near the top of the tree where it looks down on the dog and hisses angerly. Using a powerful flashlight, the men shine light up into the critter's eyes while one of his buddies blasts the cornered victim with a shotgun. The dying animal topples to the ground and gives a final fight with the dogs before drawing its final breath. The fur and hide may or may not be saved, dried, and sold as pelts.

*The Tuscaloosa News,* **Sunday May 18, 1947, page 9**
**Coon Hunters' picnic**
Tuscaloosa County coon hunters will hold a picnic Wednesday afternoon at 4:00 p.m. at the State Hospital Colony on the Columbus Road. A basket lunch will be served at 6:00 p.m. All members of the association are invited to come, bring a basket of food, their wives, and their dogs.

**Rabbit hunting**

*The Tuscaloosa News,* **January 13, 1940**
**Rabbit sales are restricted**
**Only trapped animals may be sold**
**License fee $2.50 required**
Life is not as glamorous as it might have been for the lowly rabbit once ranked as a "fur-bearer." Last August 8, the Alabama Conservation Department raised the rabbit to the lofty estate of "game animal."

It's all because the rabbit is still liable to find his way across market counters in grocery stores, in stews, or on café tables — legally.

Beware! The fellow who killed the rabbit better be careful or he will be in trouble too. As a matter of fact, only a trapper can legally take rabbits to market and he must have a $2.50 fur-trapper license and he must offer only the dressed carcass for sale. Under the new rating of "game animals," the rabbit must be shot only between October 1 and February 20 and the hunter must have a license. The "cotton-tail" may be hunted with sticks and dogs anytime without a license.

"We have tried to be lenient in enforcing the law" said Ben C. Morgan conservation game chief "but market hunters slaughtering our local game and selling them under the guise of imported rabbits must stop."

"It is therefore necessary that we stick to the strict interpretation of the law which says that only the dressed carcass of fur-bearing animals can be sold for food purposes. We will enforce the law making it necessary for anybody offering dressed rabbits for sale to have a $2.50 fur-trapper license where they are trapped. This will permit them to sell dressed rabbits."

None shot as game animals may be sold legally and likewise none taken with dogs or sticks.

**Boyd comment:**
Rabbit hunting in the Lafoy Community could be divided into two broad categories—as a sport and as a means of keeping predators out of gardens.

As a sport, I use the examples of Mackey Deason, Johnny Rushing, and the late Dr. Charles Sprayberry, all dear friends of mine.

These men kept large kennels of beagles, dogs that are not only excellent rabbit hunting dogs and loyal companions, they are also happy-go-lucky, funny, and have pleading expressions. They were bred to hunt in packs so they enjoy company. My three friends often called each other on the spur of the moment and said, "Let's go rabbit hunting after work. I will meet you in an hour."

My father-in-law, Roy Rushing, hunted and killed rabbits in an effort to protect his vegetable garden from being invaded by rabbits. He often walked over his property, shotgun in hand, scouting out rabbits to kill. He even resorted to enclosing his several-acre vegetable gardens with chicken wire trying to keep the pesky rabbits away.

Some Lafoy Community women served rabbit on their tables. My mother-in-law did not.

**Bird dog**

***The Tuscaloosa News*, date not known but likely in the 1950s**
**By Bob Kyle**
A canine that would make Pistol Packing Mama lay down her guns has turned up at Northport. The canine, a bird dog, will point whisky in stump holes and hollow logs. But take it easy folks, the dog isn't for sale. Not in these times.

Huston Thomas, widely known singer who resides in Northport, comes up with the strange tale of the whiskey pointing canine owned by Hayes Rushing.

While hunting with Leon Chism in the Piney Woods community, Rushing's dog pointed a covey of birds on one of the long Piney Woods ridges. The men killed two birds on the covey ridge.

Old Bill, the dog, retrieved the two birds and went on down the ridge where he pointed again. Hayes and Leon walked up to Old Bill with both barrels cocked. Nothing moved. They kicked around but still no bird fluttered out.

Directly in front of the dog stood a hollow tree inside of which was a pint bottle of pure Tuscaloosa County wildcat whiskey. The men, thinking it to be a bottle of kerosene left by loggers or woodcutters, went in to investigate. After uncorking the bottle, there was no mistaking the fact that it was liquid corn.

Looking further, they discovered there was a crippled bird behind the bottle.

So old Bill, Houston concluded, makes a double "pint," one on the bird and one on the pint of moonshine. Rushing makes the point the dog will be kept tied.

**Boyd comment:**
Bob Kyle (1909-1990) wrote a folksy column for *The Tuscaloosa News* for several decades. His columns were filled with humor about "down-to-earth" events, especially about country folks.

Hayes Rushing was a great uncle to my wife, Peggy, and a brother-in-law to Houston Thomas.

Kyle creates a nice pun on words in using "pint" and "point." Country folks often pronounced the word "point" as if it were spelled "pint."

**Music on the Crabbe Road**
Music in the form of singings, fiddling events, and dances was an important part of recreation on the Crabbe Road during the early decades of the 20$^{th}$ century. Many residents of the community were gifted musicians.

***The Tuscaloosa News*, February 21, 1929**
The singing at Lafoy School was enjoyed by a number of friends last Sunday evening. The people are always glad to have Prof. Adam Lesley and the other good singers with them.

***The Tuscaloosa News*, December 7, 1933**
**Fiddling planned**
The Lafoy School Parent-Teacher Association will sponsor a fiddlers' convention and Christmas playlet, a short and entertaining play, in the school Friday night, December 22 at 7:30 o'clock. A contest will be held to decide the ugliest man and woman. Proceed from the entertainment will be used for school equipment. All fiddlers and the public are invited.

***The Tuscaloosa News*, December 24, 1933**
**Large crowd attends Lafoy fiddlers' match**
A large crowd enjoyed the fiddlers' convention and a playlet presented Friday night by the Lafoy Parent Teacher Association at the school. Herman Purdue of the First National Bank personnel presided as master of ceremonies.

John O. Hamner won first prize with Artamus K. Callahan second, and Bill Johnson of Cottondale third. Special selections were given by the Lafoy String Band with Dee Hamner playing the violin and Harwood Hamner handling guitars.

A short play "A Saturday Night Social" was directed by Miss Lenora Hyche. It was a blackface minstrel production which caused much merriment.

Last Wednesday, as a closing exercise for the holidays, the Lafoy School gave a community Christmas tree ceremony that was attended by many patrons.

### *The Tuscaloosa News*, March 14, 1934
A fiddlers' convention will be held Friday night at Lafoy school which is located eight miles from Tuscaloosa on the Crabbe Road. Sandwiches, Eskimo pies, and a pretty girl cake will be sold. All fiddlers and candidates are invited.

**Boyd comment:**

Fiddling contests occurred frequently. Lafoy had its own renown band, the "Lafoy String Band," made up of Oll Dee Hamner (1927-1980), son of Oliver "Ollie" Jackson Hamner and Mary Louise Rigsby, and his brothers Hollis Harwood and John O'Neil, along with their friend Richard Patrick. The band played widely at square dances, political rallies, community gatherings and fiddlers' conventions.

Lenora Hyche, noted in the December 24, 1933, article was the daughter of Lenora Bell "Lou" Rushing Hyche. She later married Ed Earnest. Her name appears often in news articles concerning Lafoy Community. She was my wife's cousin.

### Honoring World War II veterans
Strong patriotism has characterized the people of the Lafoy community since its first residents arrived. Many young men of the area volunteered to serve their country when World War II broke out. Some gave their lives so that freedom might rule in our nation. A returning home welcoming party was given for these men. The following article tells the story.

### *The Tuscaloosa News*, June 6, 1946, page 6
### Lafoy Club Entertains Returning Servicemen
The members of the Lafoy Home Demonstration Club entertained the returning servicemen of the community at a picnic supper Saturday night at the home of Mr. and Mrs. Albert Hagler. The young people enjoyed swimming in the lovely lake on the grounds near the home, and enjoyed other social features.

An old-fashioned supper was served to about 100 people of the community, friends of the servicemen and their relatives. The tables were spread with all kinds of home-prepared dishes—fried chicken, chicken pies, ham, salads of all kinds, and cakes and pies. Music and dancing were enjoyed.

Those that played string music included Mitt Lary and four of his sons—Alfred, Frank, Gene, and Raymond. Ice cream was served to all at a late hour. Mrs. T. S. Black, president of the Lafoy Home Demonstration Club, and the members of the club all served admirably as hostesses.

The following boys were special guests of honor for the dinner party: Terrell Rushing; Bernard Rushing; James Rushing; Buck Rushing; Howard Rushing; Devaughn Black; Pat Rigsby; Almon Rigsby; Grady Shirley; B. F. Shirley; Ed Earnest; Tuck Mathis; Dick Hagler; Narley Walters; J. D. Hamner; Clifford Davis; Elmer Smelley; Raymond Lary; and Daniel Morrison.

**Boyd comment:**

Albert Hagler and his wife, Patty Helen Elizabeth "Patty" Parizek Hagler were the parents of seven children: Henry Albert, Jr.; Alene; James "Jimmy"; Patty Jean; twins Mary and Martha; and Nina Sue. The Henry Albert Hagler property joined the Macedonia Methodist Church property on its southern border. The Hagler residence, a large rustic, two-story, wood house, sat on a hill overlooking a small manmade swimming hole, Hagler's Lake, a favorite community site for swimming and other social functions. The water was so cold I could stay in it for only short periods of time. A deep gorge lay between the residence and the swimming hole. In order to create a direct walking path from the house to the lake, the Haglers had constructed a wood "swinging" walking bridge over the gorge. As a kid, I enjoyed jumping on the bridge making it "swing" from side to side. Without a bridge to get from the Hagler house to the swimming hole, one would have to walk east on the long dirt driveway until the gorge ended and then walk west toward the Crabbe Road for about a hundred yards.

The cost of admittance was a dime. A level area beside the lake was an ideal site for picnics, dancing, and just hanging out. Electric lights allowed the area to be used at night. Drinking alcohol and loitering were not allowed. The event honoring returning veterans was long remembered.

**The history of the Albert Hagler house**
The history of the unique Albert Hagler house was unknown to me until February 2024 when my good friend Hilary Shirley, whose property adjoins the former Hagler property, told me he thought the house was originally built as a summer home for Frank Fitts, Sr. (1881-1979) and his family who lived in Pinehurst near downtown Tuscaloosa. Hilary then contacted Lewis Fitts who is the grandson of Frank Fitts who gave me the following information.

Interview with Lewis Fitts 205-7925-0224
The Fitts family is a very prominent family in Tuscaloosa history dating back to the mid-1800s. During the 1920s, Mr. Frank Fitts, Sr. built the house as a summer house on the Crabbe Road on a bluff overlooking Northport River 8 miles north or Northport. The house was a two-story very rustic structure built out of used lumber. The exterior plywood boards had numerous nail holes indicating it had been used earlier. A large bedroom for Mr. and Mrs. Fitts overlooked a steep bluff of North River. A thick growth of trees on the bluff obstructed a view of the river itself.

It is not certain, but it is thought that initially there were no glass windows upstairs. Large wood shutters covering the window openings could be opened and closed depending upon the weather and outdoor temperature. Later, more modern windows were installed.

The Fitts created a swimming hole just west of the house by using dynamite to blow out a cavity for the water reservoir. Pieces of rock from the explosion were used to create a dam for the swimming hole. Mrs. Frank Fitts was an artist and created a lovely mosaic using some of the rock. A flat area served as a picnic area in which concrete tables and benches allowed picnicking.

The Fitts installed a zip line that allowed swimmers to "zip" down the bluff from the house and drop into North River. On one occasion, the force of the splash into the river ripped off a girl's bathing suit.

The Fitts property in Pine Hurst consisted of three or four acres and included a barn and small pasture for several ponies. Lewis says that his father in the 1920s occasionally rode his pony from Pine Hurst to the summer house on the Crabbe Road, a ride that took a half a day.

The year Albert Hagler purchased the Fitts summer home is not known but likely was in the 1930s. During the 1940s and 1950s, I was in the house on several occasions when my mother visited Mrs. Hagler. The house in 2024 remains a private residence.

***The Tuscaloosa News*, circa 1950**
**Widows enjoy themselves even if the fish weren't biting**
More than 30 women, mostly elderly widows from the Northport area, met Thursday at Clara Rushing's Lake for a picnic and fishing.

Mrs. Clara Rushing and Mrs. Edna Watkins spearheaded the drive to get the ladies together. It went so well another one is planned for Christmas.

"The meeting gave us a chance to get together

Josh and Clara Rushing home in 2024
The appearance is the same as when the Rushings lived there in the 1940s-1960s. A separate chapter is devoted to the Ezra Jonah Shipp family, who built this house in 1925. From the exterior, the house is unchanged from its original appearance.

to talk about old times," said Mrs. Watkins.

Rushing's Lake is located about nine miles from Northport on the Crabbe Road. The fish were not biting very good, but 88-year-old Mrs. Jureda Carnathan caught a small brim while fishing from the bank. Some of the ladies took their cane poles and boarded one of the two small boats in the lake to try to catch the "big ones."

The picnic dinner had a "home cooked flavor" and featured Southern fried chicken, potato salad, pies, and cakes.

**Boyd comment:**

Mrs. Rushing's farm was less than a quarter of a mile south of our home. Her only grandchild, Ray Rushing, was my age. He lived in Northport and occasionally came to spend the day with his grandmother. When that happened, I was invited down to play with him and we spent a lot of time by the lake.

## 4-H Club works to build a church

It may seem odd to include 4H Club activities in a chapter on "recreation." However, in the following instance it is very appropriate.

4-H clubs were originated in the early 1900s to allow young people to have a "four-square education," the 4 H's representing Head, Heart, Hands, and Health. The organization seeks to promote positive youth development, facilitate learning, and engage youth in work of their community through the Cooperative Extension Service to enhance quality of life. Both the boys' club and the girls' club were well established in our community. It was a great experience for me. One of the major projects of our neighborhood youth is discussed in the following news articles.

### *The Tuscaloosa News*, July 1, 1950
### Lafoy 4-H Girls Club

The members of the Lafoy 4-H Girl's Club elected leaders for the new season when the group held its first meeting at the home of Mrs. Trimm Hamner.

Miss Ramona Hamner, president for the past year, presided at the business session. Carol Kay Hamner led the group in songs. The devotional was given by Ruby Nell Sanford. Members answered roll call by naming their projects for the summer.

Edna Earl Williams was chosen to serve as the new president. Elected with her were: Ramona Hamner, vice president; Nell Sanford secretary/treasurer; Carol Kay Hamner, song leader; Sarah Shirley, reporter. Mrs. W. A. Glover is their adult leader.

After a discussion, the members decided to present a play as the summer project. At the next meeting, to be an all-day session on July 13 at the home of Mrs. Bill Glover, they planned to make a 4-H quilt. Each member has been asked to bring a covered dish to that meeting. Mrs. Glover and Mrs. Hamner served cake and cold drinks to the members.

Eleven club members and Miss Mary Jo Spencer, assistant county agent and 4H club leader, were present.

# RECREATION ON THE CRABBE ROAD

**Boyd comment:**
All three of the Hamners noted here were members of the William Trimm Hamner family. Mrs. Hamner, the former Anna Velma Rice, was the mother of Ramona and Carol Kay. Other children of the William Trimm Hamner family included Thelton Max Hamner, Donald Rice Hamner, Alton Rice Hamner, William Wayne Hamner, Carl Hoyt Hamner, and Anne Wanita Hamner.

According to an article in *The Tuscaloosa News* December 7, 1927, Mrs. Trimm Hamner was in charge of the Lafoy School library.

### *The Tuscaloosa News*, April 1950, from Peggy's clippings
### 10-acre Cotton Patch to Build Lafoy Church

If the boll weevils aren't too bad this summer, and if weather continues as normal, the people of the Lafoy Community expect to make a bale to the acre in their 10-acre "community cotton patch." With that yield, they can repay seed and fertilizer loans and the rest of the money will be profit for the construction of a new Lafoy Baptist Church [Carrolls Creek Baptist Church]. Then the old church building, the Lafoy School which had closed in 1941, will be transformed into a community house for all organizations in Lafoy, a community three miles from Northport on the Crabbe Road.

This 10-acre plan is being jointly sponsored by the Lafoy Farm Bureau Home Demonstration Club, and the communities' 4-H clubs.

It all started when two well-known farmers, Ed Earnest and Robert Rushing, offered to lend 10 acres of fine land for the project. Now nearly every person in Lafoy, man, woman, boy, and girl, has signed a pledge or volunteered to plant, chop, plow, and even pick the cotton in the community cotton patch.

Several farmers of the community have offered to lend their machinery and motorized equipment so there will be no expenses except for the feed and fertilizer. Farmers hope to gross $200-300 for each bale of cotton. They believe ten bales will complete their project.

Not all the plan is complete, but the land has been prepared and committees appointed. Some 4-H Club members are already at work on the patch including DeVaughn Black, Alton Hamner, Betty Drew Black, and Bobby Fields. Chairman of the project is Ed Earnest with Robert Rushing and Spurgeon Black serving as members of the Farm Bureau Committee. Other committees are to be named.

Further discussion of the cotton patch project was discussed last week at a meeting of the Agriculture Committee. DeVaughn Black presided with Carol Kay Hamner leading the singing and Mrs. Trimm Hamner giving the devotional. Mr. Earnest reported cotton patch progress and County Agent Beverly Holstun urged farmers to produce more cotton to meet domestic and foreign demand.

Mr. Holstun presented to the Lafoy committee a certificate of "Superior Rating" for accomplishments in 1950 awarded by the Alabama Extension Service in Auburn.

### *The Tuscaloosa News*, June, 1950 from Peggy's clippings
### Lafoy Groups Put in Hard work on Community Cotton Patch

It was work day Wednesday at Lafoy and despite humid 93-degree heat, more than 30 people plowed, chopped, and put soda under 10 acres of cotton.

They were member of the Lafoy Farm Bureau 4-H Club and Home Demonstrations Club who plan to use the funds from this cotton project to help build a new Baptist Church, Carrolls Creek Baptist. The old church building will then become a community center.

The project is expected to yield about ten bales of cotton which should bring about $2,500.

More than 30 people aided with four tractors and did an estimated 1,000 manhours of work on the project. The tractors were donated and operated by Burton Dunn, DeVaughn Black, Ed Earnest, and Hugh Spencer.

4-H Club members headed by Mona Lisa Earnest, president, chopped most of the cotton. Members included Wayne Hamner, Olan Montgomery, Roland Fields, Nella Jean Rushing, Juanita Hamner, Rayburn Brown, Larry Rushing, Grover Earnest, Peggy Rushing, Shelby Rice, Patsy Brown, Carol Hamner, Laura Dean Montgomery, Barbara Rice, Nina Hagler, Mary Hagler, Betty Black, Sarah Shirley, Herman Boyd, Jr., Milton and Warren Rice, and Jan Earnest.

Woman of the Home Demonstration Club served a delicious lunch at noon under large shady oaks in the front yard of Mrs. Trimm Hamner's home. Club members serving lunch were Mrs. Roy Rushing, Mrs. Trimm Hamner, Mrs. Harwood Hammer, Mrs. Herman Boyd, Mrs. Spurgeon Black, Mrs. Hugh Spencer, Mrs. Bill Glover, Mrs. Burton Dunn, Mrs. Ed Earnest, Mrs. Robert Rushing, Mrs. Vernon Rice, and Mrs. J. D. Hamner. Mrs. Bill Glover, president, was in charge of the food.

The group plans to work the cotton about every ten days to two weeks until the later part of July when it is "laid by" until cotton picking time.

**The game of double six dominoes**

*The Tuscaloosa News*, June 13, 1938, page 6
**Domino party is given**
**Windham Springs**
An enjoyable domino party was recently held at the home of Mrs. Joe Christian. Among the guests for this event were Homer Majors, Leonard Homan, Perry Davis, Mr. and Mrs. P.P. Falls, Erastus Wilson, Mr. and Mrs. Clarence Hagler, Moody Fields, Hester Barnett, Roy Chappell, George Davis, Cecil Gregory, Murry Walker, Whitt Jones, and Willie Long.

Delicious refreshments were served to the group by Mrs. Christian.

**Boyd comment:**
A set of well-used double-six dominoes could be found in most homes in the community. On cold winter nights after supper, a family could sit around the kitchen table and enjoy several games of dominoes before bedtime. On special occasions, as noted in the above article, a few friends would be invited over for a "party." The game called for four people although domino games could be played with only two or three people. Experienced players had a knack of knowing which dominoes his partner held, and by playing in tandem they could win.

When our children visited their grandparents, Roy and Faith Rushing, soon after arriving they asked their granddaddy, "When can we play dominoes?" Roy was a champion player and on the rare occasions when one of the kids won, he would crack a big smile and say, "Just wait until next time."

A group of retired old men met in downtown Northport almost every day to enjoy several hours playing dominoes, commenting on local politics, complaining about the weather, and chewing and spitting tobacco. On Saturdays when many country folks came to town to buy groceries, feed, and clothing, some of the male farmers joined in the domino game while their wives shopped.

**Recreation of young people in Lafoy**
Recreation refers to activities that people choose to do to refresh their bodies and minds and make their leisure time more interesting and enjoyable. Unlike city kids in Northport, children and young people in Lafoy had no sidewalks on which to roller skate and no community center that offered dances on Saturday nights.

Much of the recreation enjoyed by the young people of Lafoy was through church activities at Macedonia Methodist Church and Carrolls Creek Baptist Church. I have fond memories of MYF parties including going to town on Sunday night after church to play carpet golf.

# RECREATION ON THE CRABBE ROAD

**Etta Rushing Thomas' Scrapbook, November 7, 1933**

The Macedonia Epworth League entertained recently the members of the organization and a few intimate friends at a beautiful Halloween party at Lafoy School.

The school rooms were decorated with orange and black paper with Jack-O-Lanterns artistically arranged.

Games appropriate for the season were enjoyed with Curtis Hamner and Howard Rushing capturing the prize in a banana and cracker contest. Music by the Lafoy String Band was enjoyed. At a late hour, a delicious course was served carrying out the Halloween colors.

**Boyd comment**:

Etta Rushing Thomas was the granddaughter of Joseph Enoch and Samantha Lenora Rushing. She collected a large stash of newspaper articles, and it is from her collection that I draw. In some instances, dates are missing.

The original Epworth League was a youth organization within the Methodist Church. It was established 1889 to encourage spiritual growth among teenage members of the denomination. In 1939, following denominational mergers among several Methodist groups during the 1930s, the Epworth League became known as the Methodist Youth Fellowship, MYF.

**Etta Rushing Thomas Scrapbook, Cabinet meeting of Macedonia Epworth meeting**

Miss Mable Hamner will act as hostess for the monthly meeting of the Epworth cabinet meeting Saturday night. All officers are to bring their report.

Miss Annie Snow Rushing was elected president. Other officers elected were Frances Shirley, Vice president, Azilee Rushing secretary-treasurer, John E. Shirley, corresponding secretary, Roy Rushing, sergeant at arms, and Glyndon Newman, advisor.

**Boyd comment**:

The date of this article is missing. However, it was prior to November 4, 1934, the day Azilee Rushing married Glyndon Newman.

Of the young people mentioned in the article, four married fellow members. As noted, Azilee Rushing married Glyndon Newman and Azilee Rushing's sister, Annie Snow Rushing, married John Shirley on January 13, 1937.

**Etta Rushing Thomas Scrapbook, *The Tuscaloosa News*, July 8, 1934**

Twenty-four members of the juvenile set of Lafoy and Union Chapel Churches motored to Spencer's Mill for a picnic on July 4. Chaperoning the happy group were Mr. and Mrs. Josh Rushing, Mrs. Early Ramsey, and "Uncle" Gus Kennedy. Boating, swimming and kodaking [sic] were enjoyed. At noon a delicious picnic lunch was served on the ground followed by homemade ice cream and cake.

**Boyd comment**:

Most Lafoy folks did not own a camera in 1934. The notation of "kodaking" acknowledges that at least one person in the group owned this newfangled black box that made photos.

The Kodak camera was first offered for public sale in 1892. In 1934, the gadget sold for $2.50. As a result, during the depths of the Great Depression, it remained a novelty and was considered too expensive by most people in Lafoy.

Mrs. Early Ramsey, formerly the Miss Susan Roberta "Birdie" Baggett, was my wife's maternal grandmother. Josh Rushing, son of Joseph Enoch Rushing, was my wife's paternal great uncle. Uncle "Gus" Kennedy drove the school bus that transported area kids to school.

The comment "motored to Spencer's Mill" is interesting. A few of the people in the community owned automobiles, but the cost of cars prevented others for enjoying that privilege. In the same edition of *The Tuscaloosa News,* on page 5 there was an ad from Tuscaloosa Motor Company, the local Chevrolet dealer. The ad reads:

"Drastic Price Reduction of $50 Brings Chevrolet up to the record low price of $465 and up, F. O. B. Flint, Michigan."

As with all advertising, one must read beyond the bold headlines to get the whole story. The only model priced at $465 was the Sport Roadstar. A Chevrolet Coach was priced at $495 and a Chevrolet Coupe cost $485. A Chevrolet Sedan carried a price of $640 and a ½ ton pickup cost $495.

Not to be overlooked is the fact that these prices were F. O. B. at Flint, Michigan, not in Tuscaloosa, Alabama. F.O.B. means "Free On Board" which is the price General Motors placed on the vehicle when it was loaded onto a transport truck, or train, that took it to Tuscaloosa. So, the cost to the customer in Tuscaloosa included the F.O.B. price General Motors gave in the newspaper ad plus transportation charges from Michigan to Tuscaloosa.

Daddy was truck sales manager at Tucker Motor Company. Occasionally he and a fellow salesman drove to Dearborn, Michigan to pick up a large commercial truck of the F-8 series, the largest engine Ford made. Daddy would drive the brand-new truck home as his salesman followed in their car. On one occasion, Daddy got caught in a terrible ice and snow storm typical for that area during the winter. He had a lot of trouble keeping the truck out of the ditch.

1934 Chevrolet Coupe

1934 Chevrolet four-door sedan

1934 Chevrolet ½ ton pickup

1934 Ford F-8 commercial truck

### The Lafoy Home Demonstration Club

Home Demonstration Clubs were a program of the U.S. Department of Agriculture's Cooperative Extension Service. Their goal was to teach farm women in rural America better methods for getting their work done, in areas such as gardening, canning, nutrition, and sewing, and to encourage them to improve their families' living conditions. Home demonstration agents worked with local clubs to provide teaching services. The clubs also took on other education and charitable roles.

I was privy to attend the monthly meetings of the Lafoy Home Demonstration Club meeting when I was four and five years old and too young to be in elementary school.

Mother was very active in the club and having no one to stay with me while she was gone, she took me along. I got to know the ladies very well. It was fun to be a "fly on the wall" as they shared community news.

### *The Tuscaloosa News*, June 20, 1946, page 7
### Lafoy Home Demonstration Club Meets in Rushing House

The Lafoy Home Demonstration Club met Tuesday, June 11, in the home of Mrs. Roy Rushing with Mrs. Ed Earnest serving as co-hostess. Mrs. Spurgeon Black, president, presided.

The members joined with Miss Elizabeth Collins in singing "Work for the Night Is Coming." The devotional was led by Mrs. Roy Rushing, and the Lord's Prayer was repeated in unison by the members.

Each member answered roll call by mentioning their favorite flower. Mrs. Trimm Hamner read a very interesting article on "Gardening is a Happy Way of Life." During the recreation hour, Mrs. John Shirley led the group in two contests which the members thoroughly enjoyed. Mrs. Bruce Hamner gave a very interesting demonstrator on the "Ease of Cooking." She prepared and cooked an entire meal in a pressure cooker as the ladies looked on. The menu consisted of roast chicken, potatoes, carrots, stewed apples, and squash which was served along with chicken salad, sandwiches, cake, and iced punch.

**The Tuscaloosa News, April 17, 1950**
**Lafoy Club Hears Interesting Talks**
"New health developments" was the topic under discussion at a recent meeting of the Lafoy Home Demonstration Club. The meeting was held in the home of Mrs. Trimm Hamner with Mrs. W. B. Glover as assisting hostess.

An interesting talk entitled "Future achievement for our home clubs" was given by Miss Elizabeth Collins, county agent. Mrs. Albert Hagler gave the demonstration on casserole dishes. The dish she used for the project was scalloped eggs and ham which was served later with additional refreshments.

Games and contests were enjoyed during the social hour. Mrs. Comer Montgomery was welcomed as a special guest.

Roll call at this meeting was answered with something each member had done to improve her health.

**Tuscaloosa County Times, October 25, 1951**
The Lafoy Home Demonstration Club was organized in September 1941 as a result of a course taught in homemaking by Miss Nancy McPhail, vocational home economics teacher at Tuscaloosa County High School. Charter members included Mrs. John Shirley, Mrs. Roy Rushing, Mrs. Bruce Hamner, Mrs. G. O. Newman, Mrs. Vera Channell, Mrs. Mary Hamner, Miss Nannie Bell LaFoy, Mrs. Charlie Newman, Mrs. Fanny Rushing, and Mrs. Con Bolton. Mrs. John Shirley served as the first president. Mrs. Shirley served as president until 1943 when Mrs. T. S. Black was elected president. Mrs. Trimm Hamner was elected president in 1946 and served until 1950 when Mrs. Bill Glover was elected to serve.

The Lafoy Home Demonstration Club celebrated its 10$^{th}$ anniversary with a supper honoring their husbands on Friday, October 19.

The basement of Macedonia Methodist Church was decorated with autumn leaves, yellow corn, and pumpkins. The tables covered with white linen cloths held beautiful flower arrangements. Place cards were green and yellow in the shape of leaves. A delicious supper was served buffet style.

After the supper, Mrs. Ed Earnest gave the welcome and introduced the guests and officers of the club.

To better acquaint the husbands with the work of the club, a meeting was presided over by the President, Mrs. W. R. Glover. Mrs. Trimm Hamner gave the devotional followed by a prayer by Mrs. John Shirley.

The secretary, Mrs. Hamner, called the roll. Two charter members were present, Mrs. John Shirley and Mrs. Roy Rushing. Each club member was asked to answer "present" by naming an ambition she had as a child. After the club members answered the question, each husband was asked to name his secret ambition. This created a good bit of laughter. After the reading of the minutes, a business session was held.

Mrs. O'Neal Snow made a motion that a supper honoring the husbands become an annual affair. It was seconded at once by all the men and passed by the club.

Mrs. Polk Rushing gave an outline of all the programs that had been presented throughout the year.

Mrs. John Shirley took each demonstration

and gave a brief report of what had been done on them. It was reported with pride that the club had placed shrubbery around two churches in the community—Macedonia Methodist Church and Union Chapel Methodist church. Each church was given $50 for grounds improvement. An equal amount has been set aside for Carrolls Creek Baptist Church to be used when the new church construction is completed. Each club member gives 10¢ per month to buy a gift for some elderly person.

Mrs. Snow told something of the new feature added to the club this year, music appreciation. The meeting was turned over to the recreation leader Mrs. Albert Hagler. She led the group in several contests which afforded much fun. One activity had Miss Elizabeth Collins, Tuscaloosa County Home Demonstration Agent, sit at a table by John Shirley and she answered "Yes" or "No" as Mr. Shirley was asked to name twelve items in her handbag. Another activity divided those present into groups and each group was given a jigsaw puzzle to complete in a specified time. The team consisting of Mrs. Julia Chism, Mrs. Clara Rushing and Mr. and Mrs. Burton Dunn finished first and won the prize.

The following, listed alphabetically, were present: Mr. and Mrs. M. D. Black; Mr. and Mrs. Herman Boyd; Mrs. Julia Chism; Mr. and Mrs. Burton Dunn; Mr. and Mrs. Ed Earnest; Mr. and Mrs. W. H. Glover; Mr. and Mrs. Albert Hagler; Mr. and Mrs. Trimm Hamner; Mr. and Mrs. Vernan Rice; Mrs. Clara Rushing; Mr. and Mrs. James Rushing; Mrs. Polk Rushing; Mr. and Mrs. Robert Rushing; Mr. and Mrs. Roy Rushing; Mr. and Mrs. John Shirley; Mr. and Mrs. Lonnie Shirley; Mr. and Mrs. O'Neal Snow; and Mr. and Mrs. Hugh Spencer.

Guests included Mr. and Mrs. Bill Jones of the *Tuscaloosa County Times*. and Miss Elizabeth Collins.

The 4-H girls of the community "baby sat" so that the members of the club could have a night out.

A beautiful birthday cake baked by the first president of the club, Mrs. John Shirley, was cut and served with ice cream.

**September 1981**
**Lafoy Home Demonstration Club**
The Lafoy Home Demonstration Club will celebrate its 40$^{th}$ birthday during the month of September 1981. The club was organized in September, 1941 as the result of a course in homemaking taught by Miss Janette McPhail, Vocational Home Economics teacher at Tuscaloosa County High School. She taught one afternoon each week for six weeks, and classes were held at the Old Lafoy schoolhouse which was a historical landmark in our community for many years, but no longer stands. The school was discontinued by the Tuscaloosa County Board of Education shortly after 1941.

The very first lesson taught by Miss McPhail was on the making of bound buttonholes. Other lessons taught were mattress-making and the making of aluminum trays. These trays were made from actual sheets of aluminum and were very pretty, along with being useful. The last class Miss McPhail taught was a lesson on "Simple Entertaining." At this meeting, the County Home Demonstration Agent, Miss Elizabeth Collins, was introduced and gave a very interesting talk concerning the Home Demonstration Work of Alabama. It was at this time that Miss Collins agreed to help organize a club in our community.

Much interest was shown in organizing this club which grew in number to twenty-five members. The first officers of the club were Mrs. John Shirley, President, Mrs. Bruce Hamner, Vice-president, and Mrs. G. O. Newman. Secretary-treasurer.

Being a community-minded organization, the club has worked hard to make our area one to be proud of. One of the first, and perhaps if not the best, projects the club has undertaken was the purchasing and planting of shrubbery around our churches. These churches include Macedonia

# RECREATION ON THE CRABBE ROAD

Methodist, Union Chapel Methodist and Carrolls Creek Baptist which was constructed during the time period. This was a large project, but one to be especially proud to be a part of.

The club had many ideas for additional projects, but found that finances were low. Members went to work on money-making projects for the club by presenting plays (which were so much fun), sponsoring political rallies, cake walks, etc. This gave the club the opportunity to get together more often in friendship and fellowship, along with helping the club finances.

There are many and varied demonstrations we have learned from putting many of these into practice in our homes. Just a few of these include canning, home management, decorating, cooking, freezing, and serving. All of these demonstrations have helped us make our homes better places in which to live, thus making our community one we can be proud of.

Our regular monthly meeting is always most enjoyable. Rollcall is answered by reciting your favorite Bible verse, by naming a county or city official, a favorite song, favorite presidential book, hobby, fruit, or flower. This is followed by the pledge of allegiance to the flag and a special or favorite hymn. During the holiday season, Christmas or Thanksgiving music is substituted.

Without a doubt, the most rewarding projects we do are giving to the needy or shut-ins in our community. Along with food, fruit, clothing, and gifts, the most important thing to us has been the giving of our time to those who need us. Another expression of love for others is shown in the quilts made for the children in the orphanage.

Another interesting demonstration we have had was patriotism, learning to care for our flag and learning to display our flag. In addition, we have done volunteer work for the Red Cross by sewing garments, making bandages, and donating money to use for entertaining veterans. We sponsored parties for our veterans and sent letters, cards, and packages to our servicemen stationed overseas. It was during this time that some of our members had sons or loved ones stationed overseas. Along this same line, our demonstration on citizenship was useful to all age groups within our community.

We have always worked with the youth in our area through such organizations as the 4-H Club, F. H. A., and others. We have invited them to our demonstrations on many and varied subjects such as freezing food, entertaining, cooking, canning, citizenship, and many others. They have been given the opportunity to prepare and serve refreshments at our club meetings. Working closely with the youth of our community has been another rewarding project our club has undertaken. Mrs. O'Neal Snow gave a program on "Helping Rural Youth to a Happy Living" which dealt with beatification of the interior and exterior of homes, thus, making for a happier life for rural young people. A demonstration of "Developing the Personality of the Child" was given by Mrs. John Shirley. Socials were also planned and given each month for these young people. Additionally, our club worked together with the 4-H Club girls, one of which, Miss Mona Lisa Earnest, won a scholarship to Auburn University through her 4-H Club work.

The club has also worked with the boys of the community giving them the opportunity to join the "Calf Chain" and supporting them in their work. The Farm Bureau was another organization we supported and helped in acquiring new members.

Through the years, our club has worked with county officials and has given interesting programs on Tuscaloosa County's progress from year-to-year with demonstrations on the "Outlook of Community, County and State."

On February 8, 1949, the club appointed a committee to check into the possibilities of getting telephone service in the homes on our community. This committee, consisting of Mrs. W.B. Glover, Chairman, Mrs. N. J. Hamner, and Mrs. Devaughan Black. Members, spent much time and effort in securing telephone services to our community.

Many programs and demonstrations have contributed toward making our community one of the very finest in Alabama. Among these are creative arts, home furnishings, clothing, family life, health, food, food preservation, rural, Farm Bureau, citizenship, community activities, defense, along with many others which have all played an important part in keeping us abreast with our changing world today. We ae very proud of Pam Robertson, our latest recipient of a scholarship for her 4'H club work.

Mrs. Margaret Shirley, president of the Lafoy Home Demonstration Club for 1980-1981, has done an excellent job, along with the officers and members of the club. The club is striving, thriving, and continues to grow. One project recently undertaken which has done so much for the community is the improving and updating of each member's mailbox. With mail being delivered on several different routes in the area, the boxes needed numbering according to route, along with making them more attractive. We feel this project was a great success. Club members have also collected aluminum and glass to be recycled. This money collected from this project has been donated to the "Love Boys Home." We have quilted quilts for our churches and taken them to patients and friends in nursing homes in our county.

We must not forget to mention our Charter Members of the club, who have done such a wonderful job through the years. There are: Mrs. G. O. Newman, Mrs. Vera Channell, Mrs. Mary Hamner, Mrs. Fanny Rushing, Mrs. Bruce Hamner, Mrs. John Shirley, Mrs. Roy Rushing, Miss Nannie Bell LaFoy, Mrs. Charlie Newman and Mrs. Con Bolton, a teacher at Lafoy School. Four of our veteran members have recently passed away and are missed very much. They are Mrs. Annie Snow Shirley, Mrs. Jene Hamner, Mrs. Loubelle Rushing, and Mrs. Lenabelle Black.

Past presidents are: Mrs. Annie Snow Shirley, (1st 1941-1943); Mrs. T. S. Black (2nd 1943-1945; Mrs. Annie Velmer Hamner (3rd 1946-1950). Subsequent presidents include Mrs. W.R. Glover, Mrs. Faith Rushing, Mrs. Reba Rushing, Mrs. Geneal Black, Mrs. Emile Snow, Mrs. Maggie Sudduth, Mrs. Jane Hunt, and Mrs. Margaret Shirley.

The Lafoy Home Demonstration Club has very much enjoyed and is very proud of its first 40 years of club work and is looking forward to many more years proud of fellowship, friendship, hard work, and helping others.

Respectfully submitted,
Mrs. M. S. Medders
Historian  September 8, 1981

CHAPTER 13

# The Curb Market

A farmer's curb market is a place where local farmers come together to sell home-grown produce, dairy products, nuts, pumpkins, canned goods, honey, bouquets of flowers, and other items produced on their farms.

A 1982 issue of *The Tuscaloosa News* contains an article giving a report of the Tuscaloosa Truck Growers Association that includes the history of the Tuscaloosa Curb Market. The first record of a curb market in Tuscaloosa dates to 1924. Its location is said to have been on Broad Street (identified as University Boulevard today) at its intersection with 21st Avenue. By 1929, the facility had been moved to 7th Street on the north lawn of the Tuscaloosa County courthouse.

Between its opening in 1924 and its closure in the early 2000s, the curb market occupied six locations. The curb market remained beside the courthouse until the 1950s when it was moved to 4th Street between Greensboro Avenue and 23rd Avenue near Tanner Brothers Produce Company behind the First National Bank Building.

The next move of the curb market came in 1982. The Tuscaloosa Truck Growers Association, the parent organization of the curb market, moved the facility to the intersection of Jack Warner Parkway and Greensboro Avenue a few yards from the banks of the Warrior River. The site was almost under the northbound lane of the Hugh Thomas Bridge. Locals refer to the area as at the bottom of "River Hill."

Tuscaloosa County courthouse 1930

Early in the 21st century, the Tuscaloosa Curb Market closed and the City of Tuscaloosa opened a new market, River Market of Tuscaloosa, on Jack Warner Parkway near 21st Avenue.

Seventh Street at the courthouse was very congested on Tuesdays, Thursdays, and Saturdays, the days the curb market was open for business. Items for sale were sold from the backs of

189

# A ROAD, A CEMETERY, A PEOPLE

The Tuscaloosa County jail in 1910
In the photograph on the previous page, it is to be noted that the roof and chimney of a residence is located south of the jail. The courthouse sits to the left of the jail. Not seen, but a second residence is located a few feet south of the courthouse. It was only in the 1940s that those residences were purchased by the county and removed making the entire block available for county use and for the building of the current courthouse in 1964.

7th Street
The Courthouse is to the left, the jail to the right. Curb market vendors and their vehicles made 7th Street so congested as to block the passage of firetrucks during emergencies.

Tuscaloosa County courthouse built 1964

pickup trucks and automobiles that were parked in the 7th Street. A section of the courthouse lawn had had concrete poured over it and vending tables set up on which sellers displayed their goods. A cheap wood roof provide shelter from rain. The curb market was open year-round.

Farm trucks and automobiles created so much street congestion that fire trucks could barely pass through in case of an emergency. It had been realized for several years that a new location was needed, but finding the right spot proved difficult.

Several Crabbe Road neighbors and friends were regular vendors at the curb market, including our next-door neighbors Octavia and John Hagler. The following clippings from the *Tuscaloosa News* portray events of the era.

### *The Tuscaloosa News*, July 19, 1929
**Tables are stolen from curb market**
Tables have been disappearing from the local curb market, Mrs. John L. Seay, market master, said this morning. Mrs. Seay was unable to determine whether the tables are being stolen at night from the courthouse or being taken away by market sellers.

The market provides free use of tables to sellers and about twenty tables have been missing in the past six weeks.

# THE CURB MARKET

**Tuscaloosa County Curb Market, 1929**
The building in the background is Allen and Jemison Hardware. The picture of the Tuscaloosa Curb Market was made in 1929. The street is 7th Street. Allen and Jemison Hardware Company was a four-story building that sold almost any hardware item one could desire. A rail spur off the nearby L & N Railroad track terminated inside Allen and Jemison at its rear. A loaded railroad boxcar often remained inside the building for several days while merchandise was unloaded. In 2024, the renovated building, among other uses, serves as an art exhibition hall.

**Boyd comment:**
Nine days later, *The Tuscaloosa News* carried an interesting article about the Tuscaloosa County jail and its proximity to the curb market. The jail was about twenty feet from the courthouse.

*The Tuscaloosa News*, **July 28, 1929**
**Tuscaloosa County jail gains 192 inmates**
**Total is 1,038 with high day of 37**
**Greatest gain is noted with white women**
As compared with the 846 prisoners who saw the inside of Tuscaloosa County's jail in 1927, there were 1,038 in 1928, according to the report of the state inspector which has just been issued. In 1927, about 14 percent of the prisoners taken to the county jail were released on bond on the day of arrest. In 1928, about 18 percent were released on the day of arrest.

As compared with the remainder of the state, it is harder to get out of the jail in Tuscaloosa County than it is in an average county in Alabama. The state average for those released on the day of arrest was 20 percent in 1927 and 22 percent in 1928.

State pays $2,197.00

It cost the state $1,917.28 to feed the prisoners in the Tuscaloosa County jail during the year 1927 and $2,197.96 to feed the increased number of prisoners in 1928, according to the report. The largest number of prisoners in the Tuscaloosa County jail on any one day in 1927 was 28, and the smallest number was 4. The largest number in jail on any one day in 1928 was 37 and the smallest number was 4.

In the state, the white male prisoners increased 0.05 percent in 1928 compared with 1927, with a 14 percent increase among white women prisoners. Negro male prisoners increased a little more than 3 percent while Negro women increased more than 4 percent. Violations of the prohibition law increased 18 percent in 1928 compared with 1927 in the state, and that increase was exceeded only by 25 percent in cases in which the charge was assault with a weapon and 33 1/3 percent increase in fraud cases. The greatest decrease was 18 percent shown in gaming cases.

**Some cases decrease, some increase**

Abusive language cases decreased 15 percent. Assault and battery cases decreased 9 percent. Assault to murder cases increased 7 percent. Assault to rape and rape cases decreased 4 percent. Carrying a concealed weapon deceased 13 percent. Grand larceny cases increased 9 percent. Petit larceny increased 5 percent. Forgery cases increased 6 percent. False pretense cases increased 1 percent. Fraud cases increased 33 1/3 percent. Perjury cases decreased 17 percent. Worthless checks decreased 1 percent. Embezzlement decreased 3 percent. Dispensing of mortgaged or stolen property decreased 15 percent. Reckless driving decreased more than 1 percent. Burglary increased more than 13 percent. Robbery and attempt to rob increased 5 percent. Homicide increased more than 6 percent. Unlawful riding of trains decreased 8 percent. Adultery decreased 16 percent. Vagrancy decreased 3 percent.

*The Tuscaloosa News*, **July 28, 1929, page three**
**Local curb market**
Baby chicks were offered on the curb market yesterday for the first time in some time. Buying was a little slow but there was a large volume of produce on the market. Almost the only shortage was in eggs, squash, Rocky Mountain cantaloupes. There was a surplus of Crowder peas and turnip greens. There were visitors on the market yesterday from Chicago, Birmingham, and Bibb County.

Items that were plentiful on the market included okra, dill, corn, Crowder and field peas, snap beans, spinach, mustard, turnip greens, carrots, beets, radishes, eggplants, butterbeans, sweet potatoes, Irish potatoes, peanuts, hot and sweet peppers, corn meal, sorghum and ribbon cane syrup, butter and buttermilk, ripe and green tomatoes, blackberries, grapes, pickling peaches, cakes, figs, apples, friars, roosters, brush brooms, cut flowers, jellies, preserves, pickles, canned fruits and soups, canned chicken and vegetables, watermelons and cantaloupes, onions, split bottom chairs, ironing boards and pure-bred pigs.

The following prices were posted on the curb market yesterday morning for the guidance of both the buyers and the sellers: standard butter 50 cents a lb.; hens 24 cents; friars 35 cents; eggs 35 cents a dozen; infertile eggs, 40 cents a dozen; squash 5 cents a lb.; Crowder peas 7 ½ to 10 cents a lb.; green peas 7 ½ to 10 cents a lb.; bunch beans 15 cents a lb.; pole beans 15 to 17 ½ cents a pound; butterbeans 10 to 12 ½ cents per lb.; tomatoes 2 ½ to 5 cents a lb.; corn 20 to 30 cents a dozen; okra 8 to 10 cents a lb.; turnip greens and other greens 10 cents a bunch; cabbage 5 to 10 cents; corn meal 25 cents a gallon; ribbon cane syrup $1.25 a gallon; sorghum syrup 75 cents a gallon; beets 5 to 7 ½ cents; Irish potatoes 3 ½ cents per pound; sweet potatoes 7 ½ cents per pound; cucumbers 4 ½ to 5 cents a lb.; bell peppers 2 or 3 for 5 cents; honey 25 to 30 cents a lb.; egg plants 5 to 7 ½ cents a lb.; grapes 10 cents a lb.; figs 7 ½ to 10 cents a quart.

**Boyd comment:**
The array of offered items for sale at the curb market was staggering. It included not only food-related items but also live chicks and little pigs, along with handcrafted chairs and ironing boards, plus much more.

I thought it interesting to compare a few curb market prices with the prices for the same items in a local grocery store. In the August 30, 1929 *Tuscaloosa News*, an A&P ad listed Brookfield butter at 43¢ cents a pound versus 50¢ on the curb market. A 5-pound sack of potatoes was 19¢ versus 17¢ on the curb market. Store-bought tomatoes were 6¢ per pound as compared to 2 ½ to 5¢ on the market. Ground corn meal that sold for 50¢ cents a gallon at A&P sold for 25¢ a gallon on the curb market.

*The Tuscaloosa News*, **September 1, 1929 page 3,**
**Curb Market Sets New High Sales for late August**
Sales of farm produce by the Tuscaloosa Curb market reached a new high record Saturday morning for this period of the year. While an exact total of Saturday's sales was not available, the new seasonal record was indicated by Mrs. John L. Seay, market director.

The total number of cub market produce sellers has grown to a new number of 934 compared with a beginning of 19 on the first day of the market in 1924.

A reduction in produce sales by the farmers' market is usually evident at this season.

However, produce selling on Saturday gave no indication of a drop said Mrs. Seay. Every variety of late summer garden produce was on display. Approximately 75 farms were represented.

**November 7, 1933 *The Tuscaloosa News*, page 3**
**Market to Move into basement**
**Transfer from curb set for Thursday**
**Buyers urged to remember change**
With winter approaching and cool weather already here, the Tuscaloosa Farmers Market will migrate Thursday from the open spaces on 7th Street to the basement of the courthouse, Mrs. John L. Seay, director, announced today.

Mrs. Seay pointed out that the basement has been renovated and a partition erected providing commodious and comfortable quarters for the market during the cold and rainy weather. She urged that buyers remember to transfer and s said the basement would be more comfortable for them as well as the sellers.

At today's session, 61 sellers were present and a surplus appeared, especially in green vegetables, apples, and tomatoes. There was a shortage in fresh county eggs however, and one seller who brought about 50 dozen ears of corn sold his entire offering.

Magazines were contributed to the library by Mrs. Grady Hansard and Mrs. W. B. Keller.

**December 7, 1933 *The Tuscaloosa News***
**41 Sellers appear for curb market session**
**Supply of Christmas offerings grows larger**
Forty-one sellers were present on the Market today for a session which saw a still larger supply of Christmas offerings. Many decorations were bought. One woman seller appeared with a wide variety of holiday cakes and candies as her sole offering.

The market has acquired a large supply of cellophane in red, green, and violet colors with which to decorate the Christmas purchases.

Two new permits have been issued by Mrs. John L. Seay, market director, these going to Miss Lizzie Crim of Gordo and Mrs. O. B. Shows of Tuscaloosa Route Two.

**December 24, 1933, *The Tuscaloosa News*, page 7**
**Curb market sellers give Mrs. Seay a shower**
A Christmas shower characterized as a "Slight token of appreciation for invaluable services rendered during the year" was given honoring Mrs. John. L. Seay, market master, at noon on Saturday by the Tuscaloosa Curb Market. Mrs. Will Dugger, a member of the Hargrove Road Home Demonstration Club, made the presentation in behalf of the sellers. Mrs. Seay briefly replied in thanks to all who participated in the shower.

Gifts of many types were showered upon her including flowers, canned goods, produce of all kinds, nuts, candles, fruits, meats, and Christmas decorations. The items filled a large box.

Many sellers were on hand and demand was swift for Christmas delicacies. It was estimated that 500 Christmas trees had been sold during the week. Magazines were given for the market library by Miss Mary Burnett, Mrs. Josh Baker, and Mrs. John M. Hagler.

The curb market will be open for business as usual on Tuesday.

**Boyd comment:**
Mrs. John M. Hagler (Octavia Tierce Hagler) was my next-door neighbor on the Crabbe Road. I share interesting snippets of their lives in another chapter.

***The Tuscaloosa News*, May 1937**
**(This article is from Peggy Boyd's clippings)**
**Strawberries offered at Curb Market for first time**
The first ripe strawberries of the year were offered at the Curb Market today as 35 sellers were present. Many calls for dressed friars, hens, and sausage were unsupplied. The market reports a surplus of wild flowers and turnip greens.

Mrs. Jimmy Coleman and Mrs. W. S. Thomson brought magazines to be distributed to the sellers. Permits issued since the last market day included Mrs. J. R. Wilson of Moundville, Route 1 and Miss Emile Shirley of the Crabbe Road in Northport and Mrs. L. C. Hayes of Tuscaloosa, Route 2. This brings the number of permits issued for the year to 160.

**Boyd comment:**

A primary source of reading material in many rural farmers' homes during the Great Depression was farm-and-home-related magazines. Outside of the family bible, the *Sears and Roebuck Catalogue*, and the *J. C. Penny Catalogue*, rural folk often had very limited libraries composed of books. So, it was a great joy to get a recycled magazine from a neighbor or fellow curb marker seller.

Miss Emile Shirley was the daughter of Tom and Ida Shirley and a sister to Mrs. Josh (Clara) Rushing. A chapter in *A Road, a Cemetery, A People* is devoted to the Joel Tom Shirley family.

*The Tuscaloosa News*, **January 4, 1938**
**Curb Market has 733 sellers during month**
**(This article is from Peggy Boyd's newspaper clippings.)**

A total of 733 persons offered farm produce at the Tuscaloosa Curb Market during the past month. Records compiled by the market director show that the number of permits sold during the year totals 311. Permits for the new year were recently issued to:

Atchison, J.W.
Barksdale, Mrs. H.
Barringer, Mrs. W.B.
Booth, Mrs. Beuna
Booth, Mrs. Monroe
Bradley, Asa
Burns, Al
Burns, R.H.
Cabiness, H.
Camp, Mrs. C.H.
Channell, Mrs. R. A.
Cork, Mrs. G. S.
Cork, Mrs. Jim
Cork, Miss Ocie
Cork, Mrs. Thelma
Cunningham, Mrs. Pinkie
Deal, Mrs. Festus
Deason, T, J.
Dockery, Mrs. A. J.
Duncan, Charles
Dunn, H. M.
Farmer, Mrs. W. C.
Faulkner, G.
Gooden, A.J.
Hagler, Mrs. John
Hagler, Mrs. Wiley
Hamner, Bruce
Hamner, Dee
Hamner, J.E.
Hamner, J.W.
Hamner, Pruitt
Hannah, A.A.
Holley, Mrs. H.A.
Holmes, Marvin
Johnson, Mrs. M.E.
Lancaster, H.A.
Lavelle, Mrs. C.H.
Marlow, Mrs. Annie
McCracken, Mrs. J.D.
McFerrin, Miss Leona
Montgomery, Mrs. B.K.
Pate, D.L.
Pate, Mrs. T.J.
Pate, Mrs. Mae
Patterson, Mrs. C.C.
Patterson, Mrs. R.E.
Reese, C. H.
Reese, Mrs. M.F.
Shirley, Miss Frances
Spain, Mrs. R. B.
Spiller, Mrs. J.E.
Springer, Mrs. L.
Stamps, E.E.
Swindle, Charles
Styes, J.E.
Thomas, Mrs. V.M.

# THE CURB MARKET

Thompson, Mrs. W.S.
Tingle, Mrs. L.C.
Yow, Mrs. A.E.
**Boyd comment:**
Of the above listed names, the following people were residents of the Lafoy Community whom I frequently saw at church and community gathering: Mr. and Mrs. John Hagler; Mrs. Wiley Hagler; Mr. and Mrs. Bruce Hamner; Mr. Dee Hamner; Mr. and Mrs. Pruitt Hamner: Mrs. Frances Shirley who later married Dee Hamner. It is possible others lived in the Lafoy Community, but I cannot attest to that.

**June 30, 1946 *The Tuscaloosa News* front page**
**New farmer's market sought**
**Site away from courthouse sought**
A movement was set in motion Saturday by the Tuscaloosa County Board of Revenue to seek a new location for the construction of a new and more modern curb market away from its congested courthouse current location.

Herman Boyd, board member, offered a resolution, seconded by John E. Walker, that was unanimously approved. The resolution called for Tuscaloosa County and the City of Tuscaloosa to get together with the Curb Market Association and plan and project such a project for the future.

The action followed a discussion with a large delegation of farmers who appeared before the board to lodge a complaint against the recent roped off section between the curb market and the county jail and prohibiting its use by the curb market. In the past the area had been used by vendors selling watermelons.

County jailer Burrell Hughes told the board that the state jail inspectors have complained that the odor from watermelon rinds "created a nuisance to the health of the prisoners and other people who live in the jail."

Hughes suggested that the section under discussion be concreted so that it could be washed off regularly.

As a temporary measure, the board agreed to cooperate with the city in concreting the area and allowing watermelons to be sold there. The sellers promised to cooperate in eliminating any unsanitary conditions that might exist.

Boyd, in offering his resolution, stated that a new location away from the congested area would be more acceptable to both the farmers having produce to sell and to the buyers.

It was brought out that having the curb market adjacent to the jail created an additional hardship on the sheriff's force in escorting prisoners from the jail to the courthouse.

**Boyd comment:**
I addressed this concern earlier. The previous comment did not include the subject of selling watermelons. Daddy was very concerned about this matter. I am proud of his effort to solve the problem, and it was solved.

***The Tuscaloosa News*, July 1, 1946**
**A new curb market**
The Tuscaloosa County Board of Revenue is to be commended for its announced move to seek a new site for the curb market away from the congested area around the courthouse and jail.

As pointed out by Herman Boyd, a member of the Board of Revenue, a new location for the curb market would be advantageous for the farmers and purchasers of their products.

There is a definite need in Tuscaloosa for a farmers curb market but the present location is not the place for it.

The curb market, like Tuscaloosa and many of its enterprises, has grown up and the courthouse space is not large enough nor is it suitable for many other persons to use it as a curb market.

Seventh Street adjacent to the courthouse has become a madhouse on curb market days, especially on Saturdays, and the crowded traffic condition creates a serious hazard. Although the Tuscaloosa No. 1 fire station is located only one block from the courthouse, the firemen would be

# A ROAD, A CEMETERY, A PEOPLE

seriously handicapped fighting a fire at the courthouse, the jail, or nearby buildings should the alarm come when the street is blocked on market days.

Firemen are slowed up in answering a call anywhere east of the No. 1 station because of the bottleneck on the courthouse block.

There are many more Tuscaloosa householders who would trade at the curb market if they could park their automobiles close by. Getting a parking place anywhere around the courthouse on Saturday is like looking for a needle in a haystack.

The present location for the curb market was okay for a smaller city than Tuscaloosa has now become. Farmers have learned more about growing and preparing produce for market. They are now bringing in more produce than can easily be handled in the limited space. It is time for expansion of the curb market in a roomier space.

A very serious accident could occur in transferring dangerous criminals from the jail to the courthouse and through the curb market grounds crowded with people.

We have known one occasion in which an innocent bystander was shot and wounded when a deputy sheriff was forced to fire his pistol to halt a prisoner who made an escape attempt while being transported from the jail to the courthouse. Had the attempt been on a day when the curb market was in session, more than one innocent person might have been wounded or killed.

**Boyd comment:**
Unfortunately, progress was slow in relocating the curb market. As is seen in a *Tuscaloosa News* article dated October 24, 1947 presented later in this chapter, the curb market was still located on the courthouse steps.

### August 9, 1947, *The Tuscaloosa News* first page
### Newfangled berries put cash in farmer's pocket
Blackberry picking is out of style and strawberries are good things for other folks to grow, says J. Pruitt Hamner of the Lafoy Commjnity a few miles from Northport on the Crabbe Road.

He grows a newfangled berry he calls "Logan berries," and he is getting rich at it.

The Logan berries grow on a vine that closely resembles what some folks call "young berries," Mr. Hamner pointed out. Some six years ago he planted 60 plants. Today, he has a half-acre of berries. He sells an average of 3,000 quarts of berries from the patch every year. They bring about 25¢ a quart. You can make pies with them, conjure up a variety of different drinks, and prepare them in other ways for human consumption, Mr. Hamner says.

What would happen, he was asked, if you put a little sugar on them and let them sit for a few days and strain out the juice?

"I don't know much about that," he answered.

His neighbor said, "The stuff will make you whistle."

The berries start ripening about the first of May every year.

You don't have to reset the plants. They come up from the roots year after year.

Logan berries, the plants of which can be obtained at nurseries, will grow in common hillside land and do well, Mr. Hamner said.

**Boyd comment:**
Pruitt Hamner and his wife, Ruby, were close friends with our family. I recall eating Sunday lunch in their home on several occasions.

### August 15, 1947, *The Tuscaloosa News* front page
### Lightening "tingles" curb market seller
Mrs. Frank (Fog) Garner of Keene's Mill Road was truly "electrified" yesterday afternoon when a lightning bolt apparently struck a power line pole at the Tuscaloosa Curb Market, coursed down the pole, and skipped to a Chinaberry tree on which Mrs. Garner was leaning.

Sparks flew out of her finger tips and elbows witnesses said, although she received no permanent injuries from the shock. Mr. Garner, who

# THE CURB MARKET

was a block away when the lightening stuck, said his wife told him she was stunned for about two minutes, either from shock or fright.

For the moment, she could not move although she felt only a tingling under the arm pits. She had one hand and an elbow on the tree when the lightning struck.

Mrs. Garner is the former Miss Gladys Kane of New York. Her husband is the son of Mr. an Mrs. Ollie Garner of Keene's Mill Road and was a former New York newspaper man. They came south several years ago. Mr. Garner was born in this vicinity. Mr. and Mrs. Frank Garner are curb market sellers.

**October 24, 1947, *The Tuscaloosa News*, page 1**
**New Location for Curb Market is Requested**
A formal request to the Tuscaloosa City Commission and the Tuscaloosa County Board of Revenue for a new location of curb market was announced today by Henry H. Hales, Chairman of the Curb Market Committee.

He said their action was taken at the committee's quarterly meeting with directors unanimously approving the resolution.

"We have realized this need for a long time" Mr. Hale said. "Various sites have been proposed and discussed over a period of years. We know that our market has far outgrown its present location.

"The committee appreciates the cooperation accorded by the City Commission and the Board of Revenue in the past, and sincerely hopes that some satisfactory solution can be reached to provide a better site for our operations."

Mr. Hale pointed out that the curb market has no funds with which to acquire or provide the necessary buildings. The present market is located on the courthouse grounds. The area by the curb market and its covering overhead was financed through a WPA project.

Mrs. John L. Seay, market master and committee secretary, said today that she had notified the Board of Revenue and City Commission by letter of the committee's action.

Lawrence W. "Dutch" Smith, Chairman of the Tuscaloosa Chamber of Commerce Rural Relations Committee, said that this committee is much interested in the project and anxious to cooperate in efforts to secure a better location and improved facilities.

A recent report by Mrs. Seay shows that approximately 300 sellers are licensed to operate at the market. Attendance averages 100 on each of the three selling days, Tuesdays, Thursdays, and Saturdays, and sellers average about $20 each day. Total yearly sales are estimated conservatively at $175,000 she said.

**Boyd comment:**
As noted earlier, the next location of the Tuscaloosa Curb Market was on 4$^{th}$ Street between 23$^{rd}$ and 24$^{th}$ Avenue. I have been unable to verify the date of its move there.

In 1982, the Tuscaloosa Truck Growers Association, the parent organization of the curb market, moved the facility to the intersection of Jack Warner Parkway and Greensboro Avenue. The site was almost under the northbound lane of the Hugh Thomas Bridge over the Warrior River. Locals refer to the area as at the bottom of "River Hill." Early in the 21$^{st}$ century, the Tuscaloosa Curb Market closed and the City of Tuscaloosa opened a new market, River Market of Tuscaloosa, on Jack Warner Parkway near 21$^{st}$ Avenue.

**Northport Curb Markets**
A curb market was located in Northport on the north bank of the Warrior River on Bridge Avenue behind a feed store during the 1970s. I am not sure when it was established but during the 1970s, my father-in-law, Roy Rushing, sold produce there. Our two oldest children, Tara, born in 1964, and Cinda, born in 1966, often spent Friday nights at their grandparents' home and enjoyed getting up at 4:00 a.m. and going to the Northport Curb Market with their granddaddy. Their job was to be in charge of the cash box, a

# A ROAD, A CEMETERY, A PEOPLE

Northport curb market, circa 1970s

Roy Rushing loads watermelons to go to Northport Curb Market

Roy Rushing grew magnificent collards

One of Roy Rushing's gardens

large cigar box, and make change for the customers. Eager buyers were present when he arrived at 5:30 a.m., and by 8:00 a.m., he likely would be sold out and ready to head home. Curb market buyers knew that to get their first choice of wares, they had to be at the market early. I am not sure when that market closed.

It was not uncommon to have a late frost after the plants were planted. This called for covering each plant with newspaper or other wrappings to protect from the freezing frost.

In the early 2000s, a new Northport farmers market opened at 4150 5th Street near the Tuscaloosa Regional Airport.

# THE CURB MARKET

Northport Curb Market 2023

**Tribute to Andre Robertson
(December 8, 1962-August 21, 2013)**
I close this chapter with a tribute to Andre Robertson, a young man of the Lafoy Community that I watched grow up. His parents, Joe and Sirley Robertson, along with his brother Duane and his sister Pam, have been dear friends over the years. Joe, the father, died August 13, 2013. Twelve days later Andre, the son, died of cancer. Our community lost two fine men within a span of just days.

Andre was a school teacher. He taught Computer Science at Holt High School, but his first love was farming, especially growing tomatoes and other vegetables. In fact, he was lovingly called the "tomato man."

The tomato growing season began in February in his cellar greenhouse with the planting of tomato seeds. After the seeds sprouted and young plants started to grow, they were transplanted into cup containers and kept in the cellar. He cared for his "babies" by watering and providing artificial light for a specified time each day with the rapt attention a mother gives a newborn baby. In late March or early April, he transplanted the plants into his outside garden. The bane of any tomato farmer is a late killing frost after the plants have been planted in the garden. When that happened, he covered each plant with newspaper or other wrappings to protect it from the freezing frost.

Andre served in leadership roles as president of the Farmers Curb Market Association that oversaw the management of the facility. He was the most popular tomato vendor at the River Hill Curb Market.

Andre lived across the Crabbe Road from his parents. As a result, motorists could keep tabs on the growth in his garden. It was an interesting sight to see him working in the garden. He always wore a straw hat, blue-jean cut-off shorts, and boots. Few men could match his physical stamina.

# A ROAD, A CEMETERY, A PEOPLE

CHAPTER 14

# The History of the Crabbe Road

Alabama attained statehood in December 1819. Two of the earliest Acts of the Alabama Legislature was the creation of the Byler Road and the Crabbe Road. Both roads would become vital to the development of not only the new state but to Tuscaloosa County in particular.

The Byler Road, named for John Byler the individual who was awarded a contract to construct a road from the Tennessee River at a point near Florence to Mobile, was built in 1821-1822. Today, that road is US Highway 43. It enters Tuscaloosa County from Fayette County near New Lexington and exits the county south of the Ralph Community, passing through Northport and Tuscaloosa.

The Crabbe Road was named for Thomas D. Crabbe, the individual who was awarded a contract to construct a road from near Decatur on the Tennessee River to the Black Warrior River in Tuscaloosa. Now identified as Alabama Highway 69, the Crabbe Road enters Tuscaloosa County from Walker County a few miles north of Windham Springs. The Crabbe Road terminates at the Warrior River in Northport. Many years later, a road from Tuscaloosa to Greensboro was named Highway 69 South. That road is not a part of the Crabbe Road.

Both the Byler and Crabbe Roads originally were called "turnpikes" and were toll roads. Tolls were identical for each road. The toll for a four-wheel vehicle such as a wagon or buggy was 75¢; a two-wheel vehicle toll was 50¢; the toll for a man riding a horse was 6 ¼ ¢; a pack horse, 6 ¼ ¢; a cow, 1¢; a hog or sheep, ½¢. Toll fees increased with time.

**The December 18, 1820 Act of the Alabama General Assembly creating the Crabbe Road**
An Act to establish a public road from the southern boundary line of township eight, in range four or five, west of the basis meridian of Huntsville, to the Falls of Tuskaloosa.

Section 1. Be it enacted by the Senate and House of Representatives of the State of Alabama in *General Assembly convened*, That a public road leading from the southern boundary line of township eight, in range four or five, west of the basis meridian line of Huntsville, by the nearest and best route to the Falls of Tuskaloosa river, be, and the same is hereby established.

Sec. 2. *And be it further enacted*, That Thomas D. Crabbe, and his associates be, and they are hereby authorized and empowered to lay out and open said road from the said eighth township line, in range four or five west as aforesaid, by the most eligible route which they have or hereafter may discover.

Sec. 3. *And be it further enacted*, That the said Thomas D. Crabbe, and his associates be, and they are hereby authorized, so soon, as they shall have layed [sic] out and opened said road, to erect

201

two turnpike gates thereon, at some convenient places, as nearly equidistant from the two extremes of said road as may be practicable. And the said Thomas D. Crabbe, and his associates may demand and received of, and from each and every person who shall or may travel on said road, and pass through the said gate or gates; at each gate the following rates of toll, to wit: For every four wheel carriage, thirty-seven and a half cents: for every two wheel carriage, twenty-five cents: for every man and horse twelve and a half cents: for every pack horse, six and a fourth cents: for every loose horse, six and a fourth cents; for every head of cattle, one cent; and for every head of hogs or sheep, one half cent. And if any person shall pass round, or through said gate, with intent to avoid the payment of toll, he or she shall for every such offence forfeit and pay to the said Thomas D. Crabbe, and his associates, treble the amount which his, her, or their toll would have been: to be recovered before any justice of the peace, with legal cost for the same.

Sec. 4. *And be it further enacted,* That the County Court of Cotaco (later renamed Morgan County), shall appoint two or more persons, who shall view said road established by virtue of this act; and they shall decide, whether in their opinion the road is completed in a good and sufficient manner, that wagons carrying two thousand pounds, and drawn by four horses, can conveniently pass the same.

Sec. 5. *And be it further enacted,* That it shall be the duty of the County Court of Cotaco, when application is made, or in their opinion it is necessary to appoint two or more commissioners to examine said road, and report their opinion to the county court. And if, in the opinion of the commissioners appointed by virtue of this act, the road is not in good and complete order, they shall direct the turnpike gates to be opened, and no toll shall be demanded or received, under the penalty of twenty dollars. And should the said Thomas D. Crabbe and his associates be convicted of receiving toll, when the gates are directed to be opened the second time, they shall forfeit all rights, privileges, and immunities under this act.

Sec. 6. *And be it further enacted,* That when the turnpike gates have been opened, and the said Thomas D. Crabbe and his associates shall conceive the road repaired in a good and sufficient manner, they shall apply to the County Court of Cotaco, to appoint two commissioners to

view and report said road, under their hands and seals; and the report of the commissioners shall be entered of record by the clerk of the county court, and then it shall be lawful for the said Thomas D. Crabbe and his associates, to receive the tolls allowed by virtue of this act; *Provided,* the commissioners are of opinion, the road is in sufficient repair. And the commissioners appointed by virtue of this act, shall receive such compensation, as the County Court may direct; to be paid by the said Thomas D. Crabbe and his associates.

Sec. 7. *And be it further enacted,* That the said Thomas D. Crabbe and his associates shall commence the said road within six months, and the same shall be completed within eighteen months. And the said Thomas D. Crabbe and his associates shall have all benefits and profits arising from the tolls, for the period of twelve years.

[*Approved December 18, 1820.*][1]

**Personal and family experience**

As with other chapters in *A Road, A Cemetery, A people,* material in this chapter comes from several sources including stories I heard my father share about his life on the Crabbe Road during the decades 1900s-1930s, old *Tuscaloosa News* articles, and my personal experiences. Another treasured resource of information comes from tales told me by some of my medical patients who were lifelong residents of the Crabbe Road.

The area of the Crabbe Road under discussion here is limited to the twenty-mile segment of

---
[1] http://www.legislature.state.al.us/misc/history/acts_and_journals/Acts_1820/Acts_71-75.html.

# THE HISTORY OF THE CRABBE ROAD

road between Two-mile Creek in Northport and Windham Springs.

The Crabbe Road of my youth in the 1940s was a narrow, crooked, dirt road barely wide enough to allow flow of traffic in opposite directions. Deep ditches lined both sides of the road. The original Crabbe Road followed old Indian trails from its origin at Guntersville near the Tennessee River to its terminus at the Black Warrior River in Northport. The road was laid out to follow along mountain ridges. The landscape changed frequently due to an unending series of bluffs, hills, hollows, creeks, and rivers. The road itself on many of the hills was so steep and slick with mud in rainy weather that cars and trucks in the 1910-1940 era often could not travel.

In the 1940s, I often rode with my father when he delivered new or used cars to customers in the Windham Springs area, and beyond. The road had not yet been paved. The Turkey Creek section of the Crabbe Road was an easy place to get the car stuck. The hill was very steep, and when wet "slippery as soap." A 1939 V-8 Ford carried either a 60 or 85 horsepower engine. (For comparison, most modern cars have 300-400 horsepower engines.) Daddy would always laugh and say, "Hayse, the car may not have enough power in all this mud to get us to the top of the hill, or we may slide into a ditch. We are just five miles from home. We may have to walk." The same situation was found as the road approached North River and was even more dangerous because there were deep ravines on both sides of the road. In my young mind, I knew we would be killed if the car slid off the road and plunged to the bottom of the gorge.

### Maintenance of a gravel road

Prior to the paving of the Crabbe Road, the graveled road surface was graded (scraped) at regular intervals by a Caterpillar Road grader to level out bumps, fill in ruts created by car and truck tires, and clean out ditches and stopped up culverts. Even so, the ride to town was bumpy in our 1940 Ford sedan that did not have modern shock absorbers and springs. It seemed as if the car was running over a never-ending scrub board like those used in washing clothes. During dry weather, clouds of dust from passing cars was so thick it was hard to see the road. When the road was wet following a rain, the road surface was so slippery drivers had to use extra care to prevent sliding into the ditches.

Parts of the road passed through very deep sandy areas. It was not uncommon for cars to get stuck in sand and had to be pulled out by mules from nearby farms.

Before the Crabbe Road was paved, in the late 1940s and early 1950s, the old bridges across Two-Mile Creek, Carrolls Creek, North River, and Turkey Creek were narrow one-lane wood structures that groaned and shook when vehicles rumbled across them. This always unnerved me, but Daddy assured me the bridges were safe and our car would not crash into the water below.

A safe speed was forty-miles-per-hour, or slower. As a kid, the ten-mile ride from our house to and from town seemed to take forever. I was so tired that sometimes I fell asleep before we got home.

### The Crabbe Road is paved

The first section of the Crabbe Road in Tuscaloosa County to be paved was the ten-mile span from Two-Mile Creek in Northport to North River. Our house was a half mile south of North River. We were lucky to be included in the first section to be paved. The road north of North River was not paved until the early 1950s.

### Other roads in Tuscaloosa County.

The following *Tuscaloosa News* articles do not relate directly to the Crabbe Road. I include them because they are representative of local road issues of the time.

**July 26, 1929 *The Tuscaloosa News* page 6**
**Good Roads Board Talks with Revenue Body About Activity**
The Good Roads Committee of the Chamber of Commerce meet Saturday with the Tuscaloosa County Board of Revenue for a discussion about some of the roads of the county, particularly the road from Ralph to Jena by way of the Shiloh Church. The condensary milk truck on that road, it is said, was discontinued last winter because the road was impassable. The condensary patrons on the route have hesitated about purchasing cows for fear the milk truck might be discontinued again in the coming winter.

The Board of Revenue agreed to begin work on the road at an early date and to fix it so that it would be passable the year around for the milk truck. Condensary workers are pointing out that use of the road by milk trucks forms a good argument for good roads, and it is an added reason for the keeping of dairy cows.

**July 28, 1929 *The Tuscaloosa News* page 8**
**State Highways in Good Shape, Report Shows Roads in Tuscaloosa All Passable**
Alabama highways remain in good condition, according to the report of the Alabama Highway Department. Relative to the roads that serve this portion of the state, the report states:

From the Mississippi line to Livingston, by way of York, the US 11 Road is paved, and from Livingston to Eutaw and to the Tuscaloosa County line the unpaved road is good. There is a ferry at Gainesville and one-half mile on the east side of the river the road is bad in wet weather.

There is pavement from the Greene County line to Tuscaloosa and for eight miles east of Tuscaloosa towards Birmingham. The road then is slate chert to Bessemer. From Bessemer, the road is paved through Birmingham to Huffman.

Between Moundville and Tuscaloosa there is a graded and graveled road (today this is Alabama Highway 69 South). From Tuscaloosa to Fayette and to Winfield there is a gravel road in good condition (today this is US 43).

From Tuscaloosa city to Holman the road is graded and fair condition (today this is US Highway 82) and from this point to Reform, there is a gravel surface. From Reform to the Mississippi line the road is under construction but is passable.

**July 28, 1929 *The Tuscaloosa News* page 5**
**Paving Ready for Three Miles Along the Columbus Highway**
Plans for the paving of three miles of the Columbus Road from a point about Deal's Lake to Coker was completed Friday.

Work will begin Monday at the end of the paving just beyond Northport and paving will continue in the direction of Coker.

Meantime, the Columbus Road out of Northport will be closed to traffic, and it will be necessary that all traffic detour by way of the Byler Road to a point about four miles out, leaving the Byler Road at the John Smith dairy and cutting through to the Columbus Road to strike that road about four miles from Northport.

It is expected that about six weeks will be required to pave the road from Northport to Coker, and there will remain about eight miles of the road to be paved before November. Contractors have announced, however, that if satisfactory progress is not made, additional workmen and machines will be placed on the road in order the contract may be completed by the specified time.

All material for the paving will be brought from Coker to the Northport end of the road.

**April 2, 1935 *The Tuscaloosa News*, page 7**
**Road Tax**
This tax is due Jan. 1 and is delinquent after April 1

Persons liable for road duty may:
First: commute same by paying $3:50
Second: work on roads for four days
Failure to do either:
(*Acts Alabama Legislature 1927,* page 400)

# THE HISTORY OF THE CRABBE ROAD

guilty of misdemeanor and upon conviction fined not less than $3.00 nor more than $10:00 for each day he fails or refuses to work. May also be imprisoned in county jail or put to hard labor. Until the law is repealed, it is the duty of the Board of Revenue to enforce it impartially.

**October 29, 1939** *The Tuscaloosa News* **page 2**
**Byler Road project to get underway soon**
Final arrangements in the participation for the blacktopping of the Byler Road from the end of the present pavement beyond Samantha to the Fayette County line has been made by the Board of Revenue, Probate Judge Chester Walker said Saturday.

At a special meeting of the body held Friday, the group agreed to purchase eight dump trucks to be used on the Byler project. Two trucks were purchased from each of the four local motor companies.

Work on the grading and graveling of the road for preparation will begin as soon as the project is released by the WPA. It was pointed out the release of the project is expected to not be later than November 15.

The county and the state will cooperate with each to contribute 25% to match WPA funds Walker said.

The blacktopping materials cannot be placed on the road during cold weather and that part of the work will be delayed until spring.

The Board of Revenue did not meet Saturday.

**January 30, 1940,** *The Tuscaloosa News*
**Damaged Roads Bring Holiday Extension in County**
**River Ice sheet sets record**
Tuscaloosa's unprecedented cold wave which brought a record of ten below zero Saturday morning January 27 set another historic mark today when the Warrior River was frozen bank to bank at the river bridge which connects Tuscaloosa and Northport traffic. Older residents said they had never seen such a condition and newspaper reports of the big freeze of 1899 make no mention of the Warrior River in Tuscaloosa being frozen over. The ice sheet had disappeared by noon today, four days later.

Meanwhile, this section sought to work its way back to normal with snow remaining on the ground for the eighth straight day. Weather forecasters predicted somewhat colder temperatures tonight, possibly down to 20 degrees. Last night's low was 23 degrees at Lock 10 and 23.6 degrees at the municipal airport.

County superintendent Rabun Fisher announced that schools which were scheduled to resume classes on Thursday will remain closed until next Monday. He said this was necessary because of hazardous conditions remain on the dirt roads in the county which are traversed by school buses. He said he had conferred with school board officials and principals from various parts of the county. He said snow was much heavier in the Brownville, Gorgas, Buhl, and Elrod areas. Residents of Buhl said that six inches of snow remained on the ground. They said the snow of Monday night January 22 and the following Tuesday ranged from 16 to 20 inches.

**Bridges over North River on the Crabbe Road**

**December 3, 1940** *The Tuscaloosa News,* **front page**
**Truck Hits North River Bridge**
**Damage Estimates $40,000**
**Two Men Hurt as Span of 80 Feet Is Thrown into Stream**
**Blocking Crabbe Road Traffic**
Damages estimating approaching $40,000 was caused Monday afternoon when a heavily loaded lumber truck struck the north end of the North River Bridge on the Crabbe Road totally wrecking the 100-foot span and injuring two persons. Probate Judge Cheater Walker said today that the financial loss would approach $40,000. The bridge was at a point nine miles north of Northport.

205

# A ROAD, A CEMETERY, A PEOPLE

The Hagler Bridge spanned North River on the Byler Road
The bridge is very similar to the Crabbe Road bridge over North River built in 1900.

Members of the Board of Revenue visited the scene this morning and planned to meet later today for a discussion of steps to replace the bridge. From four to six months will probably elapse before a new bridge can be constructed, it is understood.

Vernon Chappell, 24, of Oakman Route 3 in Walker County and Mose Walker, a Negro of Wiley, were in hospitals here today undergoing treatment for injuries sustained in the accident. The two were riding on the lumber truck which was driven by Irvin Dalkins of Oakman, who was not seriously injured.

**Victims seriously hurt**

Chappell was reported in a serious condition at the Druid City Hospital. He suffered a severe back injury. The Negro was in Stillman Hospital. He was believed to be not seriously hurt, but the full extent of his injured could not be determined, it was said.

The bridge built of wood and concrete with steel braces was constructed about 1900. All but about 20 feet of the south end of the structure crumbled into the river when the truck struck the first brace on the right at the north entrance. All the steel of the bridge fell into a mass of twisted wreckage.

State highway patrolman Henry Johnson who investigated the accident said the driver of the truck apparently lost control of the vehicle on the downhill curve approach to the bridge. The front left wheel of the truck struck the brace on the right side of the bridge knocking the structure from its moorings on that end, Johnson said. He said the truck dropped about eighteen feet from the roadbed.

The Crabbe Road is one of the main arteries of traffic connecting Tuscaloosa and Walker Counties. Residents of the Windham Springs community and others who reside beyond the river will be forced to travel on cut-off roads that connect the highway with the Watermelon Road and Byler Road in order to reach Tuscaloosa.

Detour signs were being made today to place at various places. Tucker Mathis and B. J. Chastise, two residents of the North River section, were stationed on either side of the river all last night to stop the traffic. Ample barricades were also placed on both sides of the river. Plans have not been completed as regards new routes that might be taken by school buses that travel along the Crabbe Road.

Larkin Rogers Hamner, a resident of the North River community, said the bridge that was wrecked was constructed about 1900. The 1900-built bridge replaced another bridge that was destroyed by high water, he said.

The bridge was said to be one of the strongest in the county. It was repaired about two years ago at which time the abutments and the floor were replaced, officials said.

The noise made by the falling bridge was heard for several miles residents of the area said.

The truck did not strike the water. The wheels of the truck were said to be buried in the mud when it finally came to a stop. The injured were taken to a hospital by a motorist.

Members of the Board of Revenue expressed the opinion that little of the material in the

# THE HISTORY OF THE CRABBE ROAD

wrecked bridge could be used in building another.

**March 8, 1942, *The Tuscaloosa News* front page**
**New Crabbe Road Bridge Serves Broad Section**
**Span Replaces Wrecked Structure**
**Formal Dedication To Be Held Later**

Tuscaloosa County citizens can be justly proud of the county's new bridge across the North River on the Crabbe Road. This span was opened recently to traffic. The bridge, which has been described by engineers as one of the most modern of wood and concrete structures of its kind in the South, replaces an old one that toppled on December 2, 1940 when it was struck by a loaded lumber truck.

The new bridge and approaches on each side were constructed as a WPA project with the county cooperating. The cost of the project to the county, counting both the bridge and approaches, was $58,942. The WPA contribution on the bridge itself amounted to approximately $18,000 and for the approaches about $27,000 according to Powell Baker, WPA road supervisor.

Construction was started in July 1941 and the bridge was competed in January. The approaches were finished only recently. The bridge span is 322 feet in length. It is located a quarter of a mile downstream from the old structure the change necessitating the building of new approaches.

The bridge rests on mass concrete piers that go down to solid rock. Col. Woolsey Finnell, county engineer, supervised the construction.

J. J. Cox was WPA supervisor on the job and has received high praise for his work. The bridge was designed by Dr. Donald duPlantie of the University of Alabama engineering faculty.

It is the firth bridge to be constructed at that

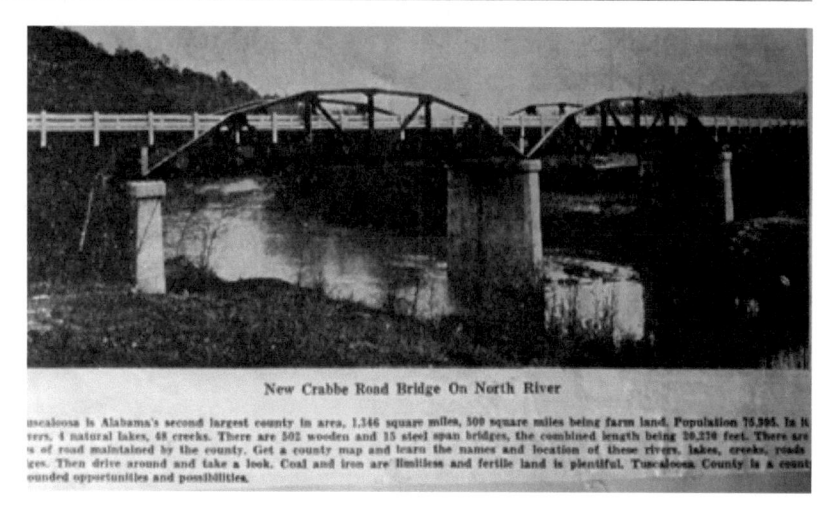

### Crabbe Road North River Bridge

This is the Crabbe Road North River bridge of my childhood. It replaced the old bridge that was destroyed in 1940. The view is looking downstream of the river.

point of the river since the Crabbe Road was built in 1823, according to Col. Finnell. The first bridge was built in 1828 about the time Andrew Jackson was elected president of the United States. That bridge was replaced in in 1894. Part of an old span of the bridge across the Warrior River at Tuscaloosa/Northport was used to rebuild the bridge across the North River in 1894, it is said.

In 1900, this bridge was washed away by high water. The one to replace it lasted until it was toppled by the truck in 1940.

A sharp curve on the north approach to the old bridge was eliminated by the new road. It was necessary to cut into a rocky hill and remove some 40,000 yards of rock Col. Finnell said.

The structure is equal in strength to one of steel and should last at least 50 years, the engineer said.

The Crabbe Road is one of the main county arteries of traffic that serves several commutes of this county including Windham Springs and the Brandon School Community. It is one of the main connections between this county and Walker County.

Plans for being made to hold an official ceremony at some later date for the dedication of the new bridge.

Col. Finnell prepared pictures and information about the bridge which will be published in the *Wood Preserving News*, a publican at Chicago.

### April 19, 1942 *The Tuscaloosa News* page 4
### Tuscaloosa County Board of Revenue

Tuscaloosa is Alabama's second largest county in area and is composed of 1,346 square miles of which 530 square miles are farm land. Its population is 75, 995. Three rivers pass through the county: the Black Warrior River, the North River, and the Sipsey River. Four natural lakes and 48 creeks supply the county with an abundant water supply. Five hundred and two wooden bridges with 15 steel spans of a combined length of 20,270 feet are part of 956 miles of roads that are maintained by the county. The Board of Revenue is made up of Chester Walker, Chairman, Pat Lancaster, John B. Taylor, and John E. Walker

### March 8, 1942 *The Tuscaloosa News* page 3
### WPA Work on County Roads May Stop

The County Board of Revenue on Saturday acknowledged the receipt of a message from Col. W. G. Henderson, State WPA Administrator, in which he stated that many current activities of the Works Progress Administration in this division will be discontinued immediately.

"It will be necessary, starting immediately, to discontinue many current activities in this division in order that all available employment can be used either for civil services which are essential to the basic needs of human life or to direct war services," Henderson said.

The message was interpreted by the Board of

Piers Rise for New Bridge on North River.
In the late 1960s, a dam was constructed on North River just north of the point where it empties into the Warrior River near Holt. The reservoir of water became Lake Tuscaloosa. This aerial view of North River and the Crabbe Road is seen from a northern view. The series of rectangular objects in the foreground are concrete piers that will support the new bridge. The light tan areas devoid of vegetation have been clear-cut and will be covered by the waters of the lake. This U-shaped bend in the river bed is typical of many such bends North River makes on its journey from Fayette County to the Warrior River. The Boyd property lies just beyond the upper right-hand corner or the photo.

Revenue to mean the immediate curtailment of WPA work on county roads unless the project is adjudged necessary for the prosecution of the defense program.

### April 30, 1944 *The Tuscaloosa News*, page 3
### Crabbe Road Placed on Post-war Program

The Crabbe Road, leading out of Northport, has been incorporated in the post war program and will be improved as soon as practicable after the present wartime restrictions are removed, G. R. Swift, Director of the State Highway Department, has notified Probate Judge Chester Walker.

Records of the highway department, Swift wrote, show that this road has been incorporated as Road Number 69 from Tuscaloosa to Cullman, which will provide a shorter route between those points.

Swift stated that the section of the road from

Northport to Windham Springs is on the federal aid secondary program.

Tuscaloosa county constructed a new and modern bridge across North River on the Crabbe Road about two years ago.

**December 24, 1969** *The Tuscaloosa News* **front page**
**Old Bridge Sinks into North River**
The old bridge seen in the preceding photo trembled on obliterated piers after the blast, then sank into the boiling waters of North River.

But the old bridge on Highway 69, the Crabbe Road, wasn't completely destroyed after the first big blast Tuesday afternoon. Not until about an hour later when the third and final charge were set off did the last pier of the old bridge sink into the mudded waters.

Nearly 100 spectators watched the demolition of the bridge from the safety of a newly completed bridge several hundred yards upstream.

Blasting of the bridge began Friday when a section was blasted loose and dropped into the water.

The Tuesday afternoon charge was bigger, rigged as a final blow to the old bridge. But, one of the charges misfired, and demonization experts had to try again.

Thus, Alsey C. Parker Engineering, Inc. won a rare race with the rising waters of Lake Tuscaloosa, formerly known as the North River Reservoir.

The reservoir dam had been backing up water since late summer. It was known the water would soon rise over the old bridge, but engineers delayed destroying it until a new one could nearly be completed.

The new bridge is not quite finished, but waters in the lake bed were rising so fast that the old bridge had to be blown anyway. After weekend rains, water had risen to within only a few feet of the top of the old bridge.

Detours are now being used to route motorists around the old bridge site.

## A ROAD, A CEMETERY, A PEOPLE

CHAPTER 15

# The LaFoy Family

The date the first members of the LaFoy family arrived in the area is not known. It is likely it was during or soon after the American Civil War, 1861-1865. The family was so well thought of that the community became known as the LaFoy Community.

LaFoy archives affirm that James and John LaFoy came to the United States from France in 1770. James was ten years old. The genealogy record between those LaFoys and William H. LaFoy and his wife Elizabeth Caroline LaFoy, the first known LaFoys to settle in the LaFoy community, is not available.

I wish to acknowledge the tireless work of research done by Brenda LaFoy, a great, great, granddaughter of William H. LaFoy and Elizabeth Caroline Cottrell LaFoy. Without Brenda's research and her willingness to share it with me, the story would not have been written.

Frances Albert LaFoy was the son of William H. LaFoy and Sarah Cottrell. Frances Albert was born October 26, 1824, in South Carolina. He married Elizabeth Caroline Cottrell prior to February 10, 1851, the exact date is not known. In 1860, they lived in Fort Motley, Greenville, South Carolina where he worked as a blacksmith and farmer. The 1880 Federal Census showed they lived in Tuscaloosa County near Northport. Frances Albert LaFoy died on December 1, 1887 and is buried in grave #113 in Macedonia Cemetery. Elizabeth Caroline Cottrell was born June 30, 1830 in Georgia. She died on December 29, 1906, and is buried in grave # 112 in Macedonia Cemetery.

Frances Albert LaFoy and Elizabeth Caroline Cottrell were the parents of thirteen children: (1) Mary F. Taylor LaFoy; (2) Henry Clay LaFoy; (3) Thomas Daniel LaFoy; (4) Sarah Elizabeth LaFoy; (5) Martha C. LaFoy; (6) Nancy A. LaFoy; (7) William LaFoy; (8) Susan C. LaFoy; (9) John Albert Lafoy; (10) William R. LaFoy; (11) John M. LaFoy; (12) John Henry LaFoy; (13) William H. LaFoy

**Brenda's great grandparents**

Thomas Daniel LaFoy, third child of Frances Albert LaFoy and his wife Elizabeth Caroline Cottrell LaFoy are Brenda Lafoy's grandparents.

Thomas Daniel LaFoy was born in July 1871. He married Addie Elizabeth "Lizzie" Brown on August 24, 1896. Thomas Daniel died on November 11, 1946, and is buried in grave # 121 in Macedonia Cemetery. Addie Elizabeth "Lizzie Brown LaFoy died on April 2, 1961 and is buried in grave # 122 in Macedonia Cemetery. Their daughter Essie Queen Lafoy married James Webster "Jay" Hamner the son of Oliver Jackson "Ollie" Hamner and Mary Louise Rigsby. Jay and Queen are buried in Carrolls Creek Baptist Church Cemetery.

# A ROAD, A CEMETERY, A PEOPLE

**Brenda's grandparents**
Brenda LaFoy's grandfather was Emil Frances LaFoy, a son of Thomas Daniel LaFoy and Addie Elizabeth "Lizzie" Brown LaFoy born December 2, 1910. Emil Frances "Frank" LaFoy married Frances America Broughton, who was born in the Cowden Community near Samantha on May 1, 1914. Emil Frances LaFoy died on May 24, 1983, and is buried in grave # 282 in Macedonia Cemetery. Frances America died June 2, 2005, and is buried in grave # 284 in Macedonia Cemetery.

**Brenda's parents**
Brenda LaFoy's father was Charles Ray LaFoy, the second of three sons born to Emil Frances LaFoy and Frances America Broughton LaFoy.

Charles Ray LaFoy was born on July 5, 1938 and died on March 16, 1992. He is buried in Salem Cemetery in New Lexington. Charles Ray LaFoy married Nella Jean "Jeanie" Rushing on May 2, 1958. Nella Jean was born December 20, 1939. She is still living in 2024.

Charles Ray LaFoy and Nella Jean Rushing LaFoy have three children and have one adopted grandchild. Brenda LaFoy is their second child. She was born March 28, 1964.

Brenda's uncle and brother to Charles Ray, Tony LaFoy was born November 18, 1936 and died February 4, 2021. He is buried in Sunset Cemetery.

Another brother to Charles Ray was William Thomas LaFoy. He died at the age of one month on January 27, 1941, and is buried in Macedonia Cemetery in grave # 283.

**The discovery of two old family letters**
In 2022, while cleaning out an old cabinet that had been abandoned for years, Brenda LaFoy's first cousin, Randy Frank LaFoy, son of Tony Lafoy, discovered two letters. The first, written in 1974, was penned by his great grandmother Allie Elizabeth "Lizzie" Brown LaFoy. Randy was about nine years old at the time the letter was written. The second paper was written by his grandmother Frances Broughton LaFoy after "Grandma Lizzie" died. She merely added a few notes to the original letter.

The letters were lovingly written in longhand to a grandson and a great grandson. The dear ladies were not writing formal letters for public viewing. They never dreamed their remarks would be included in a book discussing the history of LaFoy Community. If an author such as I merely typed the messages found in those letters and inserted them into this story, most readers would be unfamiliar with the names, places, and events noted resulting in a loss their historical significance. So, I decided to present their message in the following manner.

Sentences taken verbatim from the letters are shown in *italic print* and are bracketed. This allows the personal spirit of the letters to remain. Personal comments made by me are in normal print.

I was born and reared in the LaFoy community. Over the past 84 years, I have had the joy and privilege of sharing life with the LaFoys.

A copy of Randy LaFoy's note to his grandparents reads:

1. The first person who lived on this street (LaFoy Road) and why is it called that?

2. Name of our community, road, etc.?

3. People who live in community?

4. What was this like before houses were built?

5. When was this road built?

6. Any information about Northport long ago?

Randy's great grandmother Allie Elizabeth "Lizzie" Brown LaFoy and his grandmother Frances America Broughton LaFoy wrote the following answer to Randy's questions noted above.

*Dear Randy,*

*James and John LaFoy came over with our father from France in 1770. James was ten years old. Brother (who is this???) was born September 20, 1751 so LaFoys have been in the USA for a long*

# THE LAFOY FAMILY

*time.*

*Your great, great grandfather, Frances Albert LaFoy, was the first LaFoy to live in the LaFoy Community, as I get it from my survey. The old LaFoy log house stood where Mable Hamner now lives.* [The old house site is located on the west side of the Crabbe Road at its intersection with Alton Drive 100 yards north of Carrolls Creek Baptist Church. No structure stands there in 2024. The log house was torn down several years ago.] *Their names were:*

*Albert LaFoy, born 1827, married Caroline Atkins, born 1830. I don't know what year they married, but their children were: Sarah LaFoy married Tommie Gray.*

*Mattie LaFoy married Hattie Griffin from Birmingham.*

*Addie LaFoy never married.* [She is buried in Macedonia Cemetery. The tombstone for grave # 114 reads "Addie LaFoy, December 29, 1867-February 17, 1924."]

*John LaFoy never married and is buried in Arkansas.*

*Dr. Henry LaFoy, married Addie Griffin. He lived in an old log house that was torn down by Spurgeon Black until he and Addie separated. One daughter_____. Later Henry LaFoy married _____ at Searles.* [The Spurgeon Black house was located on the west side of the Crabbe Road at its intersection with House Bend Road. It was next door to his wife Mrs. Lena Bell Black's parents, Mr. and Mrs. Charlie Newman.]

*Will LaFoy was killed in a hunting accident.* [He is buried in grave # 111 at Macedonia Cemetery.]

*Your great grandfather, Thomas Daniel LaFoy, was born July 3, 1876. Thomas Daniel LaFoy married Addie Elizabeth Brown on August 24, 1896*

## LaFoy Road and farm

*Thomas "Tom" Daniel LaFoy and his wife Addie Elizabeth Broughton bought land about 1900 and cut a narrow little dirt road through the woods to it from the Renfro Road. Soon afterwards, they built a house. It was the only house on the road. They had to clear ground of trees and bushes in order to plant a garden and raise corn and a little cotton for a cash crop. Tom worked the land and sold timber to earn a living to provide for nine children.*

*Caroline Atkins LaFoy donated land from their farm for a school which was named LaFoy School.* [The school opened in the early 1900s. The story of LaFoy School is told in Chapter 5, "The Lafoy School."]

*These are the nine children of Thomas Daniel LaFoy and Addie Elizabeth Brown LaFoy. They were born when Thomas and Addie lived on the LaFoy Road:*

*Verna M. LaFoy, born May 25, 1898*
*Mary Lee LaFoy, born August 26, 1900*
*Maggie Lou LaFoy, born February 20, 1902*
*Essie Queen LaFoy, born August 25, 1903*
*Thomas Coleman LaFoy, born May 8, 1905. He died 1908 and is buried in grave #119 in Macedonia Cemetery.*
*Thurman Britton LaFoy, born January 3, 1907*
*Nannie Bell LaFoy, born May 3, 1909 married Narley Walters*
*Emil Frances LaFoy, born December 2, 1910. He married Frances Broughton.* [As noted earlier, Frances Broughton LaFoy added comments in the letter to Randy LaFoy originally written by her mother-in-law Grandma Lizzie LaFoy after Grandma Lizzie died.]
*John Wilton LaFoy, born July 24, 1913. He was his mother's birthday son.*

*Your grandparents, Emil Frances LaFoy and Frances Broughton LaFoy, have put 40 hard and stormy years here. Today, our LaFoy family lives in Tuscaloosa, Northport, Searles, Brookwood, Bessemer, Birmingham, and Cardona. Aunt Queen Hamner, papa's sister and our family are all the LaFoys left in LaFoy Community now.*

## Randy's questions to his grandmother

**"Who were the people in the LaFoy community?"**

213

*She replied, "Really too many to name now. Some kinfolks also live in about four housing projects. But other older generations who made up the LaFoy Community included these families: the Rushing family; the Clements family; the Shirley family; the Hamner family; the Robertson family; the Jones family; the Tierce family, the Hagler family; the Turner family, and many others."*

**"When was the LaFoy Road built?"**

*"The LaFoy Road was built about 1900 when Thomas Daniel Lafoy acquired land and built his home on it."* [Today, the LaFoy Road carries the name Fire House Road. Several LaFoy families continue to live there having built new houses and renovated old houses.]

**"Do you have any information about Northport long ago?"**

*"All I can say is our old faithful Dr. Samuel T. Hardin was a doctor, a friend in need, and never turned a person away. Faithful Northport store merchants included — Christian and Faucett, Barnes and Norris Gin, and Rice's Gin and Warehouse. Farmers depended on them. Up until some years ago, Northport would flood when the Warrior River would rise after big rains. I have seen the water up in the stores on Main Street. Many years ago. Sitting in the boat, I could touch the telephone wires. Northport was completely destroyed by a storm (tornado in 1932), but, like always, the town built back and keeps going. Where Lake Tuscaloosa is now just a few years ago was a small river called North River. Now just look at the progress."*

**LaFoy odds and ends**

The LaFoy Road currently is identified as Fire House Road. It exits the Lary Lake Road ¼ mile from the Crabbe Road. The Lary Lake Road originally was called the Renfro Road as it led to the Anthony Renfro farm, an area of about 1,000 acres. The farm was bisected by North River. The Crabbe Road's old name was the Jasper Highway; today, it is known as Alabama Highway 69 North.

*Tuscaloosa Weekly Times*, Oct. 7, 1874 — H. C. LaFoy, registered voter Moore's Bridge Community

*Tuscaloosa Weekly Times*, March 9, 1976 — Frances Albert LaFoy, property tax notice of $5.85.

*Tuscaloosa Gazette*, March 11, 1880, William H. LaFoy — Petit Jury duty.

*Tuscaloosa Weekly Times*, Feb. 15, 1882 — William H. Lafoy, making settle for Homestead Application

*Tuscaloosa Gazette*, March 23, 1882 — Henry Clay LaFoy — petit jury duty

*Tuscaloosa Weekly Times*, January 30, 1889 — J. A. Cottrell acting as administrator of Frances Albert LaFoy's estate, offered Frances Albert LaFoy's property for sale to the highest bidder.

*Tuscaloosa Gazette*, April 13, 1896 — marriage license issued to T. D. LaFoy and Lizzie Brown.

*Tuscaloosa Gazette*, March 23, 1899 — J. W. LaFoy has employed Mr. Fletcher Jennings, a sterling young man, on his farm.

**Summary**

The LaFoy family's contributions to the LaFoy community have been many. The one most recognized is the donation of land on which the LaFoy School was built. Family members have been hard-working, dependable, honest, self-reliant, citizens who have been eager to assist neighbors, supported law and order, and were, and remain, God-fearing men and women.

CHAPTER 16

# Cost of Living

The essentials of life include food, clothing, and shelter. To provide those necessities during the first half of the twentieth century, the people of Lafoy, most of whom had very limited income, put forth a valent effort to see that these needs were met. A discussion of the following topics tells how Lafoy community residents dealt with economic hardship.

The average family income in Alabama during the Great Depression of the 1930s fell from an already low of $311 in 1929 to $194 in 1935.

**Electric power**
In 1906, 90 percent of Alabama had no electric power. In that year, Alabama Power Company was organized. In 1926, only half the homes in the United States had electricity. Electric service from Alabama Power Company first became available to residents in the city of Tuscaloosa in the mid-1920s but was not available in the Lafoy Community until 1940. However, there is one known instance in which a house did have electric power prior to 1940. It was the home of Ezra Jonah Shipp located across the Crabbe Road from Macedonia Methodist Church. Mr. Shipp used a series of batteries to generate electricity for his home. Periodically, Mr. Shipp took the batteries to Northport to be re-charged. The Shipp farm and house was only a quarter mile south of my boyhood home. An entire chapter in *A Road, A Cemetery, A People* is devoted to the Shipp family.

**Carbide system**
A second home, that of John and Octavia Hagler, had a carbide lighting system that provided flames of light in ceiling fixtures throughout their home, a three-bedroom, kitchen, dining room,

The Shipp House retains its original appearance after 95 years.

living room, indoor bathroom, a front porch and screened-in back porch. The system provided light only. They slept year-round on the back porch regardless of the outdoor temperature.

The use of carbide as a source of light in

215

homes in rural areas not served by electricity began shortly after 1900 and continued in some areas past 1950. Calcium carbide pellets were placed in a container outside the home where water was piped to the container. As water dropped on the pellets, acetylene gas was produced. The gas was piped to lighting ceiling fixture in each room and porches. When the switch to a fixture was turned on, a very bright flame illuminated the entire ro
om.

The Hagler house was built circa 1915. I assume the acetylene lighting system was installed at the time of construction. In 1940, Alabama Power Company extended power service from Northport to the Lafoy Community. The power line ended at our house. Extension of service to our next-door neighbor to the north, Tuck and Louise Matthis, and all areas north of us did not receive power service until the late 1940s.

Even though the Haglers did not continue to use the carbide system after electricity became available, they did not disassemble it. I was fascinated each time I visited their house, it was next door to our house, and examined each fixture and the pipe leading to it. It was fun to sit and listen as they told stories about carbide lighting.

**The following ad comes from the January 6, 1930, *Tuscaloosa News*. Subscribers to the newspaper must have read this article with envy of the luxury that city folks had but was not available in rural areas for another decade.**

It is no job at all to manage a completely equipped electric home at all.

With electricity it takes less time to do the household activities, and less effort, and now it is far cheaper. So much cheaper that any housewife who wants swift electric service can afford it. Indeed, she can NOT afford not to use electric service if she wants economy and ease and efficiently, all at once.

The new rate makes it economic for you to let electricity do all these tasks: cook the meals, clean the floors, do the laundry, freeze the ice. The more electricity you use the cheaper it gets.

There is an electric appliance to lighten almost every task. Find the ones you need in our salesroom, so they can soon start their comfort making in your home.

Do not forget our special 10% discount on all ranges.

Alabama Power Company

**January 2, 1930, *The Tuscaloosa News*
Montgomery Ward and Company
Across the street from the post office
An ad
Genuine Tungsten light bulbs**

**25, 30, 40, 60 watts    Six for a dollar**

What a substantial saving. The inside of the bulb is frosted to insure a bright light without a glare. Soft pearl color is a relief from eye strain. Easy to clean. Made under patent of General Electric.

**A 2nd ad from Montgomery Ward**

Wardway electric gyrator washer    $73.50

Wash your clothes the modern way. Do not buy any washer until you have tried the Wardway. All copper tub, no center post to tear dainty fabrics, 8 position safety wringer. Washes clothes clean in seven minutes. Guaranteed for ten years. Zero to 8 sheet capacity.

**A 3rd ad from Montgomery Ward**

Super charged automobile battery $10.79. Three-year warranty.

**March 2, 1930, *The Tuscaloosa News*
Buy now to use your refrigerator all season**

The saved cost of ice alone will be and important item and you will know the satisfaction of knowing your food is well kept.

In our large stock are models for every home staunchly constructed and perfectly insulated. Come in an select yours tomorrow. $19.50 and up. Sokol Brothers.

**Commercial ice for those without electricity**
How did people in Lafoy keep dairy products such as milk and butter from spoiling prior to the availability of public electrification in the area? Often, dairy products were kept in the well that supplied water for the family or in a nearby spring of water or in an icebox. For those who lived in town, commercial blocks of ice were delivered to their home by an ice wagon several times a week. However, ice wagons rarely made trips to rural areas such as Lafoy. To purchase a 50- pound cube of ice, which would last three days in an icebox, Lafoy folks had to make a trip to town. That was not feasible most of the time.

The following is an ad by City Ice. Co. in the July 28, 1929, issue of the *Tuscaloosa News*.

*The Tuscaloosa News*, **July 28, 1929, page 6**
**City Ice Co. Ad**
**15th Street and Queen City Avenue**
    Station # 1, Jack's Place, Birmingham Highway
    Station # 2, 8th St. and 32nd Avenue
    Station # 3, Junction of 14th and 15th St. by M & O Railroad
    Station # 4, Junction Bridge St. and Watermelon Road, Northport
    Station # 5, Main Street downtown Northport
    Station # 6, 8th Street and 11th Avenue

| Prices at listed locations | | Prices at plant | |
|---|---|---|---|
| 100 pounds | 30¢ | 100 pounds | 20¢ |
| 50 pounds | 15¢ | 50 pounds | 10¢ |
| 25 pounds | 10¢ | 5 pounds | 5¢ |

**A work ethic and trait of honesty from the 1930s**
The Great Depression of the 1930s brought very difficult times to most Americans including the good people of the Lafoy Community. They buckled down, carefully budgeted what little cash they earned, did without "luxuries," and survived by growing most of their food, made their own clothing, and helped their neighbors in times of crisis. In general, life in rural areas like Lafoy was much better than in large cities.

Following the election of Franklin D. Roosevelt in 1932, the Federal Emergency Relief Administration, a grant-making agency authorized to distribute federal aid to the states for relief was established. The small government checks were used to help ward off starvation. The distribution of government checks in Tuscaloosa County was under the supervision of Mrs. Phyllis Frances, Tuscaloosa County Relief Director. By the end of December 1935, FERA had distributed over $3.1 billion and employed more than 20 million people nationwide.

The work ethic of the era was anchored in a sense of responsibility that was vastly different from today. The following news article captures the work ethic and sense of honesty exhibited by the people of Tuscaloosa County during that era.

*The Tuscaloosa News*, **July 8, 1934**
Many dollars have been sent out by the Tuscaloosa County Relief Committee and several of them have come back "declined with thanks."

Yes, believe it or not, the case records of field workers under Mrs. Phyllis Frances show that three checks have been recently returned uncashed by persons to whom they were sent. In each case the person to whom the check was sent informed the Relief Committee "I have got a regular job now and do not need the money."

The very people who returned the checks, one was a white man and two were Negroes, had been virtually on starvation until given aid by the relief committee. They had been unemployed for months. After their case had been investigated, the relief committee sent them checks in small amounts, just enough to meet the budgetary needs for food.

One of the Negroes in returning his check uncashed wrote the relief committee as follows: "I received the check today, and I thank you very much, but since I have a job maybe you can help some other person who is unemployed. If I get out of work again, I will thank you all to help me."

The writer of the letter is a thirty-eight Negro laborer. His case is regarded by the field workers as typical of the spirit of a host of persons who are receiving relief checks.

Many of the men on relief rolls have returned their work cards to the relief committee accompanied by letters of gratitude and expressions of pride in getting a "regular job" so relief work is not needed.

A similar spirit of pride in helping themselves is reported among the 150 subsistence homestead families in Tuscaloosa County. Farm foremen who inspect these farms each week report that entire families are taking great interest in their projects and respond quickly to the encouragement given them.

Of courage with many hundreds of families on work relief and direct relief, there are cases where the spirit shown is not in line with that exemplified by the three men who returned the checks. But these cases do stand out in the minds of the relief workers and they prove an inspiration to those whose task it is to help families in need.

## AUTOMOBILES 1910s-1950s

From the years 1900 to 1919, some 2,000 American companies were involved in some way with the construction of motor vehicles. Some companies made only one car. Henry Ford receives credit for building the first mass-produced car in 1908, the Model T.

The number of active automobile manufacturers dropped from 253 in 1908 to only 44 in 1929 with about 80 percent of the industry's output accounted for by Ford, General Motors, and Chrysler which was formed from Maxwell in 1925 by Walter P. Chrysler.

I have a lifelong love affair with automobiles. I guess its beginning lies in the fact that my father was in the automobile business all his adult life and I spent many hours hanging out at Tucker Motor Company, the local Ford dealership. I have selected a few articles from the *Tuscaloosa News* relating to the subject.

### *The Tuscaloosa News*, March 20, 1919
**A new car in the community**

Lafoy School is progressing, and we are delighted with our teachers, Miss Anabel McElroy and Miss Annabel Beaver, both of Cuba, Alabama. We believe they are trying to do the right thing for the children. Health, is good in our community. Mr. Bernice Whatley has purchased a new motor car.

**Personal note:**

The brand and cost of Mr. Whatley's new car is not stated. Perhaps it was a Ford Model T. In 1919, Ford Motor Company produced 498,342 new cars. The average cost was $500. Very few people in Lafoy had the financial means to spend that amount of money for a car.

The terrible Great Depression of the 1930s following the Stock Market crash in October 1929 profoundly affected the automobile industry. The highly profitable luxury end of the automobile market virtually disappeared. The lower-priced segment grew from 40 percent of sales in 1929 to 80 percent of sales in 1933 and remained at 60 percent through the upturn and beyond. As a result, half the automakers ceased production. The only major auto companies to survive the Great Depression were General Motors Corporation, Ford Motor Company, Chrysler Corporation, Hudson Motor Car Company, Nash-Kelvinator Corporation, Packard Motor Car Company, Studebaker Corporation, and Crosley Motors.

### *The Tuscaloosa News*, February 2, 1930, page 3
**Automobile makers big user of national resources**

That the automobile industry is a large consumer

# COST OF LIVING

of raw products of other industries is shown in the following figures of consumption in 1929.

Carloads of automotive freight, 3,600,000; rubber, 85%; plate glass, 67%; iron and steel, 19%; copper, 15%; lumber, 18%; lead, 27%; gasoline, 80%; cotton fabric, 278,000,000 pounds.

*The Tuscaloosa News*, **June 2, 1930**
**An ad by Ford Motor Company**

| | |
|---|---|
| Standard coupe | $495 |
| Sport coupe | $525 |
| Two door sedan | $495 |
| Town sedan | $660 |
| Pick up open cab | $425 |
| Pick-up closed cab | $455 |
| Station wagon | $640 |

All prices f.o.b. Detroit. (FOB shipping point, also known as FOB origin, indicates that the title and responsibility of goods transfer from the seller to the buyer when the goods are placed on a delivery vehicle.)

*The Tuscaloosa News*, **July 8, 1934**
**An ad by Tuscaloosa Motor Company (Chevrolet)**
**Sport Standard models**

| | |
|---|---|
| Sport Roaster | $465 |
| Coach | $495 |
| Coupe | $485 |

**Master models**

| | |
|---|---|
| Sport roadster | $540 |
| Coach | $580 |
| Town sedan | $615 |
| Sedan | $540 |
| Coupe | $560 |

All prices f.o.b. Flint, Michigan

*The Tuscaloosa News*, **April 5, 1939**
**An ad by Lancaster's Garage (Oldsmobile)**

$777 and up. Check Olds delivered prices and check up on Olds values as compared with any other car in the lower price market.

This year's Oldsmobile Sixty Sedan with built-in trunk sells for $105 less than last year's Oldsmobile model with built in model. Prices have absolutely been reduced on the Oldsmobile Seventy and the Oldsmobile Eighty. For quality, value, and all-around satisfaction, this year its Oldsmobile!

Delivered prices are at Lancing, Michigan and are subject to change without notice. Price includes safety glass, bumpers, bumper guards, spare tire, and tubes.

Transportation, state, and local taxes, if any, optional equipment, and accessories are extra.

**Personal note:**

From the beginning of the automobile revolution, many people could not afford a new automobile. As a result, used cars have played an important role in the industry. The August 18, 1940, issue of the *Tuscaloosa News* on page 11 has side-by-side used car ads by Tucker Motor Company (local Ford dealer) and Tuscaloosa Motor Company (local Chevrolet dealer).

*The Tuscaloosa News*, **August 18, 1940**
**Tucker Motor Company (Ford dealer)**

1938 four-door Pontiac sedan, radio, good tires, good motor $495

1939 Chevrolet business coupe, driven less than 12,000 miles, radio, car is just like new $595.

1938 Ford coupe, radio, new tires, extra clean $465.

1937 Plymouth two-door sedan, motor reconditioned $325.

1936 Plymouth two-door sedan, tires, motor, and entire car is in good condition $195.

Ten Model A Fords all in good running condition priced from $25 up to 95.

**Tuscaloosa Motor Company (Chevrolet dealer)**

| | |
|---|---|
| 1930 Chrysler coupe | $45 |
| 1925 Chevrolet sedan | $85 |

1934 Chevrolet sedan, looks good and runs good $150

1934 Buick sedan, looks and runs good and has practically new tires all way around    $175

1936 Ford two-door sedan. This car has a new paint job and the upholstery is protected with seat covers, motor is reconditioned    $245

1938 Chevrolet deluxe town sedan with radio. It is in perfect condition and priced low    $475

1939 Chevrolet master deluxe with built in trunk, like new, tires in perfect condition $545

**Personal note:**

It is interesting that the term "built-in trunk" is used in several of the automobile ads. Automobiles with a built-in trunk was first available circa 1934. Almost all cars had them it within a couple of years although you could buy a car without a trunk for a while, but by 1939, all cars had trunks.

I remember my father telling me as a child that bootleggers often rigged their cars with special shock absorbers so that the rear end of the car did not sink low when the trunk was filled with many gallons of moonshine whiskey.

*The Tuscaloosa News*, **October 15, 1941**
**An ad by Anders Motor Company**
**Studebaker dealer**
New 1942 Skyway Series, Studebaker Commander

You do not have to give up the satisfaction and prestige of driving a big impressive car merely because you feel you must cut down on your motoring expenses.

You can easily settle that problem for years to come with the distinctively flight-streamed, finely finished, roomy, new 1942 Skyway Studebaker Commander. It saves gas sensationally every mile.

Come in and drive this wonderful car. You may use your present car as part payment.

*The Tuscaloosa News*, **October 15, 1941**
**An ad by Austin Motor Company**
**Dodge dealer**
There can be no curtailment of Dodge quality

No substitute for Dodge dependability

In this Dodge you find the brilliant climax of a long development. You now have power that ebbs and flows with hushed and cushioned energy. It is a power transmitted in an oil encasement where wear and tear cannot occur. You find a car in which the driver rests, freed of shifting and clutching fatigue, yet free to clutch when need arises. Lifetime qualities are moving into this new car. They strongly invite your ownership for they will be with you at their finest a year or many years from now. Dodge dependability becomes more than ever an investment for the years. All you must do is give the accelerator a touch and fluid drive provide marvelous flexibility.

**Personal note:** power flow engines and all fluid drive were percussors to automatic transmissions in automobiles. The first fully automatic transmission appeared in the 1940 Oldsmobile. It was a $50 option and very popular. By the early 1950s, almost every nameplate offered an automatic transmission.

## WORLD WAR II AFFECTS AUTOMOBILE PRODUCTION

War had been raging in Europe since 1939 but the United States had not been in active war mode until after the Japanese bombing of Pearl Habor on December 7, 1941. The war effort immediately affected the automobile industry in the United States. On February 22, 1942, all manufacturers ended their production of automobiles and no new cars were sold from that date until 1946, except for special exceptions. The January 1942 production quota had been a little over 100,000 automobiles and light trucks. The units manufactured at the beginning of February would bring up the total number of vehicles in a newly established car stockpile to 520,000.

# COST OF LIVING

*The Tuscaloosa News*, January 30, 1942, page 1
**Auto tax penalty to take effect February 1, 1942.**
Approximately one-half of the Tuscaloosa County registered motor vehicles had been provided with auto tax stamps at noon today according to reports from the Tuscaloosa and University post offices. The Tuscaloosa office has sold 4,500 and 300 have been disposed of at the University.

Deadline for the purchase of the stamps without penalty is Saturday afternoon according to federal officials. The Tuscaloosa office will remain open till 4:00 p.m. and the University office till 1:00 p.m.

Treasury officials have announced that owners of automobiles using public highways will be liable for penalty unless automobiles have tax stamps conspicuously displayed upon them by Sunday, February 1. The penalty set by law may be $25 fine or 30 days in jail.

*The Tuscaloosa News*, February 22, 1942
**New car ration eligibility set**
Farmers, if they have no other means of transportation, defense workers, taxis operators, and essential traveling salesmen will be eligible to buy new automobiles, under rationing regulations announced today.

Aside from these groups, the eligible list follows in general that for rationing new tires and includes, physicians, visiting nurses, firefighters, policemen and others regarded as essential to the protection of health and safety.

No one will be permitted to buy a new automobile unless the local rationing board is satisfied that the applicant's present car is not adequate for the duties he performs.

Rationing is in effect starting March 2 and will govern the sales of 340,000 new automobiles made available this year.

The Office of Price Administration directed that local rationing boards require an applicate to prove his need for a new car in light of conditions peculiar to his community. Officials predicted that less than 10% of last year's production would be available for sale in the next twelve months. Many persons on the eligible list will not be able to get a new car.

Within these qualifications, the following will be eligible to purchase certificates: physicians; surgeons; visiting farm veterinarians; clergymen; ambulances; visiting nurses; fire departments; police departments; mail carriers; executives, technicians, engineers, and workers directly or indirectly connected the prosecution with the war; persons carrying newspapers for wholesale delivery.

Approximately 140,000 new cars will be made available to sale for eligible civilian individuals and various federal, state, and local agencies between March 2 and May 31.

The rationing regulations do not apply to the approximately 135,000 new automobiles that had been ordered and stored for sale in 1943 and after. The regulations provide for persons who made downpayment on new automobiles prior to January 1 when all stocks were frozen may obtain refunds if they are unable to meet eligibility requirements.

*The Tuscaloosa News*, March 2, 1942, page 3
**New Car Ration Program Begins**
**Detroit, March 2**
Far from popular with the automobile manufacturers and the retail dealers, the new automobile rationing program got underway today with the average individual having only the remotest chance of getting one of the 144,000 vehicles to be allotted during the coming three months.

"Almost like registering for the draft" said one intending applicant for a certificate authorizing delivery of a new car.

Aside from providing necessity for the vehicle, the applicant is required to say exactly where he is going to keep it, where he is going to use it, and why a car owned by some other member of his immediate family is not "available and adequate" for his use. He is called upon to also explain why transportation facilities other than an automobile car are not adequate for the work he believes entitles him to eligibility classification.

Just when delivery can begin will depend largely upon the volumes of applicants in the different communities. Besides, the allocation of new vehicles, the local rationing boards have new tire and tire recapping certifications to act upon and the supervision of sugar rationing will come under the direction of most of these local committees.

## NEW CAR PRODUCTION AFTER WWII

As noted, no new cars, commercial trucks, or auto parts were made from February 1942 to October 1945. On January 1, 1942, all sales of cars, as well as the delivery of cars to customers who had previously contracted for them, were frozen. After 1945, the government relaunched commercial production and carmakers debuted their 1946 models to a public that was eager to get back on the road. However, the waiting list for a new car was long and many people became very impatient and frustrated. This is illustrated in the following want-ad from the April 21, 1946 issue of the *Tuscaloosa News*.

### *The Tuscaloosa News*, April 21, 1946, page 19
**Want ad**

I would like to trade my 1938 model Chevrolet in good condition, plus my high place on the list for a new 1946 Ford for a 1940 or 1941 Ford or Chevrolet. I am tired of waiting. Phone 4171.

**Personal note**: After World War II was over, people were desperate for new cars, especially returning veterans. My father often talked at the supper table about some customers whose names were on the new car waiting list at Tucker Motor Co who would approach him and offer to slip him $100 under the table if he would bump their name up to number one on the list. Of course, he did not do that.

### *The Tuscaloosa News*, April 21, 1946, page 3
**An ad by Tuscaloosa Motor Company**

Again, in production!
The New Chevrolet
Bringing you big car quality at low cost
The new Chevrolet is the big-quality car of low price — large, roomy, with big car styling, big car comfort, big car performance and it saves you money on gas, oil, and upkeep as well.

### *The Tuscaloosa News*, May 16, 1950 page 11
**An ad**

Again, Mercury leads the way
Earlier this year, the big new Mercury proved its amazing performance by winning top prize in the Mobil Gas Grand Canyon Economy Run!
From coast to coast, it became America's "Number 1 Economy Car."
Now, Mercury has been chosen to set the whirlwind pace at the Memorial Day Indianapolis 500-mile Race.
Here is the car that has everything that America wants. Prize-winning economy plus performance that is truly in a class by itself. And moreover, owners say it is the smartest looking, smoothest riding car on the road as well.
Come in today and drive it. Once you do, you will go for Mercury. Mercury goes for you.
Tuscaloosa Lincoln Mercury Company
Greensboro Avenue and 11th Street
**Personal note**: Ford Motor Company first introduced the Mercury brand in 1939, and it sold for $ $916 and had a 95-horsepower V-8 engine. More than 65,000 were built the first year. The offerings included two and four-door sedans, a sports convertible, and a town sedan.
Back on Feb. 4, 1922, Henry Ford, with encouragement from his wife Clara and his son Edsel Ford, had purchased the Lincoln Motor Company from inventor and automotive engineer Henry Leland for $8 million. The transaction set in motion the creation of an iconic American luxury brand, Lincoln, that would be sold at Ford dealerships.

# COST OF LIVING

In the late 1940s, Ford Motor Company required that the Mercury and Lincoln marques be sold under different roofs from Ford automobiles. This brought about a significant change at Tucker Motor Company owned by Hayse Tucker. Previously, all three marques — Ford, Mercury, and Lincoln — had been sold at the dealership.

Based on the requirement by Ford Motor Company, Mr. Tucker opened Tuscaloosa Lincoln Mercury Company on Greensboro Avenue and transferred Mr. Shorty Foster from the position of general sales manager at Tucker Motor Company to the new dealership as general manager. My father replaced Mr. Foster and moved from the position of sales manager for trucks at Tucker Motor Company to general sales manager at the Ford dealership, a position he held until his death in 1964.

*The Tuscaloosa News*, **June 18, 1946**
**Passenger car tire prices raised**
Washington, June 18: OPA today announced an immediate increase of 3.3% in retail ceiling prices for passenger car tires.

The same percentage increase, granted to offset producers' higher wages and material costs, was also granted to manufacturers and wholesalers. It also applies to motorcycle tires.

The new retail ceiling for the popular size 6:00-16 4-ply passenger cars, which OPA said represented 70% of all passenger tire sales, is $15.70 on a nation-wide basis. This is an increase of 50 cents.

The higher prices apply only to tires for replacement purposes. Last week OPA granted manufacturers an increase on tires for new cars, but automakers were not permitted to pass this on to the public in higher prices for new cars.

*The Tuscaloosa News*, **May 19, 1947, page 2**
**An ad by Pullen Motor Car Company**
**Pullen Motor Car Company**
**527 22 Avenue          Phone 3183**
**Tuscaloosa's Buick Dealer Since 1908**

That you may know the selling price of the following new Buicks delivered to Tuscaloosa

|  | Two door | Four door |
|---|---|---|
| Buick Special | $1840.64 | $1896.93 |
| Buick Super | $1986.41 | $2067.82 |
| Buick Roadmaster | $2276.81 | $2364.29 |

These prices are established under handling, delivery and transportation charged as allowed under the O.P.A. and are given you with the hope that you will refuse to pay the excessive prices asked by some used car dealers during this unfortunate shortage of automobiles. Help us stamp our this "Black Market."

The acronym ABCD is an acronym used by local car dealerships to steer customers away from unethical advertising by other dealerships. The four letters represent:

A. Sell cars to dealers you trust.

B. Require a trade-in to obtain delivery of a new car, but if you do have a car for trade-in, we would appreciate your trading it to us.

C. Require you to purchase any accessory you do not want.

D. Penalize you by making an unjustified low allowance for the car you trade.

**When can you expect delivery?**
If you are one of those individuals who placed a signed order and a deposit with our company, we estimate at the present rate of production it will take approximately six to eight months to liquidate these orders. Deliveries are being made in rotation with the older orders being filled first.

The waiting period can be drastically reduced by an increase in production which we hope will come in early summer when more steel becomes available. In the meantime, your patience and understanding will be of great assistance in dealing with the temporary shortage of automobiles and on over which we have no control.

**Personal note:**
As noted earlier in an article from the *Tuscaloosa News* of March 2, 1942, production of automobiles and trucks was stopped in March 1942

due to the World War II effort and did not resume until after World War II ended in 1945. All 1946, 1947, and 1948 car models essentially were duplications of the 1942 models with modest style changes here and there. Ford was the first to introduce an entirely newly redesigned automobile, in 1949.

The buying public was eager to get back on the road, but production lagged demand by far. As a result, a "Black Market" developed in which some automobile dealers and used car dealers resorted to very unethical practices — price gouging, false advertising, undeliverable promises, "below the table" deals and other unethical shenanigan practices.

In this ad by the local Buick dealership, Pullen Motor Company, warns the buying pubic to be diligent in noting false advertising by other automobile dealerships.

**Cost of new 1947 Fords**
The following prices for Ford cars can be compared with the prices of Buicks in the Pullen Motor Company ad.

    Deluxe 2-door sedan    6 cylinder    $1212
    Deluxe 4-door sedan    6 cylinder    $1270
    Deluxe coupe           6 cylinder    $1154
    Super deluxe 2-door sedan   6 cylinder $1309
    Super deluxe 4-door sedan  6 cylinder $1346
    Super deluxe coupe     6 cylinder    $1409
    Super deluxe 4-door wagon 6 cylinder $1893
    Deluxe 2-door sedan    8 cylinder    $1288
    Deluxe 4-door sedan    8 cylinder    $1440
    Deluxe coupe           8 cylinder    $1230
    Super deluxe sportsman convertible   $2282
    Super deluxe convertible coupe 8 cylinder $1740
    Super deluxe coupe     8 cylinder    $1409
    Super deluxe 4-door wagon 8 cylinder $1972

1947 Chevrolet four-door sedan

**Cost of new 1947 Chevrolets**
**Stylemaster**
    4-door Sport Sedan    6 cylinder    $1276
    2-door Town Sedan     6 cylinder    $1219
    Sport Coupe           6 cylinder    $1202
    Business Coupe                      $1160
**Fleetmaster**
    4-door Sport Sedan    6 cylinder    $1345
    2-door Town Sedan     6 cylinder    $1286
    Sport Coupe           6 cylinder    $1281
    Convertible Coupe     6 cylinder    $1628
    4-door Wagon, 8 passenger 6 cylinder $1893
**Fleetline**
    Sportsmaster 4-Door Sedan 6 cylinder $1371
    Aerosedan 2-Door      6 cylinder    $1313

*The Tuscaloosa News*, **August 1, 1947, front page**
**GM Announces hike in auto prices**
**Detroit, Aug. 1, 1947**
General Motors Corporation today announced a two to six percent increase in the list price of all passenger cars effective immediately.

"Price adjustments on specific models and body styles will be established individually by the divisions involved," the announcement said.

Cadillac, Buick, Oldsmobile, Pontiac, and Chevrolet were affected.

President C. E. Wilson said the company's first general price increase since last November

# COST OF LIVING

was necessitated because of increased cost of both labor and materials are too great for General Motors to possibly absorb through improved processing and the use of better machines and tools or from the potential increase in volume.

***The Tuscaloosa News*, August 13, 1947 page 2**
**New cars due to increase**
**Washington, D.C.**
Your chances of getting a car, new or used, will be a little brighter in the fall organized dealers and manufacturers said today.

But do not expect a return anytime soon to the days when salesmen chased customers instead of ducking them. Dealers still have a 5,000,000-car deficit to fill.

Both new and used car dealer associations said the removal of curbs on easy payment buying in November may cause a further temporary boom in the car market. But they believe new efforts by manufacturers and dealers to stamp out black market merchandising, the addition of more than 1,000,000 new cars over last year's output, and the end of the vacation season will combine to help bring used car prices down to a better level.

One of the strongest new weapons against black market, according to dealers, is a new type of conditional sales contract adopted by several large manufacturers and several individual dealers.

It is designed to keep buyers from grabbing 1947 models to turn over to used car dealers. Under this contract, the buyer promises for six months he will not sell the car to anybody except the dealer who sold it to him.

The National Automobile Dealers Association, representing about 40,000 new car dealers reports that already there are fewer 1947 models on used car lots as a result.

The Association says several courts have already approved the legality of the contract.

William Shuman, manager of the National Used Car Dealer Association, reported that his dealers have observed a leveling off since July.

"I look for a more sensible market by the end of the year," Shuman said. "After Labor Day, a lot of people who bought cars for vacation trips will find them a burden and get rid of them."

Shuman said used car dealers are making less than 10% gross profit. He said their prices are dictated by the high prices they are forced to pay. He blames price gouging on "bootleg" and "fly-by-night" operators and on individuals who sell their cars directly to other individuals.

These outrageous prices are caused by segments of the public with easy money who get on several dealers' list and speculate in cars," he said. "It is your own neighbors across the street who are to blame. We have had reports that doctors and other professionals who have turned over as many as 15 to 20 new cars."

The New Car Dealers Association surveyed 68 cities and found the average dealer had on hand twice as many orders for new cars as he expect to obtain from the manufacturer during the rest of this year.

Since production has resumed, dealers have resorted they had been able to deliver only about 30% of cars their customers have ordered.

## ODDS AND ENDS REGARDING COST OF LIVING

### Control of flies and bugs
During the period 1910s-1940s, many houses in Lafoy neither had screen doors nor screens on windows to keep out flies, mosquitos, and other flying pests. As a result, a market for many pesticides to help kill these unwanted critters evolved. The following is one example.

***The Tuscaloosa News*, July 1, 1929**
**An ad**
If you want to rid your home of flies, mosquitoes, every pest
Get the deadliest killer known
Black flag liquid meets the test

Spray black flag within the room,
Watch the bugs begin to fall
Every bug will meet his doom
For Black Faly liquid kills them all
Money back if not absolutely pleased
**Black Flay 35¢ for a half pint.**

**Wood burning kitchen stove**
*The Tuscaloosa News*, **February 2, 1930**
**An ad**
**Standard Furniture Company**
Wander range — $25,
Six eyes, large oven, warming closet, porcelain door and splasher. Clean and in perfect condition.
$1.00 down and $1.00 a week.

*The Tuscaloosa News*, **August 1, 1929**
**A want ad**
For sale: Four-gallon Jersey cow and young calf $35

**Providing milk for the family**
Almost every family in Lafoy had a milk cow, sometimes two cows if the family was large, that provided plenty of butter, sweet milk, and buttermilk. Therefore, a cow that produced a lot of milk was essential. The following article about pure-blooded Jersey cows is interesting.

*The Tuscaloosa News*, **July 7, 1929, page 4**
**For the farmer**
J. T. Powell of the firm Powell-Brothers Farmers and Merchants of Northport on last Friday bought of the Duloc Breeders Farm Corporation a pure blood Jersey cow "Violet Fontaine Rose" in a lot of three other cows of high grade and large production.

Experts who have looked over the abstracted pedigree of Violet Fontaine Rose pronounce her blood lines and production records of ancestry as taking high rank, and it is possible this cow is as well-bred as any yet raised or brought into the Tuscaloosa district. Her sire Fontaine's You'll Do

Wood burning kitchen stove

was imported in dam (dam is the word for mother of a calf) by W. R. Spann and won second prize at the Tennessee State Fair in 1914 as a yearling bull, his progeny having commanded good prices and a half-brother on the sire side of the bull You'll Do Victor that sold in 1925 for $10,000.

The grandsire of this cow on her sire side being the famous bull Imported Oxford You'll Do who won first prize over Jersey Island in 1911 and the sire of 60 daughters that sold for an average price of $1,015, also the gold and silver medal cow now selling for $3,000 at auction with a record of 16,361 pounds of milk, 1128 pounds of butter, and the cow Oxford You'll Do Imbellus with a gold medal record of 16,662 pounds of milk.

On the dam's (the mother of a calf) side of this cow's pedigree, is found many good bulls and heavy producing cows with records of 5500 butter and up and many prize winners at Kentucky and Tennessee fairs of recent years. Mr. Powell will of course keep abstracted pedigrees and other records of Violet Fontaine Rose for inspection by anyone interested in Jersey cow and Jersey history.

While this cow is advancing in age, she herself has a record of 10,965 pounds of milk, 531 pounds of butter at 1 year and seven months of age. It is the purpose of Powell Brothers to make careful selection of the sire of some brought into the district recently in the last breeding of this cow with the result that the calf, whether bull or heifer, shall bring the price paid for the cow in addition to the high production in the meantime and the hope of more pure bloods to follow. Local dairy enthusiasts are extending Mr. Powell many congratulations.

*The Tuscaloosa News*, February 2, 1930
**Herrin Piper Mule Company**
**2701 2nd Ave. North, Birmingham**
When you are in the market for good mules and horses, come to see us as we always carry a full stock of farm and draft mules and saddle horses.

We have a truck to deliver for no extra charge for two or more horses or mules if delivered in a fifty-mile radius of Birmingham if you are on a good road. That makes us just as close to you as your barn door and prevents you having to walk your mule home.

It will pay you to shop before buying, and we trade too.

## NEW CEMETERY IN TUSCALOOSA

The first cemetery in Tuscaloosa was the Greenwood Cemetery. It had its first burial in 1820. The first cemetery in Northport was the Old Northport Cemetery later known as the Stone-Robertson Cemetery. It dates to 1823. The Evergreen Cemetery adjacent to the University of Alabama was established in 1857. Most of the early rural cemeteries in Tuscaloosa County were located beside little country churches. The oldest was Bethel Baptist Church and Cemetery on the Watermelon Road near North River which was established in January 1818.

The burial ground for most residents in Lafoy prior to 1930 was the Macedonia Methodist Church Cemetery. However, from the time of the opening of Tuscaloosa Memorial Park Cemetery on the Old Birmingham Highway near Hurricane Creek in 1930 became the burial ground used by several Lafoy families. The following ad from the February 2, 1930, issue of the *Tuscaloosa News* is very interesting.

*The Tuscaloosa News*, **February 2, 1930, page 10**
**An ad**
A beautiful monument will be erected at the entrance to Tuscaloosa Memorial Park dedicated to the fine Tuscaloosa County lads who lost their lives in the wars of their native lands.

The names of each one is to be engraved upon it. This monument will be a thing of which all Tuscaloosa people will be proud. Plans for this magnificent memorial shaft are now being drawn. Therefore, we ask your cooperation in securing the names of all who lost their lives in the Civil War, the World War, the Spanish War, and all other wars of this country.

Drive our now and see this beautiful future spot of Tuscaloosa. Driveways through the park have already been graveled — a large fine nice-looking entrance has been decided upon.

Beautification starts immediately. Shrubbery, grass, and flowers will soon adjoin the first section of Tuscaloosa Memorial Park. Contrite curb, gutters, and storm sewers are called for in contracts now being let.

The perpetual upkeep plan means that the plot where your dead loved ones' sleep will forever be properly cared for. A reserve fund for that purpose is being laid aside from the sale of each lot. Funds built up to be placed in hands of trustees, under bond, to be used for that one and

# A ROAD, A CEMETERY, A PEOPLE

only purpose.

To you who have already bought their lot in Tuscaloosa Memorial Cemetery, you are urged to come by Duckworth-Morris' office at once so as the record of your transaction may be properly verified and closed.

Tuscaloosa Memorial Park officers and directors:

Fleetwood Rice, Vice President
J. F. Alson
W. P. Bloom
G. R. Brown, Secretary/Treasurer
J. C. Austin
Duckworth-Morris Real Estate and Investment Company
Exclusive agents

*The Tuscaloosa News,* **July 1, 1929, page 3**
Round trip excursion Tuscaloosa to Birmingham via Southern Railway $1.50

*The Tuscaloosa News,* **July 28, 1935, page 3**
**An ad by Brown's Dollar Store**

Linoleum rugs — 3 feet by 9 feet, felt base, $2.47

Special bath towel set — one large group, extra-large triple weight, beautiful pastel colors, five for 77¢

Window shades — 3 X 6 six feet, green, cream, and tan; 2 for 77¢

Boy's overalls — good weight denim, well made, size 4-12, two pair for 77¢

*The Tuscaloosa News,* **March 6, 1938**
**An ad by Sokol Brothers**
For the spring bride, a complete three-room outfit for $175 or buy any room individually.

Ten piece living room set $69 — sofa, four chairs, three lamps, coffee table, lamp stand.

Complete bedroom set $69 — bed, dresser, highboy, lamp, lamp stand, box springs and mattress, and two chairs.

A modern kitchen set for $49 with kitchen table, four chairs, pie chest, and large cabinet.

*The Tuscaloosa News,* **October 5, 1939**
**Yellow Front Store**
**An ad**

Matches, 2 boxes for 5¢
Peaches #2 Can, 2 cans 17¢
Delta Crackers 1# box 8¢
Soap Triple cake 3 bars 10¢
Corn flake package 5¢
Coffee 1# Wonder brand 10¢
Potatoes 5 12¢
Cabbage firm head 2¢
Delicious apples 1 dozen 15¢
Shoes, children oxford 98¢
Toilet tissue, 1000 sheets 15¢
Union under ware full cut 65¢
Men's felt hats 98

*The Tuscaloosa News,* **June 21, 1942**
**Hill Grocery store**
**An ad**

White Tulip flour 48# bag $1.85, 24# bag, 95¢
Sunnydale oleo 18¢ a pound
Del Monte coffee 1# tin 33¢
Kellogg's' Corn Flakes 3 packages 17¢
Bama grape jam 2# jar 27¢
Skim milk powder 7-ounce package 10¢
Jazz dogfood 5# bag 37¢
Mason pint fruit jars 59¢ per dozen
Prince Albert tobacco 2 can 25¢
Quaker grits 3 packages 25¢
Hills' special sliced bacon 32¢ per pound
White House apply juice 6 ounce can 5¢
Fresh crowder peas 7 ½ ¢ per pound
Fresh okra 12 ½ ¢ per pound

*The Tuscaloosa News,* **April 30, 1944**
**Baby chicks**
**An ad**

Thousands of baby chicks for sale
Assorted heavies (hearty back yard chickens of both sexes) $6.90 per 100, 500 $33.50
Strong healthy breeds — Barred Rocks, Wyandolies, White Rocks, Rhode Island Reds,

# COST OF LIVING

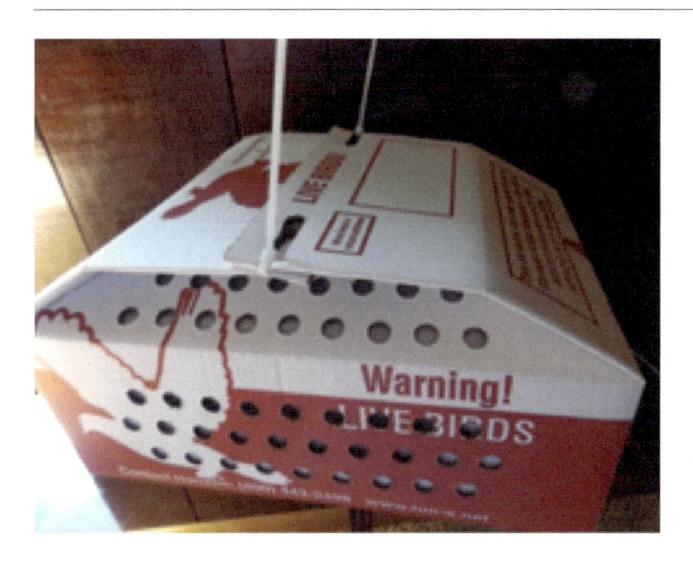

*Box used to ship one-day-old baby chicks*

White Gianis.

Shipped by US Postal Service, we pay the postage

Live delivery guaranteed

Atlas Chick Company, Saint Louis, Missouri

**Personal note:**

The idea of shipping one-day-old baby chicks is intriguing, but it was a common practice in the 1930s and 1940s. The shipping box was made of sturdy cardboard and petitioned inside for a set number of chicks — usually 50 or 100 chicks. Each chick had its own cubicle. The box had ventilation openings to allow air flow inside the box. Each cubicle held a tiny container of water. Shipping was given priority status and one-day-delivery was the standard. As soon as the chicks arrived at the local post-office, they were hand delivered to the customer. There were many venues available to the public for ordering chicks including Sears and Roebuck and J. C. Penny.

An article in the July 7, 1929 states that baby chickens can run about and feed within a few hours after they leave the egg.

**The Tuscaloosa News, June 1, 1944, page 6**
**Meat rationing to remain the same**
**Cheese and products reduced two points**

All meats not ration-free will continue so through June 1, the Price Administration said today in announcing these principal changes starting Sunday, in the point value of other commodities:

Canned carrots, orange juice, grapefruit juice, and blended grapefruit and orange juice are added to the long list of point-free processed foods.

All varieties of cheese and cheese products are reduced two points a pound to a new value of ten points.

The ration cost of canned evaporated and condensed milk is halved dropping from one point a pound to a half point.

The only increases are for pineapple juice up to 15 points for a No. 2 can and grape juice boosted 4 points to 10 for a pint container.

Butter stays at 10 points a pound and margarine at 2 points a pound.

Choice beef steaks and roasts continue to be the only meat cuts requiring ration points. Values are unchanged except for one exception. Chuck steaks and roasts are cut two points a pound. Flank steaks remain ration-free.

All grade D meat is removed from rationing for the months of June, but OPA said very few steaks and roasts of this low quality are sold at retail. Most of the meat from these animals is made into hamburger and sausage.

In continuing the ration-free meat bargains, the agency said overall civilian supply for June averages 310,136,000 pounds a week, a 9.6% increase over the 282,259,000 pounds in May.

Beef, veal, lamb, and mutton and variety meats will be in more plentiful supply in the new period. Pork, while still coming to market in excess of demand, will fall slightly in volume.

Allocations for cheese for June total 67,000,000 pounds as compared with 55,000,000 pounds for May accounting for the two-point reduction in ration values.

An increase in 50% to butter set aside for the army and navy reduced the monthly allocation for civilian use to 133,000,000 pounds from 145,000,000 in May when 50% of production was put aside. This tightens the supply but the over-all distribution situation is "regarded as good" said OPA.

It explained the point value on evaporated milk is being cut in half because with most meats being removed from rationing only 30 red points instead of 60 are being validated each month.

Evaporated milk is an important part of infant feedings and halving the point value will permit purchase with the same amount with 30 points as previously could be bought with 60.

The point increase for pineapple juice and grape juice reflects short supply and too rapid movement into consumption. Slow movement on the other hand brought carrots into to the list of point-free canned vegetables. Carrots go to a zero rationing from 3-point for a No. 2 can.

**Personal comment:**

During World War II, food supply in the United States had to be divided into foods needed by people on the home front and foods needed for the military men fighting on foreign soil. A very complicated system of rationing food developed and a point value assigned for each food and for each family.

Each civilian person started with 48 blue points and 64 red points each month. Thus, the shopper for a family of four had a total of 192 points for processed food and 256 points for meats, fish, and dairy products. Each month brought new ration stamps as the old ones expired.

*The Tuscaloosa News* **November 3, 1948 page 2**
**Christmas Lay Away Plan Offered Here:**
Santa Claus' modern right hand is neither Donner nor Blitzen but the lay-a-way plan. Besides making it possible for the reindeer to spend Christmas with their family at the North Pole, the plan that is featured by most Tuscaloosa merchants is a great help to Santa himself.

The lay-a-way plan reduces last minute Christmas shopping rush, reduces pocketbook strain, and encourages customers to buy early before merchandise has been picked over by holiday crowds. In society's effort to build a saner world, it builds a saner shopping system.

Quantities of Christmas merchandise has already been received by local stores, and the customary holiday atmosphere has set in. The stores are not too crowded yet, clerks are not too rushed, and there are many useful and lovely would-be gifts on display for the customer to choose from.

In general, the lay-a-way system requires a down-payment on the goods, and the remainder of the amount paid on installments. Some stores keep the article "laid-away" until it has been paid for in full. Others allow a certain portion of it to be charged.

Lay-a-way articles eliminate good hiding places for little children's toys and insure their surprise right up to the last minute. Santa will not be worn out after last minute shopping trips either, and can join the holiday festivities with as much vigor as the rest of the family.

Gifts from make-up kits to men's suits and from silver to cedar chests have already been purchased on this plan. Announcements from many Tuscaloosa stores that are sponsoring the lay-a-way plan can be found in today's *Tuscaloosa News*.

CHAPTER 17

# Windham Springs

Windham Springs is a community on the Crabbe Road ten miles north of my boyhood home. The area was home to several sulfur springs. In 1848, Levi Windham of nearby Pickens County discovered the area. The land was fertile and excellent for growing cotton. After obtaining title to the land, in 1850 Mr. Windham returned to settle there. He brought along fifty slaves to clear the land, and upon completion of that work he possessed a beautiful farm. The immediate area surrounding the springs was left in its natural state because of its picturesque beauty.

In 1850, Mr. Windham built a hotel and six cabins. He claimed that the mineral waters on his place had curative qualities. The news spread throughout Tuscaloosa and adjacent counties like news of a new patent medicine. The water was said to cure rheumatism, toe itch, colic, stomach acidity and most any other sort of ailments. George Christian, father of Northport businessman T. W. Christian, had supposedly been cured of a severe case of eczema on his legs, an ailment doctors were unable to cure.

After the Civil War, Mr. Windham lost his slaves and couldn't operate the farm or hotel anymore. The acreage and resort were sold to Sam Friedman and Company of Tuscaloosa.

Sam Friedman added several new cabins, bringing the total to twenty cabins. He also leased the hotel and cabins to local operators. The curative effects of sulfur water continued to attract people to the resort, and often there were three to four hundred people there at one time. Travelers who made trips out from Tuscaloosa, Jasper, Fayette, and Carrollton stopped at Windham Springs regularly because of the good hospitality, cool nights, and good meals.

The resort remained open until May 1917 when the hotel, several houses, and a church were destroyed by a tornado. The church and several houses were rebuilt, but not the hotel or resort cabins. A post office under the name of Oregonia operated there from 1848-1907.

When I was growing up, the only remains of

Windham Springs Hotel in operation 1850-1917

the resort were the springs and a shed over one of the springs where visitors could access the water, fill a cup, and drink it. I visited the area on several occasions, but the foul, rotten-egg odor kept me from even tasting the water, much less drinking it.

Visitor area at one of the mineral springs

CHAPTER 18

# The Joseph Enoch Rushing Family

The Rushing family has been an integral part of the Lafoy Community dating to the arrival of the first Rushing family member shortly prior to the Civil War. The 1860 Federal Census shows Prudence Melvina "Sook" Rushing" living in the Northport area. She was a sister to Joseph Enoch Rushing, the patriarch of the Rushing family in the Lafoy Community. Sook is buried in Macedonia Cemetery.

John Culpepper Rushing was born in 1846. He married Margaret Laird. Margaret was born about 1842. Both were born in Alabama. They had three children: (1) Prudence "Sook" Rushing. Her grave marker gives no date of birth. The year of death is 1917; (2) Joseph Enoch "Joe" Rushing was born on January 14, 1850, and died on November 28, 1936. He married Samantha Lenora Deason who was born on May 16, 1852, and died on August 5, 1911. They are buried in Macedonia Cemetery; (3) John D. Rushing whose date of birth is not known.

The Rushings of Lafoy Community descend from the second child of John Culpepper Rushing, Joseph "Joe" Enoch Rushing. Joseph Enoch Rushing and Samantha Lenora Deason were the parents of eleven children, ten boys and one girl.

I was born in 1939. My parents, Herman C. Boyd, Sr, and Lucille Farquhar, along with my brother Herman C. Boyd, Jr. and me moved to the Lafoy Community in 1940 and quickly became neighbors and friends with the Rushings. I had the privilege to see them frequently and to worship with many of them weekly at Macedonia Methodist Church. That association grants me the unique opportunity to share personal stories in this memoir. However, the most important connection I share with the Rushing family is that on June 2, 1962, I married Peggy Ann Rushing, a great granddaughter of Joseph Enoch Rushing and Samantha Lenora Deason.

After Peggy and I married, I was welcomed into the Rushing family. Peggy is the "official" Rushing historian of the family. She has spent many years assembling pictorial scrapbooks about the Rushing family. Her contributions here are invaluable. Without her help, I could not have produced this document.

A memoir is not a work of genealogy. It is a collection of reminiscences. However, in the instance of the Rushing family, I include some Rushing family genealogy. The first members of the Rushing clan's immigration from Germany that ultimately led them to Tuscaloosa County circa 1860 began in 1684.

**First generation**

Matthew M. Rushing was born before 1684 in Germany along the French border. He and his wife, Vrow, settled in Virginia. They had two children. The second child, William Rushing, is the line from which the Lafoy Community Rushings descend.

233

## Second generation

William Rushing was born circa 1720 and settled in North Carolina. He and his wife, Mary Paul, had ten children. The firth child was Robert Mark Rushing. It is through Robert Mark that the local Rushings descend.

## Third generation

Robert Mark Rushing married Jemima Jackson. They had ten children. The third child was John Rushing and is the line through whom Peggy's family descend. Three sons of Robert Mark and Jemima Rushing married three daughters of William Enoch Deason and Rebecca Shepherd Deason. Subsequently, there were several marriages between the Rushing and the Deason families.

## Fourth generation

John Rushing was born circa 1776. He married Amelia "Millie" Deason in North Carolina. John and Amelia had eight children. The fourth, John Culpepper Rushing, is the line through whom the local Rushings descend.

## Fifth generation

John Culpepper Rushing was born in 1846. He married Margaret Laird. Margaret was born circa 1842. She was born in Alabama. They had three children: Prudence "Sook" Rushing; Joseph Enoch "Joe" Rushing, born January 14, 1850; John D. Rushing. The Rushings of Lafoy descend from the second child of John Culpepper Rushing, Joseph "Joe" Enoch Rushing.

Sook never married. She lived with her brother, Joseph Enoch "Joe" Rushing. Family tradition holds that she had a disability the nature of which is not known. It is thought possibly to have been blindness. She is buried at Macedonia Cemetery in Northport, between her brother Joseph Enoch "Joe" Rushing and her nephew, Hayes Rushing. Joseph Enoch "Joe" Rushing's wife, Lenora Deason Rushing is buried on the other side of her husband.

## Sixth generation

Joseph Enoch "Joe" Rushing was born in Tuscaloosa County. His tombstone in Macedonia Cemetery reads "January 14, 1850." Family records state that he was born in 1852, not 1850. He died on November 28, 1936. On June 27, 1872, Joseph Enoch "Joe" Rushing married Samantha Lenora Deason. Samantha Lenora was born in Northport on May 16, 1852, and died on August 5, 1911. Joseph Enoch and Samantha are buried in Macedonia Cemetery.

Joseph Enoch and Samantha Lenora Deason Rushing had twelve children, eleven of whom lived to adulthood. They include: (1) John Gilbert "Gib" Rushing was born July 28, 1873 and died December 30, 1939; (2) Joseph David "Gin" Rushing was a twin to Thomas Hillman "Jack" Rushing and was born on October 15, 1876 and died April 22, 1943; (3) Thomas Hillman "Jack" Rushing was a twin to Josepha David "Gin" Rushing and was born October 15, 1876 and died November 9, 1942; (4) James Willie "Will" Rushing was born on August 20, 1879 and died January 1, 1934; (5) Lenora Belle "Lou" Rushing was born on February 14, 1882 and died on March 19, 1954; (6) Marvin Goldman Rushing was born on October 8, 1884 and died on February 17, 1947; (7) Joshua "Josh" Mills Rushing was born on April 25, 1887 and died on June 30, 1961; (8) an unnamed infant whose date of birth is not known is buried in an unmarked grave at Macedonia. (9) Sylvester Hayes was born on September 11, 1889 and died on May 25, 1953; (10) Hewitt Ashley Rushing was a twin to James Knox Polk Rushing and was born on September 9, 1892 and died on March 1, 1947; (11) James Knox Polk was a twin to Hewett Ashley Rushing and was born on September 9, 1892 and died on August 18, 1967; (12) Robert Edward Lee Rushing was born on May 15, 1895 and died on March 15, 1982.

Joseph Enoch and Samath Deason's fifth child, Lenora Belle "Lou" Rushing, married Early Monroe Hyche. That marriage produced two

# THE JOSEPH ENOCH RUSHING FAMILY

The Ed Earnest family

children; (1) Wayland; (2) Lenora. Lenora married Ed Earnest.

**Obit for Mrs. Lou Hyche**
Mrs. Lou Bell Rushing Hyche, 72, of the Crabbe Road died Thursday afternoon, March 19, 1954, at Druid City Hospital. Funeral service will be held March 20 at Macedonia Methodist Church with the Rev. J. E. Horton and Rev. Tim Powell officiating with burial in the church cemetery with Jones and Spigener in charge.

Surviving is: one son, Wayland Hyche; a daughter, Mrs. Ed Earnest; three brothers, Polk, Josh, and Robert Rushing; seven grandchildren.

Active pallbearers will be nephews, Roy Rushing, John Rushing, Preston Rushing, Minor Medders and David Rushing.

Honorary pallbearers will be Dr. Luther Davis, Spurgeon Black, Gil Hamner, Anthony Renfroe, Ed Turner, Nathan Chism, Sam Palmer, Carl Adams, Belton and Elmer Earnest and Curtis Hamner.

**The Joseph Enoch Rushing farm and home**
Joseph Enoch Rushing and his wife Samantha Lenora Deason purchased land on the east side of the Crabbe Road starting at the Carrolls Creek bridge and extending north to what is now identified as Chism Road. Their home was at the intersection of what in 2024 is Rushing Loop and Sleepy Valley Road. The dates of the births of their children extend from 1873 to 1895, but it is not known if they were living in the house at the time all their children were born.

The house as seen in the following photograph portrays a sturdy wood-plank exterior building with a wood-shingle roof. The house faced west and a long porch extended across the front of the house. At the time of this photograph, the house sat only thirty or so feet off the original Crabbe Road. The Crabbe Road was paved with asphalt circa 1947. When the road was paved, the long curve in the road that ran in front of the Rushing house was made straight. The old curve segment was named Rushing Loop Road.

Following Samantha Lenora's death, Lenora Belle "Lou" Rushing and her husband Early Monroe Hyche and their children Wayland and Lenora lived in the house, along with Hayes Rushing who never married.

Over the years, additions to the house have been made. It still stands but has little resemblance to the original structure.

**Obit for Joseph Enoch "Joe" Rushing**
Joseph Enoch Rushing, prominent Tuscaloosa County farmer and known by many as "Uncle Joe," died on August 5, 1911 and was buried Saturday afternoon in Macedonia Cemetery following services in the church there. He died at his home on the Crabbe Road on Friday after a prolonged illness.

Mr. Rushing, who was 85 years old, was a lifelong resident of this county and prominent in all community activities at Macedonia. He was a

235

# A ROAD, A CEMETERY, A PEOPLE

The Joseph Enoch Rushing family standing in front of the Rushing house, circa 1921
Based on the ages of the children identified in the photo, the date is circa 1921. Joseph Enoch is standing in the second row, the sixth person from the left and is between two females, Clara Bell "Jim" Rushing and Mrs. Mittie Williams Snyder Rushing the wife of John Gilbert "Gib" Rushing. Samantha Lenora Deason Rushing was deceased at the time. She died on August 5, 1911. Joseph Enoch would die a few years later, on November 28, 1936.

Joseph Enoch Rushing and his eleven children
Front row L-R: Joseph Enoch "Joe" Rushing; John Gilbert "Gib" Rushing; Joseph David "Gin" Rushing; Thomas Hillman "Jack" Rushing (Roy Rushing's father); James Will Rushing
Back row L-R: Robert E. Lee Rushing; James Knox Polk Rushing; Hewett Ashley Rushing; Sylvester Hayes Rushing; Joshua Mills "Josh" Rushing; Marvin Goldman Rushing; Lenora Belle "Lou" Rushing

trustee of the church for many years and active in church life. He was a trustee of Lafoy School for many years and active in school affairs. Friends from all parts of the county gathered for the last rites.

Surviving Mr. Rushing are 10 children and 41 grandchildren and 11 great grandchildren. The children include one daughter, Mrs. Lou Rushing Hyche and nine sons: Gilbert "Gib" Rushing; Joseph David "Gin" Rushing; Thomas Hillman "Jack" Rushing; Goldman Rushing; Josh Rushing; Hayes Rushing; Polk Rushing; Hewitt Rushing; and Robert Rushing.

Pallbearers for the funeral were grandsons Howard, John, Roy, James. and Joe Rushing and Wayland Hyche.

Honorary pallbearers were Joe Rice, R. L. Shamblin, Frank Rice, L. C. Curry, Hull Cummins, O. J. Hamner, B. A. Renfroe, C. S. "Boss" Hinton, Bill

# THE JOSEPH ENOCH RUSHING FAMILY

The Joseph Enoch Rushing house in the 2020s
The long front porch was removed years ago.

Koster, J. I. McGee, H. G. Shepherd, and Gary McGee. Foster's Funeral Home was in charge.

**Memories**
It is not my intent here to provide a family history of all the eleven children of Joseph Enoch and Samantha Lenora Rushing. I limit comments to the names of spouses and their children. In instances where I had closer contact, I present more information, especially in the case of the Thomas Hillman "Jack" Rushing family. He was my wife's granddaddy.

**John Gilbert "Gib" Rushing, 1st child**
John Gilbert "Gib" Rushing was born July 28, 1873. He married Millie Williamson Snyder on June 9, 1910. They both are buried in Williamson Cemetery in Northport. They had four children: Josephine (NMN) Rushing, born November 6, 1910; John Emil Rushing, born March 2, 1913; Joe Raiford Rushing, born March 10, 1916; Betty Ruth Rushing, born December 10, 1927.

**Joseph David "Gin" Rushing, 2nd child**
Joseph David "Gin" Rushing was born on October 15, 1876. He was a twin to Thomas Hillman "Jack" Rushing. "Gin" married Permelia Alma Hamner on March 16, 1903. "Gin" and Permelia are both buried in Macedonia Cemetery. They had six children: John David Rushing, born December 21, 1904; Etta Alma Rushing, born May 17, 1906; Theo Mae Rushing, born October 4, 1907; Margaret Lucille Rushing, born January 6, 1910; Woodrow "Bunk" Rushing, born June 23, 1912; James Cleveland Rushing, born June 24, 1916.

**Thomas Hillman "Jack" Rushing, 3rd child**
Thomas Hillman "Jack" Rushing was born on October 15, 1876. He was a twin to Joseph David "Gin" Rushing. "Jack" married Annie Brazile "Brizzie" or "Peggy" Hamner on October 15, 1902. Annie Brazile was a sister to Permelia Hamner, wife of "Gin" Rushing. Twin Rushing boys married Hamner sisters.

"Jack" and Annie Brazile are buried in Macedonia Cemetery.

Thomas Hillman and Annie Brazile had ten children: Ozella Bertice "Bert" Rushing was born on February 21, 1904; Clara Bell "Jim" Rushing was born December 26, 1906; Edward Nathan Rushing was born on July 2, 1908 and died two days later; Joseph Howard "Runt" Rushing was born on March 4, 1910; Temperance Hagler "Temp" Rushing was born on January 17, 1911; Roy Marshall Rushing was born on September 11, 1912; Nell Irene Rushing was born on December 22, 1914; Truman Hillman Rushing was born on October 1, 1916; Annie Gladys Rushing was born on December 30, 1918; Anthony Leon Rushing was born on March 9, 1921 and died on January 12, 1923.

**Obit for Thomas Hillman Rushing, November 9, 1942**
Thomas Hillman Rushing, widely known Tuscaloosa farmer, died Monday afternoon at his home on the Crabbe Road after an illness lasting a year. He was a lifelong member of Macedonia Meth-

odist Church and was active in religious and social affairs of his community.

Funeral services were to be held this afternoon at 3:30 from the Macedonia Church with the Reverend J. C. Maske and the Rev. I. T. Carlson officiating. Jones and Spigener will direct internment in Macedonia Cemetery.

He is survived by his widow, Mrs. Pearl Rushing and eight children: Mrs. Herman Thomas; Mrs. Clyde Utley; Miss Temp Rushing; Howard Rushing; and Roy Rushing all of Northport; Mrs. Ed Owens of Monroeville; Mrs. Robert Romaine of Gordonsville, Tennessee; and Truman H. Rushing of Fort Brady, Michigan; and a stepson, Truman Smelley.

He is also survived by four grandchildren and seven brothers: John Gilbert "Gib" Rushing; Marvin Goldman Rushing; Joshua Mills "Josh" Rushing; Sylvester Hayes Rushing; James Knox Polk Rushing; Robert E. Lee Rushing; and Hewett Ashley Rushing; and one sister Mrs. Lou Hyche.

Active pallbearers for the funeral were to be Wayland Hyche, Nathan Chism, James Rushing, Woodrow Rushing, Joe Rushing, and Harwood Hamner.

Honorary pallbearers will include Charlie Newman, Gus Kennedy, B. A. Renfroe, Wiley Hagler, Billy Clements, John Cole, Lester Taylor, U. P. McKinly, Judge Herbert Findley, Dr. W. M. Faulk, Judge Chester Walker, Judge Fleetwood Rice, J. E. Barrett, Dewey Lunceford, Festus Shamblin, C. E. Lamb, and Howard Maxwell.

### James Willie Snow "Will" Rushing, 4th child
James Willie Snow "Will" Rushing was born on August 20, 1879. "Will" married Fannie Lee Gay on February 13, 1907. "Will" and Fannie had two children: Azilee "Dee" Rushing was born December 27, 1907; Annie Snow "Sally" Rushing

Will Rushing family: Will, Azilee and Fannie Gay Rushing
Note the dogtrot in the middle of the house.

was born May 13, 1913.

### Obit for Will Rushing
### January 1, 1934
An extended illness resulted in the death this morning at 3:00 o'clock for Will Rushing, widely known Tuscaloosa County resident, at his home on the Crabbe Road. His passing is mourned by many friends and family.

He is survived by his widow, Mrs. Fannie Gay Rushing; two daughters, Azilee, and Annie Snow Rushing; nine brothers: Gilbert; Jack; Gin; Goldman; Polk; Hewitt; Josh; Hayes; and Robert; one sister, Mrs. Early Hyche and several nieces and nephews.

Funeral services will be held Tuesday at 11:00 o'clock in Macedonia Methodist Church of which he was a member. The Rev. Trimm Powell, the Rev. M. R. Smith and the Rev. C. L. Manderson will officiate with Jones and Spigener in charge.

Pallbearers will be B. A. Renfroe, Roy Faucett, Lev Anders, Jimmy Maxwell, Charlie Shirley, and B. V. Chism.

### Lenora Bell "Lou" Rushing, 5th child
Lenora Bell "Lou" Rushing was born on February

# THE JOSEPH ENOCH RUSHING FAMILY

The Goldman Rushing family

Josh and Will Rushing

14, 1882. She married Early Monroe Hyche on November 16, 1904. "Lou" and Early Monroe had two children: Wayland Monroe Hyche who was born on January 15, 1913, and Lenora Bell Hyche who was born on July 14, 1917.

**Marvin Goldman Rushing, 6th child**
Marvin Goldman Rushing was born on October 8, 1884. He married Ozella Judson "Juddie" Hamner on December 20, 1905. "Juddie" was a sister to Annie Brazile Hamner Rushing, wife of Jack Rushing and a sister to Permelia Alma Hamner Rushing, wife of "Gin" Rushing. A niece, Loubelle Hamner, married a fourth Rushing, Robert E. Lee Rushing, brother to Marvin Goldman and Thoams Hillman "Jack" Rushing.

Goldman and "Juddie" had eight children: Thelma Ann Rushing was born on September 29, 1906; Lottie Snow Rushing was born on October 5, 1908; Marvin Bernard Rushing was born on July 3, 1911; Alda Judson Rushing was born on June 7, 1914; Mary Lenora "Nona" Rushing was born on September 24, 1916; Buna Etteline "Dick" Rushing was born on March 21, 1920; Charles Preston "Pete" Rushing was born on September 24, 1922; Billy Gean Rushing was born on May 15, 1926.

**Joshua Mills "Josh" Rushing, 7th child**
Joshua Mills "Josh" Rushing was born April 25, 1887. He married Clara Barton Shirley on March 2, 1919. Josh and Clara had one child: Joseph Thomas Rushing who was born December 9, 1919.

**Unnamed child, 8th child**
Unnamed infant boy who died at birth. He is buried in Macedonia Cemetery

**Sylvester Hayes Rushing, 9th child**
Sylvester Hayes Rushing was born on September 11, 1889. He never married. He grew up in the Joseph Enoch Rushing house. After his sister Lou married Early Monroe Hyche and purchased the family house from her father, Hayes continued to live there the rest of his life.

**Hewitt Ashley Rushing, 10th child**
Hewett Ashley Rushing was a twin to Polk. They were born on September 5, 1892, He married Nora V. Turner on May 4, 1919. Nora was a sister to Annie Elizabeth Turner who married Hewitt's twin brother James Polk Rushing. Hewitt and Nora had seven children: James Enoch Bernard who was born February 20, 1922; Aimon Terrell Rushing was born August 2, 1925. Terrell was killed in a military airplane crash June

L to R: Hewett Ashley Rushing, 1943; Annie Brazile "Brizzie" or "Peggy" Hamner Rushing; Thomas Hillman "Jack" Rushing holding granddaughter Peggy Rushing. Peggy was born January 13, 1940.

3, 1963 and his body was never recovered; Susie Veteria Rushing was born April 9, 1929; Sylvester Hardin "Sam" Rushing was born on June 16, 1931; Billy Frank Rushing was born on May 28, 1933; Patsy Joann Rushing was born on January 1, 1936; Emily Nella Jean "Jeanie" Rushing was born December 20, 1939.

**James Knox Polk Rushing, 11th child**
James Knox Polk Rushing was a twin to Hewitt Ashley Rushing. They were born on September 9, 1892. He married Annie Elizabeth Turner on February 6, 1921. Annie Elizabeth was a sister to Nora Turner the wife of Polk's twin brother Hewett Ashley. So, Turner sisters married twin Rushing brothers. Polk and Annie had five children: Frances Kathleen Rushing was born October 17, 1921; James Valentino Rushing was born December 13, 1923; Eddie Ormand Rushing was born on April 3, 1927 and died two weeks later on April 17, 1927; Lessie Elizabeth "Boots" Rushing was born on October 3, 1928; Hazel Annette Rushing was born on August 14, 1932.

**Robert Edward Lee Rushing, 12th child**
Robert Edward Lee Rushing was born May 15, 1885. On February 11, 1923, he married Lou Belle Hamner. She was a niece to Alma, Ozella, and Annie Brazeal Hamner, wives of Rushing brothers "Gin," Goldman, and Jack Rushing. Robert and Lou Belle had five children: Wilma Maureen Rushing was born on November 26, 1923; Margaret Louise Rushing was born on August 4, 1925; Melba Lee Rushing was born July 13, 1927; Mary Evelyn "Cricket" Rushing was born on February 2, 1929; Mildred Denese Rushing was born on April 19, 1931.

**The Thomas Hillman "Jack" Rushing family**
Greater attention is given to the Thomas Hillman "Jack" Rushing family than to the other ten children of Joseph Enoch and Samantha Lenora Rushing for it is from this family that my wife descends and it is a family about which I have much greater research material.

"Jack" married Annie Brazile "Brizzie" or "Peggy" Hamner on October 15, 1902. Annie Brazile died May 21, 1927. Later, Jack married Pearl Hamner Smelley.

**The Thomas Hillman "Jack" Rushing home**
The Rushing property was first obtained by Benjamin Whitfield as a land grant in 1825. It was later sold to Joseph Enoch Rushing but the year

# THE JOSEPH ENOCH RUSHING FAMILY

The Jack Rushing house circa 1900
From: L-R. Clara Bell Rushing, born December 26, 1906; Thomas Hillman Rushing, born October 15, 1876; Annie Brazile Hamner Rushing, born April 10, 1982; Ozella Bertice "Bert" Rushing, born February 21, 1904

Due to the ages of the children, this photo was likely made in 1908. It is not known when the house was built or by whom. It was the house in which Jack reared his family and the one in which my wife lived until 1957 when a new house was built adjacent to the old structure. The house sat about twenty feet from the Chism Road. The exterior boards never were painted. In its original form, the house had only three rooms and two dogtrots. The section of the house shown in the left side of the picture had two rooms, a living room and bedroom separated by a dogtrot. An open hall separated the front rooms of the house from the kitchen shown in the right side of the house. The roof was made of wood shingles.

is not known. Notation of the location of Joseph Enoch's house, about a hundred yards southeast of Jack's house, has already been given. The builder of Jack's house remains unknown.

The picture below was made several years later during the 1910s. Another bedroom/sitting room with a fireplace and chimney was added next to the kitchen. It served as the bedroom for the four kids. A tiny bedroom not shown behind this room served as the bedroom for Peggy's parents.

Clara Bell and Bertice Rushing in front of the Jack Rushing house
This picture was made during the 1910s, several years after the picture on the left. Another bedroom/sitting room with a fireplace and chimney was added next to the kitchen. It served as the bedroom for the four kids. A tiny bedroom not shown behind this room served as the bedroom for Peggy's parentsisThe original porch was extended turning the porch into a "L" configuration. A new set of steps was built next to the chimney. Washed clothes are seen as they hang out to dry on washday. The family well was near the clothesline. The open area seen beyond the clothes is the west end of the dogtrot that separated the two front rooms. The young ladies are Clara Bell and Beatrice Ozella "Bert" Rushing.

**Educational opportunities for the Rushing children**

The Rushing children received their public education at Lafoy School located a half mile north on the Crabbe Road of the Jack Rushing home. An entire chapter in *A Road, A Cemetery, A People* is devoted to Lafoy School which opened in 1911 and closed in 1941. Jack Rushing was a farmer with limited income, especially during the 1930s when the Great Depression robbed many Americans of their financial reserves. However, Jack sacrificed in order to see that his children were afforded as much schooling as possible. An article in the October 1, 1933, issue of *The Tuscaloosa News* states that he, along with J. Hamner, were trustees of Lafoy School. Times were so hard that many children, especially boys, had to drop out of school around the age of twelve to stay home and work on the farm to help earn a living. That was the case with Roy Rushing, my father-in-law. Family tradition holds that in the 1930s, some siblings had to stay home in order that other brothers and sisters could attend school.

**Clippings from old newspapers noting Rushing children**

*The Tuscaloosa Breeze,* **March 13, 1913**
An article regarding a drama put on by the students at Lafoy school notes that Clara Bell Rushing performed a recitation "Writing Grandma." In adulthood, Clara Bell "Jim" married Clyde Utley. In the same news article, it is noted that the recitation, "Neberkenezer" was given by Herman Thomas. In adulthood, Herman Thomas married Bertice Rushing, a sister to Clara Bell.

*The Tuscaloosa News,* **March 20, 1919**
Miss Bertice Rushing is spending the week in Northport with her cousin, Miss Thelma Rushing.

*The Tuscaloosa News,* **December 8, 1932, page 2**
Students with 100 percent perfect attendance at Lafoy School during November were Rachael Grammer, Myrtle Ester Hamner, James Rushing, Maurine Rushing, J. D. Hamner, Frances Rushing and Joe Rushing.

Education was important to the Rushing family and parents saw that their children were in school unless providentially hindered.

*The Tuscaloosa News,* **December 24, 1933**
A large crowd attended Lafoy School's fiddlers' match on Saturday. A short play "A Saturday Night Social" was directed by Miss Lenora Hyche. "A Saturday Night Social" was a blackface minstrel production which caused much merriment.

Last Wednesday, as a closing exercise for the holidays, the Lafoy School gave a community Christmas tree ceremony that was attended by many patrons.

**Boyd comment:**
Lenora was the daughter of Lenora Bell "Lou" Rushing who married Early Monroe Hyche. Lenora Hyche married Ed Earnest, by whom she had six children. Later in life, she married Roy McAlister. Lenora is buried in Macedonia Cemetery.

**Making a living**
Joseph Enoch Rushing was a man who loved the good earth, a place that with toil and hard work provided a living for him and his family. The love for farming was passed on to his children.

The soil on the large Rushing farm was rich in natural resources good for growing cotton, corn, vegetables, and fruit trees. Several of his children — Hewett, Polk, Will, Robert, Lou Belle, and Roy — spent much of their adult years farming parcels of original Rushing land.

None of Joseph Enoch's children loved farming more than my father-in-law, Roy. After his marriage to Faith Vivian Ramsey on July 2, 1938, he turned to farming to provide for his family. However, earning a living at the end of the decade of the Great Depression proved inadequate to meet the needs of a growing family. He accepted a job at Gulf States Paper Corporation in Holt. After a short time, he knew shift work in a factory was not the life he desired. He turned in a resignation and returned to the farm. But God opened another door.

Roy's youngest sister, Gladys, had married Robert Romaine on December 23, 1939. Robert had just opened a new business, Romaine Concrete. He offered Roy a job that led to a long tenure. Roy was a very hardworking man and very skilled in concrete work. He remained with Romaine Concrete many years, but in his later years as aging took its toll he reluctantly "retired"

# THE JOSEPH ENOCH RUSHING FAMILY

Mules working in the Rushing field

following which he worked with Joe Hutt construction performing less strenuous tasks.

Throughout his work in construction, Roy maintained a large garden growing delicious tomatoes, watermelons, and vegetables of all types.

The desire to earn a living in the concrete business flows in the veins of the Rushing family. Roy's two sons, Larry and Randy and Larry's son Lance and Randy's son Shane and Shane's son Hunter all worked in the concrete businesses. Also, Robert Romaine's son, Jimmy and Jimmy's son, Rob, worked in the concrete business.

## The Enoch Rushing family in Lafoy Community affairs

The entire Rushing clan could be described as solid, hardworking, honest, civic-minded, middle-class people who befriended all. They were God-fearing men and women many of whom were leaders in church. Macedonia Methodist was the church in which Enoch's children were reared. As some married and moved away, they became active in other local churches. Goldman, Jack, Robert, Polk, Lou, Will, Hayes, Eddie Ormand, Joseph David, and the unnamed infant are all buried in Macedonia Cemetery.

The involvement of the extended Rushing family in Lafoy Community life is noted in other chapters relating to recreation, farming, Lafoy School, Carrolls Creek and Macedonia Methodist Churches, politics, the curb market.

## Faith Vivian Ramsey Rushing

### The cow story

The saying "a man's work is from sunup to sundown but a woman's work is never done" characterizes the life of Faith Rushing, my mother-in-law. Examples are numerous, but once again, sharing my memories must be confined to just a few. I will start with the story of her and her rebellious milk cow.

Like most families in the community during the 1930-1950 era, the primary beverage served at mealtime was milk, except for a cup of coffee for the adults at breakfast and iced tea on very special occasions. Faith milked the family cow twice a day regardless of rain, sleet, or snow during the cold months. The task was equally difficult in hot weather, and in fact was made worse in summer by biting black flies and horseflies that swarmed around the cow while being milked. To brush off the flies, the cow was constantly swishing her tail which usually had briar tips, little sticks, and cockle-bur in it which caused much pain when it was flung full force against the skin on Faith's face. There was yet another frustration with which Faith had to contend, the mighty kick of the cow's hind legs.

She once had a cow that was bad to kick when being milked. As Faith milked the cow, she sat on a little milking seat that had a board attached on which to set the milk bucket. The bucket was directly under the cow's udder. With the bucket resting on the stool, Faith could use both hands to milk the warm milk from the cow. Everything worked well if the cow stood still. However, the old hussy unexpectedly would give a strong kick trying to dislodge the biting flies from her hair. This of course, turned over the milk bucket and milk spilled into the dirt in the cow stall. One day Faith was frustrated beyond measure when this happened. Roy was nearby in the barn doing other chores. She screamed as loud as she could. "Roy, come here and do something to this cow." He grabbed a large old baseball bat and walloped the cow's rearend so hard the bat broke in two. That cow never kicked again while being milked.

**Learning to drive a car**
At the time Roy and Faith married in 1938, Roy had never owned a car nor driven a car. Soon thereafter, he purchased a used vehicle, possibly a Ford or Chevrolet. But by the time of Peggy's first memory in the mid-1940s, the only source of family transportation was an old Ford pickup truck. The family traveled little except to go to church and to visit relatives. On such trips, all six — Roy, Faith, Peggy, Larry, Linda, and Randy — loaded into the little one-seat truck and off they went. It was a tight squeeze as truck seats of that era were much more narrow than modern pickups.

In 1957, Roy's boss offered to buy the old truck from Roy but allow Roy to continue to use

1957 Ford station wagon

it to get to and from work if Roy would buy a new vehicle to be used by the family.

My father was a salesman at Tucker Motor Company, the local Ford dealership. Daddy sold Roy a new 1957 Ford station wagon. Owning a family vehicle to be used by Faith and the children was a major advance. Soon thereafter, Peggy passed her driver's license test. This allowed her to chauffeur her mother when she needed to run errands. 1957 was a banner year in yet another way; they build their new home on the site next to the old Jack Rushing house.

Faith had been a stay-at-home mom when the children were young. She depended on the hospitality of friends and relatives for transportation to home demonstration club meetings and WSCS church meetings, both organizations in which she was very active.

A few months after buying the station wagon, one morning she told Peggy as she was preparing to leave for school, "I am tired of looking at that car just sitting in the garage all the time when I could use it to go places. Today, I am going to practice driving it back and forth on the driveway. Go out there and back the car to the end of the driveway and show me how to operate it. I am ready to get a public job now that Randy is ten years old. You kids are old enough to take care of yourselves after school until I get home."

She succeeded. After passing her driver's license test, she got a job with Co-ed Collar Company, a fabric manufacturer in Northport. She had always enjoyed sewing and enjoyed her work

# THE JOSEPH ENOCH RUSHING FAMILY

but the job did not offer the opportunity to meet the public. So, she accepted a job in the children's department at Wiesel Men's Store in Tuscaloosa. She loved getting to meet people and help them select clothing for their children. She worked there until retirement.

There is yet another chapter to her learning to drive an automobile. That part of the tale was not discovered until many years later.

When Grady Shirley built their new home in 1957, the front porch was at ground level. However, the terrain sloped to the back and the back porch was high off the ground. This called for a long concrete staircase led that led from the back porch to the ground. The concrete steps were flush with the back wall of the garage. There was no separating distance between the steps and the back of the garage.

Probably thirty or more years after Faith's practice driving lessons driving back and forth from the garage to Chism Road which ran in front of the house, Roy discovered one day that the concrete staircase had come disjointed from the rear of the garage. He was very puzzled. Since he was the man who poured the concrete originally, he knew something had caused the dislocation. So, he walked around the house and examined the rear wall of the garage. There he found a surprise. The wood wall in front of the front bumper of the car was badly dented in. It was then learned that in Faith's initial driver's lesson, she had banged the front bumper of the station wagon into the wall. The shocking jolt had dislodged the concrete stairs from their anchor. It appeared Faith had conveniently forgotten to tell anybody.

### The collapse of the dining room table

One of the most exasperating moments that I recall in Faith's life during the years I was a part of the family occurred when the dining room table collapsed. Her dining room table was long and seated ten or twelve people. The mahogany table top was supported by a large single wood pedestal. A lovely linen tablecloth covered the table.

On a very special occasion, the table was set for twelve people. Tea had been poured into the glasses. Six or eight large vegetable bowls filled with peas, corn, potatoes, and other vegetables and cooked fruits were placed on the table. The meat platter at the center of the table was filled with a large delicious roast surrounded by its juices. Guests and family were standing around the table waiting to be seated. Suddenly, without warning, the pedestal snapped in two at the floor. The table top and all the delicious food quickly slid off onto the floor as we all helplessly looked on. Amazingly, most of the food stayed in its containers. A few glass containers were broken. Faith burst out in tears. "Roy, I want that table thrown away. I never want to see it again."

### The Joseph Enoch Rushing family and Macedonia Church

The history of the founding of Macedonia Methodist Church is given in another chapter. I merely note here that the *Tuscaloosa County Deed Book 55 of June 12, 1902* shows on page 247 that Mr. and Mrs. Eugene Benjamin Tierce, Sr., deeded land on which to build Macedonia Methodist Church.

The earliest date that Rushing names appear on Macedonia Church records is December 1904. They include Thomas Hillman "Jack" Rushing, his wife Brazile Rushing, and Jack's brothers Goldman Rushing and Josh Rushing. They joined by transfer of letter, probably from Northport Methodist Church which had been established in 1837. Jack's brother Robert Rushing joined Macedonia by faith on August 14, 1907.

Jack's daughters Clara Bell Rushing and Bertice Rushing joined the church in 1916. Azilee Rushing, daughter of Jack's brother Will Rushing and his wife Fanny Gay Rushing joined in 1916, as did Jack's brother Hewitt Ashley Rushing and his wife Nora v. Turner Rushing.

# A ROAD, A CEMETERY, A PEOPLE

CHAPTER 19

# The Mitt Lary Family

Joseph Milton Lary, better known as "Mitt," was a peach farmer who settled in the Lafoy Community in the early 1900s. His farm was located between the Crabbe Road and Highway 43 North, the Byler Road, just north of Carrolls Creek. During my childhood, the road passing through his property was a narrow dirt road. I traveled the road frequently. Today, the road is a major thoroughfare and carries the name *Mitt Lary Road*. The road had four narrow one-lane bridges to allow passage over four small creeks as they made their way into Carrolls Creek.

The Lary house was a small structure that appeared to be almost square, and from the outside one might guess it had only four or five rooms and a front porch. My parents frequently mentioned that the house was home to Mitt Lary and his wife, Margaret Rancher Lary and their family of seven boys — Joe, Jr., Frank, Al, Gene, Ed, James, and Raymond — all of whom were star baseball players. In my child's mind, I was amazed that so large a family could live in such close quarters.

Today, many sports minded individuals would say that the Lary family was the winningest sports family in Alabama history. It began with Mitt, the daddy. In 1916, Mitt was promised a tryout for both the New York Yankees and the Boston Red Sox. However, when the United States declared war on Germany on April 7, 1917, Mitt enlisted in the US Army before his tryout and served in Germany as a machine gunner.

When Mitt returned to the United States after the war, he met the love of his life, Margaret Rancher, in New York. They married and rather than pursuing professional baseball, they returned to his roots in Tuscaloosa County and to life on the farm growing peaches and other crops including cotton and corn.

The first son, Joseph Milton Lary, Jr. was born in 1922, and subsequent sons came along every couple of years, or more frequently, the last being Gene who was born in 1933. Life on the Lary farm was busy and difficult as the Great Depression swept across the United States during the 1930s. Earning a living during such times was not easy. The seven boys were kept busy with farm chores and attending school. The love of baseball was so ingrained in Mitt, that when the boys were not busy performing farm tasks, he had his sons practicing baseball. He made a baseball diamond in the front yard of the farmhouse and stood on the front porch instructing the boys in the art of pitching. He also instilled in them the history of American baseball, a national sport that began in June 1846 when the first official baseball game in the United States took place in Hoboken, New Jersey. In 1869, the Cincinnati Red Stockings became America's first professional baseball club.

# A ROAD, A CEMETERY, A PEOPLE

Six of the seven boys followed in their father's footsteps and perfected their craft as pitchers. James was the designated catcher in the bunch. James, the second son born in 1923, was also a musician and an all-state tuba player while a student at Tuscaloosa County High School.

Patriotism ran strong in the blood of the Lary family. Like their father, the Lary brothers served their country in its armed forces. James served in the US Army in Italy. Joe Jr., Raymond, and Ed served in the US Navy. Frank was a member of the Alabama National Guard and Al served in the Korean War. The boys joked that Al was the luckiest as he was assigned the duty of being Marilyn Monroe's personal escort during her trips to Korea.

Each of the Lary boys attended the University of Alabama all earing prestigious sports awards. Joe Jr. was the first Lary to enter the University of Alabama after World War II ended. He earned two letters in baseball and was a part of the 1947 Alabama SEC championship team. Joe Jr., Al, Ed, Frank, and Gene earned athletic scholarships to the University of Alabama. Frank and Al were part of the 1950 SEC championship team and secured a spot in the university's first college world series. Ed and Al were the only two brothers who also played football at Alabama. Al became a first-team All-SEC and All-American selection in 1950 and held almost every receiving record at Alabama during his time on campus. He was named the top all-around athlete at Alabama in 1950. Gene was the last Lary to attend the University of Alabama. He earned four letters in baseball and helped lead Alabama to the 1955 SEC championship.

After graduating from college, Joe Jr., Ed, Al, and Frank all played on the Tuscaloosa Indians semiprofessional baseball team before entering the professional ranks. The story of the Tuscaloosa Indians semiprofessional team began with the 1950 UA baseball season. The 1950 UA season began with a 2-3 record as the Crimson Tide lost two separate road games to Stetson University in DeLand, Florida and Rollins College in Winter Heaven, Florida. The games were Alabama's first appearances in the College World Series, a fledgling organization only in its fourth season. Following the unsuccessful trip to Florida, the Tide baseball coach, Tilden "Happy" Campbell, had already penciled in his team to play the first of two exhibition games against the Birmingham Barons, then a minor league affiliate for the Boston Red Sox. Frank Lary had been the standout on the Florida trip. He posted the lowest earned run average, 2.3, the statistic used to measure a pitcher's effectiveness obtained by calculating the average number of earned runs scored against the pitcher in every nine innings pitched. An ERA between 2.00 and 3.00 is considered excellent and is only achieved by the best pitchers in the league. Brothers Ed and Al also scored well.

The Tide beat the Barons 23-5 in Rickwood Field in Birmingham. Happy Campbell played all 21 players he took to the ballpark that day. The Tide continued to win in March and April posting a 14-4 overall to clinch a spot in the SEC playoff against Kentucky. Alabama took the best-of-five games with Frank Lary getting the win over the Wildcats in game one.

As professional athletes, Frank led the way for the Lary boys. He was a Major League baseball pitcher for the Detroit Tigers (1954-1964), New York Mets (1964, 1965), Milwaukee Braves (1964) and Chicago White Sox (1965). He led the American League with 21 wins in 1956 and ranked second in the same category with 23 wins in 1961. He was selected to the American League All-Star team in 1960 and 1961 and won the Gold Glove Award in 1961. He was known as "Taters," "Mule," and the "Yankee Killer." The later nickname was won due to his 27-10 record against the New York Yankees from 1965-1961. At one point, Frank beat the Yankees 14 or 15 games.

Frank had an apartment in Detroit. Family legend states that Frank would invite Mickey

# THE MITT LARY FAMILY

Mantle, Yogi Berra, and Roger Morris to his apartment to hang out the night before a ballgame and enjoy being together. Then the next day, he would go on the field and strike them out.

Al Lary was six 6 feet, 3 inches tall and weighed 185 pounds. He signed his first contract with the Chicago Cubs before the 1951 season. He spent 1953 in military service. He was a right-handed pitcher who appeared in 29 games—16 as a pitcher and one as a pinch hitter—for the Chicago Cubs of Major League Baseball from 1954 and again in 1962 with a seven-year lapse.

Gene was the last of the Lary boys to attend UA. He earned four letters in baseball and helped lead Alabama to the 1955 SEC championship. He was also named to the Alabama all-century team.

After the Larys completed their baseball playing careers, most returned to their roots in Tuscaloosa County. Frank opened a Phillips 66 filling station and was involved in the Tuscaloosa County Commission until his retirement. Gene opened a trophy shop in Northport, and after his death, his family continued to operate the business. Joe Jr. was a baseball coach and school teacher at Holt High School and also operated a radio repair shop. Al, too, was a school teacher and opened a carpet cleaning business. Ed was employed by B. F. Goodrich Tire until his retirement.

Al was the last Lary brother to die, December 2017. The original Lary house still stands. Four roads near the family farm carry the Lary name—Mitt Lary Road, Frank Lary Road, Lary Lake Road, and Lary Cutoff Road.

# A ROAD, A CEMETERY, A PEOPLE

CHAPTER 20

# The Joel T. Shirley Family

~

The following memoir by Sara Shirley Brown is a collection of memories she has of her beloved maternal grandparents, Joel Thomas 'Tom" Shirley (March 6, 1866-July 9, 1943) and Sara Ida Curry Shirley (August 16, 1873-July 29, 1961). Tom and Ida were married January 12, 1893. They lived their early married years in Pickens County. Sara does not know when they moved to the Crabbe Road near Carrolls Creek in Tuscaloosa County but it can be concluded with a high degree of accuracy that it was between April 20, 1904, and 1911. The April 20, 1904 date is the day they lost to death an infant daughter and buried her in Backbone Cemetery in Elrod, Alabama, near the Pickens County/Tuscaloosa County line. In 1911, they lost another child to death, M. T. Ormand Shirley. He was buried in Macedonia Cemetery on the Crabbe Road in the Lafoy Community, not in Elrod.

To affirm their residence in Pickens County, family records, including a receipt from T. L. Holman General Merchandise in Sipsey Turnpike, Alabama, a community in the eastern edge of Pickens County, show that Tom did business with the company on July 18, 1894. The earliest date of Tom's receipts from a Northport merchant, J. H. Anders Mercantile Company, is in 1912.

Tom and Ida had seven daughters and one son: an infant daughter died at birth, April 20, 1904 and is buried in Backbone Cemetery in Elrod; Mary Irene Shirley Pierre (6/9/1895-3/26/83) is buried in Backbone Cemetery; Maude Shirley Bobo (1/9/1898-5/3/84) is buried in Memory Hills Garden; Clara Barton Shirley Rushing (2/16/1900-10/22/84) is buried in Memory Hills Gardens; Pricey Gibson "Ted" Shirley White (1903-1933) is buried in Macedonia Methodist Cemetery; Julia Estelle Shirley Robertson (5/9/05-7/25/29) is buried in Macedonia Methodist Cemetery; Emile Mae Shirley Snow (2/11/12-5/28/96) is buried in Backbone Cemetery, Elrod; M. T. Ormond Shirley, (1909-1911) is buried in Macedonia Cemetery.

Sara Shirley Brown is the daughter of Emile Mae Shirley Snow and was born on July 16, 1933. Sara has one sister, Melanie Dianne Snow Jackson. Dianne was born September 6, 1944. Sara and her mother lived with Tom and Ida during the first years of Sara's life.

The house and farm Tom and Ida rented was owned by Mrs. Lola Rice Anders. The following is a copy of the rental agreement dated November 5, 1928.

"Whereas the said Mrs. Lola Anders does lease to the said J. Tom Shirley, for the term of three (3) years, all lands she owns on the south side of Carrolls Creek, and a parcel of land on the north side of said creek, where the residence of the said J. Tom Shirley now is and bounded on the east by the Crabbe Road, and on the west and north by an agreed turn row between J. W. Hallman and J. Tom Shirley, said being a part of the old Gay place .

In consideration of the use of the above-described land, the said J. Tom Shirley, agrees to pay $167.00 on the 15th day of November 1929, and $167.00 on the 15th day of November, 1930, and $166 on the 15th day of November 1931, making the total of $500 for the three years, and he further agrees to keep the place in as good condition as his means will permit, using his best judgment in the same.

Witness our hands, this 5th day of November, 1928."

Sara Brown tells the following story in the first person. Few changes have been made from the original transcript written in cursive penmanship.

**The Shirley house and yard**
In the 1930s during the years of the Great Depression, to reach Tom and Ida's place a person would travel north from Northport on the Crabbe Road, a narrow, crooked dirt road that after a rain was muddy and slippery and in dry weather hot and dusty. My grandparents made trips to Northport by mule and wagon as they never owned an automobile.

Six miles north of Northport, the Crabbe Road crossed Carrolls Creek and entered the Lafoy Community "way out in the country." The area was named for one of the first families to settle there, the LaFoy family. The Lafoy Community was a country neighborhood that was home to many families including the Shirleys, Hamners, Rushings, Clements, Tierces, Haglers, and LaFoys. Note: the family spelled the name "La-Foy." Others generally spelled the name "Lafoy."

Just past Carrolls Creek on the left was a little sandy dirt road winding its way through the fields to a small modest house and farm. This was home to Tom and Ida Shirley until his death in 1943. After he died, Grandma could no longer manage a farm and had to relocate. Shortly thereafter, the Trimm Hamner family rented the farm and lived in the old Tom Shirley house for many years. Previously, the Trimm Hamner family lived in a rented house on the east side of the Crabbe Road a few yards south of the Carrolls Creek bridge. That was the house my mother and my sweet stepfather, "Pop" Snow, my sister, Diane, and I lived in until I was grown.

The front porch of my grandparents' house was in the shape of a "L." I recall with fondness Granddaddy's routine on the front porch when he came in from working in the fields or from doing other farm chores. Near the steps and at the edge of the porch, there was a homemade stand that was similar to an old-fashioned sewing machine. The stand had boards across the top where he kept a bucket of clean water brought in from the spring behind the house. An enamel wash pan was kept beside the water bucket. The most cherished item to me was the soap dish. It has a special design in it. It is a family heirloom that I have and it will stay in the family. There was always a bar of that reddish-colored Lifebuoy soap. I thought it was so colorful.

Granddaddy would stop at the washstand, lather his hands with the sweet-smelling soap and rinse them in the pan. He then would reach up and dry his hands on a towel hanging on a rack nailed to the front wall of the house. The rack, too, is special to me; it is still in the family. He then would take off his hat, hang it on the rack and go inside to the kitchen to enjoy a good hot dinner (lunch) meal. As busy was life was, after eating he would take a short nap before going back to the field.

A door at each end of the front porch opened into the house's two front rooms. The rooms served not only for sleeping quarters but also as sitting rooms during the daytime. Heat from open fires in the fireplaces was the sole source of heat for the entire house, except for the wood-burning stove in the kitchen at the back of the house. There was no back porch.

Sheets for the beds were made of fertilizer

sacks that had been boiled in an iron wash pot in the back yard. Boiling the sacks was to "soften" the material. Even so, the cloth was still very coarse, not nice and soft like modern sheet material.

The house was built up off the ground with no underpinning. This allowed cold winter winds to blow under the house and up into the bedrooms through cracks in the floor. On really cold winter nights, flat irons used to iron clothes were kept in front of the open fire in the fireplace. The metal became really hot. When we went to bed, the irons were wrapped in cloth and put between the sheets at the foot of the bed to help keep our feet warm during sleep.

Like most items in the house, bed mattresses were homemade. I don't remember exactly how the process got started, but people in the community would gather at a common location, probably the Lafoy School house, and would work together in making several mattresses. The affair was similar to having quilting parties to make quilts. Someone brought the heavy blue and white thick mattress ticking, along with cotton that would be stuffed inside the mattress once the ticking was stitched together. A set of instructions gave directions. The final step was to sew the mattress covers together starting at the top and going to the bottom using large needles and heavy threads. Bed springs were the old open coil metal springs, not the nice box springs of today. The beds were not real comfortable, but it beat sleeping on the floor which was the only other option.

The front, back and side yards next to the house were bare dirt, not pretty grass lawns that were kept cut by push lawnmowers. In fact, no grass was allowed to grow in the yard. If sprigs of grass appeared or weeds shot up, they quickly were scrapped off using a sharp hoe and swept away by a brush broom made of tree or bush limbs bundled together and held in place by tightly wound and knotted strips of coarse cloth.

A dirt yard presented no problems in dry weather. However, after a rain the yards became one big mud pie. Since children went barefoot from mid-May until school began in September, mud got caked between our toes after walking in a muddy yard. Grandpa's yard had no sidewalks. So, to help us not walk in mud, large flat rocks taken from the bottom of Carrolls Creek were laid in linear fashion leading up to the front and back steps to form "sidewalks."

Grandmother and Granddaddy's yard was very neat and pretty. She planted and maintained beds of beautiful roses, verbena, petunias, zinnias, and marigolds. Something was always in bloom from spring until fall.

**Granddaddy and Grandmother**
Granddaddy was a stern, to the point person, as I remember him. I was only nine years old when he died. He had been sick for some time. He had started his farm crop in 1943 but was unable to finish it. Until harvest time, friends, neighbors, and family came in to help when farm work needed to be done.

Grandmother and Grandaddy were married on January 12, 1893 in Pickens County. At that point in his life, he apparently exhibited a more romantic personality than when I knew him near the end of his life. He wrote the following love poem to his sweetheart.

Many a leaf may cover with snow,
Many a year may come and go,
Many a sun may rise and set,
But you, Miss Ida, I still will never forget.

He was a hardworking man always able to make something of whatever little he had. Though seemingly an intelligent soul, he had little financially. As with many farmers in Lafoy Community, in the spring, he bought all his fertilizer, seeds and crop supplies on credit from Northport merchants. Repayment of debt was done when the crops were harvested and sold in the fall. Whatever money was left was used for general needs until the next crop and harvest time a year later.

Although there was not a lot of money for extras, there was always plenty of clothing which Grandma would sew. She was great at making and quilting quilts. Some of the quilt tops were made of recycled fabrics from discarded garments. She made pretty dresses, scarfs, table cloths and anything to dress up the home. The kitchen chairs were simple straight back wood chairs. Nothing fancy. She had a small dresser and a little table on which she set a kerosene lamp. Light for the house came from kerosene lamps or candles. Electrical service was not available in the Lafoy Community until 1940.

**The kitchen**
There is something special about kitchens, and hers was no different. It was the greatest room in the house. It was simple with no sink, running water or built-in cabinets.

In one corner, there was a wood-burning cook stove. Its cooking surface could accommodate six pots, skillets or kettles at the same time. A warming area was located over part of the rear one third of the stove. Left overs were placed there to stay warm until the next meal. At the back of the stove, a metal stovepipe allowed the escape of smoke and soot from the house. The stovepipe would get really hot and had to be spaced two or three feet from the wall to prevent the house from catching on fire.

Attached to the right end of the stove next to the oven was a metal tank reservoir that held about two gallons of water. Heat from the stove heated the water so that it could be used as dish washing water. If really hot water was needed to sterilize dirty dishes, it was heated in large kettles on the stove. There was no "water heater" in the house.

The stove was the only source of heat in the kitchen. During cold weather, it was wonderful to sit behind the stove in the afternoons after school. But, in hot weather, the kitchen room temperature could get mighty hot. Regardless of the heat, Grandma would do lots of canning and jelly making under these conditions.

There were two small tables in the kitchen. One was for water buckets and one for use as a work table. All water for cooking, household use and bathing had to be brought to the house in large buckets from a spring that was quite a distance from the house. We had to cross over a branch and go across the field to get to the spring. As a result, our family conserved on water usage.

The long homemade eating table was on the back wall in front of the window. On the back side, we kids sat on a bench. The adults sat on the other side in straight back chairs. When dinner was finished, all the dishes were cleared from the table. The food was pushed to the center of the table and covered with a big tablecloth. With food readily available, it was easy to go back to the table for an afternoon snack. Dishes were kept in a homemade cabinet known as the kitchen safe.

One of the most important items in the kitchen was the meal box, a wooden box built by my Aunt Irene Pierre's husband. The box was about waist high, two feet in depth and four feet wide. Two lids at the top of the box were hinged at the back. Under the first lid was a large compartment that was divided into two sections, one bigger than the other. Flour was kept in the bigger section. A big wood bread bowl or tray, the meal and flour sifter, her rolling pin and a cloth used for making biscuits, pies, teacakes were stored in the smaller section.

Corn meal was stored in the bin under the second lid of the meal box. Granddaddy raised the corn that he took to Northport to be ground into meal. He was very particular in selecting the corn that was to be ground. Only well-filled-out ears would do. After shucking the corn, he removed all immature kernels at the end of the cobs. After having about a bushel of corn shucked and inspected, he was ready to shell it using his hand-cranked faithful mechanical corn sheller. I enjoyed turning the handle but I was not as strong as he and gave out soon.

The metal corn sheller was in a wood box that was about four feet tall and about a foot wide. The round disc in the sheller was covered with tooth-like nubs. Ears of corn were fed into the opening at the top of the sheller and as they passed through the machine, the corn was "shelled." Shelled corn dropped to the bottom of the box. Corn shucks and cobs were fed to the mules. Grandaddy wasted nothing.

There was still one more inspection Granddaddy made before taking the corn to the gristmill. He would select only the cleanest and best corn to go in a clean cloth sack. Only then could it go to the mill. The miller took a portion of the meal as pay for milling. The finished product was rather coarse. So, when Grandma got ready to make cornbread, which was served at most dinner and supper meals, the meal had to be sifted to remove husks.

**Alabama Power brings the first electric utility service to Lafoy in 1940**
Available family records of Tom and Ida reveal that on January 16, 1940, Tom paid a $5.00 deposit to Alabama Power "to connect services to the stated address" Even so, at the time of his death in 1943, my grandparents continued to cook on their old wood-burning black iron kitchen stove. Their Alabama Power bill for the month of May 1943 was paid on June 3, 1943. The amount was $4.05.

The icebox, not a refrigerator, was located on another kitchen wall. As electricity was not available in the Lafoy Community until 1940, the only means of keeping food cool was to use an icebox. Her icebox had several doors. The top door opened into a shelf where a fifty-pound block of ice could be placed. As the ice melted, water drained into a pan at the bottom of the icebox. The pan was emptied when full but not before because melted ice water added some cooling effect to the interior of the icebox. If my grandparents had lived in town, the "Ice Man" would have brought a new block of ice as soon as it was needed. In rural areas, he came less frequently. Therefore, the doors to the icebox were opened only as needed and quickly shut to make the ice last longer. Only perishable foods got put in the icebox. It was not uncommon for all the ice to have melted prior to his next run. Most county people could not afford to make a long trip to town to buy ice every three or four days. The July 29, 1929, issue of *The Tuscaloosa News* contains an ad by City Ice Company listing the price of 50 pounds of ice at a cost of 15¢.

When we were without ice, to keep milk and butter from spoiling, other means were used. We were blessed with several streams of water nearby including the good spring where we got our drinking water. Milk was stored in glass jugs and butter put in water-tight jars that were placed in the very cold spring water behind the house. I don't reminder food spoiling

We ate breakfast by lamp light because their workday started before daylight. Dinner was served around noon, and supper was usually early, before sundown.

Granddaddy had a unique way of telling time. He wore no timepiece. When plowing in the fields, he could accurately tell the time of day by looking at his shadow. When it was cloudy and his body made no shadow, he and the mules seemed to know when it was dinner time. He would head to the house to eat and take a short rest.

There was always plenty to eat. Vegetables of all kinds, chicken, pork and sometimes beef were raised there on the farm. In winter, Granddaddy hunted squirrels and rabbits. Boy, could Grandma make a wonderful stew using wild meats! If he tired of these foods, he would rig up a fishing pole made from one of the stalks of cane in the cane patch. He attached a little fishing line, gathered his hooks, dug a worm or caught a few crickets for bait and headed for Carrolls Creek which was just behind the house. Before long, he would have caught several brim or catfish ready for Grandma to fry and make good hushpuppies.

When making teacakes, Grandma used no recipes. She would put flour in the wood bowl mixing tray, make a hole in the flour with her fist large enough to accommodate eggs fresh from the chicken yard, add butter that was freshly churned, along with sugar and just the right amount of vanilla flavoring. Sugar and flavoring were about the only ingredients not produced on the farm. Sugar was bought in large quantities on infrequent trips to Northport. She would work the mixture together, roll out the dough and put it in the oven to bake. The cookies always tasted delicious.

When all the housework was done and other duties completed, Grandma spent much of the time in the field or garden. Little time passed that she was not busy gathering fruit or berries or drying apples she would use to make wonderful fried apple pies.

**Grandpa's blacksmith shop**
Tom Shirley was a good farmer. He always managed to have the equipment and tools he needed for a task. Proper care of his tools was important to him. Everything was put in its place when not in use. His blacksmith shop was in a building nestled under a big tree out back near Carrolls Creek. Even though there was a large door at the end of the shop to allow smoke to escape from the room, the place was very sooty and smelled of stale smoke. Nevertheless, it was one of my favorite places to go.

The main function of the blacksmith shop was to sharpen metal plow points and to use in shoeing horses and mules. The fire used in blacksmithing was built in a metal bed supported by four legs made of rocks or metal. The fire was made from chunks of coal. A set of hand-operated billows was used to fan the fire into action. Once the fire had a blue blaze indicating it was at its highest temperature, Grandaddy, wearing heavy work gloves and using metal tongs, would hold the plow point or horseshoe/mule shoe in the fire until the metal turned red from extreme heat. He then would take the point out, hammer it hard on the anvil, sharpening its edges. He then put the metal into a pan of water to cool. The process was repeated several times until he was satisfied the point was sharp. When plowing, dull plow points do not turn the earth smoothly. What fun it was to watch him at work.

Granddaddy was one of the few farmers in the neighborhood who had a blacksmith shop. As a result, neighbors often brought their mules and horses to be reshod by him.

**Corncrib, mule stables and wagon shed**
The cribs and mule stables were the two biggest building in the barnyard. The floor of crib house was built a couple of feet above the ground. It was a favorite place for me to go. The area between the cribs and stables was wide enough so that the wagon could pass through. Depending upon the season of the year, the wagon might be loaded with cotton, corn, or hay. To pass through the area, Granddaddy had to open and close a big gate that was anchored to the post by heavy duty gate hinges. I enjoyed swinging on that gate as he opened and closed it. I did not weigh enough to make the gate swag.

The crib had two rooms, one to store corn and the other to store cotton that had been picked and was waiting to be carried to Northport for ginning. Once cotton was picked in the field, it was never left out in the field for fear of being rained on. If cotton got wet, the quality of its lint was reduced and the amount of money he received when it was sold was less. So, each day's picking was stored in the cotton shed.

A bale of ginned cotton needed to weigh between 450 and 500 pounds. A farmer could not take a wagon load of cotton to the gin until he had an amount of unginned cotton that would yield a 450 or so bale of ginned cotton. Granddaddy always knew when the wagon held just the right amount of cotton to warrant taking it to the gin, a six-mile one-way trip from his farm.

Several mule stables were across from the

cribs, one for each of the mules. A crib for mule feed was next to the stables. Mule feed included cottonseed meal and cottonseed hulls, both made from cotton seeds after the ginning process. Cottonseed hulls have little nutritional value. They are used as ruffage. Cottonseed meal has good nutritional value. Feed was placed in a wooden trough in each mule stall at feeding time. The mules also were fed hay that was stored in the loft.

The barn loft made a good place to play. To get to the loft, I climbed a wood ladder nailed to the side of the crib. Hay was stacked in bales, and we kids could rearrange them and make a nice sitting area. To get the bales of hay into the loft from the hay wagon, he, or a helper, pitched them through a large opening, or wide door, at the front of the loft. This was a job for strong men and older boys, not for girls like me.

The mule lot was behind the crib and stables. Mules were not allowed into the open pasture as were the cows. The mules got their water from a stream of water that flowed through the lot. A wood rail fence enclosed the lot.

The wagon shed was located behind the crib house and the mule shed. There, the wagon, plows, and slide were kept, always out of the weather. Granddaddy was very picky about caring for all his farm implements. All kinds of plow points and miscellaneous tools were hung on nails nailed into the wagon shed wall.

The slide was a homemade rig probably about one half the size of a wagon. It had sides similar to a wagon but not as tall. The slide was built on shaped hardwood rudders. It was perfect for hauling fertilizer, seeds, and tools to the fields. It was easy to be pulled along the ground when hitched to a mule. Also, it was fun to ride in. I liked to run to the fields about quitting time in hopes of catching a slide ride back to the house.

**Cow pen and pig pen**
Behind the mule stables was the fenced area called the cow pen. There were several stables for the cows. Cows were milked under a tin-roofed covered area separate from the stables. After milking, the cows and calves were turned into the adjoining pasture for the day. In the late afternoon, someone, often me, would have to go to the pasture and drive the cows home to the cow lot.

Granddaddy's livestock were well cared for, even the pigs. The pigs lived in a log-fenced pen near a branch of water. One side of the pen was dirt. The other side was floored with small logs or poles. The pen was on a slope. The boarded area was periodically washed out with water from the branch. Granddaddy occasionally would dig a deep hole in the pigpen, hoist and secure a pole in the hole and wrap crocker sacks around the pole. He then would soak the fabric with motor oil. The pigs enjoyed rubbing against the oiled rag. He said the oil would relieve their itching and help with dry skin.

**Chicken house, smoke house, potato house**
The entire farm was well organized. In addition to those already mentioned, there were several other outbuildings.

The chicken house and chicken yard were fenced in by a tall chicken wire fence to keep out foxes, weasels, and other predators. Inside the chicken house, neatly-cut roosting poles provided safety for the chickens at night. Nailed to one inside wall were several boxes lined with straw where the hens laid eggs. During the daytime, the chickens were allowed to roam freely near the house and barn. Occasionally, a stubborn hen would not lay her eggs in the hen boxes but out somewhere else in the yard. This made Grandmother mad. I enjoyed gathering eggs as long as there was no chicken snake in a box.

The smoke house was near the back of the family home. There, hams, bacon slabs, and sacks of sausage were hung up to cure in the smoke that came from a smoldering fire made of history sticks. Once the meat was cured, it did not spoil so it was left hanging in the smokehouse until needed. Anytime one went into the smokehouse, the delightful aroma of cured hams, bacon, and sausage filled the air.

Salt meat is the part of a hog's belly and sides used mainly as seasoning, i.e., grease. It was "salted down" or buried in salt in the roughly-made wooden box in the smokehouse. Grandmother used salt meat in cooking all those wonderful vegetables. Salt meat was very tasty when sliced, soaked in water to remove the salt, and then fried.

Potatoes had to have a house too. It was a roughly-built small log house not very tall. The roof was so near the floor that you could hardly stand up in it. The room had no windows and only one door. In the spring after the Irish potatoes were dug, the log house was called the potato house. Granddaddy would build a little frame around the wall with a board around its bottom. It was just high enough to keep the potatoes in place. The potatoes were spread on the floor to dry or cure out. The room needed to be dark to prevent the potatoes from sprouting. In addition to having no window, Granddaddy would tack up croaker sacks, burlap bags, to keep light from coming in through cracks in the log walls. Croaker sacks were burlap sacks in which livestock food, such as cottonseed meal or cottonseed hulls, came. After a certain period of drying out, the Irish potatoes were moved into the cellar, a dug-out area under our house. The cellar was a good storge place as it provided warmth during the winter and coolness in summer.

After the Irish potatoes were removed from the potato house, the empty house was made ready for sweet potatoes that were dug in early fall. As the sweet potato crop dried, they were moved into another small section to make room for the peanut crop.

The first step in harvesting peanuts was to pull the entire plant, vines, roots, and nuts, up from the ground. They laid open in the sun in the field for a few days to dry. Then the plants were stacked against a pole on a round platform there in the field. A cover was placed over just the top of the stack to prevent rain from getting into the stack. After thorough drying, they were moved to the potato-peanut house for storage. The vines were laid on the floor against the walls to help insulate the room. Then during the winter, when there was not as much activity, we would spend many hours picking peanuts off the vines and putting them in a crocker sack for storage. With no windows in the room and surrounded by peanut vines around the wall, we did not get very cold while working with the peanuts. On occasion, Grandmother would parch a few peanuts in the old kitchen stove oven. Boy, they were so good.

The fodder, or peanut vines, were used for food for the cows and mules. Few things were wasted on the farm.

**The farmland**
The farm was fenced and cross fenced. Any needed repairs were made after all the harvest was over. The fields were terraced to prevent erosion. To take advantage of every foot of land, Granddaddy planted fruit trees on the wide terraces. This provided fruit for the family and some shade from the sun for an occasional stop while working in the field. In addition to fruit trees, they had fig bushes and arbors for scuppernongs. A grape vine ran along the garden fence. There was a big strawberry patch that ran the full length of the garden. A big persimmon tree stood between the barn and the field. It made an excellent shade for the watermelons Granddaddy brought in from the patch. The pear tree was right near the back door opening off the kitchen. It was just to the right of the high wide steps. Grandmother made a lot pear preserves. A jar was kept on the kitchen table through those years just waiting to be eaten when Grandma got out the dough tray and mixed those wonderful scratch biscuits. It was interesting to see her pinch off portions of dough for each biscuit. All seemed identical as she laid them on the old black cast-iron baker to bake.

Not only were there tame fruit trees on the farm, there was a huge crabapple tree that was covered with beautiful flowering buds in the spring. The crabapples were about half the size of a regular apple. Although very tart, they were good to nibble on in the afternoons when driving the cows from the pasture to the barn to be milked. For variety, you could add a dash of salt. Wild huckleberries grew on the banks of Carrolls Creek. They had the same taste as tame blueberries.

There were many areas of Carrolls Creek on the farm that were shallow enough to wade in. The bottom of the creek was covered with smooth large flat rocks. It was a perfect place to wade barefooted during the hot summer days when the huckleberries were ripe. They were easy to pick because they hung over the edge of the creek.

In late summer and early fall, you could take a walk in any direction and find vines of muscadines hanging from tall trees. They were really good to eat just plain, or of course Grandma could take them and make jelly from the juice and preserves from the hulls.

**Granddaddy's interests**
Granddaddy had many interests. In the early 1900s, he was a lumber scaler, keeping records of timber cut from certain properties. He was always interested in news items from around the country. He subscribed to *The Atlanta Journal*, *The Birmingham News*, *The Tuscaloosa News* and other publications. During the time they lived in Pickens County, he was an active member of the Piney Grove Alliance which was formed in 1890. He served as secretary. His father, Little Berry Shirley, a Methodist minister, was chaplain of the organization. The purpose of this organization is not clear, but it could have been similar to the Odd Fellows of which he was a known member from 1908-1934. This is one of the oldest fraternal organizations in the United States. Its symbol stands for Friendship, Love, and Truth. He was also a member of the Woodmen of the World.

The many wooded areas on the farm and the good water supply were a perfect environment for wildlife. Granddaddy trapped animals for their furs. Once he trapped an animal, he would cut and shape boards of various sizes and stretch the animals' skins over the boards to dry. Animal hides were in demand in those days. He received a good price for the skins. His picture once was in a publication that told the story of his trapping.

On another occasion, his picture was in the newspaper featuring his well-known pole bean patch. The area of the farm across Carrolls Creek from their house was damp rich land. He cleared a portion there for a garden and planted pole beans. Due to its location, he often had a good supply of beans when other farmers had none. Sales from the beans brought additional income to the family. Once after his picture was in the paper and a story told of his abundant crop, a thief came in from the back during the night and stole a lot of beans and did much damage to the crop. The vines were hanging full of beans almost ready to be picked, He never learned the identity of the thieves.

The bean patch was across Carrolls Creek from Granddaddy's house. An area in the creek just downstream from the bean patch was shallow enough for the wagon loaded with garden equipment to ford across. But, the nearest route to the patch was just behind blacksmith shop where the water was too deep to ford. He solved the problem by having a foot log across the creek.

Could you walk a foot log? Well, you learned or fell off into the creek. The foot log was simply a big tree cut so that it fell across the creek and made a walking bridge. Granddaddy, or someone else, had taken an axe and chipped foot holes on the top surface of the log just the right size to fit your feet. Strips of wood were nailed along the side of the log to help keep you from slipping off. There was a crude handrail. Learning to cross the foot log was a little scary to begin with, but with some experience, I could practically run across the log.

The scariest time in walking across the foot log came when a snake decided to sun himself on the log. You might try to scare the snake off by throwing rocks at it, but if it did not move, you just went back to the house and waited a while before going to the bean patch.

**The pet cemetery**
Just between the blacksmith shop and the foot log was Granddaddy's pet cemetery. He had always been an animal lover and showed his respect to his pets as they passed on by burying them in their own little plot. He would place a river rock slab at the grave for a headstone. There was a dozen or so graves as best I remember.

**Using tobacco**
Grandma was a calm, peaceful little lady. She always had some funny little story to tell. You would not see her without her apron over her dress. She always had a handkerchief in the apron picket, along with a little worn tin snuff box and a little "tooth brush" which she made from a tiny branch from a black gum bush. She would break the little branch to about a three-to-four-inch length stick and fray it on one end. She used this to pick up the snuff and transfer it to her mouth.

Granddaddy dipped snuff also, but he had another use for tobacco. He grew his own tobacco crop. He gathered the leaves, let them dry and then ground them into a powder and used the mixture to dust his watermelon and cantaloupe plants to keep off bugs. Collard bugs were treated differently. This was a job I got to do many times. I would be given a little can or jar with a small amount of kerosene in it. The object was to hold the can under the collard leaf that had a bug on it and flip the bug into the kerosene which would kill it.

**Washing clothes in a washpot**
What did you do when your few changings of clothing were all dirty? You declared it was washday and got started.

The wash area was in the back yard near a stream of cold clear water. It consisted of a large black iron washpot and a wash bench with three No. 2 galvanized washtubs.

The first job was to get the water in the washpot as hot as possible by building a fire under it. Once the water was hot, dirty clothes were dumped into the pot and allowed to boil until Grandmother felt they were clean enough to be put in the first of two rinse waters in the galvanized tubs. Clothes worn while working in the fields, at the blacksmith shop, and while tending farm animals got very dirty. The same clothes might be worn for several days before being changed.

Upon taking the clothes out of the washpot, they were scrubbed on the scrub board, a rectangular board with a corrugated metallic surface. This removed dirt from the clothes prior to being put through two rinse waters. The only soap used was amber-colored octogen bar soap. Grandmother used no bleach or fabric softener.

Once they were deemed "clean," they were placed in the first of two rinse waters where again they were stirred vigorously by hand and beat with the paddle. After the second rinsing, the clothes were rung out by hand and hung out on clothes lines that were strung between trees to dry in the sun. Boy what a wonderful fragrance—clear sun-dried clothes.

**The rolling store**
My first memory of a rolling store is from the 1940s when Mother, "Pop" Snow, Diane and I lived on the hill beside the Crabbe Road near the Carrolls Creek bridge.

The rolling store was a kind of small grocery store on wheels. The vehicle was like a school bus whose interior had been converted into a small store. The ceiling was high enough so that one could stand upright inside. The shelves were stocked with cans of staple foods, sewing needles, cloth, magazines, matches, patent medicines, baking powder, soda, candy treats and other things. A few small windows on the sides of the bus provided light for the interior.

Two wood platforms separated by a set of steps were attached to the back of the bus. The steps led to the back door of the store. Two large barrels were anchored to the rear platforms; one held kerosene. I am not sure what was in the other barrel. The rolling store came frequently, but not more than once a week.

**Fun and games**

Despite chores, school and whatever else came up, there was time for fun but only when all tasks had been completed.

There were lots of children nearby. The Hewett Ashley Rushing family, a family with seven kids, and the Polk Rushing family, a family with four kids, lived across the Crabbe Road from my grandparents. These kids merely had to cross the Crabbe Road, a small narrow dirt road, crawl through a barbwire fence and run through the pasture or field of cotton or corn and they would be at Grandaddy's house. The Trimm Hamner family lived in a house beside the Crabbe Road just south of the Carrolls Creek bridge. They had eight children. One was Ramona Nell. Ramona died July 12, 2021. In August 2007, Ramona wrote me a letter recalling an event from our childhood. I share it here.

"I had gone over to visit Sara one evening and they had just finished eating supper and were cleaning up the supper dishes, putting the food away and "Miss" Emile asked me if I had ever eaten a pear salad, which I had not. So, she fixed me a pear salad which I relished with every bite. After all these years, when I eat or fix a pear salad, I always think of "Miss" Emile and how much I enjoyed that first pear salad.

"One Sunday afternoon, Mother dressed up us children in our Sunday clothes and we went over to visit Mr. and Mrs. Shirley and Miss Emile. We children were playing out in the yard, and Miss Emile called us to come to the kitchen door. She gave us each a sliver of chocolate pie. We went back out into the yard to eat the pie. There were a lot of chickens in the yard. I had taken one bite from my pie when a huge rooster jumped up and my pie hit the ground. He gobbled it up in just a few bites. Naturally, my heart was broken, but I didn't dare ask for another slice of pie. So, Max, my brother, gave me the last bite of his.

"When I was about five or six years old, Mother sent me on an errand to Mrs. Shirley's house. Instead of going around the pasture, I cut through it, not realizing that Mr. Shirley had a ferocious bull in there. He happened to see me walking through the pasture. He met me halfway, grabbed me by the hand and hurriedly got me out of there, at the same time telling me what a dangerous thing I had done. When we got out of the pasture, he said, "Child, don't you ever do that again." That scared me. When I got home, Daddy explained what the bull would have done if he had seen me.

"Miss Emile was always up to date in all areas of homemaking, cooking, sewing, yard maintenance, and gardening. She would have made an excellent Home Economics teacher. She was a very smart, self-taught person. She was a person whom you would be glad to call a friend."

We played jump rope using ropes that were used to hitch the mules to plows. Annie Over was played by tossing a rubber ball across the roof of the house to others who were on the other side of the house. The object was to catch the ball before it landed on the ground. Sometimes, we would draw a rectangular grid in the dirt yard and throw a rock into one of the grids. Standing balanced on only one foot, you hopped to the grid containing the rock, picked up the rock and hopped back to base, all the time balanced on one leg, without falling. Boys enjoyed shooting marbles. We often looked for an old discarded round metal rim that once had served as a band around a wooden barrel. We then would find a stick of wood and start the rim rolling and keep it rolling using only the stick. Girls played house using discarded cans or jar lids to make mud pies.

**The Carrolls Creek swimming hole**
One of the most popular places in the community was the Carrolls Creek swimming hole located beside the Crabbe Road bridge. The land belonged to the Polk Rushing family. They were glad to share the area with the community. There was no cost to swim or picnic. The swimming area was about half the size of a football field. The part next to the road was shallow, ideal for wading and for young non-swimmers to play in. The water next to the far side was deep, ideal for older daredevil boys who wanted to show off by diving from steep rock clefts that overshadowed the creek. Sometimes community picnics were held there as well.

The area around the swimming hole was a good place for teenage courting to take place. Lafoy Community was made up largely of Hamners, Shirleys, Rushings, LaFoys, Clements, Haglers, and Tierces with a few other families add in. Intermarriage among neighborhood families was common, including cousins marrying cousins. The "love bug" for many young men and ladies first appeared at the swimming hole.

The swimming hole was also used by Carrolls Creek Baptist Church for baptisms.

**Home remedies**
Doctors in Northport and Tuscaloosa made house calls to families who lived on the Crabbe Road, but many rural families first tried home remedies such as these.

Castor oil, an almost clear liquid, was used as a laxative. It had a terrible taste.

Sulfur powder, a bad-smelling substance, in small quantities was taken to help resist red bugs. Mixed with petroleum jelly or lard, it was applied as a paste to wounds on farm animals.

Baking soda mixed with water was taken in small quantities to help indigestion. Commercial toothpaste was expensive and hard to come by. So, baking soda also was used to clean your teeth.

Vicks Vapor Rub was rubbed on the chest if one had a cold, cough or congestion. Just prior to getting in bed, you stood before the open fire and let the fire warm your chest. Then, the Vicks was rubbed on the chest skin and a soft cloth was placed over the area under the pajamas.

Turpentine was rubbed on strains, sprains and as an antiseptic on open wounds.

Rock candy/whiskey was made by putting chunks of rock candy in a jar of whiskey. The whiskey would gradually dissolve the rock candy. The liquid was used as a cough syrup prior to bedtime.

Sweet oil was warmed and then a few drops put into the ear for ear aches.

**Obituary for Joel Thomas Shirley**
*The Tuscaloosa News*, **July 11, 1943**
Funeral services for Joel Thomas Shirley, 77, who died Friday night at his home on the Crabbe Road after an illness of six months, were held at 4 o'clock Saturday afternoon from the Jones and Spigener Chapel with interment in the Backbone Cemetery near Elrod.

Mr. Shirley was a native of Pickens County but had resided in this county most of his life. He is survived by his widow, Mrs. Sara Ida Curry Shirley, four daughters, Mrs. Frank (Irene) Pierre, Mrs. Ray (Maude) Bobo, Mrs. Josh (Clara) Rushing, and Miss Emile Shirley, all of Northport. He was preceded in death by two daughters: Pricey Gibson Shirley White and Julia Estelle Shirley Robertson.

Active pallbearers for the rites were Joe Rice, Jr., Howard Hagler, Woodrow Rigsby, Lonnie Shirley, Herman Boyd and Roy Rushing.

Honorary pallbearers were T. W. Christian, Roy Faucett, C. S. Hinton, Harry May. R. G. Parker, Ed Turner, Walter Bertels, Dr. G. W. Hall, C. P. Homan, Ollie Ramsey, Robert Rushing, James Anders, Verner Robertson, John Shirley, A. C. Kenney, John Hagler, and Wiley Hagler.

# THE JOEL T. SHIRLEY FAMILY

**Obituary for Sara Ida Curry Shirley**
*The Tuscaloosa News*, July 30, 1961

Mrs. Ida Curry Shirley, 87, of Northport Route 2 [Crabbe Road], widow of J. T. Shirley, died at noon Saturday at Druid City Hospital.

Survivors include four daughters, Mrs. Irene Pierre of Tuscaloosa, Mrs. Ray (Maude) Bobo of Ashville, North Carolina, Mrs. Clara Rushing and Mrs. O'Neal (Emile) Snow, both of Northport; two sisters, Mrs. H. T. Ramsey and Mrs. Lillie Anders of Northport; two brothers, J. C. Curry of Elrod, and William Curry; four grandchildren and seven great grandchildren. She was preceded in death by two daughters: Pricey Gibson Shirley White; Julia Estelle Shirley Robertson.

Funeral services will be conducted Monday at 11:00 a.m. at Macedonia Methodist Church by Rev. Bobby Shaw, the Rev. T. H. Wilson and the Rev. David Lewis. Burial will be in Backbone Cemetery in Elrod with Spigener-Brown Service in charge.

The body will lie in state at the church from 10:00 a.m. to 11:00 a.m.

Active pallbearers will be John Hagler, Albert Hagler, John Shirley, Lonnie Shirley, Herman Boyd, and Roy Rushing.

Honorary pallbearers will be Robert Rushing, Polk Rushing, Bernard LeSueur, Hayse Boyd, Albert Taylor, Dr. Joe Davis, Dr. Albert Folsom, W.M. Marable, W. H. Chism, John C. Brown, Jody Allen, Keener Berry, James E. Hocutt, Vincent Glass, Owen Rice and Billy Church.

Tom Shirley with his shotgun

J.T. Shirley setting muskrat trap

Mrs. Joel Thomas (Ida) Shirley

Maxine Robertson Davis, daughter of Julia Estelle Shirley Robertson and granddaughter of Tom and Ida Shirley

**Boyd comment:**

The following is a copy of an article in *The Tuscaloosa News* whose date has been clipped off. It gives interesting information regarding automobiles in early Tuscaloosa County. The article includes comment about the Crabbe Road.

The first car, a Locomobile Steamer, came to Tuscaloosa in 1900. It was owned by D. L. Rosenau. The car needed about an hour for the boiler to generate enough steam to put the heavy machine in operation.

# A ROAD, A CEMETERY, A PEOPLE

W. S. Persinger was the first car owner in Northport bringing a steam-driven automobile back from Birmingham in 1905. In his 1931 *Early History of Northport,* Persinger described the trips he used to make on the Crabbe Road to Windham Springs twenty miles north of Northport to a resort there. He wrote of the sand beds along the way that were almost impassable due to the steamer miring down in the sand. One is sand hill in the Lafoy Community two hundred yards south of Macedonia Methodist Church.

**Personal memories of some of Tom and Ida's family**
**By Hayse Boyd**

I had the joy and privilege of being longtime friends and neighbors with two of Tom and Ida's six children, Clara Shirley Rushing and Emile Shirley Snow. I share a few memoires of each starting with Emile.

**Emile**
Emile, Sara Brown's mother, married who was lovingly called "Pops." Pops was a well-known and respected local law enforcement official. Their home sat upon a little hill on the east side of the Crabbe Road a few yards south of the Carrolls Creek bridge. A large relatively flat area between the house and the road made an ideal garden spot. When going to and from town during gardening season, I often waved to Emile as she worked in her garden. She nearly always wore a wide-brim straw sunhat as protection from the sun.

Family records show that O'Neal H. Snow was enlisted for a three-year term into the United States Army Air Forces at Fort McClellan, Alabama on April 11, 1946. On July 9, 1946, he wrote a postcard to his wife stating he had just arrived in Greensboro, North Carolina.

In a letter dated November 16, 1949, G. A. Rudes, Fire Chief, Ladd Air Force Base, Fairbanks, Alaska wrote the following recommenda-

Joe Rushing, son of Josh and Clara Shirley Rushing, standing on his grandparents' (Tom and Ida) front porch

The former home of Josh and Clara Shirley Rushing as seen in 2022 across the Crabbe Road from Macedonia Methodist Church

# THE JOEL T. SHIRLEY FAMILY

tion for O'Neal Snow.

"The bearer O'Neal H. Snow has served in the Ladd Air Force Base Fire Department under my supervision for the past ten months. I do not hesitate in recommending O'Neal H. Snow for any position in firefighting work."

One of O'Neal's hobbies was coin collecting. In the June 16, 1966, *Graphic* newspaper, he said that he had attended coin conventions in Atlanta, New Orleans, Birmingham, and Montgomery. He became interested in collection after he got his first coin from Dr. Walter B. Jones, Alabama geologist and archaeologist for thirty-four years. O'Neal saw his interest as both a hobby and an investment.

Emile was a community pillar and leader. She served in leadership positions in the Tuscaloosa County Home Demonstration Club. Articles about her work often appeared in *The Tuscaloosa News*.

Emile was a faithful member of Macedonia Methodist Church, the church I attended. She was one of the first to arrive each Sunday. She parked in the same spot under the big oak tree in the parking lot right next to the cemetery fence. The front of the car faced the Crabbe Road. She taught the adult Sunday School class and was active in the women's organization, the WSCS (Women Society of Christian Service). We enjoyed chatting and catching up on the week's news. Sara's sister and Emile's other daughter, Diane, was a member of our youth group.

**Clara**
Clara Barton Shirley Rushing married Joshua "Josh" Mills Rushing. Josh was the son of Joseph Enoch Rushing and Samantha Lenora Deason. One of Josh's brothers was Thomas Hillman Rushing who was the grandfather of my wife Peggy Rushing Boyd. Thus, Peggy called her "Aunt Clara."

Josh and Clara's house and farm were on the west side of the Crabbe Road directly across the road from Macedonia Methodist Church. The

1904 steam engine car

1905 steam-engine car ????

Model T circa 1920 at Tom and Ida's house
The sailor is unidentified. Tom and Ida never owned an automobile.

265

Sarah Shirley Brown with her beloved doll

distance from the Boyd farm to the Josh Rushing farm was less than a quarter mile. As a result, I often was in and out of their home growing up.

Clara and Josh had only one child, Joseph "Joe" Thomas Rushing (1919-1995) who married Vera Hawthorne (1919-1998). Vera and Joe had two children, Ormand Ray Rushing (1939-1988) and Audrey Aleen Rushing. Audrey married Clyde Frank Kemp.

Ray and I were the same age and close friends in school. He and his family lived in Northport, but Ray often visited his paternal grandparents. When he did, I was invited to spend the afternoon. A special treat was to walk barefoot down the hill behind "Miss" Clara's house to her fishing lake. We were careful to watch for water moccasins, as careful as kids our ages were. Since I had no neighborhood playmates, it was a special treat for the two of us to just sit and talk. Years later, I had the privilege of being the family doctor for all the members of the Josh Rushing family, including Ray. Unfortunately, he died of heart disease at age forty-seven.

One of my favorite memories that occurred at the Josh Rushing home was the "welcome home" party given in honor of Joe when he returned home from World War II. The event was in the summertime. Activities began just before dark, but light bulbs attached to electric cords that had been strung around the yard provided light after the sun set. The yard was filled with people. Music was played. Ice cream was served. I was so sleepy when we finally got home, Mother had to prod me to get out of the car and into the house and into bed. I was a walking zombie. I had never stayed up that late.

In closing, I again express sincere appreciation to Sara Shirley Brown for sharing family pictures, news items, memorabilia, and most of all for her friendship without which I never could have written this story about a truly amazing family, the Tom and Ida Shirley family. In 2022, Sara is still very busy. She volunteers four days each week at the Christian Ministry Center in Northport. She is also involved in other community and church organizations. Thanks, Sara.

CHAPTER 21

# The Byrd Franklin Shirley, Sr., Family

The Byrd Franklin Shirley, Sr, family is one of the largest and most prominent families in the Lafoy Community. I have been blessed to live a lifetime surrounded by and loved by members of this dear family. First and second-generation members are now deceased. Many of the third generation, my generation, continue to live in the Lafoy Community and our bond of friendship grows deeper with the passage of time.

**Byrd Shirley and Matilda Smith marry**
Byrd Franklin Shirley was born on March 17, 1880, and died on November 17, 1932. He was the son of John Lewis Shirley and Anna Key Chism Shirley. At the time, his parents lived in what in 2024 is part of the Northwood Lake area in Northport near the Shirley Cemetery that is located on Union Chapel Road West.

Byrd married Matilda Ann Smith who was born on September 9, 1886, and died on January 6, 1957. The Smith family lived in the vicinity of Piney Woods/Windham Springs twenty miles north of Northport on the Crabbe Road. Byrd and Matilda were the parents of twelve children, eleven of whom lived to adulthood.

Byrd Franklin Shirley, Sr., as a young man.   Shirley Cemetery, Northwood Lake, Northport, 2024

# A ROAD, A CEMETERY, A PEOPLE

**Resource material**
Most of the information presented in *A Road, A Cemetery, A people* comes from personal experience. I was in and out of the Shirley homes countless times. I worshipped with them regularly at Macedonia Methodist Church. I served as family physician to several. We shared fellowship at community picnics. We stood beside one another and shared common grief as deceased family members were lowered into their graves in Macedonia Cemetery.

Shirley grandchildren Naomia Shirley Brown, Charlotte Shirley Hardison, Carol Shirley Booth, Hilary Shirley, Robert Shirley, Emma Jean Hamner, along with great-granddaughter Beth Sherman all provided rich memories of their families. They not only shared personal stories but also allowed me to examine their collections of documents, photographs, and newspaper clippings.

On-line copies of many issues of *The Tuscaloosa News* beginning in 1929 are available to researchers. A weekly column in the *News*, "Lafoy News," was written by Lafoy resident Ida Clements (1902-1975) and appeared throughout the 1930s and 1940s. They contained many articles about the Byrd Shirley family.

Brenda LaFoy, a descendant of another Lafoy Community family who arrived in the area in the mid-1800s shared her research material. (The LaFoy family spells its name with a capital "F." However, newspaper articles and other research sources spell Lafoy with a lower case "f.")

*Hamner Heritage—Beginning Without End* is a book of history and genealogy about the descendants of William T. Hamner, Sr., a very early settler in Lafoy dating to circa 1830. It was written by Geneal Hamner Black and Mary Clark Ryan. Geneal was the granddaughter of Byrd and Matilda Shirley. *Hamner Heritage . . .* has been an invaluable research source.

**Piney Woods, sawmilling and turpentine**
When Byrd Shirley was born, the ten-mile stretch of the Crabbe Road between Carrolls Creek and Windham Springs was sparsely settled. Prior to his marriage, Byrd found day work in sawmilling and related jobs near Turkey Creek and Piney Woods as it became available.

Piney Woods was about fifteen miles north of Northport. The area was aptly named due to thousands of acres of virgin pine forests that grew in abundance on its steep hills and in its deep ravines. In 2024, the Fire Tower Road connecting the Crabbe Road with the Watermelon Road traverses the area.

Pine trees not only were sawmilled into lumber for building purposes, pine rosin was distilled into turpentine, a liquid with many uses. It is used to ignite kindling wood when starting a fire in a stove or fireplace. It is a paint thinner and has medicinal use in treating wounds and burns. When mixed with animal fat, it has been used as a chest rub or inhaler for nasal and throat ailments.

Byrd worked at sawmills, but a more interesting job was his work in gathering decaying pine stumps to be used to make turpentine. The steep hills, large rock boulders, cliffs, and deep ravines made road construction difficult in the area. An alternative was to lay a several-mile-long dead-ended railroad line that was called the "Dinkey Line." The word "dinkey" is defined as "a nickname for a short railroad line." The rail track followed the crests of hills, but it did not connect to another rail line. It had no locomotive. Teams of mules pulled the open rail cars up and down the track. Pine stump gatherers walked through the woods, pulled up decaying pine stumps and loaded them into the rail cars. At the end of rail line, the stumps were loaded onto wagons and taken to a turpentine mill.

**The Byrd Shirley Farm and the Renfro family**
Another of the early families to settle in the Lafoy Community was the Renfro family. Little is known about Mr. Renfro, but much has been written about his wife, Susan (January 2, 1851-December 31, 1936) and his son, Benjamin An-

# THE BYRD FRANKLIN SHIRLEY, SR., FAMILY

thony (1872-1957). Both are buried in Macedonia Cemetery.

In the early 1900s, Susan and Anthony Renfro owned 1,900 acres of land on the south and west sides of North River between the Crabbe Road and the Fayette Highway. The Renfro land adjoined on its northern border a large farm owned by Memnon Tierce, Sr. A narrow dirt road led from the Crabbe Road near Lafoy School to the Renfro farm. Today, that old roadbed is part of the Lary Lake Road. The Renfro Road had no bridge over North River. However, at one point in North River on the Renfro farm the river was shallow enough to allow wagons, buggies, and later automobiles to ford the river.

Byrd Shirley bought about 120 acres of farmland from the Renfro family and built his home on the property. The year is not known with certainty, but it probably was prior to the birth of Byrd and Matilda's first child, John Ester, who was born in 1907. The Byrd Shirley property was bordered on the east by the Crabbe Road, on the south by the Lark Hamner property, on the west by the Renfro property and on the north by the John and Octavia Tierce property.

Hiliary Shirley, grandson of Byrd Shirley, recalls that Anthony Renfro was a tall man who had Indian blood in his ancestry. He never married. He always wore liberty overalls and a denim jacket. The overalls had an upper pocket in which he always carried a can of Prince Albert smoking tobacco and a packet of cigarette paper. Like many men of the time, Mr. Renfro rolled his own cigarettes by pouring a small quantity of ground tobacco leaves onto a tissue-thin sheet of cigarette paper and rolling the paper into the form of a cigarette. Once the cigarette was rolled, a good lick of saliva onto the forefinger and then rubbed onto the paper sealed the cigarette so that tobacco did not fall out. It was cheaper to make your own cigarettes rather than buy packaged readymade cigarettes. Hilary also recalls that Mr. Renfro always carried candy in his pockets that he shared freely with children whom he met.

*Byrd Shirley house and farm buildings, Lonnie Shirley Road, circa 1970s*

**The Byrd Shirley home**

Shirley family tradition holds that Byrd probably met his future wife, Matilda Ann Smith, while sawmilling in Piney Woods. As noted, it is not known with certainty when they bought their farm and built the house. The house originally had only four rooms, an open dog trot and a front and back porch. The house faced southwest. The east wing, shown in right side of the painting, included three rooms—a bedroom, dining room and kitchen. The west wing initially was made up of only one room that was used as a second bedroom. (This painting of the house was done after an addition was made on the west wing circa 1950s.) The front porch swing and straight back chairs shout "welcome" to all who pass by.

The floor of the house was about two feet

# A ROAD, A CEMETERY, A PEOPLE

A painting of the Byrd Shirley house by granddaughter Emma Jean Hamner

L-R- Byrd Shirley, James Wesley, Lonnie Lee, Fannie Lou, John Ester, Circa 1912

above the ground and was supported by several columns of stacked rocks. There was no underpinning until many years later. The family well was located under the back porch at the end of the dogtrot.

A family of a mother, a daddy and their twelve children made up of seven boys and five girls lived within the confines of this limited space until the older kids began to marry and leave home. The children and their dates of birth were: (1) John Ester Shirley (January 17, 1907); (2) Fannie Lou Shirley Hamner (April 30, 1908); (3) Lonnie Lee Shirley, Sr. (December 9, 1909); (4) James Wesley Shirley (September 2, 1911): (5) Emma Frances Shirley Hamner (June 9, 1913); (6) Grady Edward Shirley (February 20, 1915); (7) Joan Shirley Davis (September 2, 1917); (8) Ruby Alene Shirley Mills (June 8, 1919; (9) Byrd Franklin "B.F." Shirley, Jr. (July 4, 1921; (10) Sue Shirley Lake (February 14, 1924); (11) Martha Nell Shirley Turner (September 24, 1926); (12) Bobby Renzo "Buddy" Shirley (February 4, 1933).

### The death of James Wesley Shirley in 1914
James Wesley Shirley (September 2, 1911-February 2, 1914) was the fourth child of Byrd and Matilda Shirley. At age three, he was standing in the yard before an open fire when his gown caught fire. In a state of panic and terror, he began to run wildly about the yard. This served only to fan the fire. He was quickly wrapped in quilts to extinguish the fire, but he had inhaled a lot of smoke and heat and died of pneumonia the next day.

### Life in the Byrd Shirley family
Like most other families in the Lafoy Community, life in the Byrd Shirley family during the era 1900-1950 was difficult. It is often said that many people in the rural South never noticed any major change in their lives during the years of the Great Depression of the 1930s. They were poor before the Depression; they were poor during the Depression; they remained poor after the Depression.

Honesty, commitment to hard work, thrift, devotion to God and to Macedonia Methodist Church characterized the Byrd Shirley family. They raised most of their produce, vegetables, and fruit. Hunting provided venison, quail, and rabbit meat. Fish caught in traps in local streams were fried and often served outdoors picnic style. The family cow provided milk, butter, and cheese. Hogs were slaughtered; their meat smoked and salted down for preservation, and the fat was made into lard. The brood of chickens laid plenty of eggs for the large family and young fryers provided tasty meals when fried in grease and served with homemade biscuits and gravy. However, it took hard work by all family members to keep the food chain in smooth operation.

As soon as a Shirley child was old enough to assume responsibility, he/she was put to work in the garden and fields, in the house, at the barn and in other places. As babies were born into the family, older children helped take care of their younger brothers and sisters.

Harvest from a few acres of cotton provided a "cash crop." All members of the family worked in the fields from planting time to harvest time. When they finished tending their own crops, they hired out to nearby farmers for a little cash spending money. It usually was spent at James Clements' store near Lafoy School less than a mile away. Seldom did Shirley kids get to go to town.

## The tragic death of Byrd Franklin Shirley, Sr. in 1932

The following article is found on the front page of the November 17, 1932, issue of *The Tuscaloosa News*.

## Farmer Struck by Automobile, Injuries Fatal
## Byrd F. Shirley Hit While Crossing Street in Northport, Dies

Birdie F. Shirley, Crabbe Road farmer, was fatally injured this morning when struck by an automobile driven by A. D. Lindsey, repair and sales representative for a Detroit adding machine concern, in the business district of Northport at the intersection of Main Street and Columbus Road.

Shirley was taken to Druid City Hospital immediately, but he died within four hours. Spectators to the accident said that the car struck him while he was walking across the street, dragging him several feet, and cutting a severe gash in the left side of his forehead.

Sheriff's attaches and Northport officers are investigating. Lindsey stopped his car immediately and offered assistance to the officers in the investigation. No charges have been preferred in the case.

The wife and several children of the injured man were summoned to his bedside today shortly after the accident. They reside eight miles from Northport on the Crabbe Road.

Funeral services will be arranged by Foster's."

## *The Tuscaloosa News*, November 18, 1932 (page 3)
## Last rites held for B. F. Shirley
## Widely Known Farmer Killed When Struck by Car, Laid to Rest

Funeral services for Byrd Franklin Shirley, Sr., 52, who died yesterday in Druid City Hospital following an accident in Northport when he was struck by an automobile while crossing the street, were held at the Macedonia Methodist Church at 2:00 p.m. today with the Rev. Marvin Manderson officiating.

Mr. Shirley, a well-known farmer of this section, had resided on the Crabbe Road for the past 20 years and was a steward of the Methodist Church. He received injuries about the body, a broken leg, internal chest and thorax injuries, as well as bruises about the head, in the accident which caused his death. Internment in the church cemetery will follow the funeral rites with Foster Funeral Home in charge.

He is survived by his widow, Matilda Ann Smith Shirley, ten children: John Ester, Lonnie Lee, Grady Edward, Joan, Ruby Alene, Emma Frances, Sue, Fannie Lou Shirley Hamner, Martha Nell, B. F. Jr., and an unborn child (Renzo).

He is also survived by a brother, Virgil F. Shirley of Coker who was born December 22, 1892 and died November 17, 1959 and is buried in Sand Springs Cemetery and a sister, Mrs. Cherry Smalley of Star Route, Samantha who was born January 3, 1879 and died September 8, 1960 and is buried in Jennings Chapel Methodist Church Cemetery.

Active pallbearers include: B. B., D. H., J. F., J. S., R. H. and A. L. Smalley.

Honorary pallbearers include: J. S. Clements; C. D. Newman; B. A. Renfro; Jack, Will and Robert Rushing; A. J. and N. J. Hamner; Collier Tierce.

A.D. Lindsey, well known representative of an adding machine company, driver of the car that stuck Mr. Shirley, was released on $500 bond yesterday afternoon pending an investigation of the grand jury on a technical charge of manslaughter."

Matilda Smith Shirley

### Memories of Matilda Smith Shirley

Matilda Shirley's grandchildren have fond memories of her. She wore long dresses that came to her ankles. Few respectable women in Lafoy during the 1900-1940s wore pants, except for overalls when working in the fields. Many of Matilda's home-made dresses were made from feed sack material. Her dresses were long-sleeved for warmth in cold weather and to protect her skin from the sun in hot weather. She was seldom seen without a full body apron over her dress. The apron had a nice little chest pocket where she kept her snuff can. She was a "clean" snuff dipper. One might not know that she had a dip of snuff stuffed away inside her mouth between her inner cheek and her tongue. She wore her long hair twisted into a bun at the back of her head. Mrs. Shirley loved Luzianne coffee, but her grandchildren recall that it was "thick as syrup."

At the time Matilda lost her fifty-two-year-old husband in 1932, she was pregnant with her twelfth child. Bobby Renzo "Buddy" Shirley was born on February 4, 1933, just as the nation was sinking deeper and deeper into the Great Depression. Matilda was a strong-willed lady. With the help of a very supportive family, she survived the loss of her husband and the economic woes of the Great Depression.

Matilda's granddaughter, Carol, daughter of Grady Shirley, recalls the day her grandmother died. The family had sent for Dr. Sam Davis, the family doctor. In those days, the Lonnie Shirley Road was still a little dirt farm road and not clearly marked. Dr. Davis had trouble finding Matilda's house. He stopped at Grady's house just a short distance away and asked for directions. After examining the dear old lady, he told the family there was nothing he could offer but his love and concern. She died shortly after the doctor's visit and joined her husband and other loved ones in heaven where she praised Jesus, her Lord and Savior.

In those days, Lafoy community families usually preferred to have the body of the deceased lie-in-state until the time of the funeral in the family home rather than at the funeral home. I recall going with my parents to the Shirley home that cold January night to offer condolences to the family. The house and porch were packed with people who had come to share their love for the entire Shirley family.

### Matilda Ann Smith Shirley obituary, *The Tuscaloosa News,* January 6, 1957

Funeral services for Mrs. Matilda Ann Shirley, 70, widow of B. F. Shirley, Sr. who died Sunday afternoon at her home on Northport Route 2 were held today at 3:00 p.m. at Macedonia Methodist Church, nine miles north of Tuscaloosa on the Crabbe Road with burial in the church cemetery by Jones and Spigener.

Active pallbearers were John Hagler, Herman

# THE BYRD FRANKLIN SHIRLEY, SR., FAMILY

Boyd, Pruitt Hamner, Frank Rutner, Polk Rushing and Newt Hamner.

Honorary pallbearers were Lester Taylor, Lattie Rigsby, Mem Tierce, Robert Rushing, Frank Clements, Albert Taylor, Spurgeon Black, M. L. Lake, Charlie Allen, Dr. Sam Davis, and Jay Hamner.

Survivors include six daughters, Mrs. Bruce Hamner, Mrs. Dee Hamner, Mrs. Howard Davis, Mrs. Erman Mills, Mrs. Thomas Lake, and Mrs. Clifton Turner; five sons, John E. Shirley, Lonnie L. Shirley, Grady E. Shirley, B. F. Shirley, Jr., Bobby Renzo Shirley all of Northport; a sister, Mrs. Lark R. Hamner; 28 grandchildren and 12 great grandchildren.

**The marriage of John Ester Shirley and Annie Snow Rushing**
John Shirley (January 17, 1907-June 5, 1996) was the oldest of the twelve Byrd Shirley children. He married Annie Snow Rushing (May 13, 1913-April 20, 1980) on January 13, 1937. Annie Snow was the daughter of James Willie Snow "Will" Rushing and Fannie Lee Gay Rushing.

Will Rushing's family settled in the Lafoy Community in the late 1800s. Joseph Enoch Rushing purchased several hundred acres of land bounded on the east by Carrolls Creek and on the west by the Crabbe Road. The Will Rushing portion of the property in 2024 includes the Telmar Subdivision.

Fannie Gay's father, Sidney Louellan Gay, another early arriver in the community, purchased land across the Crabbe Road from the Rushing property. In 2024, part of the old Gay farm is home to Publix Grocery at the intersection of the Crabbe Road and Mitt Lary Road.

**The following wedding announcement appeared in the January 24, 1937, issue of *The Tuscaloosa News*.**
The marriage of Miss Annie Snow Rushing and John Ester Shirley was quietly solemnized Wednesday, January 13, 1937, at the home of the groom's mother, Mrs. B. F. Shirley, Sr., of Lafoy. Only the closest relatives were present at the ceremony which the Rev. L. T. Selman, pastor of the Macedonia Methodist Church, officiated.

For her wedding, Miss Rushing wore a navy-blue crepe costume with gray accessories. Her flowers were rosebuds in a shoulder corsage. She is the daughter of Mrs. Will Rushing and an honor graduate of Tuscaloosa County High School and prominent in Sunday School and church circles. She has been president of the Epworth League at Macedonia Methodist Church for two years.

Mr. Shirley is the son of Mrs. B. F. Shirley, Sr., and is a prosperous young farmer and is active in the work of the Macedonia Methodist Church. He is a member of the official board. He is a regular seller on the Tuscaloosa Curb Market and is widely known throughout the county.

After a short honeymoon trip, Mr. and Mrs. Shirley have returned to reside with the bride's mother. Many friends wish for the young couple a life of joy and prosperity."

**Plans for a new house**
Will Rushing died in 1934. After John and Annie Snow married, they lived for several years with Annie Snow's widowed mother in the old Rushing house. Annie Snow's only sibling, Azilee, had married Glendon Newman in 1934 and moved away so there was plenty of room for the young married couple in the old Rushing home. However, they soon made plans to build a new house on the Byrd Shirley farm just a mile north on the Crabbe Road. The building site was on the highest point in elevation on the farm. It was about a hundred feet off the Crabbe Road and right beside the little dirt farm road that led to the Byrd Shirley house.

Lumber for the new house came from timber grown on the Shirley farm. The logs were sawed and planed, and as time allowed, John and his brothers did the carpentry work on the new house. As soon as the day ended at their public jobs, John and his helpers rushed home and worked on the new house until dark. They also worked each Saturday. Progress was slow but steady. Charlotte Shirley Hardison was born to John and Annie Snow in 1942. She is not sure when her parents moved into the house, but it was prior to her birth.

A front bedroom for Fannie Rushing was included in the blueprints. Mrs. Rushing's failing health would not allow her to continue to live alone in the Will Rushing house so she moved into the new house as soon as it was finished. Her health continued to decline to the point she became a bed-bound invalid. Mother and I often visited "Miss Fannie" when I was a child. She was a pale, sweet, softspoken lady. The bedroom was heated by a gas space heater. The room temperature was kept very warm. Once I remarked to Mother as we were leaving the house, "My goodness, that room sure was hot." Fortunately, I did not embarrass Mother by voicing my childish opinion in front of Miss Fannie and Annie Snow. Mrs. Rushing died January 1, 1967.

The layout of the house included the front porch, Miss Fannie's room at the front, living room with a brick chimney and fireplace, dining room, kitchen, and two additional bedrooms, a stubbed-in room for a future bathroom and a large back sleeping-porch. The steps leading off the back porch were steep and long. At the time construction was finished, the house had no indoor plumbing or electricity.

**The old vacant Will Rushing house burns**
James Rushing, son of Polk Rushing and a nephew of Will Rushing, lived near the Will Rushing house. One day James was plowing in a field nearby. He smelled smoke, and upon looking around, he discovered the old vacant house going up in flames. He hopped on his mule's back and went running for help, but it was too late. The house burned to the ground.

**John and Annie Snow have two children**
The first child, Charlotte Ann Shirley, was born on December 19, 1943. Charlotte is married to Thomas Welch Hardison. They have two children, Ann Rushing Hardison, and Richard Lewis Hardison.

The second child was John "Johnny" Rushing Shirley. He was born September 21, 1945. Johnny is married to Linda Gail Burt. They have one child, Victoria "Vicky" Lynn Shirley.

Charlotte and Johnny shared a bedroom when they were little. Then, a bedroom and bathroom for Johnny was built in the open space beneath the kitchen and dining room. A staircase led from the kitchen to the new basement bedroom. Two outside windows were installed letting in light. That was Johnny's "hideout" until he married and left home.

**John Shirley, the farmer**
"Mr. John" as I called him was a hard worker, honest, and a man of integrity who loved his family and God. Farming was at the center of his life from childhood. He first plowed using mules until the mid-1940s when he bought his first tractor.

After marrying at the age of thirty and moving out of the old Byrd Shirley house, John could no longer meet the financial responsibilities of a growing family on the income produced on the farm alone. He became a truck driver for a local trucking firm. He made deliveries around town and to nearby towns that did not include overnight trips away from home. Even so, growing vegetables to be sold on the curb market and to be peddled from his pickup truck remained his passion and the object of true love.

John had garden patches scattered about his farm. The main garden was in front of his house. It included about two-acres of rich soil bordered by the Crabbe Road and the Lonnie Shirley Road. Articles about his prize-winning vegetables and watermelons often appeared in *The Tuscaloosa News*. An example is found in the June 16, 1968,

# THE BYRD FRANKLIN SHIRLEY, SR., FAMILY

edition in which he is shown displaying his potato harvest. The caption reads, "Despite hot and dry weather, John Shirley of the Crabbe Road has completed the harvesting of his three-acre Irish potato garden which yielded approximately 225 bushels. Shirley retired from his lifetime occupation as a truck driver several years ago and is now supplementing his retirement income by truck farming on about 14 acres."

The June 15, 1968 news article showed his old faithful Farmall tractor. At the time, he was sixty-two-years-old. For the next fifteen years or so, he continued to drive his tractor even in the middle of hot summer days when the temperature was in the high 90s. He turned over the tractor twice and it was a miracle he was not crushed to death. But after each wreck, he had the tractor upended and got right back on and continued to plow. Everyone in our community was filled with love and respect for him. Drivers on the Crabbe Road tooted their car horns as they drove past his garden. It was inspiring to see our dear elderly friend slowly plowing his garden making sure not to plow too close to the plants.

Another article appeared in *The Tuscaloosa News* whose caption reads, "Big Melons. Umh! Good eating!" "John Shirley of the Crabbe Road, Lafoy Community, planted three acres of watermelons this year and has made a bountiful crop. Practically every day now he markets from one to two pick-up loads in the Tuscaloosa/Northport area. In order to keep disease and insect problems to a minimum, he planted his melons on land that had not previously been in melons."

John Shirley

This is not John's tractor. His was like this one, but his was old and rusty.

**A spiritual mentor**

John was a spiritual pillar at Macedonia Church. Seating in the sanctuary was divided into two sections of pews separated by a center isle with narrow isles at the outside ends of the pews. The John Shirley family sat on the second pew from the front on the left side. They were present at every service unless providentially hindered. Sitting erect and with his eyes focused on the preacher, it was evident his attention centered on being fed God's word.

Often, Mr. Shirley was called upon to pray aloud. He did not have a bombing voice, but as he stood and softly communed with God, the congregation was moved with reverence as he praised God, confessed sin on behalf of himself and the church, and humbly petitioned God to heal the sick and to meet specific needs of the day.

I never knew John Shirley to teach a Sunday School lesson. Yet his daily exemplary godly life was a great lesson as he set the standard for us young people to emulate. As I matured and aged, I often discussed matters of faith with John and always came away inspired. I never heard John Shirley use profanity. This is not to say that he was a somber person who never laughed and enjoyed having a good time. He showed personal interest in us and made us laugh.

### Social interaction between the John Shirley family and the Boyd family

Annie Snow carried the nickname "Sally." I do not know the story behind the custom. I use the word "Sally" with fondness. John and Sally were close friends with the Boyd family. We often shared Sunday lunch after church.

In the 1940s and 1950s, Macedonia shared a preacher with three other Methodist churches—Patterson's Chapel, Union Chapel, and Jennings Chapel. This meant that Macedonia had preaching only twice a month, a morning service on the first Sunday of the month and an evening service on the third Sunday of the month.

Most women in our church prepared lunch prior to leaving for Sunday School at 10:00 a.m. As a result, all that was needed when they returned from church was to heat the food up.

After church while standing in the church parking lot, it was decided who was going home with whom for lunch. If we were going to the Shirley home, we would run home, pack up the food Mother had cooked prior to going to church, and go to their home. We did this with several other church families. The memory is cherished.

After lunch, John and Daddy would invite me to get in the car with them and go for a nice long Sunday afternoon ride. They enjoyed inspecting local crops and predicting if it would be a good year for cotton and corn or not. They also talked about politics, the weather, and all sorts of subjects. I learned a great deal by just listening to their conversations. While the men were riding around, Mother and Sally stayed home and enjoyed visiting and catching up on "women talk."

In the 1950s, Annie Snow developed tuberculosis. At that time, standard medical treatment for tuberculosis patients was to be admitted to sanatoriums where they could receive treatment and have exposure to clean open-air spaces. Annie Snow was hospitalized at a tuberculosis sanitarium near Montgomery for about a year. My parents drove John to visit her frequently on Sunday afternoons. I was allowed to go and sit outside the sanitorium under the shade of trees. This experience was one of many that led me to enter the field of medicine.

John lived to the age of eighty-nine and died on June 5, 1999. The last year or so of his life he was confined to Forest Manor Nursing Home.

### My memory of Lonnie Lee Shirley

### Marriage and children

Lonnie Lee Shirley, Sr. was born on December 9, 1909, and died on June 10, 1975. He was the third child born to Byrd and Matilda Shirley. Lonnie married Estelle Wedgeworth who was born on September 1, 1915, and died on December 1, 2000. They had two children, Naomia Odell and Lonnie Lee, Jr.

Naomia was born on December 28, 1935 and died on November 12, 2021. She married Jack Randolph Brown who was born on July 13, 1930, and died on September 12, 2013. Jack was a Baptist preacher. Naomia and Jack had two children, Beth, who was born on February 26, 1960, and Brett Jeffery who was born on December 2, 1962. Brett was severely injured in a logging accident and died several years later on March 6, 2010 of ongoing complications.

Lonnie and Estelle's second child, Lonnie Lee Shirley, Jr., was born on August 3, 1942, and died on February 16, 1943. The cause of death is unknown.

### Lonnie's Lafoy School years

### Lafoy School, early 1940s

An entire chapter in *A Road, A Cemetery, A People* is devoted to the history of Lafoy School. Here, I relate a few stories of Lonnie's experiences during the years he was a student there. The school year was only five months, October through February. He and his siblings walked the half mile distance from the Byrd Shirley home to the school regardless of the weather.

# THE BYRD FRANKLIN SHIRLEY, SR., FAMILY

Lonnie exemplified an entrepreneurial spirit as a young school kid. Lafoy School served hot lunches to its students at a cost of a nickel per day. Lonnie often chose to forgo lunch and instead he walked next door to Mr. James Clements' country store and buy five one-penny sticks of candy. When he returned to school, he sold each stick of candy for two cents. As soon as he got home in the afternoon, he was hungry and would eat a hearty snack to tide him over until supper.

Lonnie had to drop out of school when he was about twelve years old and go to work on the farm to help earn a living for the growing family.

### Lonnie's life's public work
Lonnie was a longtime employee of the Tuscaloosa County Road Department, a division of county government under the supervision of the Tuscaloosa County Board of Revenue. In the 1940s, 1950s, and early 1960s, many of the rural roads in Tuscaloosa County were unpaved. Dirt roads become very bumpy and require periodic scraping. Ditches beside the road had to be kept free of debris and culverts kept unclogged. It was the road department's task to see that these things were done.

My father was elected to serve as a member of the Tuscaloosa County Board of Revenue for District One from 1944-1952. Lonnie Shirley served as supervisor for District One under Daddy's direction. Each morning the two men would confer and discuss plans for that day's work. This work relationship deepened the bond of friendship between our families, a bond that already existed as neighbors and fellow members of Macedonia Church. District One included the southwestern and midwestern areas of the county—Fosters, Ralph, Romulus, Elrod, Buhl, Coker, Echola, Brownville, Northport, and the Crabbe Road south of North River. The people of District One were very appreciative of the work Lonnie and his workers did. An example is seen in the following July 2, 1950, article in *The Tuscaloosa News*. Unfortunately, I am unable to locate the photos noted in the article.

### Feast in honor of Tuscaloosa County Board of Revenue Workers, District 1

### They prepared the feast:
Famous for their fine cooking, these women of the Romulus Community prepared the delicious picnic spread that was served in honor of the County Road Department for District 1. The affair was held at Romulus School on Thursday afternoon. The ladies providing the meal included: Mrs. F. B. Browning; Mrs. A. N. Burroughts; Mrs. Gay Dorroh; Mrs. Cordie McCracken; Mrs. Marvin Dees; Mrs. Verner Booth; Mrs. J. C. Cork; Mrs. Cliff Burroughts; Mrs. Tim Leatherwood; Mrs. Harvis Faulkner; Mrs. W. A. Cork; Mrs. Ray Burroughts; Miss Ruth Leatherwood; Mrs. A. P. Burroughs, Jr.; Mrs. W. V. Burroughs, Jr.; Miss Sally B. Evans; Mrs. Nelson Burroughs.

### They did the road work:
The men employed by the county who were the honored guests included: "Preacher" Wilbourne; Tolly Wicker; Lonnie Shirley; J. O. Allen; Jim Allen; Olen Booth; P. M. Beck; P. T. Pool; Early Grammar; Delmas Beck; Clyde Utley; Virgil Barton; James Hewett; Dewey Fair; James Robertson; Board of Revenue member Herman Boyd; County Engineer Rayburn Moore

### They did the speaking:
The following county and community leaders spoke at the Romulus picnic Thursday to honor the county road crew of District 1 and Board of Revenue member Herman Boyd: Virgil Barton, community leader and Beat 21 committeeman; Herman Boyd; Gay Dorroh, community leader; Cliff Lindsey, Board of Revenue member for District 2; Probate Judge Chester Walker; Tax Assessor, James R. Maxwell: Tax collector, Festus Shamblin; Dr. A. W. Patton, dentist who served as master of ceremonies; Board of Revenue Clerk,

Matt Maxwell."

**Politics**
Lonnie was not only Daddy's neighbor in Lafoy Community and oversaw the work of county road maintenance, he was his campaign manager at election time. Lonnie attended political rallies all over the county campaigning for my dad. Naomia Shirley recalls that during political campaign seasons, he would come in from work, take a bath, put on a white shirt and tie, and head for a political rally soliciting votes for Daddy.

**Lonnie and Estelle at home**
When Byrd Shirley bought his farm from the Renfro family in the early 1900s, a little dirt wagon road began at the Crabbe Road at the site John Shirley later built his home and circled through the Shirley and Renfro property and exited at the Crabbe Road near Lafoy School. Today, the road carries the name Lonnie Shirley Road. After Lonnie and Estelle married, they bought a few acres of land on the Lonnie Shirley Road from the Renfro family and built their first home. The house was about one hundred yards southwest of the Byrd Shirley home.

The exterior walls of Lonnie and Estelle's house was made of large round logs painted green. As with other members of Macedonia Church, our family often enjoyed sharing Sunday lunch with Lonnie and Estelle in their home.

Estelle took pride in her flower beds and shrubs around her house. She also tended a large vegetable garden. During Naomia's early years, Estelle was a stay-at-home mom. She did not learn to drive an automobile for several years after Naomia's birth. Later, she wanted to serve as a nurse's aide at Bryce Hospital. That required that she learn to drive.

She bought a blue used Chevrolet pickup and set about the task before her. Like many adults who delay learning to drive until they are well into adulthood, Estelle's learning experience was a little bumpy, but she succeeded. She and her pickup truck bonded. She enjoyed the freedom that comes with driving oneself to and from work, church, and shopping. I do not recall that she ever had a fender bender.

She was known for her beautiful penmanship. Carol Shirley Booth and Hilary and Robert Shirley told me they enjoyed perusing their aunt's letters. Her cursive handwriting was a work of art.

Country folk use jargon that is passed down from prior generations. Two expressions Estelle frequently used were, "Confound the dill" and "Come to me, Naomia." She also often said, "These *Knicky* shoes are killing me." She was referring to pain in her feet that resulted from spending many hours walking on concrete floors at Bryce Hospital.

Lonnie referred to Estelle as "good woman." As with all married couples, on occasion disagreement arose between Lonnie and Estelle. If Estelle was "chewing" on Lonnie in disagreement, he would turn to her and quietly reply, "Good woman, everything is going to be alright." He would shrug his shoulders and go on about his business paying her no mind.

Lonnie had the personality to deflect verbal injury and turn a potential conflict into a moment of humor. For example, once a person came up to Lonnie in public and was giving him a blistering scolding, almost to the point of being ready to fight. The man said, "I am so mad at you Lonnie Shirley, I feel like punching you in the nose." Without batting an eyelash, Lonnie said, "I am so mad at you that I am going home with you to eat supper." Both men laughed and went away friends.

**Outdoor shower**
The Lonnie Shirley log house lacked indoor plumbing. Lonnie rigged up a shower stall outside. First, he poured a small square of concrete that would serve as its floor. He then built a wood frame to support a 100-gallon tank that once had served as the diesel fuel tank on an abandoned

road machine. The tank was kept filled with water and was heated by the hot rays of the sun. Obviously, the shower could be used only in warm weather and on sunny days. Lonnie enjoyed coming in from work on hot summer days and showering in the warm water. Privacy was not an issue in those days as cars seldom passed by. If he heard a car coming on the dirt road, he would take necessary action. In cold weather, plan "B," bathing inside, was followed.

**The house burns**
One day while Lonnie and Estelle were at work, the old log house caught fire and burned to the ground. Word quickly spread through the community. Mother and I were among many neighbors who were there when Lonnie arrived home that afternoon. In an era of no cell phones or social media, Lonnie did not know about the fire until he got home at the end of the day. I was standing near Lonnie when he said, "I told Good Lady that the only way I would get the inside of that house warm was to burn it down." That was vintage Lonnie Shirley.

Lonnie's brother, Grady, and others in the community pitched right in and built a four-room "red" house a few feet southwest of the log house. This one had indoor plumbing. After Lonnie's death, Estelle continued to live in the house until her death. In their retirement years, Naomia and her husband, Rev. Jack Brown, lived there until their deaths.

**His work with the youth at church**
Another fond memory I have of Lonnie was that he often served as chauffeur for our youth group at Macedonia Church. Naomia was very active in the program, and after MYF meetings on Sunday night, he often would take us to town for a game of putt-putt golf and treat us to a milkshake. He would turn up the volume on the car radio and we would laugh and giggle. He loved to be around children and we enjoyed being around him.

Lonnie loved to play cards of any type including poker. Nephew, Robert Shirley recalls that Lonnie often would say to him in the late afternoon as he passed by B.F.'s house, "Boy, you want to come up and play cards after supper?" Robert always replied, "I will if Mama will let me."

**My memory of Grady Edward Shirley and family**

**Marriage and children**
Grady Edward Shirley was born on February 20, 1915, and died July 10, 1994. He was the sixth child of Byrd and Matilda Shirley. Grady married Margaret Watkins who was born on August 27, 1918, and died on August 10, 2003. They had five children: Wendall; Gary; Hilary; Mark; and Carol.

Wendell Edward Shirly was born on September 4, 1939, and died on July 23, 2019. He married Permelia Jane Cruce Rose. They had three children. Wendell Todd Shirley was born on February 9, 1966; Johanna Rose Shirley was born on June 15, 1969; Ryan Edward Shirley was born on May 9, 1971.

James Gary Shirley was born on December 1, 1942, and died on June 23, 2020. He married Sarah Frances Price. They had no children.

Joe Hilary Shirley was born on October 7, 1947. He married Betty Jean Rose who was born on December 14, 1949 and died on October 22, 2009. They had three children. Susan Hilary Shirley was born on Septrember24, 1977; Leah Hartin Shirley was born on January 21,1982; Steven Grady Shirley was born on January 13, 1987.

George Mark Shirley was born on November 22, 1950, and died on December 19, 2020. He married Patricia Jane Robertson. They had two children. Edward Mark was born on July 10, 1981. Amy Elizabeth was born on June 19, 1982.

Carol Jean Shirley was born on September 17, 1952. She married Randy Ray Booth. They have two children. Meredith Margaret Booth was

L-R- Wendell, Hilary, Gary (standing behind Trixie the cow) and Mark

born on February 21, 1981. Brandon Manly Booth was born on January 19, 1990.

**Early married life**
Following their marriage, Margaret and Grady lived in several locations including a house on Main Avenue in downtown Northport and in Oliver Heights in Northport. Grady was employed for a short time in Holt where he worked in a bag factory. Grady also worked in Decatur, Alabama for a year or so during World War II (1941-1945).

By the time of Hilary's birth in 1947, Grady and Margaret had bought property from the Renfro family adjacent to the Byrd Shirley farm. Grady built a three-room house made up of a front porch, living room/bedroom, bedroom, and kitchen. The house had no indoor plumbing. The water supply came from a spring down the hill from the house. They lived in this house for several years. Hilary remembers it as being "a very cold house." Heat came from a fireplace in the front room and a wood-burning kitchen stove. As with the John Shirley and Lonnie Shirley families, I recall our family eating Sunday lunch there on at least one occasion.

Hilary is not sure of the date his family moved into the house that became the permanent home of Margaret and Grady and the house where the children grew up. Mark was born in November of 1950. Hilary says the move occurred prior to Mark's birth. The house sits on a beautiful sloping hill at the intersection of Lary Lake Road and Lonnie Shirley Road. It has a commanding view of cultivated farm land and adjacent forests.

The house consists of three levels, a basement, the main floor, and an upstairs that has dormer windows opening on the front. The move into the house occurred in stages. The basement was finished first and the family lived in it for several years before the two upper levels were added.

**Grady Shirley Construction Company**
Grady was born with master carpenter skills. He began his construction career by working for independent contractors in Tuscaloosa, but soon he organized his own construction company. It was an instant success. As military veterans returned home after World War II, the housing industry boomed. Unlike other builders in Tuscaloosa, Grady did not want to expand his company to include several work crews. He desired to limit his work so that he could be an on-site supervisor of each project. As a result, he would take on only two or three new building projects at a time. Those who wanted Grady to build their new houses were willing to wait their turn in order to benefit from the quality of his work which was superior to that of many others.

Excellence of construction was never negotiable with Grady, but he also was interested in saving his customers money when possible. An example is found in the matter of avoiding architectural fees.

Drawing up blueprints begins the process of building a house or church. This normally involves an architect whose fee is a percentage of

# THE BYRD FRANKLIN SHIRLEY, SR., FAMILY

.L-R- Grady (face hidden), Hilary, Gary, Margaret, Carol, Mark, and Wendell

the final cost of the building. To save his clients a hefty several-thousand-dollar architect fee, Grady secured the services of O'Neal Ray, a Northport resident who was a master in drawing house, school, and church plans. Although expertly trained, O'Neal was not a licensed architect, but he had an agreement with a licensed architect who would approve O'Neal's work for a nominal fee. In my own case, Peggy and I saved several thousand dollars in architectural fees when Grady built our home on Lake Tuscaloosa in 1977 and when I built my medical office building in 1980. Not only was O'Neal excellent at his work, he was a wonderful man.

**Macedonia Methodist Church**
No resident of the Lafoy Community has had a larger role in constructing church buildings at Macedonia Methodist Church than Grady Shirley. The original church building was built in 1902/1903. In 1945, a tornado damaged that building beyond repair. I remember the event vividly. The only items saved were the piano and the pulpit chair. Both were stored in our home while the damaged building was removed and a new building constructed.

Grady and his crew, along with other helpers from the community, pitched right in and built a new church building as quickly as possible. The storm occurred in the spring and the new building was not finished until late summer. During the interval, Sunday School and preaching were held outdoors. I thought that was neat. Grady's time was given *gratis*.

The sanctuary stood at ground level with the parking lot in front. The wood structure whose outside walls were covered with asbestos was approximately forty-feet-wide and seventy-five feet long. A full basement used for Sunday School rooms were beneath the sanctuary. A few years later a kitchen opening off the basement was added. Again, Grady Shirley did the job. An entire chapter in *A Road, A Cemetery, A People* is devoted to Macedonia Methodist Church.

In the 1970s, a new sanctuary, church office and bathrooms were built. As part of the construction, the original basement was retained over which new Sunday School rooms were added. Here again, Grady stepped in and donated time and effort, at no cost to the church, to build a place of worship he loved.

**Grady, the farmer**
As with all members of the Byrd Shirley family, Grady enjoyed growing vegetables and other farm products, especially pumpkins and peanuts. Moreover, he loved to give away the fruit of his labor. He always planted more than the family could use. I often wondered if he gave away more that he kept.

Grady had health issues that in later years prevented him from stooping over to harvest butterbeans and peanuts. Grady developed a unique way to get the job done. Butterbeans can be grown in two varieties, bunch, and pole-climbing. His were of the bunch variety. Bunch butterbean vines grow only to a height of about one foot. Moreover, many pods are located on the vines just above ground level. The harvester either must bend over or get down on his knees to gather the ripe pods. Grady's inability to squat or crawl on his knees made that impossible. To solve the problem, Grady would walk down a row of butterbeans, grab each bunch and yank the entire vine, roots and all, out of the ground and toss them into the bed of his pickup truck. After pulling up all the bunches in a row, he would drive his truck to the shade of a tree and sit on the tailgate and harvest each ripe pod and toss it in a bucket for shelling. There is a major waste in this method as all pods on a vine do not ripen at the same time. The non-ripe butterbeans were thrown away. This did not bother Grady because as stated, he planted an over-abundant crop to cover the expected loss. What a wonderful guy!

Grady raised turkeys. Every time I drove up to the back of their house, I saw turkeys everywhere, in the yard and in the woods. Upon seeing a car approach, the turkeys began gobbling, clucking, yelping, and purring. The following very nice article and picture of Grady's granddaughter Meredith Booth appeared in the *Tuscaloosa News* (the date of the article is clipped away). It reads,

"These turkeys gobble down corn tossed by 6-year-old Meredith Margaret Booth at her grandparents' farm in Northport. The traditional centerpieces of today's big Thanksgiving meal seem blissfully unaware that they should be thankful they are receiving dinner rather than being dinner. Meredith's grandparents, Grady and Margaret Shirley, operate the farm off Alabama Highway 69 eight miles north of Northport. The youngster's parents are Carol Shirley Booth and Randy Ray Booth."

**Grady, a giver to the community**
In the 1960s and 1970s on rainy days when it was too wet to work, several Lafoy Community men gathered at J. M. Bolton's little country store on the Crabbe Road. The store was located at the intersection of House Bend Road and the Crabbe Road. They told tall tales and shot the breeze. It would have been fun to have been a fly on the wall and listen. Grady was always there and a major participant.

Just as Grady was generous in sharing his vegetables and construction work at his church, he helped dig many graves in Macedonia Methodist Cemetery. Until the late 1900s, if a burial was to occur, men of the Lafoy Community dug the grave at no cost to the deceased's family. John Hagler was the person who oversaw these efforts. On the day of the burial, Grady and his crew would stop work at the construction site and go to the cemetery and dig the grave quickly and without charge. He then returned to the construction site to continue the day's work.

**Margaret Watkins Shirley**
Margaret Watkins Shirley, Grady's wife, was a beloved member of the Lafoy Community. I have wonderful memories of her. She spent her life serving her family as a stay-at-home mom. She was very active in the Lafoy Home Demonstration Club, the Women Society of Christian Service (WSCS) of Macedonia Church, youth counselor to the Methodist Youth Fellowship of Macedonia and a caring and loving grandmother to her nine grandchildren.

**The lifework of Grady and Margaret's children**
It has been my privilege and joy to have grown up and know Margaret and Grady's five children. Some were patients in my practice. I could write a long story about each, but I must limit my comments.

**Wendell**
Edward Wendell was born on September 4, 1939 and died on July 23, 2019. He began his work career in his father's business but soon established

# THE BYRD FRANKLIN SHIRLEY, SR., FAMILY

his own company, Shirley Concrete. He was very successful and several members of the Byrd Shirley family were employed there. His hobby was collecting and restoring antique tractors.

**Gary**
James Gary was born on December 1, 1942, and died on June 23, 2020. Gary was a very talented mechanic. He repaired and serviced gasoline and diesel engines.

I owned a 1980 Allis-Chalmers tractor that I used to bush hogg several areas on our farm. When the tractor required routine maintenance or repairs, I would drive it over to his house and leave it for a few days while he did the work as his time allowed. It was always a pleasure to just sit and visit with him for a while.

Gary was active in 4-H Club. One of his projects was tending a beehive house near his home.

**Hilary**
Joe Hilary was born on October 7, 1974. His work career was spent in the concrete business. Working alongside his brother, Wendell, first cousin, Robert, brother-in-law Randy Booth, nephew, Brandon Booth, and son, Steven, Hilary poured curb and gutter concrete all over the state of Alabama and in nearby states. Even in retirement, Hilary's internal clock wakes him up at 3:00 a.m. and he goes to a fitness center where he exercises.

Known as "Red Man" due to his red hair, there are many complements due him. I begin with his marriage and family. Hilary married Jean Rose, a member of a very prominent Northport family. Jean was born on December 14, 1949, and died of ovarian cancer on October 22, 2009. Jean had a twin sister, Joan, and a brother Wayne.

Gary and James Cooper, Associate Tuscaloosa County Farm Agent, harvesting honey

Joan, too, died of ovarian cancer. Hilary gave loving tender care to Jean during her long illness. Hilary and Jean's home overlooks Lake Tuscaloosa. The house and grounds are meticulously maintained. Because of their love for God's wonderful creation of nature, Jean's funeral service was held outdoors in the Macedonia Methodist Church covered worship center. It was a moving service.

Jean and Hilary have three children, Susan, Leah, and Steven. Susan was born on September 24, 1977. Leah was born on January 21, 1982. Steven was born on January 1, 1987. Joan and Jean's mother, Mattie Rose was a nurse at Druid City Hospital. Jean was a teacher at Faucett Elementary School as was Susan. Leah is employed in the business world. Steven followed in his father's footsteps and worked for Shirley Concrete Co. Upon Hilary's retirement, Steven pursued other lines of work.

Susan's life is a special blessing to all who know her. Many years ago, she developed a brain malignancy. She has undergone repeated surgical procedures. She had to retire from teaching, but she is one of the most upbeat individuals and strongest Christians one will ever meet, a true inspiration.

Hilary's most important and lasting attribute is his devotion to Christ and to his church. He remains a pillar of strength at Macedonia. I am moved each time I hear him pray during public worship. He is also very involved in seeing that Macedonia Cemetery is maintained in a state that appropriately honors the memory of those who are interred there.

**Mark**
George Mark was born on November 22, 1950,

and died on December 19, 2020. He married Patricia Jane Robertson. They have two children. Edward Mark was born on July 10, 1981. Amy Elizabeth was born June 19, 1982.

Mark was skilled in all things relating to woodwork and carpentry. His life work was spent with Grady Shirley Construction Co. I had the joy of watching Mark, and his crew, build our home on Lake Tuscaloosa. Mark was a big man and strong as an ox. He could handle a fourteen-foot-long two-inch by twelve-inch board of lumber as if it were a toothpick. Like his daddy, Mark took no short cuts in making sure that the finished product would last a lifetime unless destroyed by an act of nature. We have now been in our home for forty-five years and thanks to him all carpentry work is as sound today as when it was built in 1977.

Mark was also skilled in making furniture. He and his family lived in a lovely white house with a wide front porch in Bellwood in Northport. He had a large woodworking shop behind the house that was filled with all sorts of tools. He made several pieces of furniture for us. One was a four-foot by five-foot oak table on twelve-inch legs that was a play table for our grandson Marshall Strickland. The wood was varnished so that the lines in the wood were seen. Marshall spent many hours playing there.

Like other members of the Byrd Shirley family, I had the privilege of serving as Mark's family doctor.

**Carol**

Carol Jean was the only girl born to Grady and Margaret. She was born on September 17, 1952. She married Randy Ray Booth. Carol and Randy have two children, Meredith, and Brandon. Meredith Margaret was born on February 21, 1981. Brandon Manly was born on January 19, 1990. Carol, like so many others in the Shirley family was a teacher. Randy's life work was with Shirley Concrete Company.

Following their marriage, Carol and Randy lived in a rental house nearby that had been the home of Newt and Jean Hamner. It was there their children were born and reared. Carol's mother's health declined in the early 2000s prior to her death in 2003. She no longer was able to live independently. Carol, Randy, and Brandon moved in with Margaret to care for Margaret. Following her mother's death, ownership of the Grady Shirley home passed to Carol.

Carol taught at Riverside Junior High School in Northport, and during part of her tenure there, my brother, Herman Boyd, Jr., was principal. Carol was very active in educational programs of the Tuscaloosa County School System.

As with her brother Hilary, Carol is a lay leader and very active in church affairs at Macedonia Methodist Church where she has held many positions of leadership.

Members of Macedonia frequently enjoy lunch and dinner fellowships. Carol, like other members of the church, is an excellent cook. She prepares delicious dishes that are relished by all who are present.

I cannot let pass the opportunity to share a beautiful picture. When the time comes in the worship service to collect tithes and offering, Randy and Brandon come to the front altar, pick up the offering plates, and move throughout the congregation passing out the plates. The thing that is so precious is to see father and son walking side by side down the aisle, the son being several inches taller than the father.

Carol, Randy, and Brandon grow the best tasting tomatoes one can find anywhere. The several-acre field is just west of their house. It is the same field where Grady grew the butterbeans noted earlier in the chapter. Randy begins preparing the garden soil in early spring. During the summer, it is a beautiful site to see row after row of towering green corn, tomato plants, pole beans, and other produce awaiting harvest. Peggy buys several bushels of tomatoes for canning purposes each year. Tomatoes usually do not come into season until late June. At the annual First

# THE BYRD FRANKLIN SHIRLEY, SR., FAMILY

B. F. Shirley with his sister Ruby Shirley Mills

Sunday in May homecoming at Macedonia when I first see Brandon or Randy, I ask, "Do you have any ripe tomatoes?" They smile in return.

Meredith married Danny Barringer. Danny owns a tree service business. Without doubt, his is the best in our area. Peggy and I love trees, and when we built our home, we saved as many trees as possible. Currently our lawn and natural area around the house includes several acres. About once a year, we ask Danny to raise the canopy under the trees. We also need his services when storms topple trees. When his crew finishes a project, the cleanup is so good that one cannot tell that a tree service has been at work. Danny is a dear friend. Meredith, like her mother, is a school teacher.

Brandon has never married. He is employed by the University of Alabama and owns a home on Lary Lake Road near his parents. The house first was the home of Grady's sister, Ruby, and her husband, Erman Mills.

## Byrd Franklin "B.F." Shirley, Jr.

### Marriage and children
Byrd Franklin "B.F." Shirley, Jr. was born on July 4, 1921, and died on February 17, 2003. He was the ninth child born to Byrd and Matilda Shirley. He married Mary Alice Turner on June 10, 1925.

They had two children, Robert Franklin, and Leigh Ann.

Robert was born on October 31, 1949. Robert married Cheryl Kay Elliott. They have no children.

Leigh Ann was born on November 15, 1962. Leigh Ann first married Joe Rice. They had two children, Tyler Rice, and Sarah Rice Hughes. Leigh Ann married a second time to J. C. Bowick. They have no children.

### The first home
At the time of Robert's birth in 1949, B. F. and Mary Alice lived in a small rental house owned by B. F.'s sister, Francis Shirley Hamner, and her husband, Oll Dee Hamner. The house was on land that had been settled circa 1830 by Oll Dee's great, great, grandfather, William T. Hamner, Sr., one of the area's first settlers. Robert's memory extends to circa 1955 when he was six years old.

The area around the house included several old farm buildings, a large corn crib, a barn, and a blacksmith shop. Bee hive houses were scattered about. Robert says the honey was delicious. There was plenty of fresh fruit from the peach, apple, and plum orchards. There seemed to be a never-ending supply of vegetables from the big garden.

A narrow dirt drive from House Bend Road, the Dee Hamner Road, led to B. F. and Mary Alice's house where the road forked. The left fork led to the site of the original William T. Hamner Sr. log cabin that was built in the 1830s. The only remains of the old structure were a few rocks from the fallen down chimney. The other fork, the one to the right, led to the "bottoms," an area bordering North River. The soil was exceptionally rich and produced large yields of corn and cotton. Today, the area is covered by the waters of Lake Tuscaloosa.

B.F. enjoyed fishing. He often took Robert to the bottoms beside North River. They usually had good luck, and in a short time frame. Some might say they cheated on the fish. This is the story.

# A ROAD, A CEMETERY, A PEOPLE

Hamner tradition holds that in times past, starting at the far bank of the river, Hamner men made a rock dam that extended almost to the near bank of the river. This increased the rate of flow of water in the narrow channel. The men rigged fish traps that could be lowered into the water when they wanted a mess of fish. The rapid flow of water pulled the fish downstream into the traps. Once a few fish became trapped, the nets were raised and the fish dumped into a bucket of water and taken home to be fried. Fried fish and hushpuppies were very popular in Lafoy. What a lazy way to catch fish!

**The move to the old Byrd Shirley house, 1956**
At the time of Byrd Shirley's death in 1932, several of his and Matilda's children were still living at home and were not married. In fact, the oldest child, John, did not marry until 1937. As the children married and established homes of their own, Matilda continued to live in the house. There were no changes made to the original four-room, open dogtrot house. Around 1956, Matilda's health deteriorated to the degree that she could no longer live alone. B. F., Mary Alice, and Robert moved into her home to help care for her. When Matilda died on January 6, 1957, ownership was passed to B.F.

A two-room addition was added to the west wing of the original house after B. F. and Mary Alice moved in. The addition consisted of a dining room and a new kitchen. The old original kitchen was turned into a storage room which occasionally served as a bedroom.

The old house was built with high ceilings, twelve, possibly fourteen feet. When the addition was done, the ceiling in the original four rooms were lowered to eight feet to match the ceiling height in the new rooms. There was one exception. The ceiling in the front bedroom on the east side was never lowered. Later, the dogtrot was screened and sheets of plastic applied to help winterize the house.

Like most rural houses in Lafoy built prior to 1940, the crawl space under the Byrd Shirley house was left open. This allowed howling cold winter winds to blow freely under the house and find their way into the rooms through cracks in the wood floors. The frigidness of the house was made even worse because there was no insulation in the attic or in the exterior walls. Open fires in fireplaces provided the only heat until the 1950s when butane gas space heaters were installed. All members of the family wore heavy clothing in order to keep warm. In summer the house was hot. The only fans available were hand-held cardboard fans. Electric power did not reach the Lafoy Community until the 1940s.

In 1990, the house needed repairs. The original exterior walls were made of wood boards that overlapped slightly. Never painted and approximately 90 years old, much of the exterior walls and interior flooring was rotting. Robert took it upon himself to make repairs for his aging parents.

He purchased large pieces of ½ inch plywood and nailed them to the exterior walls. Then, he nailed small strips of boards to cover the cracks between the plywood sheets. This created a board-and-batting finish. The addition made the house much warmer in winter, but it remained a cold house. He also enclosed the crawl space under the front porch by installing decorative lattice.

**Mary Alice's parents move in**
Not long after Mrs. Matilda Shirley's death, the health of Mary Alice's parents, Festus and Leona Turner, declined to the degree they could no longer live independently. They moved into the house with B. F. and Mary Alice. They lived there until their deaths. Leona died on September 27, 1959, and Festus dropped dead of a heart attack on January 20, 1971, while standing in the dogtrot of the house. Both Festus and Leona are buried in the Old Center Church Cemetery on the New Watermelon Road near North River.

Festus and Leona had nine children: (1)

Macedonia Cemetery

Daniel Harrison; (2) Festus, Jr.; (3) Ida Grace; (4) Mary Alice; (5) William David; (6) Joseph Bernard; (7) William Willard; (8) John Terrell; (9) Sara. Each of the children would invite their parents to share holiday meals with them in their homes. However, Festus and Leona most often chose to eat with B. F. and Mary Alice.

**Life work at Gulf States**
As with all the Shirelys, B. F. was a hard worker. He was employed by Gulf States Paper Corporation for many years. As soon as he got home from work in the afternoons, he worked in his garden. Growing more food than the family would consume, he often dropped off fresh vegetables at the pastor's house or at the homes of other neighbors in the community.

**Caretaker for Macedonia Cemetery**
B. F. became the caretaker for Macedonia Cemetery after he retired from Gulf States.

A separate chapter is devoted to Macedonia Cemetery. Much of the following material is included in that chapter, but it is repeated here because of the influence B. F. had on the care of the cemetery.

The oldest grave marker in the cemetery is that of Susannah Clardy Tierce who died on April 27, 1862. However, the cemetery has 128 graves that are marked only by rocks that have no names or dates. Therefore, it is possible burials occurred earlier than 1862.

Before and during my childhood, maintenance of the cemetery was haphazard and handled in the following manner. The first designated cleanup was done during the week prior to the first Sunday in May.

The first Sunday in May was the highlight day of the entire church year. The day began at 10:00 a.m. when families gathered to place flowers on the graves of their loved ones. Then around 10:30 a.m., the crowd moved into the sanctuary for the start of an "all day gospel singing." At noon, a break occurred for a "dinner on the grounds" meal outside. Delicious dishes of all varieties were spread out on long picnic tables. Most ate far too much. After lunch, the singing resumed and lasted most of the afternoon. The crowd was so large that in addition to filling the church parking lot, cars were parked on both sides of the Crabbe Road for a great distance north and south of the church.

Returning now to the care of the cemetery, it is noted that family members with loved ones buried there came during the week before the first Sunday in May and cleaned the areas where their family members were buried.

Following the cleanup in early May for Decoration Day, there was no formal schedule for maintenance for the rest of the year. The old section of the cemetery was not sodded leaving the bare earth unprotected from erosion. As summer progressed, weeds, briars, vines, and fallen leaves left the cemetery in a very deplorable state. From time to time, family members would come and scrape away the unwanted growth on their family plot but not on the entire cemetery. I performed this task about once a month on our family plot. Eventually, volunteers dwindled and it became necessary to have a paid custodian. The pay was meager. B. F. agreed to perform the task, not for the very small stipend given, but because of his love and respect for those dear souls who were interred there.

Under B. F.'s supervision, the cemetery was well kept. He did a great job. With the passing of time, his health declined. I was his personal physician. I knew his aging body was being subjected to more physical stress than it needed. But, like all members of the Shirley family, he would not give up. He developed a routine of working in the cemetery for a couple of hours, go home and rest for a couple of hours and return later in the day to continue the task. Eventually, he could do the job no more. It was a sad sight to visit him as he sat in the swing on his front porch with his legs propped up to help with the swelling he had in his legs and hear him say, "I just cannot believe I no longer am able to work. I miss it so much."

B. F. knew the history of many people interred in the cemetery. No mapping of the graves had ever been done. In 2001, he and I mapped both the old and the new sections. With pen and paper in hand, we began at the southwest corner of the cemetery and assigned the grave #1. Over a period of several weeks, as we made our way through the graveyard, he told me stories about many who were buried there. Three were murdered. One was hung for killing the sheriff of Tuscaloosa County. I made careful notes. I share that information in another chapter.

**Fannie Lou Shirley Hamner**
Fannie Lou Shirley was born on April 30, 1908, and died on August 17, 1988. She was the second child of Byrd and Matilda Shirley. She was the first to marry. On February 14, 1926, Fannie Lou married Edward Bruce Hamner. Bruce was born on August 25, 1901, and died on February 12, 1986. The marriage produced four children: (1) Ollie Bruce was born on February 24, 1927 and died on July 5, 1980; (2) Alvin Franklin was born on October 9, 1928, and died on May 12, 2016; (3) Maryann Geneal was born on November 22, 1930 and died on April 29, 2007); (4) Glenda Sherrell was born on October 13, 1942. In 2024 she is confined to a nursing home.

When Fannie Lou and Bruce married, they moved into the kitchen area of the old William T. Hamner, Sr. plantation dogtrot log cabin on House Bend Road. The story is recorded on page 194 in *Hamner Heritage—Without End*. The original two-room dogtrot house was constructed circa 1833. It was made from logs cut from the woodlands of the Hamner property. With time and the births of sixteen children, William T. Hamner added lean-to rooms and a large kitchen with a wide fireplace to the log cabin. Bruce and Fannie Lou's first three children were born while they lived there.

At the time of Glenda's birth in 1942, the family lived in a rental house on the Sidney Louellan Gay farm which at the time was owned by Mrs. Lola Anders. Today it is the site of Publix Grocery at the intersection of Crabbe Road and Mitt Lary Road. They lived in that house until the early 1950s. I recall our family sharing Sunday-after-church lunches in that house. In the mid-1950s, they bought property and built a new house at the top of Sand Hill on the Crabbe Road. The property was a part of the original William T. Hamner, Sr. plantation. Sand Hill is a half mile south of Macedonia Church. Several members of Bruce and Fannie Lou's grandchildren live on the property in 2024.

Fannie Lou was a talented seamstress who was well known for her homemade rag dolls and other handcraft articles. Her talents were passed on to her daughters. She retired after sixteen years of employment at Bryce Hospital.

**Emma Frances Shirley**
Emma Frances Shirley was born on June 9, 1913, and died on March 10, 2008. She was the fifth child of Byrd and Matilda Shirley. Frances married Oll Dee Hamner who was born on November 6, 1907, and died on September 8, 1993. Frances and Dee had one child, Emma Jean Hamner. She was born on October 27, 1942.

Oll Dee Hamner was the son of Ollie Jackson

# THE BYRD FRANKLIN SHIRLEY, SR., FAMILY

Hamner. Ollie Jackson was the son of John Pruitt Hamner and Annie Margaret Hall. John Pruitt Hamner was the son of William T. Hamner, Sr.

In 1920, Ollie Jackson Hamner and his wife Mary Louise Rigsby built a new dogtrot house that was about one hundred yards east of the original William T. Hamner, Sr. log house.

When Dee and Frances married on December 24, 1938, they moved into the house Dee's parents had built in 1920. At the time, Dee's father was deceased but his mother was still living. They lived in that house until Emma Jean was thirteen years old. In 1955, they built a new home in front of the old dogtrot house. The old house was torn down. No known photos of the 1920 house exist.

Frances was artistic and known for her handcrafts. Much of her craft work was made from pinecones, nuts, grains, and other material collected from their land. She created lovely wreaths and other objects of beauty.

Dee was a talented musician and a well-known "fiddler." As a young man, he and his brothers, Hollis Harwood Hamner, and John O'Neal Hamner, along with a friend, Richard Patrick, formed a band that often played at square dances, political rallies, community gatherings, and fiddlers' conventions.

Emma Jean, like her parents, is talented and an artist of renown. She married Billy Ray Price. They have two children. Dennis Scott Price was born on June 23, 1962. Tina Frances Price was born on February 17, 1965. Emma Jean and Billy Ray subsequently divorced.

**Joan Shirley**
Joan Shirley was born on September 2, 1917, and died on December 31, 2013. She was the seventh child of Byrd and Matilda Shirley. Joan married Howard Davis. They had one son, Ronald Howard. He was born on October 18, 1942, and died on December 30, 2021. Joan was the only Shirley child who did not live in Lafoy Community in adulthood. After Lake Tuscaloosa was developed, she built a weekend cabin beside the lake on land that originally was part of the William T. Hamner, Sr. plantation. Her nieces and nephews lovingly called her "Aunt Jo" and described her personality as "easy going and free."

**Ruby Earlene Shirley**
Ruby Earlene Shirley was born on June 6, 1919, and died on January 3, 2002. She was the eighth child of Byrd and Matilda Shirley. Ruby married Erman Wesley Mills. Erman was born on June 19, 1918, and died on May 13, 2002. They had four children: (1) Charles Earnest was born on January 5, 1942; (2) Matilda Elizabeth was born on June 28, 1944; (3) Laura Alene was born on April 3, 1947; (4) Emma Shirley was born on March 26, 1950, and died on February 11, 1970. They first lived on the Tierce Patton Road near its intersection with the Crabbe Road. Later they built a home on Lary Lake Road on land that originally was part of the Renfro property. Her family describes her as quiet and reserved.

**Mattie Sue Shirley**
Mattie Sue Shirley was born on February 14, 1924, and died on August 10, 1999. She was the tenth child of Byrd and Matilda. She married Thomas Lake. He was born on September 26, 1920, and died on January 18, 2006. They had three children: Thomas Harold was born on July 23, 1945; Emily Susan was born on November 11, 1947; Tilda Jane was born on December 31, 1954.

Thomas and Sue built a home next to Bruce and Fannie Lou Hamner in the 1950s but later moved to Northport.

**Martha Nell Shirley**
Martha Nell Shirley was born on September 24, 1926, and died on March 28, 2007. She was the eleventh child of Byrd and Matilda Shirley. She married James Clifton Turner. Clifton was born on March 15, 1921 and died in August of 2009). They had four children: (1) Shirley Ann was born

on July 28, 1947; (2) Jerry Allen was born on November 20, 1948; (3) Nancy Kay was born on July 13, 1952; (4) Thomas Larry was born on July 12, 1954.

Martha and Clifton first lived in a house located on House Bend Road on land that had been part of the William T. Hamner, Sr. plantation. Later, they bought property and built a house on the Lonnie Shirley Road between the old Byrd Shirley house and Lonnie Shirley's property.

**Bobby Renzo**
Bobby "Buddy" Renzo Shirley was born on February 4, 1933 and died on March 15, 1999. He was the twelfth child of Byrd and Matilda. He was born three months after his father was killed in the pedestrian accident in Northport. He first married Jennie Marie Sexton. They had three children: (1) Shelia Ann was born on December 29, 1953; (2) James Wesley Shirley was born on December 4, 1956; (3) Debra Jo was born on October 30, 1958. Renzo and Jennie divorced. He later married Anne Kelly. They had no children.

Buddy never saw his father as he was unborn at the time of Byrd Shirley's death. Buddy, like John, B.F., Martha, Lonnie, and Grady lived on the Lonnie Shirley Road. Buddy lived in a house trailer just across the road from the old Byrd Shirley house. I find it heartwarming that he named one of his children for his older brother, James Wesley, who died as a result of being burned at age three.

CHAPTER 22

# Marjorie Shipp

As noted in the chapter devoted to Dr. Joseph Calvin Shipp (1927-2021), he was a world-renowned physician known for his research in juvenile diabetes and a life spent in academic medicine. The love and support of his lovely wife and life partner, Marjorie Morris Shipp, played an integral role in his life. Here in this chapter, I share a few of the events in Marjorie's life that tell, in part, the story of a truly great individual.

**Marriage and Years at Gainesville Medical School, 1960-1970**

Marjorie Morris from birth had a keen interest in learning and adventure. Little did she realize how her life would follow that trajectory when she met Joe Shipp. In 1961, Marjorie was a graduate student at the University of Florida at Gainesville pursuing a master's degree in education and journalism. Dr. Shipp was fond of telling the story of meeting Marjorie for the first time. One day she was walking across campus and he saw this lovely young lady for the first time. He literally stopped in his tracks. "She was the loveliest girl I'd ever seen. I knew I had to meet her. I went up and introduced myself. She was friendly, smart, and beautiful. We've been together ever since."

After a short courtship, Joe and Marjorie were married on November 23, 1961, two days before Thanksgiving. The intensity and volume of their respective academic workloads was so great that there was no time for a long honeymoon. In choosing Tuesday of Thanksgiving week break for the wedding day, the couple knew that a holiday weekend would be enough to allow for a short honeymoon.

While Marjorie focused on her studies, she quickly adopted her husband's zeal for improving the lives of children with type 1 diabetes. The Camp for Diabetic Children near Gainesville was just the place for her to work with Joe to improve the facility. She served as camp organizer and administrator. She began an art program for the campers that would allow children to enjoy creative therapy in addition to their medical treatments. In time, the camp became one of the premier camps in the U.S. for juvenile onset diabetics. Later, she and Joe developed a program in Safety Harbor, Florida for adults with type 2 diabetes.

Marriage to Joe Shipp resulted in a lifetime of travel and adventure for Marjorie and their four children. One of the most rewarding features of academic medicine is the opportunity to participate in research sabbaticals that allowed Dr. Shipp to work with other renowned physician researchers around the world. It also provided an opportunity for Marjorie to use her ample gifts in both professional and personal ways through international work studies spanning the globe from Africa to Palau.

# A ROAD, A CEMETERY, A PEOPLE

Dr. Shipp participated in approximately thirty sabbaticals. He and the family enjoyed living in: Munich Germany; Colombo, Sri Lanka; Geneva, Switzerland; Sydney, Australia; and Vellore, India. Within the United States, his work took him to Cleveland, Ohio; Fresno, California; Gainesville, Florida; Omaha, Nebraska; Santa Barbara, California; Tallahassee, Florida; and Washington, D. C. Marjorie's favorite place was southern India.

**The Shipp children**
Marjorie gave birth to their first child, Joseph Calvin Shipp, Jr., in 1962. Shortly afterward, Dr. Shipp's first sabbatical led the family to a small town near Munich, Germany. This was an exciting time in European history. Joe and Marjorie witnessed firsthand Communism, the Cold War, and a divided Germany. They were able to visit East Germany as well. Marjorie found the German people friendly and cordial, and it was a good place to start their growing family with children who were exposed to multiculturalism at a young age. The four Shipp children received their schooling in many countries. Each school had excellent faculty and the children excelled in their studies.

Joseph Calvin, Jr. is now an appellate lawyer for the State of California. In 1963, daughter Sherise was born. Sherise now is a luxury diamond award realtor in San Diego. A third child, Dane, was born in 1970. He is currently a physician-researcher living in Santa Barbara.

The fourth and last child, Michelle, was born in 1974. She now lives in Santa Barbara and is a lawyer/banker.

**University of Nebraska Medical Center in Omaha, 1970-1985**
After their move to Nebraska where Dr. Shipp served as Chairmanship of the Department of Internal Medicine, Marjorie served as a docent director for the Joslyn Art Museum and later as an acquisitions advisor for the Sheldon Art Museum.

Majorie's vivacious charm, wit, and enthusiastic support of her husband's work were valuable assets to Dr. Shipp as he recruited young men and women to pursue their life work in medicine. Marjorie fondly recalls hosting countless potluck dinners in their small living room and getting to befriend these young people. The impact of the Shipps' recruitment of these bright students into medicine—especially in research, patient education, and clinical practice— continues to this day.

**India**
Their work in India was probably the favorite for both Dr. Shipp and Marjorie. India covers a huge landmass and is the home to several major world religions, including Christianity whose strongest base is primarily in southern India. Vellore, India is home to the Christian Medical College Vellore, a private Christian minority community-run medical college with a network of hospitals.

Founded in 1900 by American missionary Dr. Ida S. Scudder, the institution has brought many significant medical achievements to India including the first college of nursing (1946), the first reconstructive surgery for leprosy in the world (1948), the first successful open-heart surgery in India (1961), the first kidney transplant in India (1971), and the first bone marrow transplant in India (1981). For the Shipps, it was an exciting medical community as well as a colorful, vibrant culture.

When our telephone conversation turned to the topic of India, Marjorie's voice was filled with extra enthusiasm. She said that if she were a patient there, she would have full confidence she would receive excellent care.

The Indian people have a long tradition of using vibrant color and luxurious textiles in all aspects of life, art, worship, and culture. Marjorie was a wonderful fit for this environment. In this exotic, beautiful location, Marjorie used her skills in the creative arts to design models for the leprosarium and well as honing her own studies of

Indian bronze work and contemporary art.

**Fun times in the South Pacific**
Some of the Shipps' most special memories were of the time spent on the islands in the southern Pacific Ocean. Not only did they have great adventures on the larger islands including Australia and New Zealand but on some of the very tiny islands as well. Snorkeling in the clear, tropical warm water was a thrilling experience for all members of the family. They became experts on identifying species of fish and coral formations. On one occasion, they had an entire island to themselves. No other human was present. They had to take canned foods and water for the few months they were there. Electricity was provided by a generator. At night if the generator was not working, they lit a candle and played gin rummy by candlelight—a tradition of card games the family still enjoys (although with electricity!).

**At home in California**
In 1985, Dr. Shipp and Marjorie chose to spend the last years of their lives in California. The kids were excited about moving to the "Golden State." Joe continued his work with diabetes research while Marjorie cultivated her artistic endeavors—winning art awards, authoring books, serving on Museum advisory boards, and contributing to countless exhibitions. Always active and engaging, Marjorie's move to their permanent location was not about to slow her interests or professional pursuits.

Until his death in 2021, Dr. Shipp held an appointment of Professor of Medicine at the University of California, San Francisco. He served as Medical Director of the Central California Diabetes Center in Santa Barbara, Associate Chief of Medicine at Valley Medical Center, and Director of Endocrinology at the hospital.

The climate in Santa Barbara was perfect for Joe and Marjorie. When Joe called, he usually was sitting on the patio beside his outdoor swimming pool with his beloved dog Murph. Dr. Shipp's death in December 2021 left a huge void in Marjorie's life, but her life moves on with the love and support of her children and, of course, Murph. She continues to live in their lovely home overlooking the Pacific Ocean in Santa Barbara. She remains involved in the organizations that have meant so much to her over the years and maintains contact with many of the cherished friends that have enriched her life.

Marjorie Shipp—a lovely lady who has used her God-given talents to improve the lives of countless diabetic children and adults. In addition, she has brought—and continues to bring—joy to all who have been privileged to observe firsthand her contributions to the fine arts. Life on this earth is much richer because of Marjorie Shipp.

**Marjorie Shipp, curriculum vitae**

**Education**
University of Florida, Gainesville, BA Degree, summa cum laude
University of Florida, Gainesville, M.E. Degree, summa cum laude
University of Nebraska, Omaha, B.F.A. Degree in Fine Arts- painting, summa cum laude
California State University, Fresno, M. A. Degree in Fine Arts- painting and a Minor in Art History, summa cum laude

**Work experience**
WRUF University of Florida, wrote and produced educational television series
University of Florida, Organized and administered summer art program for diabetic children
Joslyn Art Museum, Omaha, Nebraska, Docent director
Sheldon Art Museum, Lincoln, Nebraska, Museum acquisition advisor with Norman Geske
Torpedo Factory, Washington, D. C., Work with co-operative gallery
Association-Leon Berkowitz, Washington, D. C., Color School (Corcoran and Marymount

Colleges)

Established Creative Travel and Import, Specific knowledge in African Masi beadwork, South Indian bronze and contemporary art from India and Indonesia

Publications of art books "The Journey" and "Silent Thoughts"

Work in Vellore, India, developed design models for leprosarium

**Awards**

Phi Beta Kappa
Alpha Lambda Theta
Alpha Epsilon Rho
University of Nebraska Art Award, 1973
University of Nebraska lecturer, Kiewit
University of Nebraska Advisory Board
Gold Discovery Award-Art of California
Silver Discovery Award-Art of California
Bronze Discovery Award-Art of California

**Exhibits/Museums**

University of Nebraska, Hatz Memorial
Crown City art Center, Kansas
Gallery 55, Nebraska
Miller-O'Brien Gallery, Nebraska
Joslyn Art Museum, Nebraska
Fresno Art Museum, California
Fig Tree Gallery, California
Gallery 25, California
Copenhagen Art Exhibit, California
University Art Museum, California
La Jolla Contemporary Art Forum, Calif.
Palm Springs Art Museum, California
San Diego Art Museum, California
Texas Fine Art Museum, Texas
Alexandra Museum of Art, Louisiana
Contemporary Arts Forum, California
Santa Barbara Art Association, California

**International work-study (1960s-1998)**

| | | |
|---|---|---|
| Africa | Hawaii | Russia |
| Australia | Hong Kong | Samoa |
| Austria | India | Seychelles |
| Bulgaria | Indonesia | Singapore |
| BWI | Iran | Spain |
| Central Asia | Iraq | Sri Lanka |
| Cook Islands | Italy | Sweden |
| Cypress | Japan | Switzerland |
| Egypt | Jordan | Syria |
| England | Lebanon | Tahiti |
| Fiji | Maldives | Taiwan |
| France | New Zealand | Thailand |
| Germany | Papua New Guinea | Turkey |
| Greece | Romania | Palau |

CHAPTER 23

# Dr. Joseph Calvin Shipp

Joseph Calvin Shipp, the son of Ezra Jonah Shipp and Norah Earnest Shipp, was born on February 10, 1927. In 1921 at the age of twenty-three, Ezra Shipp became a Rural Route mail carrier with the Northport Post Office.

In 1923 while delivering the mail, Jonah met his future wife, Norah Earnest, one of twelve children of Levi and Ellen Earnest who lived on a farm off Crabbe Road in the Windham Springs area about twenty miles north of Northport. After their marriage, the young couple purchased a 100-acre farm in the SW ¼ NE ¼ Section 3 Township 30 Range 10W across the road from Macedonia Methodist Church. In 2022, the house carries the address of 14793 Crabbe Road. Like most rural areas in Tuscaloosa County, the area was without electric or telephone service.

Jonah and Norah had two children: Joseph Calvin Shipp, born February 10, 1927, and Maxwell Jonah Shipp, born May 27, 1930.

**The beginning of the Joseph Calvin Shipp/Hayse Boyd friendship**
It was a hot day in the summer of 1956. I was sixteen years old and pushing a lawn mower cutting grass behind Macedonia Methodist as part of my youth work for the church. Dressed in shorts, I had removed my T-shirt hoping to be cooler. My hair and body were covered with dust, and sweat was running down my face. I was unaware of company when suddenly I was startled to see a well-dressed young man who was not much older than I striding toward me. I shut off the lawnmower. Embarrassed by my appearance, I waved my hand as he said, "Hi, I'm Dr. Joe Shipp. I was born and reared in the house across the road from this church. I am home from Boston visiting my parents in Northport and decided to drive up and relive some fond memories of childhood."

At the time, I was entering the eleventh grade at Tuscaloosa County High School, and I aspired to become a doctor. I said to myself, "Oh boy, what a wonderful opportunity this is to talk to a young doctor and to buzz him with questions about my future."

We chose a shady spot under a nearby oak tree, and as a hot wind blew, I was all ears. The conversation between the two of us quickly took on an aura of a high school kid and a young physician sharing their love for medicine. I do not remember the details of our visit as he talked about his medical training up to that time, but in researching material for *A Road, A Cemetery, A People*, I came across the following article from the front page of the April 20, 1954, *Tuscaloosa News* that summarizes the story very well:

"Dr. Joseph Calvin Shipp of 2215 19th Ave. Northport has been awarded a Lilly Fellowship in the medical sciences for the year 1954-1955, it is announced today by the Medical Fellowship Board of the National Academy of Science—National Research Council.

Shipp received his B. B. Degree from the University of Alabama in 1948 and in 1952 his M.D. from Columbia University College of Medicine and Surgeons. While at Columbia, Shipp received many honors but two in particular are truly outstanding. Shipp was the recipient of the Janeway Prize awarded annually for a work of prose, whether fiction or non-fiction that gave the greatest evidence of creative imagination and sustained ability. He also received the William Perry Watson Prize awarded annually to the member of the graduating class who showed the most valuable work in the study of diseases of infants and children.

Dr. Shipp's major field of interest is biophysics. As a Lilly fellow, he plans to study the function of the kidney tubule at Harvard Medical School under the direction of Dr. George Thorn and Dr. A.K. Solomon.

He served an internship in internal medicine at New York Presbyterian Hospital 1952-1953 and an internal medicine residency at Brigham and Women's Hospital 1953-1955 and at the Boston VA Healthcare System 1955-1957."

Sitting in the quietness of the church parking lot, Joe and I talked a long time. I was in awe when he spoke about his life in New York City and Boston. It is an experience I will never forget. As we parted ways, I assumed I would never see or hear from this man again. He would spend his life in academia and medical research far from the little town of Northport where I hoped to spend my life practicing medicine. But I was wrong.

After opening my medical practice in Northport, Peggy and I became dear friends with Betty and Sonny Booth. We learned that Betty and Sonny were close friends with Dr. Joe Shipp who now lived in Santa Barbara, California. Joe and Sonny had attended Tuscaloosa County High School together and while in school their lives were closely intertwined, a relationship that had continued over the decades. Each time Dr. Shipp returned to Northport to visit family, he and the Booths got together. Sonny Booth, ever the clown, told me that over the decades when Joe Shipp felt a spell of depression arising, rather than spend good money on an office visit to his psychiatrist, he would telephone Sonny, and after listening to Sonny's wild tales for thirty minutes, his depression was gone and the visit was free.

Before addressing Dr. Shipp's life in academic medicine and research, let's discuss his young years on the Crabbe Road.

**The Shipp house on the Crabbe Road**
The house Ezra Shipp had built in 1923 was without question the most "modern" in the Lafoy Community. The Shipps lived there until 1940 at which time it was sold to Josh and Clara Rushing. The house was two doors from our house and during my childhood I frequently was in and out.

The new Shipp house was sturdily constructed of wood. It faces east and sits no more than seventy-five feet from the highway. At the time of its construction, the house was by far the most modern residence in the area, and the only home with indoor plumbing. A wide screened in porch extended halfway across the front of the house. I enjoyed sitting there in a swing passing the time of day talking with Mrs. Rushing as we watched traffic pass by. In the 1940s, not too many cars made their way along the winding dirt Crabbe Road with its steep hills, sharp curves, sand traps and slippery red clay hills when wet.

The front door opened into a large living room. The dining room adjoined the living room and in the center of the house. The kitchen was to the right of the dining room. The short hallway opening off the left wall of the living room led to two bedrooms with a bathroom between the two rooms. A back porch extended across the entire width of the house. In the late 1940s, the southern two-thirds of the back porch was enclosed and formed a sleeping porch and sewing room. The northern one-third remained a porch on which the family well was located.

Electricity did not come to other homes in Lafoy until 1940. Abstract of Title records show that E. J. Shipp and wife Norah granted Alabama Power Company title to right-of-way property for power lines on December 7, 1939. However, the Shipp house had electric service starting in 1925 with a power source from batteries stored in a small building near the house. No other house in the area had this modern convenience. Mr. Shipp maintained a close watch on the charge meters in the batteries and replaced them as needed. Joe did say that his dad made sure the family was frugal in its use of electricity in order to prolong battery life.

The structure sits on level ground that gently slopes downward in the back. The flooring of the structure is supported by several columns of rocks in pillar formation. The terrain allows for a partially underground room, a cellar, beneath the back bedroom. The cellar room has a concrete floor and serves as a storage room for canned goods, peanuts, potatoes, onions and other foods. It also may be used as a storm shelter. Mrs. Rushing was always kind enough to allow my mother to store some of her potted outside plants in the cellar during the winter months.

Joe enjoyed telling the story that during the Great Depression of the 1930s his family was among the first to own a radio. As a result, neighbors sometimes came to his house to listen to radio broadcasts of the World Series. They would "watch" the radio as the exciting game was broadcast.

Each time we talked, he commented, "Update me regarding my old home on the Crabbe Road. Is it still in good shape? I am sure it is because it was of the finest quality when it was built." My wife sent him a current picture of the house. He was delighted to see it has stood the test of time so well. Its exterior is unchanged from the time of construction. He always asked about Macedonia Church and Cemetery, the church where he and his family worshipped when they lived on the Crabbe Road.

To mention even a few of the funny experiences that Joe's daddy enjoyed while delivering the mail, would make this account too long. I do include one detail. The distance from the Shipp home to Windham Springs, the northern terminus of his route was only ten miles. However, the route also included many additional miles of little dirt trails that fed into the Crabbe Road from areas around Piney Woods, Yellow Creek, Turkey Creek, Tierce Creek, and North River. In total, the route was approximately seventy miles round trip. Little one-lane roads in the mountainous terrain were so steep that his little car barely made it up the hill. When wet, the muddy road was so slippery he often slid into the ditch. Yet, people on his route said they could set their clocks because he was so punctual in delivering the mail.

Joe told me that only once did his dad not deliver the mail as scheduled. In January 1940, Tuscaloosa County experienced a "big snow," and record-breaking low temperatures. The old Chevrolet just would not crank that morning.

Ezra Jonah's last assignment was Route One, the Watermelon Road route, a ninety-two-mile route which he served from 1936 -1963 at age sixty-six. He knew most of the families on his route and shared their joys and sorrows.

**Joe Shipp attends Lafoy School**

An entire chapter in *A Road, A Cemetery, A People* is devoted to Lafoy School, the school Joe attended from 1933-1940. Here in this chapter, I include additional information that Joe fondly shared of the school. Lafoy School was one and a half miles south of the Shipp house. Established in 1912, the school served the educational needs of the children of Lafoy Community and the Crabbe Road area near North River until it closed in 1941. Joe and his fellow students walked to school regardless of the weather.

School terms in many areas in the rural South in the 1920s, and extending in some areas until the 1940s, were five or no more than six months in length—November through March. This al-

Mr. and Mrs. Jonah Shipp, Joseph and Maxwell

lowed children to be available as "free" workers on family farms during growing and harvesting seasons. Without the help of children, some families would not have survived in the economically-deprived South. Fortunately, the Shipps were better off financially than many in the Lafoy Community. They grew their own food including vegetables, produce, poultry and dairy products. The income from serving as an US Postal Service mail carrier was an added bonus.

Unfortunately, some Lafoy adults did not see the need to keep their kids in school even if their labor on the farm was not needed to make ends meet. Tuscaloosa County School Superintendent James Sellers, in an article in the September 2, 1928 edition of *Tuscaloosa News*, urged parents to please keep their children enrolled in school. The article listed the faculty for Tuscaloosa County schools. Lafoy School's sole teacher for the 1928-1929 school year was Mrs. Floyd Robertson. However, by 1932 enrollment had increased to eighty-three students according to an article in the December 8, 1932 edition of *Tuscaloosa News*. Lafoy then had a faculty of two. The rapid turnover in teachers at Lafoy School is largely due to the fact many of the teachers were young single women, and when they married, they moved to other areas with their husbands.

Joe's favorite teacher was a retired University of Alabama professor. In taking dictation during our conversation, I failed to record the professor's name and had intended to discuss the matter with Joe during our next phone visit. Unfortunately, death took my beloved doctor friend prior to that phone call.

Pupils were not assigned a grade level. Rather, upon entering school at age six, each the student was given a beginner's primer for reading and writing. When the kid completed the beginner's primer, he or she advanced to the next level. Other subjects such as arithmetic were added along the way. As a result, students were not identified as first, second or third graders. Rather, their level-of-standing was based upon the successful completion of textbooks.

Joe Shipp possessed a brilliant mind and was a self-motivated individual. He would have excelled academically regardless of the elementary or high school he attended, but he was quick to acknowledge his respect for the education he received at Lafoy School. "Lafoy School was a great school and it prepared me well," he told me in one interview.

His parents were very involved in the life of the school and according to an article in the November 27, 1938 edition of *Tuscaloosa News*, E. J. Shipp was president of the Lafoy P.T.A.

**Farming**

Joe enjoyed growing up on a farm. He was very involved in 4-H Club work and helping with farm chores. The Shipp farm was divided up into several portions—gardens, cow and mule pastures, hog pasture and pen, corn and cotton land, and timber. Mr. Shipp never owned a tractor and did all plowing using mules. The gentle sloping area next to the house was the family garden in which they grew most of the produce and vegetables they ate.

A large barn with storage space for wagons,

Joe's Prize Pig

Joe's brood of chickens

mule, cow and chicken feed, hay, and corn was built just north of the Shipp home, and adjacent to it was a large hen-laying house. In between the hen house and the back porch stood a dirt-floored wood garage with boards on which the car tires rested.

A small creek flowed northward through the property and emptied into North River three quarters of a mile north of the Shipp farm. The creek is identified as Boyd Creek and named by my paternal grandparents, Mr. and Mrs. William Aaron Boyd, Jr., who lived there in the early 1900s.

Joe loved to brag about raising pigs. He was given a sow each year that provided him with twelve to fifteen piglets which he sold to earn money. He proudly recalls that his pigs often won "best pig" award at the county fair.

As with raising pigs to earn income, Joe notes that he often picked cotton for neighboring farmers and was paid one cent for each pound he picked. Moreover, he was an excellent picker and could pick as much as 200 to 300 pounds per day. Few adults could exceed that. He was paid one cent per pound. This brought in $2 to $3 dollars per day. As a young school kid, Joe learned to work 12-hour days and to never spend more money than he earned.

**Joe Shipp and personal tragedy**
Joe Shipp experienced personal tragedy in early life, the death of his mother and the death of his only sibling. Joe's mother, Norah L. Earnest Shipp, was born January 25, 1898, and died of ovarian cancer on October 14, 1942, at the age of forty-four. Joe was a junior at Tuscaloosa County High School. The loss was devastating. Her death no doubt further stimulated him to dedicate his life to serving others in the field of medicine.

Joe's brother, Maxwell Jonah Shipp, was born May 22, 1930. During the Korean Conflict, Maxwell was killed on June 25, 1953, when the engine of the US Airforce F-86F Sabrejet fighter bomber he was piloting lost an engine and crashed. He was on a training flight and not in enemy combat. His obituary reads:

**Lt. Maxwell Shipp obit:**
Funeral services for 1st Lt. Maxwell Shipp, 23-year-old airman who was killed on May 22, in a plane accident in Korea will be held Friday at 2:00 p.m. from the Northport Methodist Church with Pastor R. D. Cook of Northport Methodist Church and Rev. B. F. Atkins pastor of Northport

Baptist Church officiating.

Burial will be in Tuscaloosa Memorial Park with Jones and Spigener in charge.

Lt. Shipp was killed when his plane lost engine power coming in for a landing after a practice flight, and he was too low to gain altitude. He had been in Korea for only a short time.

Survivors include: his widow, the former Sara Frances Bell; his parents, Mr. and Mrs. E. J. Shipp of Northport; two brothers, Dr. Joseph Shipp of New York City and Airman First Class Lucien Lewis of Germany; one sister, Mrs. Mrs. Martha Lewis Mitchum.

Active pallbearers will be William Dickon, Liege Moore, Leon Jones, Paul Robertson, Lynwood Thornton and Harold Webster.

Honorary pallbearers will be Maxie Mitchell, Lester Brock, Heflin Christian, Ray Jenkins, Roger Hansard, Russell Anders, Herbert Summerlin, Joe Langston, Keith Barge, Charlies Stone, Norman Carlson, Kenneth Bohannon, Jerald Wiggins, James L. Booth, Jr., Wyman Brown, W. N. Evans, Orman Chapel, and John B. Maxwell."

Following Norah's death, Joe's father married Marie Holley Lewis, daughter of Nathaniel Glazier Holley and Ida Frances Holley. Marie was a widow with two children, Martha Lewis (October 11, 1929-October 16, 2004) and Lucien Lewis (January 23, 1930-July 17, 2016). Martha married Wilburn Gayle Mitchum; Lucien married Sarah Frances Bell (December 31, 1930-November 1, 2005), the widow of Maxwell Shipp. Interestingly, both Martha and Lucien worked at the Northport Post Office.

Joe's stepmother, Marie Holley Lewis Shipp, was much loved by Joe and Maxwell. Sadly, she,

Maxwell Shipp

too, died of an adenocarcinoma of undetermined origin on October 28, 1976. Thankfully, Jonah and Marie were granted twelve years of good health after he retired as a rural mail carrier during which time they enjoyed traveling. Jonah was physically able to live alone after Marie's death. At age eighty-nine, he succumbed to a massive cerebral hemorrhage on December 1, 1985.

**The move to Northport in 1940**

The Shipps enjoyed life on the farm on the Crabbe Road throughout the 1920s and 1930s. In 1940, Joe would enter the ninth grade and Maxwell would enter the second grade. (At age, thirteen, Joe would normally have been entering either the seventh or eighth grade, but while at Lafoy School he had been bumped up a grade or so because of his accelerated rate of learning.) Their parents thought it best to move to town so that the boys would be near their schools. This would allow better access to afterschool activities. Jonah bought about twenty acres of land near Tuscaloosa County High School that at the time was in open farm cultivation. Milton Cooper, a prominent builder designed and built a large three-bedroom house. In 2022, the house carries the address of 2219 19th Avenue, Northport.

**The years at Tuscaloosa County High School, 1940-1944**

Joe's transition from a small, two-room, two-faculty community school where everyone knew everyone else to a high school whose faculty numbered twenty-five or more was smooth. His world expanded exponentially. He quickly made friends with kids from rural areas all over the county and with those who lived in town.

Ever the student with excellent self-motivation and lofty dreams, the faculty was delighted to feed his thirsting young mind. In fact, at the time it was a challenge for them to prepare lessons that were indeed stimulating for such an outstanding scholar.

I think Joe's most cherished achievement was serving as editor of the school's first high school annual, the TUSCOHI. Tuscaloosa County High School's first graduating class was the Class of 1927, but no student or faculty member had put forth the effort to organize and publish a yearly annual. At the beginning of his senior year in the fall of 1943, Joe determined he would see that omission corrected. It would be a difficult job, but he was the man to do it, and he did.

During our conversations in 2021, he often broached the subject of the school annual and asked if the school was still publishing the TUSCOHI. I could not answer the question, but I knew one who could, Sonya Booth Davis, daughter of Sonny and Betty Booth, Joe's dear friends from his youth. He often spoke with Sonya on the phone. She, too, had been on the TUSCOHI staff during the years she was a student at TCHS in the 1980s. They enjoyed sharing stories about the school annual. Sonya went to the high school and secured a copy of the 2021 issue of the TUSCOHI and sent it to Dr. Shipp. He was delighted to know that after seventy-seven years, the project he began remained in active mode.

**Joe Shipp at the University of Alabama, 1944-1948**

When Joe graduated from Tuscaloosa County High School in May 1944, World War II was raging and many TCHS students volunteered for immediate military service. Joe, too, was eager to join the US Navy. However, he was only seventeen and too young to join without parental consent which his parents were unwilling to grant. So, he enrolled in the University of Alabama as a pre-med student and lived in the Kappa Alpha Fraternity house. In 1945 upon turning eighteen, he joined the U.S. Navy as a paramedic. He received his basic training at Annapolis, Maryland. At war's end in the summer of 1945, the Navy offered him a deal. The Navy would provide free tuition for him to finish the two-year pre-med school in Tuscaloosa and then pay for four years of medical school training. In return, "He would be a Navy doctor for life." He was given twenty-four hours to make a decision. He respectfully declined the offer. He did not want to be a military doctor. His aspirations were for excellence in research and academic medicine.

Joe returned to Tuscaloosa from Annapolis to complete his pre-med training. As he neared the end of his second year of the two-year medical school, Dr. Stuart Graves, a man who had served as the dean of the two-year pre-medical school in Tuscaloosa since 1928, called Joe into his office one day and said, "Young man, your record is outstanding. I think you qualify for entrance to Columbia Medical School, one of the most prestigious schools in the country." Joe hardly knew what to say. As the startled student sat quietly in his chair facing the dean, Dean Graves picked up the telephone and called the dean of Columbia Medical School and after no more than a cordial hello said, "I recommend a young pre-med student here in Tuscaloosa, Joe Shipp, to your school." The two deans chatted for only a couple of minutes before Dean Graves said, "Good bye." Dr. Graves turned to Joe and said, "You are admitted to Columbia Medical School! Now go do your work."

A question arises, "Why did Dr. Graves want Joe to attend an out-of-state medical school when Alabama had just opened its own four-year medical school in Birmingham in 1944?" Herein lies the answer.

Alabama Medical College was first opened in 1859 in Mobile by Josiah C. Nott and other physicians as part of the University of Alabama. Closed by the Civil War in 1861, it reopened in 1868. The Mobile school was closed and moved to Tuscaloosa in 1920. It remained a two-year medical school offering only basic science courses until 1944. In 1944, the two-year school in Tuscaloosa closed and a four-year medical school, the Medical College of Alabama, opened in Birmingham. Dr. Graves saw the potential in Joe Shipp to become a world-class physician, educator, and researcher and at the time, Columbia Medical School was the best place for his journey to begin.

**Professor of Medicine, University of Florida College of Medicine at Gainesville, Florida**
Joe Shipp entered Columbia University College of Medicine in 1952. After completing his studies at Columbia, Joe became a teaching fellow at Harvard Medical School. Later, he was a research fellow at Oxford University. He was certified by the American Board of Internal Medicine in 1962. He was destined for a life of great achievement in not only the practice of medicine but in research and administration, particularly in the field of juvenile diabetes.

The University of Florida College of Medicine was established in 1956. The founding dean was Dr. George T. Harrell. In looking for a cream-of-the-crop young physician in the emerging new generation of doctors to help him develop the relatively new medical school into a world-class teaching, research and patient care institution, Dr. Harrell turned to Dr. Joe Shipp. In the early 1960s, Shipp joined Dr. Harrell and others at the Florida College of Medicine as Professor of Medicine. He also was a Markel Scholar in academic medicine, an honor bestowed upon few researchers.

In 1964, Dr. Harrell left the University of Florida College of Medicine to establish a second medical school, the Pennsylvania State University's College of Medicine in Hershey, PA. Dr. Emmanuel Suter replaced Dr. Harrell and served as dean in Gainesville until 1974. Working under two great physician administrators and deans, Joe Shipp contributed greatly to the up-and-coming new medical school in Florida. Joe remained in Gainesville until 1970 when he answered the call to serve at another medical center, Nebraska College of Medicine in Omaha.

**University of Nebraska Medical Center**

**Omaha, Nebraska**
A private medical college was founded in Omaha by the state legislature in 1869 and was chartered in 1881 as the Omaha Medical College. A university hospital opened in 1917. In 1968, the University of Nebraska united its health sciences forming the University of Nebraska Medical Center. Robert Grissom, M.D., served as the first chairman of the UNMC'S Department of Internal Medicine having been recruited in 1953 from the University of Illinois where he was assistant professor of internal medicine. In 1956, he became Chairman of the Department of Internal Medicine. Dr. Grissom set high standards in medical education, medical ethics and in the quality of care and dedication to patients. He stressed the importance of intellectual curiosity, research, and the fact that the physician should be a life-long learner.

In 1969, Dr. Grissom recruited Dr. Joe Shipp and offered him the chairmanship of the Department of Internal Medicine in 1970. In 1971, there were 27 full-time internal medicine faculty members that served seven divisions—cardiology, diabetes endocrinology metabolism, digestive diseases and nutrition, hematology, oncology, psychosomatic medicine, and pulmonary medicine. In 1976, Dr. Shipp issued a six-year progress report that showed significant growth in all areas. In 1980, Dr. Shipp was honored as Regent's Distinguished Professor of Medicine at the University of Nebraska College of Medicine. He began and directed the diabetes clinic at Nebraska Diabetes Center for fifteen years.

# DR. JOSEPH CALVIN SHIPP

**Visiting professor and consultant internationally**

Joe Shipp served as a visiting professor and consultant at medical schools and hospitals in the South Pacific, Near East, Far East and South Asia. He was the recipient of a Fulbright-Hayes Fellowship to study and teach medicine and diabetes in India and Sri Lanka. He served on the board of directors of the American Diabetes Association and authored over two hundred publications. He was a member of the Association of American Physicians, American Society of Clinical Investigation, the Endocrine Society, and a fellow of All India Institute of Diabetes and Research.

Throughout his career, Dr. Shipp was devoted to excellence in advancing research in the field of diabetes, including patient care and education. He was internationally recognized leader in the development of patient care systems, including the establishment of diabetes camps for the young and for adults. He was among the first to introduce insulin pumps as an option in patient care.

**The last years, California**

His last years of teaching and research were spent in Santa Barbara, California, an area he loved. Santa Barbara is a coastal city situated on the south facing section of the Pacific Ocean, the longest such section on the West Coast. The town is between the steeply rising Santa Ynez Mountains to the east and the Pacific Ocean to the west. It is referred to as the American Riviera. The city is 100 miles northwest of Los Angeles and 325 miles southeast of San Francisco.

Joe held an appointment of Professor of Medicine at the University of California, San Francisco. He served as Medical Director of the Central California Diabetes Center in Santa Barbara, Associate Chief of Medicine at Valley Medical Center, and Director of Endocrinology at the hospital.

The climate in Santa Barbara was perfect for Joe and Marjorie. When he called, he usually was sitting on the patio beside his outdoor swimming pool. He bragged on the view, the azure Pacific in one direction and the Ynez in the other. In his gated community, drought tolerant native plants covered the landscape to which he enjoyed cultivating other blooming plants that required irrigation. It was a lovely place.

Joe's vision declined with age but not his inquiring mind. Audio aids for the visually impaired offers almost endless resources. Each time we talked Joe gave me an update on his current "read." His interests were wide, but he was especially stimulated by studying the history of the Ancient East, the area of the world he often visited and served as visiting professor and consultant at many hospitals.

**The marriage of Joseph Shipp and Marjorie Morris**

Dr. Shipp and Marjorie Morris were married on November 23, 1961. At the time, Marjorie was a graduate student at the University of Florida at Gainesville pursuing a master's degree in education and journalism. Joe told me one day, for the first time, he saw Marjorie as she was walking across campus. He literally stopped in his tracks. "She was the loveliest girl I'd ever seen. I knew I had to meet her. I went up and introduced myself. She was friendly, smart, and beautiful. We've been together ever since."

*Dr. and Mrs. Joseph Shipp*

# A ROAD, A CEMETERY, A PEOPLE

Dr. and Mrs. Joseph Shipp and family
An entire chapter in *A Road, A Cemetery, A People* tells the story of Marjorie and the four children born to her marriage to Joe Shipp.

**Bringing our story to an end**
This chapter is not written to serve as a biography of Joseph Calvin Shipp, M.D. To tell that story professionally is beyond my capability. My intent is to introduce the reader to a great man of medicine who began his life on the Crabbe Road. Humanity is blessed because of his diligent lifelong dedication to medical research and treatment, especially to juvenile diabetes mellitus.

I have given Joe many well-deserved accolades, yet have not elevated him as a heroic god. That is the way Joe would prefer it. In telling his life story, especially his years prior to medical school, I trust the reader has seen a farm kid who enjoyed the simple things of life—going barefooted in summer, raising pigs, picking cotton, and attending a country church across the road from his home. Those experiences influenced his life in later years as he moved among the giants in medicine all around the world.

Joe enjoyed watching Alabama football. The subject came up during each phone call we shared. Most Alabama football games are nationally televised. However, on occasion, the game is televised only regionally. One Sunday last fall, our telephone was ringing as we arrived home from church. It was Joe. "Why was yesterday's Al-

Dr. and Mrs. Joseph Shipp

abama's ballgame not televised in California? Is something wrong with Saban? What was the score?" I replied, "Joe, Peggy and I are among a handful of people in Tuscaloosa who do not watch television, including Alabama football games." He was appalled. I turned to Peggy and asked her to give me the score from the *Tuscaloosa News*.

One of the great frustrations of Joe's was the rise in morbid obesity that has occurred in America during our lifetimes, Alabama being among the worst.

Joe often commented that at ninety-five he hoped to live to the age of one hundred. He missed the goal by less than five years. His last morning had been good. It was spent by the pool engaged in conversation with Margorie. After a light lunch, he took his afternoon nap from which he did not awake. It is wonderful that he was able to arrive at the end in such a peaceful,

# DR. JOSEPH CALVIN SHIPP

Dr. and Mrs. Joseph Shipp

quite way.

Joe Shipp strongly encouraged me, first as a sixteen-year-old Crabbe Road kid who aspired to become a physician. Sixty-six years later, as an eighty-two-year-old retired physician and author, I continue to be encouraged by his example. Robert Frost wrote the immortal words, "Two roads diverged in a yellow wood, and sorry I could not travel both, I took the one less traveled by, and that has made all the difference." Joe and I started on the same road, our beloved Crabbe Road, and each achieved the destiny God laid out for us, albeit his was one of far greater achievement.

Joe's parting words on our last telephone conversation were, "I am eager to add to my library your next book, *A Road, A Cemetery, A People*. To my dear departed friend and fellow physician, I bid you adieu with another quote from Robert Frost.

"The woods are lovely, dark and deep, but I have promises to keep and miles to go before I sleep, and miles to go before I sleep ." I hope to keep my promise to you that soon *A Road, A Cemetery, A People* will find its place in your library for your family to enjoy.

Made in the USA
Columbia, SC
06 January 2025